T0283258

Paul Celan

Letters to Gisèle
(1951–1970)

with a selection of letters from
Gisèle Celan-Lestrange

EDITED BY BERTRAND BADIOU

ABRIDGED AND TRANSLATED FROM
THE FRENCH BY JASON KAVETT

NYRB/POETS

NEW YORK REVIEW BOOKS *New York*

This translation is dedicated to the memory of
Maurice Olender, without whom this book would not exist.

THIS IS A NEW YORK REVIEW BOOK
PUBLISHED BY THE NEW YORK REVIEW OF BOOKS
207 East 32nd Street, New York, NY 10016
www.nyrb.com

Originally published in the French language as *Correspondance (1951–1970),*
avec un choix de lettres de Paul Celan à son fils Eric, edited and annotated by
Bertrand Badiou in cooperation with Eric Celan.

Library of Congress Cataloging-in-Publication Data
Names: Celan, Paul, author. | Badiou, Bertrand, editor. | Kavett, Jason,
translator.
Title: Letters to Gisèle (1951–1970): with a selection of letters from Gisèle
Celan-Lestrange / Paul Celan; edited by Bertrand Badiou; adapted and
translated by Jason Kavett.
Description: New York : New York Review Books, 2024. | Series: New York
Review Books poets Identifiers: LCCN 2023040748 (print) | LCCN
2023040749 (ebook) | ISBN 9781681378305 (paperback) | ISBN 9781681378312
(ebook)
Subjects: LCSH: Celan, Paul—Correspondence. | Celan-Lestrange, Gisèle—
Correspondence. | LCGFT: Personal correspondence.
Classification: LCC PT2605.E4 Z48 2024 (print) | LCC PT2605.E4 (ebook) |
DDC 831/.914 [B]—dc23/eng/20231204
LC record available at https://lccn.loc.gov/2023040748
LC ebook record available at https://lccn.loc.gov/2023040749

ISBN 978-1-68137-830-5
Available as an electronic book; ISBN 978-1-68137-831-2

Cover and book design by Emily Singer

Printed in the United States of America on acid-free paper.
10 9 8 7 6 5 4 3 2 1

NEW YORK REVIEW BOOKS
POETS

PAUL CELAN (1920–1970) was born Paul Antschel into a German-speaking Jewish family in Czernowitz, Romania (present-day Chernivtsi, Ukraine). In 1938 he went to France to study medicine, but the outbreak of World War II found him in his native country. His parents were deported to a Nazi camp in Ukraine and murdered. He was held prisoner in Romanian labor camps until 1944. He then moved from Czernowitz to Bucharest to Vienna before emigrating to Paris in 1948—the same year that his first book of poetry, *The Sand from the Urns*, was published. In 1951 he met Gisèle de Lestrange, and they married the following year. Though the couple separated in 1967, they remained close, keeping up a constant correspondence until his suicide in 1970.

GISÈLE CELAN-LESTRANGE (1927–1991), born Gisèle de Lestrange, was a French graphic artist. An accomplished print-maker in her own right, she collaborated with Paul Celan on two books juxtaposing her etchings and his poems.

BERTRAND BADIOU is the director of the Paul Celan research center at the École normale supérieure in Paris, and the editor of Celan's works and letters in Germany and France. He is the author, most recently, of *Paul Celan: Eine Bildbiographie*.

JASON KAVETT received his PhD in German from Yale University. He lives and works in Paris.

Contents

INTRODUCTION

PAUL CELAN WAS BORN in 1920 as Paul Antschel to a German-speaking Jewish family in the city of Czernowitz in the Bukovina, which had become part of Romania in the aftermath of World War I. In August 1942, his parents were deported to the German camp Mikhailovka in Ukraine. His father died, likely of typhus, by the fall; before the winter was over, his mother had been murdered. Their son survived in forced labor camps under Romanian authority between 1942 and 1944. In 1947, he began to publish poetry under the name Paul Celan, an anagram of the Romanian spelling of his family name. After the war, he would go first to Bucharest and then to Vienna. In 1948, he emigrated to Paris, where he made his home. Throughout his life, however, he composed his poetry almost exclusively in German.

Gisèle de Lestrange, born in 1927, came from a French aristocratic family and grew up in Paris and on the family estate just outside the city. She would make a name for herself as a painter and printmaker.

At the moment they met at a café on boulevard Saint-Germain in November 1951, Celan was stateless. Gisèle, about six years younger, was beginning to distance herself from her social background; at first, the couple felt constrained to keep their relationship secret, as we learn from their early letters. Just over a year later they were married. Their son, Eric, was born in 1955. Beyond the books, languages, and visual art the couple discussed from the start, Gisèle would teach Celan about "things of the sky"—constellations and their names—while Celan would teach her about "things of the earth": plants, flowers, and stones.

By the 1960s, Gisèle Celan-Lestrange's letters reveal an artist who had acquired a mature and distinct point of view. Arriving in sunny Antibes in April 1966 for a break from the worries of life in Paris, Gisèle writes to Celan: "A pebble, a blade of grass, the line of a hill, witnesses of the perpetual drama of nature, are realities for me, which can help me. Not to understand but perhaps to know." Similarly, Celan's letters reflect his ongoing development as a poet, as when he writes in March 1967: "I worked, yesterday and the day before yesterday, on the manuscript of *Atemwende* [*Breathturn*]. It is really the densest thing I have written so far, the most sweeping. At certain turning points in the text, I felt, I admit, pride."

The couple shared an aesthetic sensibility and supported each other's work as artists. "In Your copperplates," Celan writes in one letter, "I recognize my poems: they pass through them in order to be in them, still." But their life together was difficult. Over the years, Celan was repeatedly hospitalized or committed to psychiatric clinics for treatment. He also had meaningful relationships with other women, including the writer Ingeborg Bachmann and the actress Inge Waern—relationships that marked his poetry and that Gisèle, not without pain, accepted, believing that Celan's freedom was fundamental to his being able to write poems. The couple separated in 1967, Gisèle seeking to protect herself and their son from Celan's psychological difficulties. However, they remained deeply attached to each other, and to their son's education and well-being—and they continued to correspond and to meet sporadically until the poet's suicide in 1970.

This book offers a selection of 301 letters out of the 335 that Celan wrote to Gisèle in the course of their life together, as well as 49 documents with one or more poems and one drawing, whose date or conditions of transmission are uncertain; 67 letters Celan wrote to Eric; and 54 out of a total of 343 letters that Gisele wrote to her husband and that were published in the original French edition. The letters cover nearly the full span of Celan's literary career, from his first public reading in Niendorf, Germany, on May 23, 1952, through the publication of *Mohn und Gedächtnis* (*Poppy and Memory*) in December 1952, to the days leading up to his final readings in March 1970 in Stuttgart and Freiburg, where he read from *Lichtzwang* (*Lightduress*), the final collection, which he did not live to see published. The letters are full of Celan's love for his wife and son, his passionate engagement with his art, and his wide reading, as well as his observations from his travels in Germany and France, and reflections on current events. Gisèle's letters, for their part, bear witness to her deep compassion for her husband, while discussing her work as a printmaker as well as projects, combining poems and etchings, that the couple undertook together.

Celan's letters to Eric have a distinct interest of their own, showing us the values he sought to transmit to his young son.

I found your handwriting very good; you have made a lot of progress, and that proves that you must be working well at school. Indeed that does not surprise me, since I know that you have understood that you have to work and learn, learn and learn even more. [...]

You see, here, in Geneva, there are a lot of foreigners who come to admire the city, the lake, the mountains. At our house, in Moisville, there is neither a lake nor mountains. There are fields and, here and there, some woods. But it is much more beautiful, believe me. Speaking of that, I wonder if the hazelnuts are ripe. Mama must have found them for you, I am sure of it. And soon, you two will begin to collect walnuts.

It is very lucky, my son, to have such a pretty house. To deserve it, you have to work well.

Postcards sent to Eric starting in October 1965 constitute a kind of travel journal from a "tour de France" that Celan embarked on suddenly to escape a tense atmosphere at home. In them, Celan describes his experiences humorously and imaginatively, all the while commenting on the poems he is writing, which will constitute part of the first cycle in his book *Fadensonnen* (*Threadsuns*).

A dark thread that runs throughout the correspondence originates in the false charge first leveled in 1953 by Claire Goll, the widow of the poet Yvan Goll, that Celan had plagiarized her husband's work—a charge that gained some traction in Germany and that was a personal catastrophe for Celan, who saw it as part of a larger anti-Semitic campaign. Celan's ongoing struggle against this slander gives rise to the theme of perseverance that pervades the correspondence:

I write You, my Love, I write You—that gives me the strength to live. My Beloved! I took out, from your little Pascal, Your photo from eleven years ago. Gisèle de Lestrange, I love You. My smiling girl from back then! So tested! So courageous! I am crying, yes. But, in these tears, I join You, You and our son Eric, You and our life that belongs to us, to the three of us, and which, don't You think, conserves and will conserve its clarities, its stars, its suns, its House. And which will help us, You and me, to raise our son, to make a man of him, upright and courageous and, yes, less exposed to hardships! I will hold out, my Beloved, we will hold out.

Take this flower "outside time," plucked for You. Tomorrow—for it is the first of October, and October is the month of my return—tomorrow, I will give You Your roses.

Particularly fascinating in these letters are the translations of his own poems that Celan regularly sent his wife over the years. They began in the early 1950s as German lessons and continued as his way of involving Gisèle in his work. These texts were in his eyes literal, not literary, translations, provided as aids to understanding, and some consist of no more than a list of individual words translated into French. Literal though they may be, they are precious documents for readers and interpreters of Celan. They are windows into poems considered among the most difficult in modern literature, providing clues and contexts that may help readers appreciate the linguistic precision of Celan's work. Our edition contains the original German and French, as well as English translations, highlighting what may be described as a secret dialogue between French and German in these poems and letters.

Many of the poems in this edition are different from their published form. Others were never collected at all; they are poems that Celan abandoned, reworked, or could not publish before he died. In the context of this correspondence, the personal pronouns in certain poems (I, you, we, us)—whose referents often seem uncertain, and which have occasioned much debate among critics—can, as it were, be read "simply." For example, in April 1966, Celan, interned and hospitalized since the previous November, sends the following uncollected poem after Gisèle's visit to him in the Sainte-Anne psychiatric hospital:

Wildernesses, woven into the days around us.

Like a lone wanderer, again
and again,
beyond the message towers,
a big white bird's
right wing
rustles in.

The poem is enclosed with a letter that begins: "Here, my Darling, is the most recent of the daily poems. It would like to tell You, too, how much, in everything I set out to do, I am close to You, still and ever." And in what is to our knowledge Celan's last letter to Gisele, he encloses a poem as a birthday present, adding: "What can I offer you, my dear Gisèle? Here is a poem written while thinking of you—here it is as I noted it down, right away, in its first version, unaltered, unchanged." These letters between a great poet and his wife offer a unique and revealing anthology of his poetry.

Celan came, as he put it in his 1958 speech in Bremen, from a former province of the Hapsburg monarchy home to many of "those Hasidic tales that Martin Buber has retold for us all in German" (SPP, 305). He became a major German-language writer—a poet first of all, but also a prose writer, as the author of *The Meridian*, the title under which he published the acceptance speech he gave in October 1960 on receiving the Büchner Prize, Germany's most prestigious literary award. In that speech, he reflects on what it means to write poetry and describes the poetic imagination—in general and his own—as it seeks to orient itself with respect to history and literary tradition. Celan also wrote numerous fictional pieces and aphorisms. His letters to Gisèle are those of a first-rate prose writer. They also underscore the importance he ascribed to his work as a translator from Russian, English, Italian, Romanian, Portuguese, Hebrew, and French; the reader of these letters will find Celan having just typed up translations of Shakespeare's sonnets.

Above all, these letters from a poet to his wife provide a vivid context for Celan's poems, articulating his reflections on his poetry and its broader ethical concerns, and allowing us to see how he was altered and shaped by his experiences. Difficult as his life often was, Celan's love for his wife and his son, echoed in his poems, is palpable in letter after letter:

In the afternoon, at four o'clock, a car from the Radio Station took me, with three other participants, to Niendorf. We drove at 120 kilometers per hour, across a landscape that was almost not one: heaths without contours, hint of the sea, of a space whose space I almost no longer dared to measure—I was frightfully far from Paris, and I was afraid that You did not feel, over there, the horror of this distance.

This edition, a translation and adaptation of the original 2001 publication *Paul Celan/Gisèle Celan-Lestrange: Correspondance (1951–1970)*, edited by Bertrand Badiou in cooperation with Eric Celan, is indebted to those who made the original edition possible and whom we thank again here. We thank Eric Celan again for his long-standing support.

—*Bertrand Badiou and Jason Kavett*
Paris, June 2024

TRANSLATOR'S ACKNOWLEDGMENTS

I thank Bertrand Badiou for his unwavering encouragement and advice, and I thank Eric Celan for his steadfast trust.

I also thank Lourdes Fernández Guerrero, Russell Perkins, Michael Kardamitsis, Maria Muresan, Michael Levine, Karen Raizen, Thomas Wild, Henry Kavett, Adam Kavett, Susan Knapp, and Mike Knapp, as well as Edwin Frank and Alex Andriesse.

—*J.K.*
Paris, June 2024

1

CAFÉ KLÉBER,
Trocadéro, [Paris,]
11 December 1951[1]

My Darling,

I am still very close to you, to your caresses, to your eyes, to your beautiful sincerity and to your love.

I am so happy to tell you about all the calm in which I fell asleep yesterday. And my only desire would be to know that you too are very much at peace.

It's this calm that worries me, you know, it's not natural for me—it's not at all natural for me, and it's you who gives it to me. I cannot understand it yet. Don't ask me what I think because I cannot know it yet.

I would like to understand.

I would like to recognize.

I would like to know.

To love you more freely, but that scares me too—and then, it's so sweet loving you beyond all logic.

I would like you to be happy and I feel so distant, so imperfect for you. That too is very worrying.

It must be very difficult to Love a poet, a handsome poet. I feel so unworthy of your life, of your Poetry, of your Love—and everything that is not you already seems no longer to exist for me.

I hear your words, and I feel you very close to me. I like being even closer. I like looking at you—knowing you are there, seeing you silent and concentrating, you give me confidence, you calm me so extraordinarily.

Dear Beloved—

It seems to me that a new life has already begun for me—that you have already created in me a flower of life that I can hardly see but that is already imposing itself very softly and very intensely.

I keep it in me, I breathe it jealously all day when I cannot see you, and it has already taken a very large place, very incomprehensible. I am so slow in understanding what I nonetheless feel already so strongly.

Darling, I have to leave you now, I am glad if you have the smallest joy, even for a second, seeing my lines, even poorly written. Forgive me for not knowing the pretty words that you know—transpose them, darling Poet, into your very beautiful music.

Wednesday—it was doubtless the desire to see you that led me to invent this opening at La Hune—which isn't until Friday—and that's why I allow myself to write to you today. Unless you wish otherwise, I think that we will see each other Friday at 6:30 at La Hune. That's far away—it will be even sweeter!

Work, my darling, and don't think of me too much—if that distracts you. I would not want that.

You will work on Wednesday evening too—and I, at home, I will paint, I think—and we will be very close.

I send you my tenderest thoughts and my gaze which is all yours because you say you like it

Gisèle

GCL and PC had met a few weeks before, probably around 9 November 1951. Here and in all following letters, the format of dates has been standardized to include place, date, and other temporal/spatial details indicated by the letter-writer, as in "Café Kléber, Trocadéro, 11 December 1951."

2

[Paris,]

[t]his Wednesday, 12 December [1951]

My darling, how can I tell you the joy that I felt this morning upon finding your letter? It had to be even greater, this joy, since fear, ever present when the heart is surprised, was dangerously mixed in at first—

So I will not see you until Friday... but Saturday too, tell me, and perhaps Sunday...

I look at you, my dear, I look at you already beyond this fog which hope, don't you think, will not tire of dissipating

Paul

3

[Dedication in *Der Sand aus den Urnen*[1]]

To Maïa[2]

so that day may break at midnight

Paul

On the bridge of years[3] in Paris [31? December 1951]

---

1. (Vienna: A. Sexl, 1948.) This volume contains forty-eight poems, written between 1940 and July 1948—the month of PC's arrival in Paris. Because of the large number of printing errors, which significantly altered the poems, PC quickly had this volume removed from the market and destroyed. Today, only a few copies remain, including one at the National Library in Vienna, about which PC would later alert students and researchers.
2. Affectionate "Russian" name for Gisèle.
3. Reference to "Le Pont Mirabeau" by Guillaume Apollinaire (cf. *Alcools. Poèmes 1898–1913* [Paris: Gallimard, 1920], pp. 14–15]. The copy in the Celans' library bears the note of the date of acquisition, in GCL's handwriting: "G. de Lestrange / 1 August 1951."

4

[Paris,]

Monday, [7? January 1952], ten o'clock

Maïa, my love, I would like to know how to tell you how much I desire that all that remains, remains ours, remain ours forever.

You see, I have the impression, in coming toward you, of leaving a world, of hearing the doors slam behind me,[1] doors and doors, for they are numerous, the doors of this world made of misunderstandings, of false clarities, of mocking. Perhaps there are still other doors for me, perhaps I have not yet traversed the whole expanse over which is spread this net of misleading signs—but I am coming, you hear, I approach, the rhythm—I feel it—accelerates, the deceiving lights go out one after the other, the lying mouths close up over their slobber[2]—no more words, no more noises, nothing more accompanying my step—

I will be there, beside you, in an instant, in a second that will inaugurate time

Paul

1. This image will be employed again by PC in the epitaph written in memory of his son, "Grab-schrift für François," *Paul Celan, Die Gedichte: Neue kommentierte Gesamtausgabe in einem Band*, ed. Barbara Wiedemann (Berlin: Suhrkamp, 2018; hereafter *NKGA*), p. 75, and *Selected Poems and Prose of Paul Celan*, trans. John Felstiner (New York: W.W. Norton, 2001; hereafter *SPP*), p. 56: "Die beiden Türen der Welt / stehen offen: / geöffnet von dir / in der Zwienacht. / Wir hören sie schlagen und schlagen" (Both doors of the world / stand open: / opened by you / in the twinight. / We hear them banging and banging). Celan writes to Isac Chiva, in an undated letter: "The child is dead. He survived the delivery—very difficult; forceps three times, then finally, to save him, Caesarian—he survived the delivery by 30 hours. / My son, our son, our son François. / Gisèle is fine, poor thing, her state is evolving normally."

2. PC refers here to his conflictual relations with Claire Goll, the widow of the poet Yvan Goll, who has falsely accused PC of plagiarizing her late husband, and, in August 1953, will begin a campaign of defamation, referred to by PC as the "Infamie." Among various troubling events, in March 1956, PC will receive an anonymous letter, doubtless written by Claire Goll, in which the supposed declarations of a writer from East Berlin, Georg Maurer, are related, presenting PC as a "master plagiarizer" (Meisterplagiator). On May 3, 1960, PC becomes aware of the defamatory open letter entitled "Unbekanntes über Paul Celan" (Unknown Things About Paul Celan), published by Claire Goll in a small Munich review, *Baubudenpoet* (issue 5). These libels will soon be propagated by articles in journals with a wide circulation: with this event, the Goll Affair will enter its most virulent phase. On the "Goll Affair" and for the most relevant documents, see Barbara Wiedemann, *Paul Celan—Die Goll-Affäre. Dokumente zu einer "Infamie"* (Frankfurt am Main: Suhrkamp, 2000; hereafter *GA*).

5

[Paris,]

[t]his Monday, [28 January 1952]—17:00

Maïa, my beloved, here I am writing to you, as I had promised you—how could I not write to you—I write to tell you that you do not cease being here, right beside me, that you accompany me everywhere I go, that this world is you, you alone, and that it finds itself expanded, that it has found, thanks to you, a new dimension, a new coordinate, the one that I decided to accord it no longer, that it is no longer this implacable solitude that obliged me each instant to ransack whoever stood in front of me, to hound myself—for I wanted to be fair and spare no one!—that everything changes, changes, changes beneath your gaze—

My darling, I will telephone you right away, at seven o'clock, when I leave my class,[1] but I will not cease thinking of you as I wait to call you—I am always worried, less than yesterday certainly, even less than the day before yesterday, but I am always worried as I have never been worried because of someone—but you know it, I do not have to tell you that—

What I loved until now, I loved to be able to love you

Paul

---

1. In order to earn money to support himself (as a necessary supplement to the aid he received, as a stateless person, from the Entr'aide universitaire française), PC gives private lessons in German and French and works as a translator.

6

151 avenue de Wagram, Paris
17th [arrondissement]
Tuesday, [29 January 1952]

My darling love,

Your letter is so marvelous. I read it a long time, several times, it moved me very much, you know, and I am still overcome with emotion this evening. I want to thank you again for it, to thank you with all the best of myself. To thank you for thinking what you say. To thank you for knowing how to say it so well, to write it so marvelously.

My darling Poet, I would so much like to be able to read all you have written. But don't you think that I will always remain a bit foreign to it? Sometimes I feel you are so great, and I know you are of the race of the very rare and the very high.

Why are you attached in this way to me?

Paul, darling—it's very extraordinary what's happening to us, it's a bit terrifying when you think about it, but it's so calming to experience it.

I live now with the very great certainty of your love, deep down, and an incredible confidence that I have never known. Nor can I get used to the joy of seeing you, of hearing you, of looking at you.

Darling—I miss you terribly. I wish it were already over, this long Wednesday separating us still, and that I could already fly into your arms which, I know—sweet joy—are also waiting for me.

My Darling, maybe you have left Claire Goll by now—and you are walking, worried, your head down, still thinking of the mean filth of that vile woman. I hope so much that it went well, that you have your manuscripts, the money she owes you, and above all, peace with her.

You shouldn't give any more space to malicious people and I wish I knew how to stop them before they can touch your calm and your silence, those villainous ignorant jumping jacks.

My beloved, we will stay together forever, the two of us, and if they don't like us, we will love each other enough not to wish them to.

I cannot wait for us to begin living entirely together. I cannot wait to be—even more—your little woman, and for you to be even more my little man.

It will be marvelous to live beside you—more marvelous still maybe when François will be yelling all day and all night. We will be happy—despite his crying—and you will be too, won't you?

Darling, I have had two days of convalescence, that's a lot for me, tomorrow it will take heroism not to go out and walk wherever my steps take me.

I thought a lot about a painting I would like to do, there would be a lot of white and also lilacs—snow and forms full of calm, something like Confidence made Form, maybe tomorrow I will begin, it will become clearer, will disappear, will transform itself, and maybe it won't be that at all anymore, but I'll try.

Darling, I would like for you to be calm, to know that you will sleep, that you will be able to work tomorrow, and not be too tormented.

I will wait for you to call me and I will run very fast to say hello to my beloved, and to tell him that I am his little peach

who loves him

and whom he loves

Gisèle

[In the margin:] Darling, excuse me, despite my promises—I have to go out to do the shopping at the market. I could not refuse that to Mama, who already yesterday and the day before yesterday couldn't go. I am covered like an onion and, have no fear, I will go very quickly.

7

My Darling,

How is my Kafkaing love doing? I would so like to know that you are writing and that your ideas are becoming clear, that your degree is being enriched with a lot of rare pretty sparrows.[2]

I hope that nobody has come to bother you and that nothing has come to trouble you, and I pray to God that you have no need to get away and that you can remain for many hours writing writing [*sic*].

My darling, I would like for you not to be too unhappy—and if my will could suffice, know that all these minutes far from you are full of this wish.

My love, a magnificent storm yesterday evening, banging and booming, chased away the sun for a few hours, making the weather nasty, which had been almost luxurious.

Some news, the arrival of Sophie[3] yesterday, dissipating all worry, will calm you too, I hope, about my sad reactions the other night, absurd ideas that I couldn't chase away, and which already, with the arrival of this so material, ridiculous and frightful detail, explained to me too this state, and this lack of decisiveness and will.

Darling, yesterday I was in the forest, I wanted to pluck lilies of the valley for you, but they are very small and all green and all closed up, so I can send you only my wish for you to be the first one to have them.

The lilacs are in bloom, and this morning, beneath the fir trees, it smells of moist earth, the damp needles don't crackle, but all the birds are singing all the same, they woke me up, with the rain too. Very frightful news made us begin the day bizarrely: the announcement of the death, by gunshot, of a very brave woman whom I liked a lot. She lived in the little house we have in Évry.

Despite that, life goes on and the Earth turns, people will come, the Pastré cousins and then also . . . you know who . . . Ponty and his wife (Marie-Louise Audiberti). I will no doubt not be able to keep myself from speaking of a vague friend glimpsed one day and who said he met her.

During the thunderstorm, I thought a lot of You—maybe in Paris your little room[4] was also full of light, of this terrible fire that does nothing but enter and leave. I would have liked to be with you, and to look at it together, close to one another. I don't like being far from you when such events take place.

We have never spoken of thunderstorms, were there many in Bukovina? Northern Bukovina, sorry, I almost forgot this capital word, Northern. In my youth, at Beauvoir, it was terrifying, two long sand paths were transformed into torrents, and they told me not to look at the flashes of lightning, otherwise I would go blind. I was very afraid of that but I loved it too, that rain that blurs everything and that sky that turns cruel to the trees. But it was in the Alps that I saw the most beautiful thunderstorms, the thunder that breaks dryly and repeats for a long time in the valleys. The flashes of lightning, they are long rivers with tributaries, which seem rather harmless while—heavens!—what noise when all is already over.

My darling, family duties call me and I leave You without leaving You.

Monday. They have all left and I feel closer to you because nothing prevents me from being all yours and from thinking every minute of you without speaking to anyone.

A telephone call from Yo, this morning, tells me that she will come here for dinner tomorrow evening, she proposes to bring you if you want. I avow that, in writing her a little note on Saturday inviting her to come, I had the great hope that she would have this idea. I have nothing left to do now but keep hoping that you will be able to come.

Darling, I spent a long night of 12 hours in bed, it's been a long time since that's happened to me. I found that very pleasant, but you, my love, you will have slept badly, tormented by these pages you have to write. I am sure they are good, and I would not like for you to doubt it. Don't torment yourself about the typewriter. I've thought of a girl who has one. I'll ask her very quickly and I think you'll get it. About Monique's, make sure to return it: she was a bit furious that I didn't leave it at the house, where she went today to take it with her on her way home. But that is of no importance, all is arranged, I told her that it would be at the Museum

Tuesday around 3 o'clock. Ask the concierge to let her know by telephone that it has arrived.

Darling, I would like to be close to you and I will always know how to be, pardon me for not having always known how to be like that, as you would have liked... I would so little want to bring you uneasiness, or to bother you, my love.

I finished *À rebours.* It's extraordinary, the sensitivity of this man, and this possibility of feeling with all his senses. Smell, taste, for example.

His imagination transports you far away to places so distant, so unreal for me that it does not cease to impress me terribly. All these scents, these liquors, these beauty products, all these little pots of fragrances, these extraordinary gems, and these flowers and overlaps. What a world it is, that of Jean des Esseintes' little house! It's terribly satanic. You know, I like this book immensely, and that I don't grow tired of these extraordinary descriptions, these sensations, visions, and dreams. How rich and colorful it is! I like the extraordinary refinement of all these improbable flasks of odors—and, you know, now I would like you to find for me *Là-bas* and *En route.* My darling love, what other marvels will you still bring me to discover?

I brought the Stories of Edgar Poe here, I'd like to reread a few of them.

My love, if You come with Yoyo Tuesday evening, she will stop by to pick You up in her car, You will have a good hour's very pretty drive and You will arrive in Le Moulin, where you will find me all alone, full of the joy You know. You will hear birds singing and you will see lots of greenery, water, and flowers. We will have dinner together, the three of us. I think that it would be a nice evening, You will take a rest from Kafka and you will return home at night, not too late, so that you are fresh and in good form for the next day.

My love, do as you see fit, it's very easy to make this happen. But you know best if it is better for you to remain in Paris, if you think that you will be working and that this could take you away too much for the moment, then my darling, you will stay and you will know that I am thinking of you and wish with all my heart for you to finish this work and that you will be rid of it quickly if it makes you even a tiny bit unhappy.

Paul, darling, I will run to the post office for this letter and come back in time to call you and to hear you darling voice, and to know very quickly that all is well in Paris for my love.

I kiss you as I love you.

Gisèle

[On the back of the envelope:] Forgot the address of Mme [initial illegible] in Paris. Can you send it? Thanks.

---

1. Former water mill, property of GCL's mother, where the Celans often go for weekends and vacations in the 1950s.
2. After having received his *licence ès lettres* (bachelor's equivalent) in July 1950, PC works on a research paper on Franz Kafka in the context of a *diplôme d'études supérieures* (master's equivalent). We have no trace of this non-completed work on Kafka, and even its specific topic remains unknown. The *licence ès lettres* will remain his highest academic degree.
3. Code name inspired by the character in the novel by the Countess of Ségur, *Les Malheurs de Sophie*, used by the Lestrange sisters to refer to periods.
4. Since August 1948, PC has been living in a hotel in the Latin Quarter, at 31 rue des Écoles.

8

[Paris,]
Wednesday, [21 May 1952], 4 o'clock

My Angel,

These lines will reach You as my train stops in Hamburg, in Germany... Today, three hours before my departure, I feel how foreign this country is to me. Foreign despite the language, despite many other things... My darling, I will only ever be able to live with You, in Your house, in Your country, in Paris. Paris, I loved it before You, but for You, while waiting here for You.

I will be impatient to return, my darling, very impatient. If there is a place somewhere for me, it is surely where Your eyes open. But Your gaze accompanies me, doesn't it?

Paul

9

[Hamburg,] 21[1] May 1952

Darling Little Peach,

I write You in all haste from the restaurant where I just had lunch—quickly—with my two friends, who had come to meet me at the train station. In haste, for I do not want to leave You without news tomorrow, which would be possible if I waited for a somewhat calmer occasion (which will probably not present itself until this evening).

I had a good trip, I am not tired at all, even though I slept only two hours. Hamburg seems to be quite a pretty city—I have still seen only very little, just the way from the train station to the radio station.[2]—The others are expected this evening, six o'clock, but it is possible that I will precede them by two hours in Niendorf (near Lübeck).[3] Among the names are some that I know, two persons whom I know personally.[4] We will stay in Niendorf for three days, then two in Hamburg—that will also be the duration of my stay here. Then two, maybe three in Frankfurt.

My angel, You clearly see that I will hurry to come home—my life does not make much sense when I am far from You: so starting today, begin waiting for me.

Do not write to me more than three times at the Hamburg address—the mail will surely have to be forwarded to me, for I will fly toward You.

My darling, this is not a letter, it is but a short message, so that You know that I am well and feel fine.

While I was eating cherries on the train, I still had, on my lips, the taste of Yours.

I will always be he whom You will desire to see in me. I love You.

Paul

1. This should read "22."
2. PC went, upon his arrival, to the office of Ernst Schnabel, director general of the Nordwest-deutsche Rundfunk; this Hamburg radio station in large part financed the Group 47 meeting (see n. 3 below, and no. 12).
3. PC participates—for the first and last time—in a conference of the Group 47 in Bad Niendorf (a Baltic seaside resort). PC will always resist being identified as a member of Group 47.

4. The "two persons" are Ingeborg Bachmann (with whom PC had an amorous relationship in spring 1948) and Milo Dor. PC had met them during his stay in Vienna between December 1947 and July 1948.

10

[Hamburg, 28 May 1952]

Little angel, I have made You suffer and I do not forgive myself for it—but You, You will forgive me this too-long silence, for You well know that I have not ceased, not for a second, loving You, thinking of You. But everything was so overwhelming, so confused, full of contradictions.—Yet the result is positive: In Hamburg, I just recorded a little program twenty minutes long that we will be able to listen to together in Paris—which earned me 400 marks—around thirty thousand francs—and it is possible that another program will be made in Frankfurt and in Stuttgart (where I will see an editor who is looking for a translator for *The Human Condition* by Malraux[1]).—This will allow us, perhaps, to hasten our union, my darling, and I think about it all the time.[2]

I leave this evening for Frankfurt, from where I will certainly write You at greater length:

Paul Celan

c/o Rolf Schroers, Gangstrasse 4, Frankfurt/Main—Bergen.

[Unsigned]

I love You, my darling, I love You—

1. PC will not translate this novel by Malraux.
2. PC and GCL will marry seven months later, 23 December 1952, just over a year after meeting.

11

Eschersheimer Landstrasse 6, Frankfurt

30 May 1952

My angel, my darling angel!

It is so difficult to tell You about everything! Every time that I try to see clearly, I must resign myself to postponing all reflection until later. Without doubt I need some distance and Your presence. I do not think I will undertake such a trip again unless You accompany me. So grant me a reprieve, my darling, to tell You about things as they happened.

In general, the results are good, even if they are not extraordinary. I got to know a good third of German writers—I am thinking only of those with whom one can shake hands without feeling remorse. But among these there is a good number of uncultivated people, of braggarts and semi-failures, and they did not neglect making me their target. I resisted, and I believe I can say that I asserted myself. (That is a simplification, of course, forgive me, but I just left people among whom simplifications are common currency.)

Ilse Aichinger, the young Viennese woman of whom I've spoken to you, won the prize[1]—she truly deserved it—but perhaps not from these people.[2] But anyway...

I read on the Hamburg radio, and we will listen to the program in Paris. Two weekly reviews asked me for poems, an editor invited me—without convincing me—to show him my manuscript; I will do, for the same editor, upon my return, a sample translation (a book by Queneau: *Exercises de Style*—do you know it?[3]); all in all, the people there know that I exist and some of them will perhaps retain a rather precise memory of me.

The reader of a major publishing house in Stuttgart (the one which established the prize) told me that he had wanted to leave the meeting after the reading of my poems, and he invited me to Stuttgart, where I will read the poems on the 6th or the 7th of June.

My darling, that will make more than 10 days of absence, but You will accord me them, these few days, won't You? Tell me, my darling, tell me, Maya, my love! Wednesday evening I will read poems here in Frankfurt—this will not be paid, like in Hamburg, where I earned 400 marks (of which

I just spent 50 on books). But in Stuttgart maybe I will get the Malraux translation and I will come home rich, my pockets full of money for our vacation...

My darling, I had not read any newspapers for six days—this morning, the news from Paris is bad—tell me what You think of it.[4] Write to me at the new address:

P.C.
chez Jan Heinz [sic] Jahn
Eschersheimer Landstrasse 6
Frankfurt am Main

My angel, I embrace You, I look at You
and I embrace You again

Paul

Best regards to Yolande and Francine

[In the margin:] From Stuttgart, I come home directly.

---

1. Ilse Aichinger, Austrian writer, won the prize for "Spiegelgeschichte," a story which had appeared in the form of a feuilleton in the *Wiener Tageszeitung* in August 1949. It was the third time the Group 47's prize was awarded. The laureates of the previous years both knew PC: Günter Eich, the future husband of Ilse Aichinger (1950), and Heinrich Böll; Ingeborg Bachmann will be the laureate in 1953.

2. PC had just been the target of anti-Semitic remarks uttered by certain participants of the conference; these same people gave the award to Ilse Aichinger, who, like her whole family, had been persecuted by the Nazis.

3. PC does not seem to have done the sample translation for this unidentified publishing house.

4. On this day, the French Communist Party organized a demonstration to protest the arrival in Paris of General Matthew Ridgway (US Army), who was accused of having used biological weapons in Korea. This demonstration occasioned violent clashes (one dead and 718 arrests).

Eschersheimer Landstrasse 6
(chez Janheinz Jahn), Frankfurt
31 May 1952

My darling,

Each time I think of this village by the Baltic, I have the impression of coming back from the end of the world.

It was truly strange, all that. In Hamburg, the two friends whom I told you about had come to the train station, but I found them more embittered by their own worries—material, no doubt—than joyous and glad to see me again. I came to understand, only an hour after my arrival, that they expected from me something like an introduction to the people from the Radio Station—it was all the more absurd since I myself did not know these people who, for their part, had no idea who I was.

I was among the first arrivals. The others, and among them the Viennese group—about whom I will tell You all the details, at once strange and ridiculous, in Paris—were to arrive late in the evening, without stopping in Hamburg; they drove directly to Niendorf, the little seaside resort in the Bay of Lübeck, only a few kilometers from the eastern zone under Russian occupation.

In the afternoon, at four o'clock, a car from the Radio Station took me, with three other participants, to Niendorf. We drove at 120 kilometers per hour, across a landscape that was almost not one: heaths without contours, hint of the sea, of a space whose space I almost no longer dared to measure—I was frightfully far from Paris, and I was afraid that You did not feel, over there, the horror of this distance.

Reception with misunderstandings in Niendorf. Madame Richter (the wife of the writer who invited me) took me for a Frenchman and complimented me first of all on my so perfect German.

The others, that is to say, the Viennese, who could clear up these misunderstandings, had still not arrived. They finally arrived, belatedly, after midnight, very tired from the journey. But there was Milo Dor, whom I like, and whom the others knew already.

That went better. The next day, first readings. Around 50 people, installed in the large hall of the hotel where we were staying, in deep armchairs—it all had the air of a meeting of people reconciled, as bourgeois, with a world whose tremors they had nonetheless felt. Anyway...

First foray. Readings. Then the intervention of "criticism." Words, with or without interior horizon. But well said, at least, this first day. Beyond the windows, at twenty paces, the sea, the sea, always begun again[1]...

At 9 o'clock in the evening, it was my turn. I read aloud, I had the impression of reaching, beyond these heads—which were rarely sympathetic—a space where the "voices of silence"[2] were still taken in...

The effect was clear. But Hans Werner Richter, the head of the group, initiator of a realism that is not even of the highest quality, was revolted. This voice, as it happened, my own, which did not glide across the words like that of the others, but arrested itself often in a meditation in which I could not not participate fully and with all my heart—this voice had to be disavowed so that the ears of newspaper readers would have no memory of it...

So, those who do not love Poetry—they were the most numerous—were revolted.[3] At the end of the meeting, when we moved on to the vote, six people remembered my name.

But this account simplifies things a bit, I will recount to You the details in a few days, in Paris. In a few days only, my dear—You will accord me them, won't You?

Thursday, I will read poems—here, in Frankfurt, and there will perhaps be representatives from several publishing houses.

I have the impression that here, in Goethe's native city, all will go better. But basically, Hamburg was good for making a few friends[4]—one can count them on one's fingers, but how could it be otherwise—and those who do not like me—excuse me for the following presumptuousness—will perhaps regret it one day.

In Hamburg I saw a few very well-known writers, who do not belong to the group, and who were very friendly with me. Among them: Ernst Schnabel (the director of the Radio station), Hans Erich Nossack, and two or three others. Schnabel will come to Paris in the summer, he will come to see *us*, You will like him.

Here, I visited the director of Fischer Verlag (which published Kafka), he will perhaps come to listen to me on Thursday. I spoke to him about translation, and he proposed to me that I translate a few pages of a book by Raymond Aron.[5] So I will have a lot of work in Paris—all the better for us, isn't it?

My darling, I leave You now—but no, I do not leave You, I ask You only to stay with me during these too-long moments when I cannot speak to You in person.

See you soon, my angel.

Paul

[In the margin:] If one of these days You should receive a telephone notification, don't worry: it's just that I would so like to listen to Your voice.

1. PC cites verse four of "Cimitière marin" by Paul Valéry: "La mer, la mer, toujours recommencée!"

2. *Les Voix du silence* by André Malraux had just been published (Paris: La Galerie de la Pléiade, 1951).

3. Walter Jens, a member of Group 47 who was at the conference, expresses himself in the following manner about PC's reading: "When Celan appeared for the first time, people said: 'But who can listen to that!'. He read with very much pathos. We laughed about it. 'He reads like Goebbels!' said someone. He was mocked, so that then later a spokesperson for Group 47, Walter Hilsbecher from Frankfurt, had to read the poems aloud again. The "Todesfuge" [see *NKGA*, pp. 46–47; *Poems of Paul Celan*, trans. Michael Hamburger (New York: Persea Books, 2002; hereafter *Poems*), p. 31] was really a disaster in the Group! It was a completely different world, the neo-realists could not follow it, they had, so to speak, grown up with this program." See Hans Werner Richter, *Briefe*, ed. Sabine Cofalla (Munich/Vienna: Carl Hanser, 1997), pp. 127f.

4. Among them: Ilse Aichinger, Günter Eich, Paul Schallück, and Rolf Schroers.

5. PC does not seem to have done this sample translation.

13

Eschersheimer Landstrasse 6, Frankfurt

2 June 1952.

Where are You right now, my darling? At the Mill? With Yolande? Or in Paris? I so wanted to telephone You this morning, my angel—it is not that far away, Frankfurt—but I told myself that You had perhaps left, that I would probably find myself talking to Your sister, and that I would have a hard time playing "Monsieur Corti," inviting You to visit an exhibition[1]...

Little Peach, I've received, in all, four letters—it is my fault, I know it, and I have not written You, myself, more than four, but, You see, I would have liked so much to have more!

Did the telegram from Hamburg not surprise You too much? I hesitated a long time before sending it to You, but I had not written You for three days and I did not want to leave You without news. You were not afraid, my darling, upon finding it? Tell me.

My darling, I expect two things in Frankfurt: first, Thursday evening, at eight thirty, the hour when I will read some poems in front of a limited audience. There will be representatives from several publishing houses and the press (some). This can help me with the publication of a book.[2]

I will enumerate the people I have seen and whom I will see again in Frankfurt:

I am staying with a participant from the Hamburg meeting; first, I went to see a person—half painter, half poet—who publishes a sort of avant-garde review, the latest issue of which contains a little Austrian anthology (Hölzer, Guttenbrunner ("scraps"), me).[3] I then saw Madame von Kaschnitz (of whom I must have spoken to You in Paris); it is she who published my first poems in Germany (in the review *Die Wandlung*).[4] She received me very warmly, and her husband,[5] a professor at the University of Fr[ankfurt], who is Viennese by birth, spoke to me for a long time of his adventures in... Bukovina. It was truly nice. An Austrian the likes of which there are no more, a Viennese lost among the Krauts...

Yesterday, I went to Bergen and stayed with Rolf Schroers, another participant at the Hamburg meeting. He lives in a little country house, it is at once nice and dismal, very German, German in a sense that disgusts You at first and then invites You to reflect. But still, Schroers was very amiable, very affable—he had already invited me, in Hamburg, to stay with him—but I declined to stay with him, on the pretext that it was far away, but in reality because I had noticed too many vestiges of a past full of horrors—vestiges that could be useful for documentation, of course, and that bordered on the works of Kafka and of many anti-Nazi authors, but still[6]...

The day before yesterday I saw M. Minssen (the one who came to Paris last month—do You remember him?): he had written me from Versailles and I had not responded—and it is he who will introduce me tomorrow at M. Guggenheimer's (one of the editors of the *Frankfurter Hefte*—*Fr[ankfurt] Notebooks*—a review that corresponds, in its orientation, to *Ésprit*). The publishing house of this review will publish a series of volumes of poetry in the autumn, and I will try my luck tomorrow.

Tomorrow too, I will see the reader of a quite well-known publishing house in Germany (Suhrkamp Verlag (publisher)). Little chance for my poems, but they are looking for—Schroers told me this—a translator for part of the works of Proust[7]...

You see, my darling, I am being very active, a bit too much so, perhaps. But I want to get married—guess to whom!—and I need to find a material basis for this "adventure"...

I will probably know tomorrow which day has been set for my reading in Stuttgart. From there, I come home directly. It is not far, my angel, a few days only.

Tell me how You are doing—have You seen Babi[8]?—tell me everything, speak to me, I have only You in this world (and in all the others)—yes. I kiss You, first on Your eyelids, then on Your temples, on Your two cheeks, and on Your mouth—I have never left You during these too-long days of absence

Paul

1. GCL, who fears the hostile reaction of her mother and her sisters, is still hiding her relationship with PC. "Corti" is reminiscent of the name of the famous editor José Corti, active in the French Resistance.

2. This book, entitled *Mohn und Gedächtnis* (*Poppy and Memory*; hereafter *MG*), will appear at the end of December 1952 with Deutsche Verlags-Anstalt (DVA) in Stuttgart.

3. PC has just published the poem "Schlaf und Speise" ('Sleep and Meal') (*NKGA*, p. 54), in an anthology entitled *Kunst und Poesie aus Österreich und Dänemark* published in the review *Meta. Zeitschrift für experimentelle Kunst und Poesie* (issue 8, April 1952).

4. The four poems "Nachtstrahl" (Night-beam), "Corona," "Auf Reisen" (Traveling), "In Ägypten" (In Egypt) (*NKGA*, pp. 42, 45, 48), accompanied by an autobiographical note, had appeared in this monthly review, published by Dolf Sternberger with the collaboration of Karl Jaspers, Marie Luise Kaschnitz, and Alfred Weber (issue 3, 1949, pp. 24off.). Regarding the poet, short-story writer, novelist, and essayist Marie Luise Kaschnitz, PC will write to Karl Krolow on

20 May 1960: "It was she who in fall 1948, when I sent her poems, was the first person in Germany—in Austria I had a few friends—to notice these poems, to absorb them, to write to me. Then a few verses were published in *Wandlung*."

5. Guido Freiherr Kaschnitz von Weinberg, archeologist.

6. It is uncertain whether PC was aware that Rolf Schroers was the son of a high-ranking police officer, and had himself been an officer during World War II.

7. Despite his keen interest in Proust's *In Search of Lost Time*, PC will never translate Proust, except for some excerpts from *Swann's Way* (probably in August 1968), which form the subject of a translation class designed to prepare students for the *agrégation* exams at the École normale supérieure (hereafter ENS), Paris.

8. Babi is one of the nicknames of GCL's friend Elisabeth Dujarric de la Rivière.

14

[Frankfurt am Main, 3 June 1952]

ON THURSDAY 5 JUNE AT 8 P.M., THE AUSTRIAN POET[1]
LIVING IN PARIS

PAUL CELAN

WILL READ HIS POEMS[2]

INTRODUCTORY REMARKS   BY FRIEDRICH MINSSEN

I ALLOW MYSELF TO CORDIALLY INVITE YOU AND YOUR FRIENDS
ZIMMERGALERIE FRANCK
FRANKFURT AM MAIN   BÖHMERSTRASSE 7

1. PC liked to refer to himself, not without a certain irony, as an "Austrian poet" and emphasize that he was from one of the "crown lands," Bukovina (in fact, the region had already been annexed by Romania two years before Celan's birth in 1920), situated, in his words, "on the edge of the Habsburg Empire" (diese Randprovinz der Habsburger-Monarchie); see as well the "Speech on the Occasion of Receiving the Literature Prize of the Free Hanseatic City of Bremen," *SPP*, p. 395.

2. Next to this, Celan writes by hand: "he will read for you, my angel."

15

[Paris, 10 August 1952]

My Darling,

Two long days without You, and these are only the first . . . I have barely left the house, yesterday just to go up to the Bibliothèque S[ain]te-Geneviève[1] (open afternoons), and a bit farther, to the Maison des Mines,[2] at mealtime. I read a lot, but above all I thought of You, a bit reassured by the idea that You were in the company of Hans Castorp,[3] this old friend with whom I hoped for a moment to be able to identify myself, during his encounter with Madame Chauchat—You surely know her already—and with Joachim, with this poor Joachim and all the others, Naphta, Settembrini, etc.

But my memory probably beautifies this book—let it spare You at least from disappointments! What else have I done? (Fair question, for I am not, like You, on a "magic mountain," but in the "plains.") Oh, not very much, alas.

Today, Sunday, since the library is closed, I went to see Hagen,[4] whom I found transcribing the pages I had translated—he did not find much to change—and I borrowed three books from him—including an account by a German Resistance writer, Günther Weisenborn,[5] whom I got to know personally in Hamburg. It is an authentic, moving book.

I translated a bit (the first pages of an American article that Roditi[6] sent me), I had dinner at the canteen, sat down in Luxembourg Garden to leaf through *Arts*, which I bought at the entrance, I came home, I read until around eleven o'clock and then I went down to take a walk for a half hour.

It is, You see, very little and I am in no way proud of that. Tomorrow, I start again with my two students, in the morning the Bulgarian and around six o'clock the American (quite content, it seems to me, with my return).

Saturday, I telephoned the Cité Universitaire: no response, so I will call back tomorrow. (But I am not doing badly at all, don't You worry.)

My darling, this letter will not reach You until Tuesday, I will have left You without news for almost four days, forgive me for this. And pardon me for these lines, which are confused for my not having known how to find the true words. But You know that these words are present, and I know that You will always hear them.

I see You reading, sleeping, living. If You only knew how proud I am of Your love! And I would like to be a bit surer that I deserve it! But I kiss You as though I already deserved it

Paul

1. Large library at place du Panthéon.
2. Student residence with a dining hall where PC sometimes took his meals.
3. PC has just given GCL *The Magic Mountain* by Thomas Mann in the French translation by Betz (Paris: Librairie Arthème Fayard, 1931).
4. Friedrich Hagen, poet, translator, and editorial director at Radiodiffusion-télévision française, had emigrated from Nuremberg to Paris to escape Nazi persecution.
5. The book to which PC refers is *Memorial. Erinnerungen* (Monaco: Desch; East Berlin: Rowohlt, 1948).
6. Edouard Roditi was a poet, translator, art critic, essayist, and co-editor, with Alan Bosquet, of the Berlin review *Das Lot* (in which poems by Yvan Goll and by PC were published), as well as the biannual review for international poetry, *Exils*. PC is most likely referring to his translation of the essay "Everybody's Protest Novel" by James Baldwin (Protest-Romane für Jedermann) published in *Perspektiven* (n. 2, 1953, pp. 93–102).

16

[Paris,] [t]his Wednesday, 13 August 1952

My Darling,

I have to convey to You in all haste some very good news: "Stutt"[1] has decided to publish the entire manuscript. I just heard about it in a letter from Koch (which Max H. forwarded me from Sankt Johann). They are waiting for me to sign the contract upon my return from Carinthia.[2] This morning, a letter from Schroers, who has likewise (as a reader at DVA (the Stuttgart publishing house)) contributed to our success, who confirms Koch's decision. It seems that H. Kasack (author of *The City Beyond the River*), who was across from me at dinner, contributed to it as well.

I hope that this time it is done, for good.

My Dear, I had forgotten to tell You, in my first letter, that the film-dubbing project[3] did not lead to anything: I arrived too late. They have, however, kept my address.

At the Cité Universitaire, where I could not go until yesterday, the doctor found that there was absolutely nothing to worry about, that it was completely ordinary. He prescribed me a sort of treatment that I will have to undergo two more times (at intervals of four days).

My Dear, this solitude is but the wait for Your return. I am filling it with reading (nothing as fascinating, unfortunately, as *The Magic Mountain*). This evening, I will write many ("business") letters.

Don't You fall in love with Hans Castorp and remember that I expect a letter from You!

Oh yes, I will translate all my poems for You: already, while walking around, I auscultate[4] them a bit, to see where they will resonate in French—they are less stubborn than I had thought.[5] But even so, You will be indulgent, all right? Say yes.—Without You the world would be empty.

Don't forget that I love You!

Paul

1. Abbreviation for Stuttgart, home to DVA.
2. For unknown reasons, PC wanted to conceal the fact that he had already returned to Paris from Carinthia without stopping to see his future editor in Stuttgart.
3. Dubbing project not identified.
4. "Auscultate" is a medical term found in *The Magic Mountain*: "'Wie steht es denn mit den Stichen am rechten Hilus, wo es immer verschärft klang? Besser? Na, kommen Sie her! Wollen mal höflich bei Ihnen anklopfen.' Und die Auskultation begann." See Thomas Mann, *Der Zauberberg. Roman*, Vol. 1 (Berlin: S. Fischer, 1925), p. 300.
5. PC is responding to the following in an unpublished letter from GCL (10 August 1952): "I am happy, You do not know how happy, about the idea of learning German when I return, but it is for the sole reason of being able to read Your poems and to love You more this way. My darling, You are really going to translate all of them for me? [...] / My darling, we will have to continue to intersperse our German lessons, which will be systematic, full of declensions, of rules, and of vocabulary, with verses by You or by others You like."

17

[Paris,] Thursday, [14 August 1952]

My Darling,

I rush to send You these lines, far too cursory, I know it—excuse me, I find myself, as You well know, engaged in a dialogue without end with You, do You not feel it?—I send You these lines to go out in advance to meet You: Aren't You supposed to come home Monday, my Dear? So this is the last letter that I address to You at the Mill, it will reach You Saturday and You will know that I am expecting You in Paris at the beginning of next week. (This corresponds to Your own intentions, doesn't it?)

My girl, my darling girl, I have nothing to tell about all these days spent without You in Paris—everything is very calm, a bit too calm perhaps, except for the storm last night—I had a fright and I got dressed around two thirty in the morning, the whole sky in flames, the flashes of lightning that followed one another uninterruptedly, a true nocturnal day—did You see it, You too?

One *VERY curious* thing that happened to me yesterday evening, "in the gloaming": I found, at a bouquiniste's near Notre-Dame, a third (!) original edition of Kafka: *Das Urteil* (*The Judgment*), price: 100 francs.[1] What's more, our library has been considerably enriched these last days. I have to point out to You, among other things (oh, forgive me again for being so extravagant!), a numbered edition—a quite rare one, I believe—of *Charmes* by Valéry (200 frs). Then the Correspondence of Nietzsche with his friend Overbeck (in German) and several little brochures by Heidegger and Jaspers, all bargains and original editions.

Were You glad to hear the news from Stuttgart? I wrote to Schroers to explain to him that I could not go to "Stutt" right now.

Have You heard from Yolande? I suppose there are letters waiting for You at avenue de Wagram.

This morning, between 11 o'clock and noon, I waited for Your telephone call: all the ears around You were no doubt pricked up...

My Dear, it is rather difficult for me to go to Chartres in the next few days. Saturday, I have to return to the Cité Univ[ersitaire] and I have the impression that it would be better for me to stay at home Sunday to rest.

I read a lot in order to be able to write a new book for You one day.[2] It is especially urgent as the first one seems to want to lead an independent life.[3]

I would so like to be the one who can dare to love You!

Paul

[In the margin:] I kiss You a thousand times!

1. PC bought the majority of the rare editions in his library from the bouquinistes along the Seine, including a good number of original editions of Kafka.
2. This new book will be entitled *Von Schwelle zu Schwelle* (*From Threshold to Threshold*; hereafter *VS*) and will open with the dedication "Für Gisèle."
3. *MG*, which PC hopes will soon be published.

18

[Paris, 1952?]

Nicht immer[1]
tritt dir das Sonnenwort auf die Stirn,
das im Blut
die brennende Rose weckt
und sie groß sein läßt
unter den Feuern der Wüste.

Manchmal
schwimmt durch den Sand ein Auge heran
und flößt dir eine zweite,
feuchtere Seele.

treten, trat, getreten—poser le pied, se mettre, se poser / das Wort, die Worte—le mot, la parole / die Sonne, die Sonnen—le soleil / die Stirn(e), die Stirnen—le front / das Blut—le sang / brennen, brannte, gebrannt—brûler, part[icipe] prés[ent]: -end (fr[ançais] -ant) brennend—ardent, brûlant / die Rose, die Rosen—la rose / wecken (v[erbe] f[aible])—éveiller, réveiller / lassen, liess, gelassen—laisser / unter = zwischen—parmi / das Feuer, die Feuer—le feu / die Wüste, die Wüsten—le désert / manchmal—quelquefois, parfois / schwimmen, schwamm, geschwommen—nager / der Sand—le sable / das Aug(e)—l'œil / heran (heranschwimmen)—vers ici / durch—par, à travers / einflössen (v[erbe] f[aible], part[icule] séparable]—inspirer / die Seele, die Seelen—l'âme / feucht—humide

Not always
does the sun-word alight on your brow,

the one that in the blood
awakens the burning rose
and lets it be large
among the fires of the desert.

Sometimes
an eye swims over here through the sand
and inspires in you a second,
damper soul.

---

1. This poem, published for the first time in the 2001 French publication of this correspondence, was most likely the subject of a "German lesson" for GCL. PC worked on this poem again without, however, giving it a definitive version. It appears in English here for the first time. See *NKGA*, p. 406.

19

[Paris?, autumn 1952]

Ich hörte sagen, es sei[1]
im Wasser ein Stein und ein Kreis
und über dem Wasser ein Wort,
das den Kreis um den Stein legt.

Ich sah meine Pappel hinabgehn zum Wasser,
ich sah, wie ihr Arm hinuntergriff in die Tiefe,
ich sah ihre Wurzeln gen Himmel um Nacht flehn.

Ich eilt ihr nicht nach,
ich las nur vom Boden auf jene Krume,
die deines Auges Gestalt hat und Adel,
ich nahm dir die Kette der Sprüche vom Hals
und säumte mit ihr den Tisch, wo die Krume nun lag.

Und sah meine Pappel nicht mehr.

auflesen—ramasser

[Word-for-word French translation by Paul Celan:]

J'entendis dire qu'il y avait
dans l'eau une pierre et un cercle
et au-dessus de l'eau une Parole
qui met le cercle autour de la pierre.

Je vis mon peuplier descendre (aller vers le bas) vers l'Eau,
je vis comme son bras plongea dans la profondeur pour saisir,
je vis ses racines se dresser vers le ciel pour implorer (qu'il y ait) de
    la nuit.

Je ne lui courus pas après,
je ramassai de par terre cette miette
qui a la forme et la noblesse de ton œil,
je détachai de ton cou la chaîne des dits
et en bordai la table, où
maintenant gisait la miette.

Et ne vis plus mon peuplier.

I heard it said, there is
a stone in the water and a circle
and over the water a Word,
that lays the circle around the stone.

I saw my poplar go down to the Water,
I saw how its arm plunged into the depths to grasp,
I saw its roots rise toward the sky to beg for night.

I did not rush after it,
I only picked up from the ground this crumb,
which has the form and the nobility of your eye,
I detached from your neck the chain of sayings
and hemmed the table with it, where the crumb now lay.

And saw my poplar no more.[2]

1. This poem was most likely the subject of a German lesson for GCL. Cf. "Ich hörte sagen,"
NKGA, p. 67.
See also "I Heard it Said" in *SPP*, p. 52, as well as "I Heard it Said" in *Paul Celan: Selections*,
edited and with an introduction by Pierre Joris (Berkeley: University of California Press, 2005;
hereafter *Selections*), p. 50, and "I Heard Someone Say," *Corona: Selected Poems of Paul Celan*,
trans. Susan H. Gillespie (Barrytown, NY: Station Hill Press, 2013; hereafter *CSP*), p. 17.

20

[Paris,] Sunday, 7[1] November 1952

My Darling,

The day was long, it is finally over. Tomorrow will be a beautiful day again, like every day since a year ago. Love.

My Beloved, how beautiful the sad heather was, with you! One day we will look for white together,[2] and then the large lamp will be waiting for us. I have so much confidence, I am so sure of loving you. Nothing can make me absolutely afraid anymore.

I realize my great luck a little more every day.

Be completely calm. Nothing must worry you, my family has never been essential for me, not since a long time ago. Of course, right now they are making their presence felt. But that is not the main thing, and nothing can spoil our Love.

I love You.

Gisèle

"Au crible de la vie fais passer le ciel pur."[3]

1. This should read "Saturday, 8."
2. GCL refers to a walk in a Parisian cemetery on All Saints' Day, but also to lines 21–22 of Apollinaire's "Mareï": "Nous irons si tu veux par la triste bruyère / Dans l'espoir d'en trouver de la blanche veux-tu (If you want we will go by the sad heather / In hope of finding the white if you want)."
3. Quotation from Paul Éluard.

21

[Paris, 7 June 1953,] 9 o'clock

Mimitchi and Big Little Angel Big,

Here I am, sitting on the terrace of a café at place S[ain]t-Sulpice, more precisely at the corner of rue du Vieux-Colombier and the aforesaid Square (the trees of which I can see, which are not plane trees anymore but rather chestnuts[1]), having before me a filter coffee, capable, I hope, of resuscitating my strength—that is to say, what I have left after an auntesque and reauntesque day, begun at ten o'clock at the Station called Lyon and finished an hour ago at the Station called—and how justly!—Invalides[2]...

Hot, oppressive day, adorned, apart from the aforementioned (or maybe not, but both implicit and explicit) aunt, by a "rain coat"[3] and by a briefcase whose weight found itself increased by a can of Swiss Nescafé and by a (considerable) bar of chocolate of the same provenance.

Increased also by walks and visits (Tomb of the Emperor, Bagatelle, Bois de Boulogne, Champs-Élysées, etc.) and by a thousand words stretching across the thousand kilometers between London and Bukovina[4]...

Increased also by fortuitous encounters, including one—an agreeable one—with my brother-in-law, the Comte de Bourgies,[5] who had noticed us while we were having lunch on avenue Duquesne and who was kind enough to ask me to come dine with him this evening, an invitation I had to decline because of the plane, the departure of which was supposed to take place at 8 o'clock (a departure which, happily, indeed took place without any delay).

After which I went to eat at Rafy's, rue de Dragon (roast veal + cheese, which would surely have made me lose weight if I had not drunk 36 beers)—

Now, Chiva[6] not having responded to my phone call just now (but he responded this morning, and will expect me around 11 o'clock—I had thought that the aunt was not leaving until around then), I write You this letter which is not one, but which would like to tell You how much I am lost in this world when You are far away—

Tomorrow, a day devoted to the Authorities—the letter from the property manager has arrived[7]—I hope that all will go well.

Excuse me for speaking by stammering only: 10 hours at the side of an aunt like that—think of this and pardon me!

I cannot wait to come home.

> I love You.
>> I love You.
>>> I love You.

Yes

[Unsigned]

1. PC had a particular affinity for these two tree varieties. The chestnut is associated with the memory of his native city, Czernowitz (see "Drüben" [Over There] and "Dunkles Aug im September" [Dark Eye in September]), poems in *Der Sand aus den Urnen* written, respectively, in Czernowitz and in Bucharest; *NKGA*, pp. 13 and 39. The plane tree, the bark of which has a talismanic value for PC, is often associated with the Celans' stay in Avignon for their honeymoon at the end of December 1952.

2. PC has just spent a day with his aunt, Berta Antschel, who, after a stay in Switzerland and a brief stop in Paris, is about to return to London. She is PC's father's sister, and originally from Bukovina; she lived in Vienna until the Anschluss in 1938, when she emigrated to London.

3. In the original, PC employed the phrase "manteau de pluie," in quotation marks. Contrary to what the quotation marks might suggest, this phrase is lexicalized in French, although this seems to be a literal translation of the German *Regenmantel*. PC liked to practice this kind of "loan translation," which gives an indication of the way he wished to be read and understood: literally.

4. Originally from Bukovina, the sister of PC's father had lived in Vienna until she emigrated to London in 1938, after the *Anschluss*.

5. Christian, Comte Ricour de Bourgies, the husband of GCL's younger sister, Solange.

6. Isac Chiva, anthropologist, companion in exile and close friend of PC's.

7. A certificate of domestic address created 1 July 1953 by G. Dupêchez, the manager of the *hôtel particulier* owed by GCL's family at 5 rue de Lota (16th arrondisement). This document was necessary for PC's application for naturalization in France. PC still had the status of a stateless refugee.

22

[Paris, March 1954?]

Little Strand—who brushes against my heart—

Big Shock of Hair who covers me—

I succeeded in reaching M. Schifferli ("Little Boatman," -*li* being the Swiss equivalent of -*lein*), the Helvetian editor of whom I had the honor of speaking to Your Very-Illustrious and Very-Gracious Franco-Bukovinian Majesty. Little Boatman having made an appointment[1] with me for six thirty at Deux-Magots, I am not very sure I will be able to be back for dinner at a seemly hour. But I will do my best to be there as early as possible. For any delay I invoke Your august clemency!

Your very obedient

vagabond Subject

---

1. At this meeting, P. Schifferli will propose to PC that he undertake several translations for his publishing house, Die Arche (Zurich). In all likelihood, he speaks to PC about the idea of publishing a German translation of Pablo Picasso's *Le Désir attrapé par la queue* (*Desire Caught by the Tail*) (Paris: Gallimard, 1945) and of his poems, published in *Cahier d'Art* in 1935.

23

[Paris, 23 May 1954?]

My love, my only love!

Do not be worried during my absence! I love You and I will love You all my life.

Take care of my little branch and my big angelet big!

Make beautiful etchings and paintings that are more beautiful still!

I do not cease thinking of You.

You are my entire life and more than it!

I love You.

Your Poeter[1]

---

1. Celan uses a word of his own invention: "Poéteux"

24

My darling, my love, my big angelet big,

I am so close to You, so so close, and this trip, this absence—how to shorten them?

I arrived here Wednesday, around 11:30, a bit later than planned: I probably boarded a train that was not mine (despite the reservation, which looked right) and I had to change trains in Mainz. There I got on the wrong train again: I took the personal train,[1] slower of course, instead of the fast train that I should have waited for. So Höllerer[2] was not at the station anymore—I dropped off the suitcases at the left-luggage office and went to find him at home. He was there, and I was warmly welcomed. After lunch (for which he paid) we went to Bergen: Schroers was not able to come, he has a position in Düsseldorf, but his wife was there, very disappointed to see me arrive without You, and also his three little boys and the sick little girl. I was quite tired, the train having been overheated I had to keep the window open (it was a bit like our return from Zurich) and I was not able to sleep. The next day, I went first to Fischer, but, not having given advance notice by telephone, was asked to come in the afternoon at three o'clock. I was received, very politely, by M. Hirsch, the director of Fischer Verlag. Some words about Pessoa[3] and Marguerite Yourcenar (I had brought the manuscript of the essay on Cavafy[4]), all that in a very cordial tone, and finally, my curiosity having gotten the better of me, I questioned M. Hirsch about the matter of Claire Goll. It is an ignoble matter,[5] indeed: she has addressed a kind of circular letter to several persons, including Schwedhelm et al., in which she accuses me of plagiarism, ingratitude, etc. Vile. But no one here takes it seriously, it is in effect quite transparent in its ignominy. I will not think about it anymore. But: These humans—what imbeciles, what bastards too...

Then I went to Goetz's:[6] I had shown Klaus's[7] poems to Höllerer, he liked them, and the idea occurred to me to read these poems at the Galerie Franck. Goetz (he did not come to see me in Paris, you remember, but anyway, I do not hold it against him) detained me to have dinner (yesterday evening), then we went to Franck's—who is leaving tomorrow for Holland. So I could not read Klaus's poems until after my return from Stuttgart. But I am so eager to see You again that I hesitate to do it—in any case, I asked Franck to allow me to fix the date for *Klaus's* reading when I will be in Munich.

Tried to reach Mme Kaschnitz—she is in Rome. Milo Dor—who is in Vienna.

This evening I will read. You will think of me, my love, I will read for You.

Schroers would like for me to come see him in Düsseldorf, I will go perhaps, probably Sunday.

Let this trip end soon! I am in truth when I am with You—oh, believe me, I know it better than ever.

My dear, how are You? Do not be too sad, work, take care of Yourself, do not deprive Yourself of anything.

My love my love my love—what extraordinary luck to have met You
I am Yours, Yours, Yours

Your very little husband

---

1. Celan writes "le personnel," which is a literal translation of the German *Personenzug*, a local, slow-moving train that makes all stops.
2. Walter Höllerer, writer and academic, co-editor of *Akzente*.
3. PC is translating poems by Fernando Pessoa, which he will have finished by 12 June 1954. They are published two years later, in *Die neue Rundschau* no. 67, vol. 2–3 (1956), pp. 401–10; see Paul Celan, *Gesammelte Werke*, ed. Beda Allemann and Stefan Reichert with Rolf Bücher, 5 volumes (Frankfurt am Main: Suhrkamp, 1983; hereafter *GW*), pp. 562–93.
4. Rudolf Hirsch had asked PC, three weeks earlier, to give a critical assessment of this essay ("Essai sur Kavafis") in view of its possible publication in *Die neue Rundschau*. PC had met the novelist and essayist Yourcenar twice to discuss it. Despite the decision to publish the essay, PC will not translate it. The project will not be realized.
5. This refers to the campaign of defamation of PC by Claire Goll (see above, no. 4, n. 2).
6. The painter and poet Karl Otto Goetz edited the review *Meta*.
7. PC had met the art historian and poet Klaus Demus in Vienna in 1948.

25

[Frankfurt am Main, 27 March 1954]

My darling, my love, my darling love, everything went well yesterday evening at the poetry reading, really very well. But here I am caught up in a terrible jam, people and more people—particularly as I leave tonight at 2 for Düsseldorf to see Schroers; who just told me by telephone that he has arranged a radio program in Cologne (which is right next to Düsseldorf). I will stay there 2–3 days. Unfortunately the reading of Klaus's poems will not be able to take place—I will return home—fortunately—earlier. I will come back to You just as I left You—only a bit richer. I am coming, my love.

Your little man

Excuse these lines written too hurriedly. I do not cease thinking of You.

[In the margin:] I will love You all my life, I live only because of You and for You.

26

Düsseldorf, 28 March 1954

Among true words truly exchanged, we think of You

Paul

Ilse Schallück u[nd] Mann

Sehr sehr herzliche Grüße!
Rolf Schroers

Sehr viele, herzliche Grüße!
Heinrich Böll[1]

---

1. "Ilse Schallück and her husband / Very very cordial greetings! / Rolf Schroers / Many cordial greetings! / Heinrich Böll."

27

Düsseldorf, Monday, [29 March 1954]

My darling little branch,

Thanks first of all for your good letters, thanks for being the person who writes them, who writes them so well. Yes, so well: so true, as I like them. Unfortunately, I am deprived today of the one which was supposed to reach me, but I will most likely have it by tomorrow morning.

But now I owe You an account of the last few days—here it is. Saturday, last day in Frankfurt: little rest—on the contrary—it was the day after the reading of my poems (which went truly well), and I had to see a ton of people. The night before, after the reading, I had spent two more hours in a kind of very German tavern, sitting at a table around which were assembled some "admirers" (readers at a publishing house, Mme Suhrkamp, the wife of the editor of the same name, "alumni" of Group 47, unknowns); everyone was drinking wine, but I—to the great surprise of those who take poetry to be the result of a kind of inebriation—drank orange juice. Quite animated conversations all along this table—the essential was quickly forgotten, and I remained, a bit mute, in a great interior calm. We went back to Bergen, Mme Schroers and I, in the car of a neighbor, M. Schneider, an "alumnus," he too, of "Gruppe 47."

Saturday morning: visit to M. Hirsch, director of Fischer. I posed him the "fundamental" question whether, in about a year, he would publish a new volume: the answer came very promptly, absolutely affirmative.[1] Spoke to him as well about translations of Apollinaire: tomorrow I will send him, from here, a few of those. Perhaps he will publish them. The essay by Mme Yourcenar: he will send me the response in Paris.

After Fischer, a meeting, of around an hour, with Höllerer, very polite, inviting me to continue to contribute to his review (*Akzente*). I had asked him to come to a café, having made an appointment there, for 12:30, with Helmut's[2] aunt, who had come to listen to the poems. Until 3 o'clock, Mme Winkelmayer, lunch, coffee, cigarettes, and words exchanged. She is really a nice woman, very agreeable, very discerning too. Subject: her nephew, for whom she has an understanding one rarely encounters.

Then an appointment with M. Remszhardt, editor of the literary page

37

of the *Frankfurter Rundschau* (a daily). I have known him since my first stay in Fr[ankfurt], he had written a short, rather friendly article about the poems read at the Franck gallery. But in the newspaper's editorial office, I learn that he is delayed—I take advantage of that to go see Olaf Hudtwalcker and his wife, who are no longer in Hamburg and work—curious coincidence—in the art gallery ("Kunstkabinett") where I had read. These two, you know them, my darling, they are the "Norwegian" and his wife—he came to have dinner with us on rue des Écoles. (I had given him my book for Nossack.) They insistently asked me how you are. Finally, quite late, M. Remszhardt: a man of around fifty, with a speech impediment—words are obstacles that he only overcomes laboriously, which gives the impression that he clings to something behind them, much more important than them, the essential itself—but unfortunately difficult to understand for his interlocutor. I left him a copy of the new poems for a review he intends to publish, with the title taken from a poem: "The Water-Diviner of Silence."[3]

3 o'clock: I had to stop here, my love: an appointment (another!) with M. Nette from Diederichs Press: translations—high hopes, but not for right away.

I continue: Frankfurt, Saturday:

So I leave M. Remszhardt to go to Jahn's (with whom I stayed two years ago). Dinner with Jahn + his wife. Uninteresting, but anyway, quite cordial. He has just finished translating an anthology of black poetry[4]—it doesn't seem to be very good. Since Madame Jahn took two hours to prepare the dinner (sandwiches), I returned late to Bergen (the trip, 2 tramways—I am pronouncing it right this time, aren't I?[5]—always takes an hour).

Late: that is to say too late to be on time [for the appointment] I made for 10:30 with the Hudtwalckers, in a café in the city center. My train to Düsseldorf is at 2 in the morning: the reason for this appointment, which allows me to pass the two hours between midnight and two a.m., which I could not spend in Bergen, since there is no tram(way) that goes to the train station at this hour. Arrived quite late at Schroers's (Mme), M. Schneider (the neighbor) offers to drive me in his car. There are thus several of us with the Hudtwalckers (the 2 Jahns are there too). We go to a little Greek bistro, a sort of Catalan[6] in Frankfurt. I knew it because, two hours earlier, I had an appointment there with Remszhardt, who, moreover, introduced me to one of the two innkeepers, a lady of a certain age, who did not look very German, a former actress: she told me she knew some "very beautiful" poems by me. I was thus welcomed, with the whole band, by a "Guten Abend, Herr Celan" (pay attention to the pronunciation of this last word, please![7]) and we spent two hours there filled with gossip ...

The next morning: Met by Schroers at the train station. We first go to his house. Right away, after asking me for Your news (at which I showed him Your photos, result: congratulations and compliments), a major politico-literary discussion. He really is a good fellow, and detests bourgeoisification and the militarist spirit which is currently spreading.[8] He is very high-strung too, surely. Too many material worries, which overwhelm him. (I loaned him a little money, he really seemed to need it.)—Then, a telephone call from Cologne (which is a half hour from here): Heinrich Böll, who knew that I was there and proposed to join us, with M. and Mme Schallück. They arrive around three o'clock. Stroll in the city, which prides itself on being the most elegant in Germany—but which does not speak to me. Stroll along the banks of the Rhine—it is rather pretty, but basically quite mediocre. Then coffee, discussion: does the reader have to identify with the characters in the novel? Finally they discover that the question is not posed the right way: identification—this encompasses so many possibilities that it is really not appropriate to employ this term.

With Böll and Schallück until midnight. It is nice.

This morning: stayed at home, while Schroers goes to work. Read a new German novel that seems to be a true work of art: *The Island of Second Sight* by Thelen.[9] Schroers comes home at noon, we eat lunch, it is over quickly, he leaves again, I go to a café and write You this. It is 6:15, I am waiting for Schroers, who is coming at 7 o'clock; we will go to dinner.

Tomorrow will be the same: I will spend the day reading and typing my poems. Böll has arranged an appointment for me with a guy from the radio who has to "buy" my poems from me for a program. The guy knows me because he read this damn Cioran translation that everyone admires (...).[10]

So I will go to Cologne on Wednesday, and stay with Schallück; Böll has offered to show me the city and introduce me to his publisher (Kiepenheuer-Witsch), which will have *certain* results, as Böll has a lot of weight. Friday, I come back to Düsseldorf, from where I will leave again at 5 o'clock by car, with the editor in chief at Diederichs and Schroers, for Frankfurt—which is on the way to "Stutt" and Munich. I will thus be in Stutt[gart] the 3rd, to see Schwedhelm,[11] and leave again the following day for Munich.—My darling, I cannot wait to return, truly, I will return around April 10th.

I am no doubt lucky to know an elite here—the people you meet, you see in the street surely have nothing attractive about them, quite the contrary.

My darling, I will be deprived of Your letters between Wednesday and Friday (Mme Schroers will no longer forward the mail on these days, I will find it Friday in Frankfurt). Starting Thursday, write to me at DVA's address in Stuttgart, Mörikestr[aße] 17.

Do not deprive Yourself of anything, my love, work and think a bit of me! I will love You all my life

Paul

---

1. PC, following various disagreements with the DVA in Stuttgart, was in search of a new publisher. His "new volume," *VS*, will, however, still be published by DVA in June 1955. It will not be until March 1959, with *Sprachgitter* (hereafter *SG*), that S. Fischer Verlag becomes PC's publisher.

2. Helmut Winkelmayer, Elisabeth Winkelmayer's nephew. PC refers perhaps to the somewhat exuberant temperament of the young man.

3. PC's translation of the title is "Le Sourcier du silence." The article by Godo Remszhardt, "Rutengänger im Stillen. Paul Celan las im Frankfurter Kunstkabinett," is published on 31 March 1954 in the *Frankfurter Rundschau*. Its title is taken from the first line of "Abend der Worte" (*NKGA*, p. 81), one of the then still unpublished poems that PC had just read.

4. *Schwarzer Orpheus. Moderne Dichtung afrikanischer Völker beider Hemisphären*, ed. and trans. Janheinz Jahn (Munich: Hanser, 1954).

5. It is a matter of not pronouncing "tramway" as "tramoué" (the English-language word which was introduced into French and has its own French pronunciation). PC refers to a tendency to pronounce it as if the "e" were closed, whereas it should be open (tʁam.wɛ). See also Apollinaire, "Chanson d'un mal-aimé," which PC knew, in the third-to-last stanza: "Soirs de Paris ivres du gin / Flambant de l'électricité / Les tramways feux verts sur l'échine / Musiquent au long des portées / De rails leur folie de machines."

6. Le Catalan: a restaurant-cabaret in the 6th arrondissement frequented by Picasso, where guitarists and flamenco singers performed.

7. PC wanted his name to be pronounced in the German way in Germany, with the emphasis on the first syllable and without nasalization ('tselan) and the French way in France, with emphasis on the second syllable and with nasalization (se'lan).

8. On 26 February 1954 the German constitution was amended to allow rearmament. The BRD (Federal Republic of Germany) will enter the Western European Union and NATO in October 1954 (Paris Accords).

9. Albert Vigoleis Thelen (1903–94), *Die Insel des zweiten Gesichts* (Düsseldorf: Dietrichs, 1953).

10. *Lehre vom Zerfall. Essays* (Hamburg: Rowohlt, 1953) (*Précis de decomposition* (Paris: Gallimard, 1949). On PC's relation to Cioran, see no. 71, n. 3.

11. Kurt Schwedhelm directed the literary section of the Stuttgart radio station, the *Süddeutsche Rundfunk*.

28

[Düsseldorf,] Tuesday, [30 March 1954]

My big angelet big,

Your letter from the 26th just arrived—it finds me at home, at Schroers's, where I pass the time thinking of You and leafing through books. I have not left the house yet today, the city, which I saw a bit last night, does not interest me; at 5 o'clock Schroers will be back, we will chat a bit, then it will be dinner, then we will go out a bit—where? I do not see very well where we could go—to a cabaret possibly, it seems that there is one here that is considered the best in all of Germany[1]—then we will chat again, discuss again maybe, then it will be night, short no doubt (shortened by all these discussions, often interesting—we talked a lot about You, my darling), then it will be tomorrow, I will go to Cologne, radio and publishers, etc.

Thank you, my darling, for not having been worried by my silence—in the meantime You have probably received my letters, which follow one another, I believe, somewhat regularly.

I am here, in the midst of a rather reassuring calm, of a calm that is the wellspring of our love.

It is such certainty, my dear, loving You! I am so much in truth with You! The people—I hardly see them, I hardly saw and felt them in Frankfurt at my reading—they were there, however, and even quite numerous—I will see them even less in the other cities. Already, I have come home a bit—a long week still, and I will be there. But here I am still there, with You.

And now: say my name, say it aloud! I am saying Yours.
I love You with all my heart

Paul Little Man of Maïa's

[In the margin of the first paragraph:] Schroers finds—and he does not seem to be the only one—that there is distinct progress with my poems.

The letter from Belgium invites me to send some poems to a Belgian review published in Flemish, an issue of which will probably arrive in the next few days.

Write to me at the DVA's address in Stuttgart, please!

---

1. Das Komödchen, where there were leftist satirical performances.

29

[Cologne,] Friday, [2 April 1954]

My darling, first of all: I love you, and then: I love You, and next: I love You and love You.—I have been in Cologne since the day before yesterday and have done quite good business: "sold" poems for a program on the Radio (payments will be sent to Paris) and agreed to translate two Simenons for Kiepenheuer[1] (Böll's publisher); result: advance payment of 200 marks (on top of 1,200 marks in payments for the two books, 180 pages each). Schallück and Böll were very-very nice, it was quite pleasant to spend two days in a most comfortable apartment with Schallück (with Schroers, from the point of view of comfort, it was rather the contrary). I am leaving again now for Düsseldorf, and then from D., by car, this evening, for Frankfurt, from where I will go to Stuttgart tomorrow. The end of the trip is approaching, thank God! But I have nothing to complain about. Remszhardt has published a very laudatory review of the evening in Frankfurt.

I received all of Your letters, others are waiting for me in Frankfurt.

My little Peach, my big angelet big, my Countess of Fairies!

Your Poeter in love with You

[In the margin:] This evening I will respond to Elisabeth's letter.[2]

1. In 1954, PC translates two novels by Georges Simenon: *Maigret se trompe* (Paris: Les Presses de la Cité, 1953)—*Hier irrt Maigret* (Cologne: Kiepenheuer & Witsch, 1955) and *Maigret à l'école* (Paris: Les Presses de la Cité, 1954)—*Maigret und die schrecklichen Kinder* (Cologne: Kiepenheuer & Witsch, 1955). The first translation, submitted at the end of July, will be received very favorably by the editor. The second, submitted late, at the beginning of January 1955, will be criticized by the editor, who thought that PC had "dazu gedichtet" (taken poetic liberties). PC does not accept these criticisms and asks for detained explanations of these supposed faults. As the manuscripts have not been preserved, it is not possible to determine how, exactly, the editor modified PC's text. See *"Fremde Nähe." Celan als Übersetzer*, ed. Axel Gellhaus et al. (Marbach am Neckar, 1997; hereafter *FREN*), pp. 235–49. Elmar Tophoven comments on an early sentence in the latter translation to demonstrate Celan's knack for finding solutions to linguistic quandaries as a translator ("Translating Celan Translating," in *Argumentum e Silentio: International Paul Celan Symposium*, ed. Amy D. Colin; Berlin & New York: de Gruyter, 1987).

2. Elisabeth Dujarric de la Rivière, whose father, a person of influence, supported PC in his request for naturalization.

30

[Stuttgart,] Saturday, [3 April 1954]

My darling, I have arrived in Stuttgart, was received here very warmly by Schwedhelm, I am staying with Hermann Lenz (of whom we often spoke at Hagen's). Monday, I will go to Munich, I will read there the same day at eight o'clock, I will stay there one more day, then Wednesday: Radio Stutt[gart], Thursday evening: Stuttgart (poems), Friday: Eßlingen. So I will come home Saturday, maybe Sunday. There was no letter from You waiting for me here, I am sad. My darling, You know it well: You are the "paintress" in the same way that I am the "poeter." Me, I know how to do one thing: love You.—All the rest has but little importance. [In the margin:] And my poems: it is You, my love

Paul

Excuse me for being so brief: there are so many people!

31

22 June 1954

"Inselhin"[1]

Inselhin, neben den Toten,
dem Einbaum waldher vermählt,
von Himmeln umgeiert die Arme,
die Seelen saturnisch beringt:

so rudern die Fremden und Freien,
die Meister vom Eis und vom Stein,
umläutet von sinkenden Bojen,
umbellt von der haiblauen See.

Sie rudern, sie rudern, sie rudern—:
Ihr Toten, ihr Schwimmer—voraus!
Umgittert auch dies von der Reuse!
Und morgen verdampft unser Meer!

22.6.1954

[Word-for-word French translation by Paul Celan:]

Vers l'île, aux côtés des morts,
époux de la pirogue depuis la forêt,
les bras "envautourés" par des ciels,
les âmes "annelées saturnement":

ainsi rament les Etranges et Libres
les Maîtres de la Glace et du Roc,
parmi les cloches des bouées qui sombrent,
parmi les aboiements de la mer bleu-requin.

Ils rament, rament, rament—:

O Morts, ô Nageurs, en avant!
Ceci—encore entouré par les grilles des nasses!
Et demain notre Mer s'évapore!

Toward the island, next to the dead,
Wedded to the pirogue since the forest,
their arms vultured around by skies,
their souls saturninely ringed:

thus row the Strange and Free
the Masters of Ice and of Stone,
in the tolling of sinking buoys,
in the barking of the shark-blue sea.

They row, they row, they row—:
You Dead, you Swimmers—forward!
Enmeshed—this too—in the weel!
And tomorrow our Sea evaporates![2]

1. The poem was probably the subject of a German lesson for GCL. See *NKGA*, p. 92.
2. See also "Isleward," *Poems*, p. 76, as well as "Islandward," *SPP*, p. 84.

32

[?, autumn 1954]

"Plage du Toulinguet"[1]

Versammelt ist, was wir sahen,
zum Abschied von dir und von mir:
das Meer, das uns Nächte an Land warf,
der Sand, der sie mit uns durchflogen,
das rostrote Heidekraut droben,
darin die Welt uns geschah.

[Word-for-word French translation by Paul Celan:]

Est réuni ce que nous vîmes,
pour nous dire adieu, à toi et à moi:
la mer qui nous jeta *les nuits* sur terre,
le sable, qui *les* parcourut à nos côtés,
la *bruyère* rouge-rouille là-haut,
dans laquelle le monde nous advint.

der Abschied—les adieux / sammeln—réunir, rassembler / werfen—
jeter / an Land werfen—jeter à terre / droben = dort oben—là-haut /
der Rost—la rouille / rostrot—rouge-rouille / darin—là-dedans où /
geschehen—advenir, arriver

[In Gisèle's handwriting:] die Heide—la lande / das Kraut—l'herbe

Gathered is what we saw,
To say goodbye to you and to me:
the sea, which cast nights to us on land,
the sand, which flew across them with us,
the rust-red heath up there,
in which the world happened to us.

---

1. Poem written following the Celans' stay in Brittany between the end of August and early
September 1954. See the final version, "Bretonischer Strand," in *VS, NKGA*, p. 73.

33

[Paris, 20 November 1954]

Leicht willst du sein und ein Schwimmer[1]
im dunklen, im trunkenen Meer:
so gib ihm den Tropfen zu trinken,
darin du dich nächtens gespiegelt,

den Wein deiner Seele im Aug.

Dunkler dein Meer nun, trunken:
menschengleich Tümmler und Hai!
Leicht willst du sein und ein Vogel—
auch oben ist Erde wie hier.

trunken—ivre / der Tropfen—la goutte / nächtens = nachts / sich
spiegeln—se regarder dans un miroir, se refléter / gleich—ressemblant
à / menschengleich—comme des humains / der Hai, e—le requin /
der Tümmler [translation missing] / (sich) tummeln—s'agiter

Light you want to be and a swimmer
in the dark, in the drunken sea:
so give him the drop to drink,
in which, at night, you gazed at your reflection,
the wine of your soul in your eye.

Darker your sea now, drunken:
humanlike both porpoise and shark!
Light you want to be and a bird—
Up above, too, there is earth like here.

---

1. See the final version of the text, published only in the *Nachlaß*, "Auf der Klippe," in *NKGA*, p. 405. This poem was probably the subject of a German lesson for GCL.

34

[Paris, December 1954 or January 1955?]

Many-Strand,

It is four thirty, I am leaving. Dupêchez was not able to give me the receipt, but I will go anyway. I am sure that all will go well.

And You? Do not worry if this imbecile, F., again showed who he is.[1]

One day, we will only see beings like Char.[2]

And I will always be there to love You.

See You in a little while!

[Signed:] i[3]

1. Allusion to GCL's difficult working relations with Johnny Friedlaender.
2. At this time, PC has a profound admiration and feelings of friendship for René Char, the poet and member of the French Resistance, whom he met the previous summer and with whom he will maintain a significant correspondence.
3. With this sign, he notes—often in the margin of a book—an idea, a source of inspiration, a word or phrase highlighted in a reading, a sketch of a translation or of a poem, or an aphoristic or speculative reflection. But over time the "i" also takes on a more general, idiosyncratic value. It also indicates a source of inspiration or a text in the course of being written, sometimes even a finished poem. In signing this way, PC identifies himself in a certain way with poetry or with the "poetic idea."

35

Stuttgart, Monday, 24 [January 1955]

Almaviva, Little-Peach, My big-love-big,

Here I am in Stuttgart since yesterday, a bit lost despite everything. The Lenzes were at the train station, we took the "tramoué," I washed up a bit; then breakfast in their charming apartment, so cared for, so old-fashioned, so touching. I have the impression that Lenz is very ill, he told me, while smiling, that he had "einen kleinen Dachschaden," that is to say that his roof is a bit damaged. His wife tells me that he cannot sleep alone. So I do not know if I will stay with them for long, I am afraid of inconveniencing them. Yesterday evening I read them all my poems.[1] They liked them very much, despite my somewhat monotonous reading: I had not slept on the train. Discussion of "titles" for the volume. They like *Inselhin*, but they worry that this title will not attract a wide audience.

Your etching, which they like very much, was on the wall before my eyes.

My darling, how are You? Did my telegram reach You in time? This letter will no doubt take two long days to arrive.

My darling, I will not repeat to You here everything that I told You before my departure.

I love You, my darling, I cannot wait to come home.

Here, a letter from the mayor of Eßlingen was waiting for me: he asks me if I can spend a few hours with them on the 28th or the 29th. Perhaps I will go over there this afternoon in order to obtain more details about my reading.

This morning, in a moment, I will go to DVA, from there to Schwedhelm at the Radio.

I think I will cancel Düsseldorf, but I am not sure yet.

I got up very early this morning (after having gone to sleep very *early* yesterday evening); Lenz will go to work, I will accompany him.

Think of me, my darling, think of Yourself.

Soon I will be back with You.

I love You

Little Husband

Write to me at Lenz's.

In the row of recent German books You will find *Das Exemplar* by Annette Kolb; the book has a dedication from the author; I do not attach any particular importance to it, but it would give immense pleasure to Lenz to have it. Could You put it in a package and send it by mail (as printed matter) to his address? Thanks, my dear love.

1. The forty-seven poems, written between August 1952 and autumn 1954, which comprise *VS*.

36

[Stuttgart,] Friday, [28 January 1955]

My darling, I have left You without news for three days, for the sole reason that I did not manage—and still do not manage—to see clearly in the midst of the impressions, indeed more or less banal, which I can gather here.

Yesterday, Your letter in which You tell me that You cut Yourself made me very worried and I sent You a telegram. But no, my darling, Your letters do not bore me, quite the contrary. You are present in each line, entirely, and I love You and "re-love" You in each word that reaches me. Truly. My little darling wife. My great big love.

I wish I were able to give You an account of all that is happening to me here, but these things are still in the state of first impressions.

The day after my arrival, I saw M. Leippe, one of the directors of the publishing house, a relatively young and quite cultivated man, and I spoke to him of the anti-Semitic critique.[1] His reaction, without being disappointing, was not extraordinary, but I am realizing little by little that resignation is something like the principal feature in the attitude of people who could not imagine being suspected of Nazism. Similar reaction, a few hours later, at Dr. Mühlberger's in Eßlingen, where I had gone—it is twenty minutes from here—to make the appointments that will take place there. Something must be done: that is more or less what he told me, in a tone of sincere indignation but without the will to act. They have ordered the incriminated book to be able to respond with a review in their journal. Will they really do it?

The mayor of Esslingen and his wife have invited me to dinner tomorrow, Saturday evening; Sunday evening, another invitation in Esslingen, at the home of M. and Mme Bechtle, the editor, where a young German poet, Heinz Piontek, will be present. Monday evening, reading in Eßlingen.

Here, I saw Eisenreich[2] and Helmut Braem, a young critic, at the Lenzes. Yesterday, I saw Schwedhelm, indignant, also, about the two reviews that I showed him.[3] All that is starting to tired me out a bit, above all because I hear myself repeating the same words: "A repeated word is never true," I read in the Proust I brought the Lenzes.[4] (They were delighted with all the presents.[5])

My darling, open the letters You send me! One of them, from Munich, proposes that I do an Anthology of contemporary French Poetry—it is quite tempting and I think that You would like it if I accepted.[6] Too bad that I cannot go for a half-day to Munich to negotiate all that in person, which is always better.

M. Leippe, one of the directors of DVA, proposes to publish my volume in the fall, which is rather normal, but I will try for Easter, in order to be done with it and more free. For the honorarium, it does not promise to be extraordinary, but most people advise me to stay with DVA, despite everything, if only for this second volume. Leippe has left for Paris, and Monday I will see M. Müller, the other director, who will offer me more concrete proposals; I will not accept just anything right away.

I really have little desire to go to Düsseldorf, but Schroers will surely be offended if I do not go. If I go, it will be Wednesday, and I will stay there two days at the very most. From there, I will go to Baden-Baden, from where I will come back to Paris. So I will be back the 7th.

My love, take care of Yourself. The cut is truly not worrisome? Don't hesitate to tell me, please! And do not worry about the difficulties that You might have with this exhibition:[7] Your etchings are very-very beautiful, I swear to You, and it is unthinkable that they will not find the path that is theirs. Theirs: ours. Truly.

This morning, I went to look for the instruments (cradle,[8] etc.)—without success unfortunately. (As for the record player, there is the customs duty to pay…)

My darling love, wait for me in utter calm, without the slightest worry. Think of Almaviva whom I love and whom I will love always always always

Your little husband

---

1. PC is alluding to Curt Hohoff's essay "Flötentöne hinter dem Nichts" published in *Geist und Ursprung. Zur modernen Literatur* (Munich: Ehrenwirth, 1954, pp. 232–43). In his evocation of the difficulties posed by PC's poetry, Hohoff compares it to the Mishnah, suggesting, for PC, that it is incomprehensible or empty. Hohoff, who was in communication with Claire Goll, was one of the first critics to publish a text comparing PC and Yvan Goll; see *GA*, no. 46.

2. Herbert Eisenreich, a writer from Austria living in Stuttgart. PC had met him a few years earlier in Paris. Through him, PC will meet Brigitta Eisenreich, with whom he will have a meaningful affair, of which there are traces in his poetry. See Brigitta Eisenreich, in collaboration with Bertrand Badiou, *Celans Kreidestern. Ein Bericht* (Frankfurt am Main: Suhrkamp, 2010) and the revised French version, *L'Étoile de craie. Une liaison clandestine avec Paul Celan*, trans. Georges Felten (Paris: Éditions du Seuil, 2013).

3. PC has in mind the above-cited essay by Hohoff (n. 1) and an essay by Hans Egon Holthusen ("Fünf junge Lyriker," published in *Merkur* in May 1954), in which Holthusen establishes a link between PC and Yvan Goll, and characterizes as "trivial" the expression "Mühlen des

Todes" (death mills) used by PC in the poem "Spät und Tief." Later, Holthusen will evoke this phrase again regarding PC's "old predilection" for "surrealist," "indulgent" genitive metaphors in his review of *Die Niemandsrose* (hereafter *NR*) in the *Frankfurter Allgemeine Zeitung*, 2 May 1964. See *GA* nos 85 and 123. It was Péter Szondi who reminded him that Adolf Eichmann had used the expression "mill of Auschwitz" (*Frankfurter Allgemeine Zeitung*, 26 June 1964).

4. This phrase is from André Maurois's essay "À la recherche de Marcel Proust" in the book PC has just given to Hanne and Hermann Lenz. It is in fact a phrase from Robert de Montesquiou, recalled by Proust in a letter to him from 13 December 1895—see *Correspondance Générale de Marcel Proust* (Paris: Plon, 1930), v. 1, pp. 20–21. Proust's Baron du Charlus will utter the maxim, "In principle, a repeated word is rarely true" in *À la recherche du temps perdu: Le Côté de Guermantes* (Paris: Gallimard, 1949), v. 7, p. 216.

5. Proust's autograph and a small bottle of perfume.

6. This project will not be realized, but PC's notes for it include plans for translations of Nerval, Baudelaire, Rimbaud, Apollinaire, Éluard, Milosz, Desnos, Supervielle, Maeterlinck, Artaud, and Mallarmé. For PC's published translations of poetry from French, see *GW* IV.

7. The reference is to an exhibition devoted to the best works from the Friedlaender studio, where GCL works, at the gallery-bookstore La Hune, from 8 to 28 February 1955.

8. The cradle or rocker is an instrument used in intaglio printing, which resembles a small knife, with which the artist covers the plate with a network of fine and regular hatchings, which allow the artist to obtain a deep black upon printing.

37

[Stuttgart,]
Monday, [31 January 1955]
seven o'clock in the morning

My love, my dear love, everything I come across here seems to me distant right now: I love You, I love You, yes, and I know that this is enough for me, that my whole existence finds in this its reason. Gisèle, my love.

I sleep poorly here: the human landscape in this woeful country (unaware of its woes) is saddening indeed. The rare friends, the true ones, are disappointed, resigned, discouraged.

This evening, I will read the poems out to them over their heads, and this will be something like meeting my listeners beyond themselves, in a second reality, which I will have given them.

Then the return will be close. I do not at all feel like going to Düsseldorf, do not feel at all like going to Munich. I will stop, because I kind of promised it, in Baden-Baden, which is on the way home. Five, six days at the most to spend here.

And You, my love? How are You? I am so anxious to see You again, to wrap You in my arms, I need so much to look in Your eyes, Almaviva, my soul-who-lives.

Pardon me for writing so little, so poorly! I will tell you all the details, rest assured.

We will find a home of our own and we will be protected there from many things.[1]

What luck for me to have met You!

Think of me, my darling, think of You,

nothing will be able to separate us.

I love You

Your little Poeter

[In the margin:] My dear, I just received Your letter from Friday: take care of Yourself, my love, ask the doctor what to do about the albumin. Wednesday I will go for a half-day to Munich, to obtain the details about the Anthology; it is simpler. It is not until the 4th that I can see M. Rosengarten in Baden-Baden; the 5th I will probably be with You. Until soon.

Do not write to me anymore, think of me!

1. PC and GCL are looking for a place to live. It will not be until July 1955 that they leave the two rooms they have lived in for over a year on rue de Lota to share a four-room apartment (property of the mother of GCL) on rue de Montevideo, with one of GCL's sisters, Marie-Thérèse de Lestrange. This cohabitation will not be easy. It will not be until November 1957 that they have their own apartment.

38

Stuttgart, Tuesday, [1 February 1955]

My dear love, just a few lines to tell You that I am thinking of You, of You always. And then, that it went very well yesterday evening at the reading (in Esslingen); a lot of people, who listened to me attentively, a bit spellbound at the end. In the audience, a certain number of young poets, one of whom, Johannes Poethen (a friend of Saguer and Jean-Pierre Wilhelm's), offered to show me Hölderlin's archives in Tübingen, which is very close to here: I will go the day after tomorrow, for a half-day.—Today, I started the "negotiations" with DVA: they promise to be quite laborious, but I think that I will manage to get to an acceptable result. They are printing 2,500 copies this time![1] The book will probably appear before Easter (but there are difficulties with the title: *Inselhin* was not kept; I am insisting, with, I believe, a certain chance of success, on *Argumentum e silentio*).[2]

My love, if it were up to me, I would go to Paris tomorrow; but Baden-Baden is set for the fourth, I will spend the day there and take, I hope, the evening train. I will telegraph You from there during the day.

My love, my dear love!

Your little husband

---

1. *VS* is published in late June 1955. The first two editions of *MG* had run to 1,500 copies.
2. The envisioned title for the volume, *Argumentum e silentio*, would have shared the title of the poem dedicated to René Char, the second to last in the collection. *Von Schwelle zu Schwelle*, the final title, is taken from verse 27 of "Chanson einer Dame im Schatten" (Chanson of a Lady in Shadows) in *MG*.

39

[Paris, around 4 April 1955][1]

My darling,

There is finally a letter from DVA: these gentlemen give a little ground, while employing inadmissible language: "Your personality," M. Müller tells me, "has become a bit problematic for me"[2]... All things considered, I should not allow people to use that tone with me, but to save the volume I will pretend not to have understood anything...

That will probably still be a while, since I will insist on several things (the number for the print run mentioned in the contract, etc.), which will necessitate a new contract. Oh well, the book will be published finally and we will both breathe.

I kiss You with all my heart, my love

P.

1. This letter, not included in the original edition of this correspondence, is published here for the first time.
2. In a letter dated 4 April, 1955, Gotthold Müller rebukes PC for the demands he has made in his prior letter to the DVA. Müller contrasts PC's friendly and gracious demeanor in person with what he considers to be the "impersonal" tone of PC's letter. The sentence which PC quotes from Müller is the following: "You will understand that the personality of the author Paul Celan, with all due esteem for his poetic work, has become a bit problematic." Müller concludes by stating that if PC does not trust in his publisher, the latter will return his manuscript of VS to him.

40

[Paris?, 7 April 1955]

So rag ich, steinern,
zu dir,
Hohe:

Von Flugsand
ausgewaschen die beiden
Höhlen am Stirnsaum.
Eräugtes
Dunkel darin.

Durchpocht
von schweigsam geschwungenen Hämmern
die Stelle,
wo mich das Flügelaug streifte.

Dahinter,
ausgespart aus der Wand,
die Stufe, wo das Erinnerte hockt.
Hierher
rieselt, von Nächten belebt,
eine Stimme,
aus der du den Trunk schöpfst.

[Word-for-word French translation by Paul Celan:]¹

Ainsi je me dresse / je suis dressé, de pierre / pierreux,
vers toi,
Haute.

Par du sable volant
érodés les deux
creux à la lisière du front.
Là-dedans,
des ténèbres aperçues.—

Traversé par les battements
de marteaux brandis muettement,
l'endroit
où me frôla l'œil ailé.
Derrière (cela),
dans la paroi,
la marche où s'accroupit le Souvenu.
Vers ici
ruisselle, animé par des nuits,
une voix,
dans laquelle tu puises (ce que tu bois) le breuvage.

So I rise up, stony,
to you,
High:

By flying sand
eroded the two
hollows in the brow-seam,
darkness glimpsed
in there.

Traversed by the thumping
of silently swung hammers
the spot,
where the winged eye grazed me.
Behind,
in the wall,
the step where the Remembered hunkers down.
Over here
trickles, animated by nights,
a voice,
from which you draw the drink.

1. This poem was probably the subject of a German lesson for GCL. Cf. "Heute und morgen," *NKGA*, p. 99.

41

[Dedication in *Von Schwelle zu Schwelle*][1]

To You, my lively soul,
my soul-that-lives,[2]
on the great open path
of our Eric

Paul
Paris, 20 June 1955.[3]

1. (Stuttgart: DVA, 1955.)
2. PC here translates the first dedication, "Für Almaviva," which he had envisioned putting at the beginning of this book.
3. GCL had returned to rue de Lota two days earlier after having given birth, under difficult conditions, on 6 June 1955, to Claude François Eric.

42

[Dedication in *Von Schwelle zu Schwelle*]

[On the flyleaf:]

★[1]
Eric Celan

[Underneath the half title:]

To Eric,
our son,
for his eyes opened on Life

His father, beside his mother
Paris, 29 June 1955

---

1. PC noted in his planner for the date 6 June 1955: "22h50 / * / Eric / Villa Molière, / 57 Bd Montmorency (16th)" (the address of the private clinic where EC was born).

43

[Paris, summer–autumn? 1955]

Good evening, my Dear, good evening in our home.
    Tomorrow I will be there, be patient.
    Hug the son when you go to see if he is uncovered.
    I love You with all my heart

                    Paul

44

[Paris,] Gare du Nord
[23 September 1955], 10:10

My big Angelet big!

Here I am at the train station, ticket in my pocket, waiting for the train...

My love, how can I stay away for a long time, when all my being plunges into Your soul, while Your eyes, once again, have overflowed for me—

I cannot wait to come home to find You beside our son, who will soon realize that he lives amidst our forever united hearts—

Until very soon, my love!

Paul

45

Cologne
Saturday, [24 September 1955], 3 o'clock

My Dear, my big soul!

I arrived in Düsseldorf this morning, but since Schroers had not come to meet me, I telephoned Jean-Pierre, who came to pick me up right away in his car (driven by one of his "friends," a young sculptor) to take me to Schroers...who had left for the weekend. I was received very politely by the maid, who knew about my arrival, I washed up, shaved, I drank a good coffee, hung up the gray suit, to leave again to visit Jean-Pierre, who lives in a very pretty little apartment, furnished with, among other things, a turntable on which he played for me...Léo Ferré.[1]—Since Schroers won't return until tomorrow, I had the idea of telephoning Schallück (I did not have the patience to spend the afternoon with J.-P.)—and here I am, arrived just now in Cologne, where I will probably spend the night at the Schallücks'.

My love, how are You today, how is our son? There it is, it is all that I can tell myself that is true and joyful, there it is, one day less spent far from You.—The faces I see here are hardly those of a Hölderlinian people...

But I am doing well, thinking of You, of you both, to whom I belong. I kiss You, my Dear.

Boisgentil[2]

1. The Celans enjoyed going to the cabaret to listen to Léo Ferré.
2. *Boisgentil* (literally, "nice-wood") is the French name for the plant called, in German, *Seidelbast* (*Daphne mezereum*), referred to in English as daphne or spurge laurel. For PC, this amorous appellation also involves many associations with Bukovina, its landscape, and its vegetation. This plant, which appears in PC's early poem "Seidelbast" (see *NKGA*, p. 348), is one of the first to blossom in the undergrowth, from February to April; in his poem it appears as a stem with a red or rose-white flower without leaves.

46

Düsseldorf, Monday, [26 September 1955]

My darling love, how are You, how is our son? Oh, I really cannot wait to be with You again, I am utterly disoriented in this country where, quite bizarrely, people speak the language my mother taught me[1]...

I did not stay in Cologne. On Saturday, Schallück and his wife had just come back from vacation, were waiting for friends, and I had left my pyjamas etc. in Düsseldorf. And moreover, the climate in their house seemed to me a bit charged, so I kept my visit short, went to their neighbors', the Eich(-Aichinger)s',[2] for another visit, even shorter, and I went walking a bit in the streets of Cologne, where, in the windows of bookshops, it so happened that I sometimes saw my poems...

Yesterday, I slept late (until noon, almost), met this tiresome J.-P., went home at 4 o'clock: the Schroers had just gotten back themselves. Madame S. thanks you very much for the scarf (in my opinion, too beautiful for her...). Discussions, without much substance, Schroers read me two of his stories, which I did not find sensational, we drank this good French cognac, but I have the feeling that I will struggle to occupy my time in the days to come. The readings will not take place until the 29th and the 30th, which is far away, this time seems to me quite empty. I will probably go to Stuttgart the 31st, to leave again on the 1st, for Basel. For I decidedly do not like this country. It is curious, but I have the impression that all these problems of language that I posed myself are, fundamentally, very secondary...

My darling, I hope that a letter will be waiting for me this evening: here, as everywhere, my life needs Your presence to be true and to be mine.

Hug our son, take him in Your arms a bit, spoil him a bit for me—and spoil his mother.

My heart sends You a thousand signs.

Paul

---

1. Regarding his mother tongue, which he learned in Bukovina, PC writes in the last distich of "Nähe der Gräber" [Nearness of Graves], dated "Cz[ernowitz], 44 [after my return from Kiev]": "Und duldest du, Mutter, wie einst, ach, daheim, / den leisen, den deutschen, den schmerzlichen Reim?" [And can you bear, Mother, as before, oh, at home, / the soft, the German, the painful rhyme?] [*NKGA*, p. 17]. PC goes, and continues to go, to Germany regularly in order not to lose contact with the language as it is spoken.
2. Günter Eich, German poet, and Ilse Aichinger, Austrian writer; PC met them in May 1952, at the Group 47 meeting in Niendorf.

47

29b rue de Montevideo
Paris, 16th [arrondissement]
Tuesday, [27 September 1955]

My darling Love,

I don't like these days without You so much, not that they pass slowly, Your son takes it upon himself to fill them, but You have so marvelously made me become used to Your presence that I have a certain difficulty with being far from You. But all is well here, You must not worry. Admit that it's a pleasant thought that the two of us are waiting for You here; for me too it's easier to be with Eric. He is so nice for me.

Like you, he very much likes "There Was Once a Little Ship" and "If the King Had Given Me." Instead of Russian, he hears French![1]

I had to make a quick trip to the bank, and after many exhortations, I left Eric here with the concierge, here, and I flew for an hour and a half far from him. I admit I was not at ease and I took two taxis. He did not wake up once, and slept his "little Angel" sleep. Paris looked very well to me under a pale sun and a sky full of large gray clouds; the chestnut trees dark and severe, rejuvenated by white flowers as we like them. Place de la Concorde more grandiose than ever, under a uniform gray-blue sky, and in the Jardin des Tuileries, this very bizarre double tree. How I love Paris through You! It's You who taught me to love it.

I kiss You as I love You

Gisèle

Your Mayuschka

A bit later, with Your words that are so sweet to wait for.

My darling, I gave Your message to our son, he was so happy, he was laughing with all his heart, and when I left him, he was still laughing. You cannot imagine how nice he is. His cheeks are getting rounder and rounder, but his smiles and his gaze are getting more and more expressive.

After his bottles, it's hard to put him back in bed, and I promise you I really replace you, I believe you have nothing to fear, he has me so easily around his little finger, he is irresistible, it's a joy to see him so glad to be living—he often stays awake, he laughs all by himself, he is so well behaved! I love him very much. More and more. My son from you. What luck I have!

I love You, my little darling Man.

Till very soon.

Your little strand

---

1. PC, who knew many popular and revolutionary songs in German, English, French, Spanish, Italian, and Russian, had a preference for Russian songs.

48

My darling love, my big-angelet-big,

Yesterday evening, I received Your second letter: I am so happy to learn that everything is going well, that our son continues to smile at You all throughout your long strolls! The more I am here, the more I know that there is only one place where I can truly live: beside You and our son, in Paris.

Tomorrow is the first reading, in Wuppertal, the day after tomorrow I will read here, and the day after I will begin to return to You, to my home. If there is one thing that this trip has, once again, taught me, it is this: the language with which I make my poems does not depend at all on the one people speak here or elsewhere; my anxieties about this, fed by my worries as a translator, are baseless. If there are still sources from which new poems (or prose) could flow, it is in myself that I will find them and not at all in the conversations that I could have in German, with Germans, in Germany.

I do not like this country at all. I find the people lamentable. Of course, there are exceptions, but they are rare, and to reach them I do not need to go travelling in Germany.

You tell me not to be too severe regarding my friends, I am trying to follow this advice, but I cannot prevent myself from noting the extent to which some of them are small and petty. The impurities are truly too numerous to be bracketed.

My days here are quite empty. Yesterday evening, I made, at Jean-Pierre W.'s[1] house, the acquaintance of a poet, Emil Barth,[2] whom I vaguely knew by name, and a Catholic author, Warnach,[3] a character about whom Schroers, also present, told me that he was a murky and dubious type. All that went quite well, but essentially, despite all these witticisms, nothing important was said.

At eight o'clock, we—I, J.-Pierre, and Schroers (who had joined us)—went to Madame de La Motte's home.[4] She is an old lady, very alert, very direct, who received me, furthermore, like a prince: champagne, wines, etc. We no doubt drank too much, we had already emptied a bottle of cognac at J.-P.'s, and the discussion with Madame La Motte [*sic*] and her two sons (the second is a musician) continued to be of the kind that preceded it.

Having got home at three in the morning, I slept until eleven o'clock. Here I am now, after lunch and a stroll of the dull variety in the center of Düsseldorf, in a café where I am writing You this letter. This evening, I will go to see, surrounded by the same characters as yesterday (Schroers, Wilhelm, and Mme Schroers), a sort of cabaret that passes for the best one in Germany.

In a word: I do not feel too bad, but I am weary.

What wearies me even more is that I did not anticipate that my arrival in Stuttgart will fall on a Saturday and that I will have to wait for Monday morning to see the editor.

Monday evening I will go to Basel, Wednesday, at the latest Thursday, I will be with You, with You, with You. With You and Your son. For if I travel, it is all the better to return to Your side.

Kiss our son, my love.
I am entirely Yours

Paul

1. Jean-Pierre Wilhelm, German art critic and translator; member of the International Brigades during the Spanish Civil War; founded and directed a contemporary art gallery in Düsseldorf (Galerie 22); will publish a short introduction to PC's work and translations of four poems in *Les Cahiers du Sud* in 1956.
2. Emil Barth, German poet, novelist, and essayist, cofounder of the Akademie für Sprache und Dichtung in Darmstadt.
3. Walter Warnach, German poet and art critic, and friend of Heinrich Böll's.
4. PC met Hildegard de la Motte in 1955 through her son, Manfred, a friend of Jean-Pierre Wilhelm's; he maintained a correspondence with her from that year until 1970.

49

[Düsseldorf?,] Saturday, [1 October 1955]
six o'clock in the morning

My darling love, my soul, You spoiled me yesterday: three letters! Thank you, little Strand, for this good news: I believe I have definitively understood, here, how much our son is present in my life, how much our love is prepared to receive him in its heart, how clearly he is already defining himself in his ardor.

My darling, the readings went well; there were not too many people, just enough to fill the two little halls, but I believe I was able to reach, among the kindly people (who, always, constitute the majority of these audiences), a few others, more inclined toward the essential.[1]

In Wuppertal, I was invited over by a gentleman who has a large collection of paintings (including Klee); it was, in a house too sumptuously filled with art, a conversation that I kept going as best as I could.

Yesterday, there was again, after the reading, a reception at Mme La Motte's [sic] home, with many people and little contact.

And here I am, at six o'clock in the morning, awake in my bed—I will take the train at seven thirty for Stuttgart, from where I will leave again on Monday afternoon (for Basel).

I am so happy to see You again, my love, to see You again, You and our son. Just before, I dreamed that I was far from You, in Romania, that I did not have any chance to write to You, but then I found You again—how could I not have found You again?

I go toward You,
as always

P.

[In the margin:] Do not write to me anymore, my darling, I am coming to find all Your words, all Your silences.

Kiss my son, kiss Your son.

---

1. The Wuppertal reading took place on 29 September 1955 at the Städtische Museum (today the Von der Heydt-Museum).

50

[Avallon, 30 April 1956]

After a very beautiful excursion to Montréal and to Fontenay, from Avallon,[1] to be there a bit sooner

Paul

---

1. PC visits these important sites of Roman Burgundy in the company of his friends Gertrud and Guido Meister, on the occasion of a Franco-German writers' meeting in Vézelay.

51

[Paris, 11 August 1956]

Just a word, my love, to thank You for all that You are—

Here I am, after having walked the quays beneath "my" clock at quai de la Tournelle (I learned just this minute that that is its name), with, in my pocket, two little books, *Nous deux encore* by Michaux and *Le Merveilleux* by Pierre Mabille,[1] a coffee in front of me (and no cigarettes!),

and my heart clothed on both sides in Your presence.

Until soon, my love

P.

---

1. PC in all likelihood has just bought these two books from the *bouquinistes* (book vendors) of the quays along the Seine. Henri Michaux, a French writer of Belgian origin, exchanged brief letters with PC between 1956 and 1966; PC is the most important translator of Michaux into German. Pierre Mabille was a medical doctor and French writer and member of the Surrealist group in 1934; contributor to *Le Minotaure*; from 1949 to 1952, instructor at the École d'anthropologie in Paris.

52

Cologne, Friday, [12 October 1956]

My darling, You are doing well, aren't You, You and the son? Having just arrived, I have, as I do each time, the impression of having come for no reason to this country, whose presence, for me, is mingled with distance. I will see tons of people tomorrow, come from the four corners of Germany,[1] a good spectacle for those who know how to look. In a moment I will go to Schroers's home (an hour from here), tomorrow I will return to Cologne [in the margin: "with him"]. And Monday evening I hope to leave Cologne.

I kiss You, my darling.

Kiss the son

Paul[2]

1. In Cologne on 13 and 14 October 1956, PC participates in the meeting of the Grünewalder Kreis, an antifascist organization created by the founder of Group 47, Hans Werner Richter. PC had agreed to go to Germany also in the hope of establishing new contacts, and to obtain the support of German intellectuals in his struggle against the campaign of defamation conducted by Claire Goll (see no. 4, n. 2).
2. PC signs here using an old-fashioned German "u" with a dash above it; this way of writing the phoneme "u," which PC employs systematically (and which is unusual in modern German orthography), is a vestige of Sütterlin script, which PC had learned from his mother. What might appear in PC's writing as a sort of maternal mark (*Muttermal*) ordinarily serves to facilitate the distinction between the vowel and the consonant "n."

53

Cologne, Tuesday morning, [5 February 1957]

My darling,

Just a few words to tell You that I have arrived in Cologne, where I slept in the hotel, right next to the train station. It is nine in the morning—I slept little, it is the disorientation—I just called Schroers, whom I will go see in an hour at Kiepenheuer.[1] Over there, more ample details about Bremen.[2] Will I spend the night here again? At Schroers's probably. I do not really know.

My darling, be patient, pay attention to Yourself and to the son. I will surely not be very long.

I kiss You, my love

Paul[3]

All my best to Francine, Mme Guenepin, the kids, Henri, Rachel, and Marius.

1. Schroers is at this time a reader at the publishing house Kiepenheuer & Witsch.
2. PC will give a reading in Bremen on 7 February 1957. He is the guest of *Neues Forum*, a review which promoted contemporary literature and art, thanks to Rudolf Hirsch, the director of S. Fischer. During the discussion that followed his reading, a student posed a question about Yvan Goll and the Goll Affair. According to Oswald Döpke, of Radio Bremen, "Celan turned pale. He got up suddenly, screamed that he would not tolerate such effrontery, which was nothing other than unvarnished anti-Semitism, and ran out of the hall." While attempting to calm PC, Döpke made a most unfortunate slip of the tongue: "Dear Herr Goll..." (Cf. Döpke, "Ich weiß nämlich gar nicht, wohin ich gehen soll. Ingeborg Bachmann in Werken und Briefen aus den Jahren 1956 und 1957" in *Du*, September 1994, p. 38; see *GA*, no. 50).
3. See above, no. 52, n. 2.

54

[Paris,] Friday, [9 August 1957]

My Darling,

Here is the letter from the agency and a card from Chiva-Ariane[1] that just arrived. It is the Wailing Wall in Jerusalem.

Excuse me again for having been so miserly with my words on the telephone: there was, sprawled in an armchair, her gaze fixed on this curious beast that I am, Mademoiselle Béatrice de Béarn[2] (and of Bushybrow).

I just returned from a short walk—I had gone to see, at the Institut Germanique, the results of the agrégation in German: three students from S[ain]t-Cloud accepted, it is a quite good result.

After Your telephone call: Do not torment Yourself, my Darling, whatever happens, we will soon have a place to live, and will be sheltered a bit from human baseness.

I kiss You, my love.

Kiss our ever so naughty son.

Paul

1. Isac Chiva and Ariane Deluz, his wife at the time.
2. Acquaintance of Marie-Thérèse de Lestrange, with whom the Celans share GCL's mother's former apartment on rue de Montevideo, as well as a telephone line.

55

[Paris?] 13 August 1957

"Matière de Bretagne"[1]

Ginsterlicht, gelb, die Hänge
eitern gen Himmel, der Dorn
wirbt um die Wunde, es läutet
darin, es ist Abend, das Nichts
rollt seine Meere zur Andacht,
das Blutsegel hält auf dich zu.

Trocken, verlandet
das Bett hinter dir, verschilft
seine Stunde, oben,
beim Stern, die milchigen
Priele schwatzen im Schlamm, Steindattel,
unten, gebuscht, klafft ins Gebläu, eine Staude
Vergänglichkeit, schön,
grüßt dein Gedächtnis.

    (Kanntet ihr mich,
    Hände? Ich ging
    den gegabelten Weg, den ihr wiest, mein Mund
    spie seinen Schotter, ich ging, meine Zeit,
    wandernde Wächte, warf ihren Schatten—kanntet ihr mich?)

Hände, die dorn-
umworbene Wunde, es läutet,
Hände, das Nichts, seine Meere,
Hände, im Ginsterlicht, das
Blutsegel
hält auf dich zu.

69

Du,
du lehrst,
du lehrst deine Hände,
du lehrst deine Hände, du lehrst,
du lehrst deine Hände

schlafen.

Gorse-light, yellow, the slopes
fester against the sky, the thorn
woos the wound, bells are tolling
in there, it is evening, the nothing
rolls its seas to contemplation,
the blood-sail heads for you.

Dry, silted up
the bed behind you, grown over with reeds
its hour, above,
by the star, the milky
channels babble in the sludge, date-mussel,[2]
beneath, bushy, yawns into the blueness, a tuft of
caducity, beautiful,
greets your memory.

(Did you know me,
hands? I went
the forked path, which you indicated, my mouth
spat its gravel, I went, my time,
wandering snowdrift, cast its shadow—did you know me?)

Hands, the thorn-
wooed wound, bells are tolling,
hands, the nothing, its seas,
hands, in the gorse-light, the

blood-sail
heads for you.

You,
you teach,
you teach your hands,
you teach your hands, you teach,
you teach your hands

to sleep.[3]

der Hang: (Abhang)—pente; (die Neigung)—le penchant, propension, inclination, disposition / werben (a, o) um jemanden / etwas werben—solliciter, rechercher, demander (en mariage), briguer / der Bewerber—prétendant / umwerben—entourer de ses hommages, courtiser / sie ist viel umworben—elle a beaucoup de prétendants / erwerben—acquérir, gagner / die Andacht—recueillement (religieux), prière / seine Andacht halten—faire ses dévotions, sa prière / Neuntägige A[ndacht]—neuvaine / Andachtsübungen—dévotions, exercices / mit A[ndacht] essen—manger avec religion / auf etwas/j[emande]n zuhalten—aller droit à q[uelque] c[hose]/[quelqu'un] / das Schilf—roseau, jonc / der Priele [*sic*]—[*translation missing*][4] / der Schlamm—limon, bourbe, vase / schwatzen—jaser, babiller, bavarder / klaffen—être béant, s'entrouvrir, bâiller / die Staude—arbrisseau, arbuste, touffe / vergänglich—qui passe vite, éphémère, périssable / V[ergänglich]keit—nature périssable, caducité / die Gabel —la fourche(ette); fourchu, bifurqué / sich gabeln—se [*sic*] bifurquer / weisen (ie, ie)—montrer, indiquer / die (Schnee-)Wächte—[*translation missing*][5] / der Schotter—cailloutis, pierrailles / eine Straße schottern—caillouter, empierrer

1. "Matière de Bretagne" was probably the subject of a German lesson for GCL.
2. "Steindattel" or literally "stone-date," a variety of mussel present in particular in the Mediterranean; according to PC's Sachs-Villatte dictionary, it is a synonym of "Bohrmuschel" (French: *pholade, térébratule*) or a "datte, moule pholade ou cylindrique, dactyle (*Mytilus*

lithophagus)" (vol. 4, p. 1669). Known in English as "date shell" or "date mussel."

3. See also "Matière de Bretagne," *Poems*, p. 101, and trans. Joachim Neugroschel in *Selections*, p. 65.

4. According to the Sachs-Villatte used by PC, "Prie(h)l *m*": "passage étroit entre des bancs de sable" *[narrow passage between sandbanks]* (vol. 4, p. 1350).

5. According to the Sachs-Villatte, "Wächte" is a synonym of "Schneewächte," "neige surplombante ou tassée en encorbellement" (snowdrift, overhanging or packed, corbeled-out snow); vol. 4, pp. 1965 and 1537.

56

[Paris, 21 November 1957]

My little darling Peach,

I am—am—so happy beside You in our new abode.[1]

Truly!

Mou-mou-tschou

21 November 1957 (and so on and so forth)

1. After more than two years of cohabitation with Marie-Thérèse de Lestrange, on rue de Montevideo, the Celans have just moved to 78 rue de Longchamp, a small four-room apartment on the fifth floor which they acquired thanks GCL's inheritance. Her mother, following her retirement to a convent in Brittany three years earlier, had made a vow of poverty and split her possessions among her four daughters and the convent.

57

[Paris,] 23 January 1958

Have a good trip, my darling,[1]

May these pieces of bark protect You,[2] they in which You have always trusted, and which have deserved Your trust.

I will think of You ceaselessly. Believe in my Love, please!

Your Maya kisses You, and remains in Your house with Your son.

We are waiting for You. Come back quickly, we need You so much.

Gisèle

1. PC had just left for Germany, visiting Cologne, Bremen (for a reading and the Bremen City Literature Prize), Hamburg, and Munich (spending the latter at the home of Ingeborg Bachmann). GCL is aware that PC has renewed his amorous relationship with Ingeborg Bachmann, which will continue episodically until June 1958, during PC's trips to Germany. PC had previously had a brief relationship with Bachmann in spring 1948, during his stay in Vienna, then in fall 1950, during a trip she made to Paris.
2. The little pieces of bark to which GCL refers had for PC a talismanic quality. They are no doubt from Avignon and recall the Celans' honeymoon trip there.

58

78 rue de Longchamp,[1]
Paris, 16th [arrondissement]
23 January 1958

Happy anniversary![2] my darling, my darling Love,

My heart is full of thanks for what You are. I thank You for Your goodness, Your patience with me, I thank you for all the love you proffer me ceaselessly and that I am far from deserving. In six years of life beside You I could have raised myself to the image of me You had created. I have not managed that, and now You have succeeded, finally, in discovering me as I was, full of pettiness, without generosity, without nobility, without truth, and it is You who have revealed me, not even I who had the courage to do so. How ashamed I am! How ashamed I am! I have only known how to offer You the heavy burden of my so imperfect, so lamentably poor and egotistical love. I have felt so cold since you know what I am, I am so ashamed, I doubt myself so much, I know very well the little that I am and know also who you are and I continue with these demands that oppress you. Oh my darling, do you really forgive me for what I am and that you didn't know I was? I have disappointed you. I will make no more promises, I will try to keep those I would like to make, I must have disappointed you so much with my promises of courage and of calm, promises that I keep so badly.

But consider a bit, my darling, that I have only you, that fulfills me and is enough, but please, believe in my love, even if it is very imperfect, very egotistical, jealous, one loves according to what one is; I am of little account, I know only how to love you badly, but my life is to love you, that's my only life, I have no other.[3]

You opened my eyes wide on the world, my eyes, large maybe, but until then closed; you didn't know that the world is you and that you created it, nothing else exists for me. What have I to do with my freedom? My freedom is you, all the rest is chains, I have no use for chains, I like freedom, I like my freedom, my great, tender, and terrible freedom. Do you really know how much I am yours? Do you know that I belong entirely to you? I am so sure of being in truth on the path with you, a difficult but true path. On this path, I struggle, I fall, I stumble, I lose myself without cease, my darling, yes, but it is also the path where I find myself and where I can continue to advance with you, beside you in truth. Allow me to cover with kisses this hand that has led me for six years, which has held mine since the beginning and which helps me.

Your son is here, beside me, he is sleeping, he does not know, it is me you have chosen so that one day he may know and sleep no more.[4] Never will I thank you enough for it, I will attempt to know how to complete that task. Speaking of which, I am thinking again of this line in Trakl: "Ein blauer Augenblick ist nur mehr Seele."[5]

I will continue to read Your poems these days and all the others, they have been in me for a long time, my darling, but I did not want to accept them, they are realities, but terrible realities. I know now that one cannot escape them, they have proven it to me a hundred times already and they will save me now and will help me to experience these realities. I will refuse them no more, I have feared them, your poems, now I love them, they are true and truth and they are you.

Thanks, my darling, for having called me the other night, to look, with you, the two of us together, at the first snow of the year, from your window,[6] in our house, beside our darling son. That was such a great joy. Thanks. See you very soon, I am waiting for you, my darling, allow me to tell you again for I think it very intensely:

I love you, Paul, and I also say your name very loudly and you will say mine too, won't you?

your Maya

I don't know how to write, I don't know how to say things as you say things so well, forgive me for not knowing how to write as I would like to and for saying things banally.

1. See above, no. 56, n. 1.
2. For PC, the number twenty-three has a talismanic value tied to his birthday, November 23, and the date of his marriage, December 23, which he calls the "big anniversaries"; the 23rd of other months of the year are the "little anniversaries."
3. In this letter, GCL expresses in veiled terms her worries about the crisis she is going through with PC; since fall 1957, PC had renewed his romantic relationship with Ingeborg Bachmann. See also *Paul Celan / Ingeborg Bachmann: Correspondence*, trans. Wieland Hoban (Kolkata: Seagull Books, 2019).
4. In "Wolfsbohne," a poem dated October 21, 1959, PC cites and re-writes this passage: "Unser / Kind / weiß es und schläft" (Our / child / knows it and sleeps) (*NKGA*, p. 419).
5. "A blue instant, all is only soul."
6. GCL will evoke this memory eight years later. See no. 298.

59

Gästehaus des Senats Bremen, Parkallee 113
25 January 1958

My Darling,

Here I am in Bremen,[1] after a stay of two days in Cologne, quite tiring because of the discussions (with Schroers, Böll, and Schallück, above all with the latter...).[2]

I am living in a sort of villa, on the second floor, in a spacious room, very calm, view of the snow-covered gardens. (But it is not very cold.)

An azalea at the window, tulips on the table, it is welcoming.

I am writing to You while waiting for the arrival of M. Lutze, who is supposed to give me instructions...

In the train, this morning, I was able to think again about my little speech[3]—it surely cannot be very long, for most importantly R. A. Schröder[4] will be there—some things will be said concerning "Gedächtnis,"[5] I had a few "i," I think that it will organize itself rather well, with "no indifferent detail."[6]

I am thinking of You, my Dear, my Maïa, of You and our son—wait for me calmly, there cannot be any shocks.[7]

Yours completely,

Paul

I will telephone You from Hamburg.

Midnight

My dear, I was not able to post this letter, I have not left the house, the whole time there were visitors; after the most fattening imaginable lunch, there were people, quite pleasant, a journalist who interviewed me,[8] then Höllerer with a Korean painter, Schröder of course (truly friendly), then Müller who brought me the news of the *third* edition of *Mohn*[9]...

Now, the speech is written, I hope it is good. But this letter will probably not be mailed until Monday... Excuse me.

1. PC is to receive, the following day, for *MG* and *VS*, the Literaturpreis der Freien Hansestadt Bremen (8,000 German marks).
2. Regarding anti-Semitic remarks made by one of the participants at a recent Franco-German meeting in Vézelay, Schallück in particular argued against writing an overly complicated and intellectual letter of protest and for giving the person in question the chance to change his disposition. The Goll Affair was probably also the subject of these "discussions" with Schroers, Böll, and Schallück. On the Goll Affair, see no. 4, n. 2.
3. In English in the original ("mon petit speech").
4. The awarding of the prize took place the day of the celebration of the eightieth birthday of the poet Rudolf Alexander Schröder, honorary citizen of the city of Bremen and founder, with Rudolf Borchardt, of the publishing house Bremer Presse.
5. PC alludes to the first phrases of his speech: "Denken und Danken sind in unserer Sprache Worte ein und desselben Ursprungs. Wer ihrem Sinn folgt, begibt sich in den Bedeutungsbereich von: 'gedenken,' 'eingedenk sein,' 'Andenken,' 'Andacht'" (Thinking and thanking are in our language words of one and the same source. Whoever follows their meaning enters the semantic field of: "recollect," "bear in mind," "remembrance," "devotion"), *SPP*, p. 395.
6. Quoting line four of Guillaume Apollinaire's "Cors de chasse," *Alcools*.
7. Allusion to the possible consequences of his affair with Ingeborg Bachmann.
8. Interview conducted by Harry Newman (*Die Welt*, 27 January 1958).
9. The third edition of *MG* would appear in April 1958, with DVA (of which Gotthold Müller was one of the directors).

60

[Dedication in an offprint of the review *Botteghe oscure*: translation of "Le Bateau ivre" by Arthur Rimbaud, "Das trunkene Schiff"]

To Maïa,
who speaks to me in
my inebriations

> Paul
> 21 June 1958

61

[Dedication in Arthur Rimbaud, "Le Bateau ivre"—"Das trunkene Schiff," translated by Paul Celan][1]

To his Boatwoman

The Boatsman
in this seventh September[2]
of our sobrieties and inebriations
1958.

1. "Le Bateau ivre" —"Das trunkene Schiff," trans. Paul Celan (Wiesbaden: Insel, 1958).
2. The seventh September in the "private calendar" of PC and GCL, which begins with their meeting in November 1951.

62

[Dedication in an offprint of *Die neue Rundschau* (Celan's translation of Mandelstam)]

For Maïa, in our house, where I translated these poems
January 1959

Paul

63

[Paris, 5 March 1959]

Das Wort vom Zur-Tiefe-Gehn,
das wir gelesen haben.[1]
Die Jahre, die Worte, seither.
Wir sind es noch immer.[2]

Weißt du, der Raum ist unendlich,
weißt du, du brauchst nicht zu fliegen,
weißt du, was sich in dein Aug schrieb,
vertieft uns die Tiefe.

For Your birthday, my Love, for March 19th—this evening, March 5th, 1959.

/ Erste Niederschrift /[3]

The word of going-to-the-depths,
that we read.
The years, the words, since then.
We are still what we are.

You know, space is endless,
you know, you do not need to fly,

you know, what wrote itself in your eye
deepens for us the depths.

/ First transcription. /

1. Allusion to a reading, during a German lesson, of Georg Heym's poem, "Deine Wimpern, die langen." One version of this poem by PC is entitled "La Leçon d'allemand" (see *NR*, TCA, p. 11).
2. "We are still what we are." This line, which will occupy a particular place in the relation of PC with his wife starting in the year this poem was written, is no longer cited by the Celans after November 1965. See Jean-Pierre Lefebvre's translation of the line "Wir sind es noch immer" in "Schaufäden, Sinnfäden" (*Atemwende*; hereafter *AW*) in Paul Celan, *Renverse du Souffle* (Éditions du Seuil, 2003), p. 101. For this phrase, see also nos 106, 135, 136, 154, 186, 203.
3. See *NKGA*, p. 129.

64

[Dedication in *Sprachgitter*[1]]

For Maïa, for her eyes
where these verses were and
remain inscribed
For You, my soul and my life—
So that you open them
under our lamp,[2] next to our
son—For this 19 March 1959[3]

Paul

1. (Frankfurt am Main: S. Fischer, 1959). A four-leaf clover was inserted in front of the page bearing the dedication.
2. See no. 20.
3. GCL's thirty-second birthday.

65

[To Eric Celan]

[Dedication in *Sprachgitter*]

To *Eric*, for whom I put the
stars in the night,[1]
with my heart that thanks him for it
In our house, always

his father
April 1959

1. See no. 69, n. 3. See also "Ein Holzstern," (A Wooden Star) written 30–31 August 1958: "Ein Stern, tu ihn, / tu den Stern in die Nacht" (A star, put it, / put the star into the night), *NKGA*, p. 115.

66

[summer?[1] 1959]

See you in a bit, my Darling!
Our glowworms are still there[2]

[Unsigned]

1. GCL believed that the note dated to 1959. It was perhaps written during the Celans' stay in Austria during the summer vacation of 1959. Glowworms can be seen between May and September.
2. This note is revelatory of PC's "superstitious" or "magical" practices, which numerous poems echo. Along with plane tree bark, glowworms—in fact the wingless females of the *Lampyris* (literally "lantern-carrier") *noctiluca*—("vers luisants" in French; "Leuchtkäfer" or "Glühwürmchen" in German) are benevolent signs for PC. See the last stanza of "Lippen, Schwellgewebe" (13 May 1967; *NKGA*, p. 259; cf. also *Breathturn into Timestead: The Collected Later Poetry*, translated and with an introduction by Pierre Joris [New York: Farrar, Strauss and Giroux, 2014; hereafter *BIT*], p. 203); and the early poem "Sommernacht" (*NKGA*, p. 318); see also the chapter that Jean-Henri Fabre devotes to these insects, of the order Coleoptera, in his *Souvenirs entomologiques* (*Fabre's Book of Insects*).

67

My Darling

It is very simple and so clear:

I need You, always, I love You. What I am doing? I am waiting for Saturday.[1] Play a lot in the sand and collect a lot of shells with our son.

As for me, I will try to find something among the words.[2] Often, You know it well, I find what Your gaze puts there.

Hug our son, I kiss You

Paul

House of Three Celans, the 19th of August 1959

1. PC will join his family in Houlgate the following weekend (according to PC's planner).
2. This August, PC is working on "Gespräch im Gebirg" (Conversation in the Mountains; see *SPP*, p. 397).

68

[Dedication in Ossip Mandelstamm [*sic*],[1] *Gedichte*,[2] selected poems translated by Paul Celan]

To Gisèle
beside our candelabrum
with seven branches
beside our seven roses[3]
November 1959

Paul

1. While the typical spelling of this name, in Russian and other languages, is Mandelstam, Celan's spelling emphasizes the concrete character of the name's components: "Mandel" (almond) and "Stamm" (tree trunk, lineage, family), with the effect that the name can be read

as "almond trunk" or "lineage of the almond," which can be understood as making reference to the Jewish people (cf. no. 79). Moreover, the name is inscribed in the semantic field of "stehen" (to stand), a motif that runs through Celan's poetry.

2. (Frankfurt am Main: S. Fischer, 1959).

3. See "Wolfsbohne," written just before, on 26 October 1959 (*NKGA*, p. 419), and "Kristall" (*NKGA*, p. 50).

69

[Paris,] Monday, [4 January 1960]

My love, here I am back at home,[1] the lamp is lit[2]—the sky is very covered—and You, You and our son, You are still on the way—but calm, aren't You, but tranquil and confident? I found a very good mail delivery slipped under the door: a letter from Schroers;[3] a letter from Madame Schneider-Lengyel—you remember her no doubt, she came to rue des Écoles and, around a year ago, here: Madame-Masks, Madame-Photos-of-Greek-vases, Madame-Little-More-Or-Less-Aberrant-Poems;[4] a letter, finally, from Mademoiselle Portal, the impulsive "Sévrienne" who often exasperated me... and who feels regret for it[5]...It is, you will see (I am enclosing the letter for you), quite nice, and I ask myself if I should not give to each of the students a *Bateau Ivre*. I am also enclosing the letter from Mme Schneider: echoes of my poems, plucked with an elegantly gloved hand—rings on top, obviously!—and resewn on crowned letterhead: it is as "graphisch" as can be and it ends with a little poem, which is something like a "puzzle," which Eric will help You to reconstruct (first You cut up the words, then, to simplify it, the syllables).

I drank my "cafeton," I counted the hours until Chambéry, I am going down to post this letter, I am waiting for the hour for telephoning.

Good snow, my Love, good sun!

I hug You on the heart side, once, twice, a thousand times—"and so" do I hug Eric too.

Your husband the poeter

/ Keep both letters. /

1. PC has just returned from the Gare de Lyon, where he accompanied EC and GCL, who are leaving for winter vacation, at around seven in the morning.
2. See no. 20.
3. In a letter from 2 January 1960, Rolf Schroers refers to his rereading of "Ein Holzstern": "The last lines went into my heart like a scream. This little impetus: Eric!—how that was suddenly clear to me, the whole scene around the good round table." See above, no. 65.
4. Ilse Schneider-Lengyel was a polymath: aside from literary works, she published works on archeology and on ethnography, devoted to masks, as well as translations. PC had met her at the Group 47 meeting in Niendorf in 1952. Schneider-Lengyel visited the Celans in 1952 at the hôtel d'Orleans, where they lived then, and at rue de Longchamp in 1959.
5. In her letter, Eliane Portal, student at the ENS in Sèvres, expresses regret about a certain aggression shown by her and her fellow students toward PC during the meetings for their preparation for the oral test of the German *agrégation* exam. PC, who was not yet an instructor at the ENS in rue d'Ulm, carried out this teaching work as an adjunct instructor (*vacataire*).

70

[Paris,] Wednesday morning, [6 January 1960]

My Darling, just a word, a thought, a line written to announce the ones to follow. It is ten o'clock, I am leaving in a moment for the École,[1] I prepared at the last minute, and that is the reason for my haste, a text by Albert Camus ("La mer au plus près"), which I will have the students translate. The death of Camus:[2] it is, once again, the voice of the anti-human, indecipherable. If one could think with his teeth![3]

A letter from your mother arrived yesterday, I am enclosing it here. Schroers sends me an essay on the Jews, accurate in its general outline, but too...general, generalizing. I wrote him a letter...which I will not post. But I have to respond, absolutely. (Sunday probably.) No respite—

My Darling, I forgot yesterday that I was going to the Bollacks'[4] on Saturday; so telephone me at 5 o'clock at the latest.

How are Your snows and your suns, my love? Eric: may he find there the health and the joys that will accompany him later!

At Richter's, yesterday evening, it went well enough; few allusions; I showed lots of dental courage[5]...

Kiss Eric, I kiss You

Paul

Still no meow from Kinna-cat.

1. PC is, since October 1959, lecturer in German at the ENS, rue d'Ulm.

2. Albert Camus has just died—on 4 January 1960—in a car accident.

3. See PC's letter from 6 January 1960 to René Char in *Paul Celan / René Char: Correspondance (1954–1968)*, ed. Bertrand Badiou (Paris: Gallimard, 2015).

4. Jean Bollack, a Hellenist, and his wife Mayotte Bollack (née Beauroy), a Latinist, both of whom PC had recently met through Péter Szondi.

5. PC possibly alludes to his hard right-wing dentist's lack of reaction to recent manifestations of anti-Semitism, above all to the profanation of the new synagogue in Cologne during the night of Christmas Eve 1959.

71

[Paris,] Thursday, [7 January 1960]

Thank You for Your letter, my love, thank You for Your so beautiful, so true letter. When You say, about the death of Camus: "I do not know how to think about it"—do You know that You say all, all that one can say of it?

When I began loving You, and it was immediately, it was Your truth that received me, I am still in it, You are, and our son has been added to it, my truth, the only one, the best one.

I am here, at home, it is a quarter to six, from a whole bottle I have left a glass of Beaujolais: but yes, I find these evenings long and...the radio works...

But perhaps, since in any case it is necessary, I will go to Frankfurt next week, Thursday perhaps; I had thought of going to Méribel, but You do not seem to encourage me to do so. (My classes at Normale, I will do them *Tuesday* and Wednesday). But yes, I will go to Frankfurt, time will pass quickly there, I will have the opportunity to see the people from Insel about *La Jeune Parque*;[1] Monday I will be back.

Just a moment ago a telephone call from M. Ferriot: he has written an article (or an essay) about my poems,[2] for the review *Critique*, he is coming to see me Monday, in the morning. But he does not seem to appreciate *Sprachgitter*, he prefers the two other collections—so what has he understood? But that is sort of my destiny in France: my books encounter here, above all, the mediocre people.

A half hour ago, I telephoned Cioran to ask what is new with him; I will see him tomorrow.[3]

Do You have sun? The radio tells me that there will be frost in the Alps: have Your room well heated, insist on it!

Mail: a letter from Jokostra,[4] one from Hildesheimer (which is brown).[5] Thank Eric for his "work":[6] it is on my table.

I kiss You, my darling, I kiss You and Your son—

Paul

1. PC had sent Fritz Arnold from Insel the manuscript of his translation of Valéry on 30 November 1959; on 16 January 1960, PC will give a reading of *Die junge Parze* for a limited audience, at the publishing house in Wiesbaden.
2. See R. Ferriot, "Paul Célan" [sic]. *Sprachgitter*," in *Critique* no. 158, 1960, pp. 663–66.
3. PC does not mention a meeting with Cioran this January. Following an encounter with Cioran one year earlier, PC had noted in his calendar on 21 January 1959: "3 o'clock Cioran / (C. unchanged, unclear, false, suspect)."
4. Peter Jokostra, German writer and literary critic.
5. Wolfgang Hildesheimer, German writer and painter born into a Jewish family, who had lived in British-administered Palestine and later served as an interpreter during the Nuremberg Trials, and member of Group 47. PC refers here to the color of the paper on which Hildesheimer sent his letter (an expression of relief and best wishes for the New Year after a disagreeable exchange in the wake of a misunderstanding about an anti-Semitic critique of *SG*. See W. Hildesheimer, *Briefe*, ed. Silvia Hildesheimer and Dietmar Pleyer (Frankfurt am Main: Suhrkamp, 1999), p. 98.
6. Drawing-collage by EC, which represents, according to the caption added by GCL, "Eric on his sled, behind: the mountain."

72

[Dedication in Paul Valéry, *Die junge Parze*,[1] translated by Paul Celan]

For You, my Darling
this poem that came to be reborn
in our house
For Your birthday
for March 19th 1960

Paul

[To Eric Celan]

To Eric

for his mother's birthday
for March 19th 1960

his father—

1. (Wiesbaden: Insel, 1960.)

73

[Salzburg, 4 August 1960]

My darling,
    Mirabell, for me, it is a poem by Trakl[1]—reread it, You will find it easily.
—Until very soon!

Paul

/ In the Salzburg train station, in the midst of waiting, 4 August 1960 /

1. "Mirabell" refers to the "Mirabellgarten" in Salzburg depicted on this postcard. See Georg
Trakl's poem, "Musik im Mirabell" in *Die Dichtungen* (Salzburg: Otto Müller, 1938), p. 14.

74

[To Eric Celan]

[Stockholm,] Thursday, 1 September 1960

My dear Eric, here I am disembarked now, quite far away, it seems to me.
It is nice out, a bit cold—anyway, it is not Paris.

I hear that Nelly is doing better, I will go see her in a moment, after I have seen the doctor.[1] Until very soon, my son! Give mama plenty of hugs!

I hug you both with all my heart

Your Papa

---

1. PC is visiting Nelly Sachs, who has been hospitalized in the psychiatric ward of a hospital in Stockholm after a serious depression.

75

Stockholm, 5 September 1960, after our telephone call—

My love!

Thank You for being so courageously at my side!

What to say? They abandon me—so we should congratulate ourselves for not having to turn to them again. I just set off a telegram to Klaus:

AN DICH SOWIE INGE GERICHTETE BITTE DER NIEDERTRACHT ZU ENTGEGNEN AUSDRUECKLICH ZURUECKGENOMMEN: Request addressed to you and to I[nge] to respond to the infamy expressly withdrawn.[1]

That's it.

What to tell You of Nelly? She suffers very much. Does not want to hear her poems spoken of anymore—

"I want to keep"—and here she brings the thumb and the index finger of her right hand together into a ring—"only this little light."

Troubles coming from a thousand directions, from far and from near.

Regarding a letter from Ingeborg—written after my telephone call—with which I[nge] had sent a pair of white gloves, Nelly said: "White gloves, that means: 'I wash my hands in innocence'[2]—ich wasche meine Hände in Unschuld—thus *proof of falseness*"!!!

My love, I will try to take a train the day after tomorrow in the evening, otherwise Thursday: morning or evening—perhaps I will stop on the way, in Hamburg or in Cologne.

My love, hug our son!
I hug You, I love You, be tranquil, I love You truly

Paul

1. PC had received, a few days previously, a letter from Ingeborg Bachmann ("Inge" in the telegram) informing him of her disagreement with the text of the "Entgegnung" (Response) written by Klaus Demus intended for the press, in response to the campaign of defamation that Claire Goll relaunched in 1960. Bachmann expressed, in a letter to Demus from the same day, her concerns about the tone, which was too defensive in her view, and wondered if it would not be better for the letter to be written by the literary director of S. Fischer, Rudolf Hirsch. The "Entgegnung" will finally appear—signed by Marie Luise Kaschnitz, Ingeborg Bachmann, and Klaus Demus—the following month in *Die neue Rundschau* (published by S. Fischer), 1960, vol. 3, pp. 547–9. The debate will soon include public letters in PC's defense by Péter Szondi, Walter Jens, Rolf Schroers, and Hans Magnus Enzensberger. No demonstration of support will fully appease PC and he will in general feel betrayed or disappointed by the efforts of his defenders, who seem to him incapable or unwilling to see the affair in its true dimensions. Regarding this, PC often cited the famous lines of the "Complainte Rutebeuf," the poem sung by Léo Ferré, "Que sont mes amis devenus?" (What has become of my friends?); PC translated several lines of this poem, which should be read in this context (lines 109–14; see *GA*, no. 323). PC will, likewise, be disappointed by his French friends, such as René Char, whose lack of knowledge of the events, of German, and of PC's work prevents their showing a level of comprehension and support in line with PC's expectations. PC composes a letter to Jean-Paul Sartre, which he will not send, in which he appeals to his "sense of justice and of truth" for this "true Dreyfus affair—sui generis of course, but well characterized." See no. 85, n. 2.
2. Literal translation of the idiomatic phrase "seine Hände in Unschuld waschen" ("to wash one's hands of it").

76

[To Eric Celan]

[Paris, 5 November, 1960]

My dear Eric,

Here I am writing you with the pigeon feather found in the street that you just gave me. What can I write other than this:

I love you with all my heart, my son who also finds my feathers.

Your papa

This 5 November 1960

77

[Dedication in *Sprachgitter*, on the back of the flyleaf]

> So kam ich unter die Deutschen. Ich forderte
> nicht viel und war gefaßt, noch weniger
> zu finden.
> …
> Es ist ein hartes Wort, und dennoch sag
> ichs, weil es Wahrheit ist: ich kann kein
> Volk mir denken, das zerrißner wäre, wie
> die Deutschen. Handwerker siehst du, aber
> keine Menschen, Denker, aber keine Menschen,
> Priester, aber keine Menschen. Herrn und
> Knechte, Jungen und gesetzte Leute, aber
> keine Menschen—

/ Hölderlin, Hyperion /[1]

[On the following page, under the logo of S. Fischer Verlag:]

To Gisèle
in our house,
December
1960

Paul

---

1. "Thus did I come among the Germans. I did not demand much and expected even less. […]
It is a hard word, and yet I say it, because it is true: I can conceive of no people more torn
apart than the Germans. You see workmen, but no humans; thinkers, but no humans; priests,
but no humans. Lords and knights, youths and adults, but no humans—"; *Hölderlins Sämtli-
che Werke*, vol. 2 (Berlin/Leipzig: Tempel Klassiker), pp. 175–6.

78

Und schwer.[1]
Und schwer wie dein
nun nach Jahren zu zählendes
Da- und Um-mich-Sein.

Und schwer, Geliebte, und schwer.

Und schwer wie das Hier-
und Hinaus-ins-zweite-
Dunkel-Gewogen-
Werden.
Dreimal schwer.
Dreimal und abermals dreimal,
und immer mit dir.

Schwer und schwer und schwer.
Und niemals mit
verkleidetem Herzen.

——

Written in Paris, 15 December 1960. Transcribed in Montana, 23 December 1960,[2] "on the bridge of years,"[3] while waiting for You, with Your white lilacs.[4]

And heavy
And heavy like your
being-there and around-me
now to be counted in years.

And heavy, beloved, and heavy.

And heavy like this being-
weighed-here
and out there-into-the-second-
darkness.
Three times heavy.
Three times and again three times,
and always with you.

Heavy and heavy and heavy.
And never with
a disguised heart.

1. See *NKGA*, p. 422.
2. The poem was transcribed the day of PC and GCL's eighth wedding anniversary. PC stays with his family in Montana (Chalet Les Fougères, Valais, Switzerland) from 19 to 27 December 1960.
3. The phrase "on the bridge of years" is used in several dedications to GCL (see no. 3).
4. PC calls to mind GCL's wedding bouquet. The lilac, linked to PC's memories of Bukovina, is also associated with time and the figure of the couple in one of PC's early poems (see "Regenflieder," *NKGA*, p. 15).

79

[February 1961]

Eine Gauner-[1] und Ganovenweise, im Februar 1961, gesungen von Paul Celan[2]

"Strampelte mi, strampelte mi.
Alla mi presente, la nostra signori!"[3]

Damals, als es noch Galgen gab,
da, nicht wahr, gab es
ein Oben.

Wo bleibt mein Bart, Wind, wo
mein Judenfleck, wo
mein Bart, den du raufst?

91

Krumm war der Weg, den ich ging,
krumm war er, ja,
denn, ja,
er war gerade.

Heia.

Krumm, so wird meine Nase.[4]
Nase.

Und wir zogen auch nach Friaul.
Da hätten wir, da hätten wir.
Denn es blühte der Mandelbaum.[5]
Mandelbaum, Bandelmaum.

Mandeltraum, Trandelmaum.
Und auch der Machandelbaum.[6]
Chandelbaum.

Heia.
Aum.[7]

A brigands' and crooks' tune, sung in February 1961 by Paul Celan

*Back then, when there were still gallows,
then, isn't it right, there was
an Above.*

*Where did my beard end up, wind, where
my Jew-stain, where
my beard, which you tear off?*

*Crooked was the path I went,
crooked it was, yes,*

for, yes,
it was straight.

Hush.

Crooked, so does my nose become.
Nose.

And we too went to Friuli.
There we would have, there we would have.
For there bloomed the almond tree.
Almond tree, talmondree.

Almond dream, Dalmontream.
And also the melmot tree.
Candle-tree.

Hush.
Ree.[8]

1. In referring to himself as a "Gauner" (thief), PC ironically cites Felix Mondstrahl (pseudonym of the poet Richard Salis), who refers to PC as "Epigone und Epigauner" (epigone and epi-brigand) in an article in *Vorwärts* in July 1961 (*GA*, no. 88).

2. See the final version of the poem, with the definitive title "Eine Gauner- und Ganovenweise, / gesungen zu Paris emprès Pontoise / von Paul Celan / aus Czernowitz bei Sadagora," *NKGA*, p. 139. Not far from Czernowitz, Sadagora, a famous hotbed of Hassidism, is PC's mother's birthplace; this town also had the reputation of being a hideout for brigands and horse thieves. This poem, written in the context of the Goll Affair (see no. 4, n. 2, and *GA* n. 268), between February 1961 and November 1962, is placed here at the beginning of 1961 based on the date indicated in the title, even if this version was probably written at the end of 1961.

3. Sixteenth-century lansquenets' song (march), to which line 14 refers. In the final version, this epigraph will be replaced by a line from Heinrich Heine's "An Edom" ("Manchmal nur, in dunklen Zeiten") (Sometimes only, in dark times), the epigraph to *Der Rabbi von Bacherach*, which mentions the yellow rings Jewish men in Frankfurt were required to wear on their cloaks. PC had also envisioned citing Dante (*Inferno*, Canto XXXI, 67). Cf. no. 83.

4. On 23 February 1961, PC writes to Friedrich Torberg, co-editor of the Austrian review *FORVM*, regarding a "Hassidic interpretation" of his poetry in terms that echo this poem, including: "Yes, the Hassidic... certainly. But You know, I grew up, despite all the beards blowing in the

wind around me, despite my years spent learning Hebrew (and which did not always delight my soccer player's heart at the time), with such beardless figures as Siegfried and the Nibelungen. Oh ihr Zîten und Hochgezîten ... [...] One is Jewish (and has nothing of it). As it happens, it is possible to Judaize [allusion to the Nazi term "verjuden"] also without being circumcised—even that has been seen. My own nose has also only recently become crooked [krumm]" (PC archive in the <DLA). In PC's writing, "Nibelungen" often designates anti-Semites.

5. One can read "Mandelbaum" (almond tree) as well as "Machandelbaum" and "Chandelbaum" (candle-tree), as a variant of the name of the poet Osip Mandelstam, to whom PC dedicated NR. On the biblical theme of the almond tree and its branch, see Genesis 30:37, Exodus 25:33, and Jeremiah 1:11.

6. "Machandelbaum" (juniper tree, *Juniperus communis*) evokes the Grimms' fairy tale "The Juniper Tree" (Von dem Machandelbaum).

7. "Aum" is a fragment of *Baum*, "tree." PC added to the final version of the poem, in November 1962, the following "Envoi": "Aber, / aber er bäumt sich, der Baum. Er, / auch er / steht gegen / *die Pest*." (But, / but it resists, the tree. It, / it too / stands against / *the plague*.)

8. See also the translation of the final version, "A Rogues' and Gonifs' Ditty Sung at Paris Emprès Pontoise by Paul Celan from Czernowitz near Sadagora," *SPP*, p. 160, and "Ballad of a Vagabond and Swindler Sung in Paris Emprès Pontoise by Paul Celan from Czernowitz by Sadagora," *CSP*, p. 65.

80

[Paris, March 1961?]

A little quite idiotic idea that occurred to me: Adorno went, from here, to see Beckett[1] (no one knows where he is ...). Since I remember that Unseld met B. at the Closerie des lilas, I will stop by and see. From there, I will go by the École.

See You in a little while, my love

Paul

1. PC will not meet Samuel Beckett (1906–1989), this or any day. Franz Wurm recalls: "In the afternoon I have an appointment with Beckett. I would like for him [PC] to come along. He hesitates, tempted, then declines: 'Unannounced? That won't do.' And if I called B.? 'Like that, at the last minute? Impossible.' When I come back in the evening, convey to him the warm greetings, he becomes sad: 'He is probably the only person here with whom I could have gotten along'." See *Paul Celan / Franz Wurm, Briefwechsel*, ed. Barbara Wiedemann with Franz Wurm (Frankfurt am Main: Suhrkamp, 1995), p. 250. André Bernold notes the following, regarding Beckett's thoughts about PC: "Beckett said, 'Celan is beyond me,' and wanted to know from Elmar Tophoven [friend of PC's and Beckett's German translator], one day when we were together, if Celan, in life, showed his distress" (*L'Amitié de Beckett, 1979–1989* [Paris: Hermann, 1992], p. 58). One of the few known details documenting PC's

relation to the work of Beckett is his translation of an excerpt of the beginning of the novel *L'Innommable* (*The Unnamable*, 1953), given to his students at the ENS (from "Il n'y a donc pas à avoir peur" to "Ça donnera ce que ça donnera").

81

[Dedication in *Der Meridian*[1]]

Long live the Meridian!
For You, my Love,
who makes it live
This day after, and this evening before
an anniversary
March 1961[2]

Paul

1. Speech given in Darmstadt on 22 October 1960 on being awarded the Büchner Prize (Frankfurt am Main: S. Fischer, 1961).
2. Allusion to 19 March, the thirty-fourth birthday of GCL, and to 23 March, a "little anniversary" for PC and GCL. See no. 58, n. 2.

82

[Dedication in Sergei Yesenin, *Gedichte*,[1] selected poems translated by Paul Celan]

For You, for
the Empress of all the Bukovinas
(a bit Austrian,
a bit Russian ...)
Your very humble, Your very proud subject

Павел Львович[2]
22 March 1961

1. (Frankfurt am Main: S. Fischer, 1961).

2. Pavel L'vovic: L'vovic means "son of Leo" in Russian. Leo was the first name of PC's father. During this period, PC liked to refer to himself as a "Russian poet." PC had envisioned entitling "Eine Gauner- und Ganovenweise" (no. 79) "Eine Gauner- und Ganovenweise, / im Jahre 1961 gesungen von / Pawel Lwowitsch Tselan, / Russkij poet in partibus / nemetskich infidelium"; the phrase "in partibus infidelium" was used by the bishops whose dioceses were in "infidel lands"; "nemetskich" is Russian for "German" (see *NR*, TCA, pp. 42–43 and *GA* no. 300).

83

[Paris?, 8 June 1961]

I answer

—————————

I resist

—————————

I refuse[1]

8 June 1961.

1. These formulations are translations, of a sort, of the German verb *stehen*, which is a kind of motto for PC. On the back side of this note, PC quoted Nimrod's Babel-esque phrase: "Rafèl mai amèch zabi et almi [*sic*] / Dante, *Inferno*, Canto XXXI, 67." See no. 87, n. 10; no. 93, n. 3; and no. 123, n. 4.

84

Trébabu, 10 July 1961, 11 p.m.

Für Dich, Gisèle, für Dich,
mon aimée—

    Die hellen[1]
    Steine gehn in der Luft, die hell-
    weißen, die Licht-
    bringer.

Sie wollen
nicht niedergehen, nicht stürzen,
nicht treffen. Sie gehen
auf,
wie die geringen
Heckenrosen, so tun sie sich auf,
sie schweben
dir zu, du meine Leise,
du meine Wahre—:
ich seh dich, du pflückst sie mit meinen
neuen, meinen
Jedermannshänden, du tust sie
ins Helle, das niemand
zu weinen braucht noch zu nennen.

The bright
stones go by in the air, the bright-
white ones, the light-
bringers.

They do not
want to sink, to fall,
to touch. They ascend
opening,
like the lowly
wild roses, so do they open out,
they flutter
toward you, you my Soft,
you my True—:
I see you, you pluck them with my
new, my
everyman's hands, you put them
into the brightness, which no one
need bewail nor name.[2]

1. See the final version of the poem, "Die hellen Steine" in *NKGA*, p. 151.
2. See also "The Bright / Stones," *SPP*, p. 176 and "The Bright / Stones," *CSP*, p. 73.

85

[Paris, 5 November 1961]

My darling, I absolutely have to leave behind all that and return to myself.[1] Returned, I will return beside You and the son: beside this life that I wanted, that I *desired* to build.

Perhaps You will find, through Elisabeth or through Mme Fulda, a doctor who understands that I am not "embellishing" at all and that all that is well and truly an affair, unique in its kind and resembling at the same time so many other affairs.[2] (For, as You know, it is all there: the falsehoods, the double game, the Jewish collaboration, etc.)

Do not despair of me, my darling. I know that I exasperate You by my inaction and by these ridiculous telephone calls sent in a direction from which I can expect nothing but betrayal.

I beg You, my darling: Do not despair!

I remain. Beside You and beside the son. Stand fast!

I will manage it.

I love You.

Paul

5.XI.1961.

1. In the wake of the Goll Affair and the Blöcker Affair, PC is going through a period of grave psychological difficulties. He notes, in French, in his planner for 4 October 1961: "Dr. Vecsler [his general physician]—Try to pull myself out of it with sleeping pills and nothing else."
2. PC considers the Goll Affair to be a "true Dreyfus Affair—sui generis" in this non-dated, non-sent letter to Jean-Paul Sartre, who had just been attacked at his home on rue Bonaparte (after 7 January 1962?): "Dear Jean-Paul Sartre, / I allow myself to address You, [like so many] [others] [at a moment] without at all ignoring [the] Your current preoccupations. I write—I write poetry, German poetry. And I am Jewish. / For the past few years, and especially since last year, I have been the object of a campaign of defamation whose size and ramifications far exceed what one [calls] could call, on first glance, a literary intrigue.* I would surprise You no doubt, if I told You that it is a matter of a true Dreyfus Affair—sui generis of course, but

correctly characterized. It is a true mirror of Germany, the 'new' paths—which Nazism knows how to take—in patent collusion, in this case, with a certain 'left' with national-Bolshevist tendencies, and also, *as often in such a case,* with a considerable number of 'Jews'—that appear there clearly. (All that moreover goes beyond German borders.) I know well that You will have a hard time believing this unknown person who writes You. Allow him to come to present to You this matter (of which I ask You to believe that it is [quite] unique), with supporting documents. / I allow myself to attach to these lines a short text. I would be happy to be able to give You all that I have done. I appeal to Your sense of justice *and of the truth.* / [In 1948, upon my arrival in Paris,] The facts oblige me to [ask You] [to treat] *exercise, regarding this* letter, [with] the greatest discretion. I ask You also to accord me a personal interview. [Unsigned.] / *In addition, for a few months, there has been a true 'psychological action' that aims at my psychological destruction."* (See GA, no. 191).

86

[Paris, 19 March 1962]

One more rose has come—the Rose of life!
Happy Birthday, my Beloved!
Happy anniversaries, my Beloved!
Many happy anniversaries,
many, many!

—The father of Your child—

19 March 1962

87

Geneva, 30 September 1962

I am trying to write You, my love.

It is Sunday, it is nice out, very nice even, and I am returning from a short stroll, tired, already, at four o'clock.

Yesterday, it went better, above all after having telephoned You from Nyon. I had taken the little train that goes up to Saint-Cergue, at a little over a thousand meters' altitude, there was sun, there were very few people, there was the "cows' mountain," but very wooded, forests all around, all the trees—very varied, from the rowan to the larch—had kept their leaves—

You would surely have liked to stroll around there: I thought about that, and I thought that it would be an ideal place for Eric.

As for me, my love, I was not able to enjoy all that. A few steps, then a snack on the terrace of a hotel, in the company of words scribbled in Nyon, with a view to a poem.[1] Then, since the train was not leaving until much later, I decided to descend on foot to Arzier, by a shortcut indicated by the hotelier. It was nice, very nice to walk up there; at a certain moment, I was not expecting it at all, a flower appeared on my right: an autumn crocus. Do you remember the second-to-last poem: "Columbus, die Zeitlose im Aug, die Mutterblume"?[2] And there I had to think of my very last poem, written after the letter received from Moscow, in which Erich Einhorn told me that he was going to spend his vacation in "Colchis," that is to say, on the Black Sea.[3] "Kolchis," this was, and I only first understood it yesterday, just a secret echo of the "Zeitlose," stirred up by the real.—One would have to know how to content oneself with this kind of dialogue, a bit extra-human,[4] don't You think? And all the more so as I can communicate it to You, my Love, and, in another way, to our son, in such moving complicity with all that, for us, is the world and its truth.

A bit farther on—the meadows were soon strewn with autumn cro-cuses—in leaving the road to take the Goat Barn Path, another flower was there: the Augentrost—the Euphrasia—of which I have spoken to you, quite often, I think. During the war, in Moldova, while carrying two buckets (of water? of soup?) which I went to retrieve, before noon, in the little town, to carry to the "work site," I had encountered it, this Augen-*Trost*.[5]

But there, you see, I saw myself thrown backward again, then there was a silver thistle and a rowan illustrating, with its yellow foliage, what I had to translate in a poem by Yesenin: "Christus, deine roten sind es, deine Schwären."[6] A bit farther on, after an intersection, the path stopped. For a moment, I envisioned continuing through the woods, then, lacking courage, I preferred to retrace my steps and get back on the train in Saint-Cergue. From Nyon, I could have easily gone to Lausanne, "to change." But I was not equipped for the night, and so it was (Re-)Geneva. With its kiosks lavishly stocked with German newspapers to receive me. Sunday editions, literary pages full of "friends"... All that is well and truly at my heels,[7] it does not leave me. I stomached it—oh, it was nothing but a few small things adding themselves onto big things. I went to have dinner, right next to my hotel, like every evening in a decent enough and not too expensive café— the Café des Alpes—I digested my readings, but I had the unfortunate idea of accompanying my sausages (from Frankfurt!) with a glass of Dôle, then another, three others. The night before, I had been able to fall asleep without sleeping pills, but then, as I foresaw this interminable Sunday, I "dôli-fied" myself. Toward midnight—I had reread your letter, then, after a few Russian poems, turned on the radio—I fell asleep.—Ah, I forget: "dôlified," I had "radiated" around the area a bit more and, having arrived "at the level" of a photo booth, obtained, for two francs, six images... of which here is one...

Oh, I know well what gestures like this mean... In Nyon, after having gotten off the train, I went to the post office to call you; on my right was the rue Perdtemps. ("Oh, how to escape Signs and Numbers!")[8]

You see, I am quite low. Luckily, tomorrow I will be at the Office. Until now, I have done nothing but look through the "Conventions" and the Dictionaries, but since Friday evening, a document of one hundred pages is sitting on my table, composed in English, touching on fishing boat management; the rhythm of the translation is ten type-written pages per day— to be dictated to a stenographer—I am only on my fourth page, the words do not come to me, all this "language,"[9] I have forgotten it, but this document will *have* to be translated, and I am almost happy as I think that tomorrow I will be able to get working on it. The hours will pass, then, the evening having come, I will go home to drop off my briefcase and go to the train station—three hundred steps from here—to telephone You. It is quickly reached, Paris—our Paris, my Love.

But if you could see this world in front of the two telephone booths! A mass of Italian workers, who call Pisa and Rome and Trieste—the mass of those who, like me, have come "to enrich themselves" in Geneva, call those who... give *them* the strength to live, by their presence. And they do not have, in their pockets, the money of "international officials"...

Then others, calling France, Germany. A quite elderly lady, the other evening, asked for Bueno Aires. A well-shaped face, very Overseas and Latin American, a bit "Indio," but upon looking more closely, a...Jewish face. There was a call notice, I heard her name: Fischer...

I write You, my Love, I write You—that gives me the strength to live. My Beloved! I took out, from your little Pascal, Your photo from eleven years ago. Gisèle de Lestrange, I love You. My smiling girl from back then! So tested! So courageous! I am crying, yes. But, in these tears, I join You, You and our son Eric, You and our life that belongs to us, to the three of us, and which, don't You think, conserves and will conserve its clarities, its stars, its suns, its House. And which will help us, You and me, to raise our son, to make a man of him, upright and courageous and, yes, less exposed to hardships! I will hold out, my Beloved, we will hold out.[10]

Take this flower "outside time,"[11] plucked for You. Tomorrow—for it is the first of October, and October is the month of my return—tomorrow, I will give You Your roses.

Hug our son, hug him tight!

Paul

---

1. The poem PC refers to is "La Contrescarpe," dated "29.9.62 / rue Perdtemps, Nyon." In the first draft of the poem appears the line "Rue Perdtemps, Nyon," referring to the street in which PC will find himself in this letter. The first draft of "La Contrescarpe" also refers to the promenade des Vieilles Murailles, the footpath along the old city walls in Nyon. See *Die Niemandsrose: Tübinger Ausgabe*, ed. Heino Schmull (Frankfurt: Suhrkamp, 1996), 129–30.
2. PC cites from memory an extract of the third stanza of "Die Silbe Schmerz" (The Syllable Pain) (See *NKGA*, p. 163; see also "The Syllable Pain," *SPP*, p. 200).
3. Erich Einhorn (1920–1974), childhood friend of PC's from Czernowitz who emigrated to the Soviet Union in 1941; professor of Romanian and Italian, later an editor and translator of a political review in Moscow. See "Paul Celan-Erich Einhorn, 'Briefe'," ed. Marina Dmitrieva-Einhorn, in *Celan-Jahrbuch* 7, 1997–98, no. 6, p. 34.
4. In a letter to the Austrian writer Reinhard Federmann, PC qualifies this kind of coincidence in the following terms: "What my *so Jewish* wife, born Alix-Marie-Gisèle de Lestrange, calls, as I do, something of the...MERIDIAN" (15 March 1962, *GA*, no. 199).
5. Allusion to PC's experience as a forced laborer for the construction of a concentration camp in Tabaresti. The *Euphrasia officinalis* (whose German name means "consolation of the eyes") appears in a poem from 1942, "Herbst" (Autumn) (*NKGA*, p. 326), and later, for the first and only time in his published work, in "Todtnauberg," the poem written after PC's encounter with Heidegger in August 1967 (see *NKGA*, p. 286).

6. PC is quoting, from memory, his own translation of "Herbst" (1916) by Sergei Yesenin, which differs slightly: "Christus, deine roten küßt er, deine Schwären." On the "silver thistle," see no. 375.
7. Allusion to the Goll Affair and its ramifications.
8. This expression has two implications. The reference is to what might be called PC's compulsive habit of interpretation: counting and seeing a significance in the numbers of things, and seeing objects or events as signs; this has already manifested itself and will lead to Celan's first major crisis at the end of this year. In his journal from 8 May 1965, PC will refer to this particular expression of delusion, in quotation marks, as "Beziehungswahn"; see no. 144, n. 1. Secondly, the quotation is from the last line in "Le Gouffre," one of the last poems in Baudelaire's *Fleurs du mal* (third edition, 1868): "—Ah! Ne jamais sortir des Nombres et des Êtres!" The appearance of the word "Perdtemps" on the right is a sign for PC. See also "To the Right," in *Fathomsuns and Benighted*, trans. Ian Fairley (Manchester: Carcanet Press, 2001; hereafter *FB*), p. 133. One of the manuscripts of the poem "La Contrescarpe" is dated "29.9.62 / rue Perdtemps." PC's speculations concerning left and right are not unconnected to their significance during the "selections" in extermination camps.
9. In English in the original.
10. "Tenir," translated as "hold out," is a French variation on the German verb *stehen* (to stand), a motto for PC (see no. 83, n. 1; no. 93, n. 3; and no. 123, n. 4).
11. PC encloses an autumn crocus (in German, "Zeitlose" or "Herbstzeitlose") with this letter. The name of this flower, aside from the Colchis of the legend of the Argonauts and the place of Ovid's exile, reminds PC of his lost "eastern" "Landschaft" (see *GW* III, p. 185; *SPP*, p. 395, and *FREN*, p. 46).

88

[To Eric Celan]

Geneva, 30 September 1962

My dear son!

I thank you with all my heart for having added your little message to mama's first letter!

I hug you too—I hug you very tight.

I found your handwriting very good; you have made a lot of progress, and that proves that you must be working well at school. Indeed that does not surprise me, since I know that you have understood that you have to work and learn, learn and learn even more.

I hope that you spent a good weekend in our house in Moisville[1] and that you had a lot of fun with your little cousins.

You see, here, in Geneva, there are a lot of foreigners who come to admire the city, the lake, the mountains. At our house, in Moisville, there is neither a lake nor mountains. There are fields and, here and there, some woods. But it is much more beautiful, believe me. Speaking of that, I wonder if the hazelnuts are ripe. Mama must have found them for you, I am sure of it. And soon, you two will begin to collect walnuts.

It is very lucky, my son, to have such a pretty house. To deserve it, you have to work well.

Here, in the office where I am working, people are busy finding the means for all those who work to have everything they need.

Now, I would like to ask you a favor: it is to ask mama, after school, to loan you a little money and to accompany you to the florist at Rond-Point. There you will ask for seven red roses, Meillands if possible. And you will give them to mama, from me.

I hug you, my beloved son!

Your papa

---

1. The Celans owned, since April 1962, a country house in Moisville, around a hundred kilometers from Paris, in addition to their apartment at 78 rue de Longchamp in Paris.

89

Paris, 2 October 1962

My Darling,

I am reading and rereading your letter, I am looking at your photo, the crocus, I am thinking again of what you tell me about Erich Einhorn, it's very extraordinary. Luckily there are all the same still secret encounters and almost mute comprehensions. Of course one must experience such things and know that even if they have become rare, they are no less essential and sufficient. As for that Augentrost, of course you have often spoken to me of it and it is thanks to you that I know it and what it means. Thanks for sharing Your life with me the way You do. Thanks for having the courage to do this tiresome work, which also helps me, seeing you withstand, seeing you hold out, even if I understand each of Your relapses, it's in Your courage and in Your efforts that I too find my strength.

In Paris, it is incredibly hot and very unpleasant, everyone has a cold and is out of sorts, and I aspire to breathe the good air of Moisville tomorrow evening to get rid of my nascent flu.

Madame Collombier sent me a German girl whose father is a lawyer in Munich and who, even if she didn't seem bad, had her eyes painted and repainted incredibly. I cannot decide and am waiting for another to be sent to me.

Your mail from this morning is not very exciting. I cite it here:

1) Deutsche Akademie für Sprache und Dichtung (invitation from Kasack and festivities program)

2) Klett Verlag (prospectus: *Neue Bücher*)

3) DVA: press clippings: 1. "Büchner-Preisträger schreiben 'Gedichte gegen den Krieg,' Schibboleth von P.C." (25/26 August 62, *Darmstädter Tageblatt*, Darmstadt) 2. "Das Leiden an der Lyrik," Carl Unsöld (28 Juni 62, Darmstadt, *Trierischer Volksfreund*).

I send you the card from the Arendts and from your Chicago cousin.

3 October, morning: no mail.

Until soon, my darling. Eric is thinking of your message, we will go to the florist on Friday morning when we return from Moisville to be able to enjoy it more.

I return tomorrow evening, not too late, and I kiss you

Gisèle

90

[Geneva,] 15 October 1962

My darling,

I just moved, that is to say, I just changed offices. After having stayed, successively, in the offices of Mister Price and of Herr Berger, here I am, installed, until further notice, in the office of Señora Maria Vasquez Lopez, currently on vacation.

In front of me, on the wall, a large map of Spain, framed by Velázquez reproductions: kings, royal children, families, beards, mustaches, horses, dogs, coats of armor. And, stuck on the window pane, a Spanish stamp illustrated by the señora: Franco's head, originally bald and beardless, receives a mustache—Philippe IV—and goatee (Napoléon III–IV [sic]). It is childish, but—isn't it?—touching. Essentially, politics, often, is only *that*, on a larger scale, without admitting it. Where the gesture commits, it leaves only few traces...

Yesterday, I was in Neuchâtel, at Dürrenmatt's home.[1]—The day before yesterday, in Bern, after the Klees—above all I looked at the paintings, and admired, from the depths of my discouragement, this immense courage: *The Creator*, for example, on a violet background, labyrinths of lines seeking to perpetuate themselves at the interior of an extra-human, infra-human, animal contour (whether it was a mollusk, or a saurian, I forget)—after the Klees and a few other modern paintings, above all two Kandinskys, and, it had to be found again, a Chagall (*Dedicated to My Fiancée*, 1911, the good old times, but, with a hideous face, the fiancé with a donkey's head, sneering, the eye contemplating an upside-down woman's head[2]

[letter unfinished]

1. Friedrich Dürrenmatt, Swiss writer and dramaturg. On this day, Dürrenmatt gives to PC his just published play, *Die Physiker* (*The Physicists*) (Zurich: Die Arche, 1962), with the dedication: "An Paul Celan / Friedrich Dürrenmatt." On the relations between PC and Dürrenmatt, see the latter's recollections in *Turmbau. Stoffe IV–IX* (Zurich: Diogenes, 1990), pp. 169ff.
2. The Bern Kunstmuseum was home to the Paul Klee Foundation. PC refers to Klee's 1934 painting, *Der Schöpfer*. It has not been possible to identify which are the two Kandinsky paintings to which PC alludes, among the three exhibited at the time: *Untitled* (1916), *Pointe Jaune* (1924), and *Regard sur le passé* (1924).

91

[Geneva,] 16 October 1962

My darling,

A few lines, while waiting for you to come, for you to be here.

Still no work, the hours are becoming long again, in my new office, where until now I was alone, a gentleman named Dupont just moved in. I ceded my table to him—given his age—we turn our backs to one another, he is a former member of BIT, one feels the "weight" of his "experience." He dictates.

Just a moment ago, at the bar, I saw Lydia,[1] back from Tunis. Tanned, and having met on a beach six people who turned out to be, like her, poets... She brings back, with the smile that you know, a Bedouin proverb. About a well polluted by the poets. Then, of

[letter unfinished]

1. The writer and translator Lydia Kerr, who worked at the *Bureau international du travai* (BIT) in Geneva.

92

Saint Cergue, 21 December 1962

Eine Stunde hinter[1]
der Bussardschwinge, im Jura,
am Lärchenstein,
kam uns, auf
dem Unbeklommenen, wo
wir gingen,
etwas entgegen: das
Rohr, das
denkende.
St. Cergue, 21.X.62

An hour behind
the buzzard wing, in the Jura,
at the Larch-Stone,
something came, on
the unanxious, where
we walked,
to meet us: the

reed, the

thinking one.

1. See the last version of this poem, no. 105, and see "Eine Handstunde," *NKGA*, p. 432.

93

[Geneva,] 22 October 1962

My Darling,

Two such good days spent with You—two days of life.

Now You have left again—and the hours, long, begin again to grow longer. No work at the office, so I went to see Demonsant to set the date of my departure,[1] but I will not see him until tomorrow.

What to say? You just arrived, very soon You will go to pick up Eric at school, he will be so pleased, You will be happy to see him again, and the little presents will add to his joy. I am thinking about it, intensely, I am thinking about my coming return, of our two houses. But I think above all that God—or is it not him?—made me meet her of whom I dreamed of meeting. But yes, it is You, my Darling. So, the moment I write these lines, I find Life again, the Real, the Future. We will hold out,[2] my Love, despite everything, against everything, with our son who, already, is so marvelously upright.

Paul

1. PC will leave the translation department of the BIT, directed by Jean Demonsant, on 26 October 1962.

2. PC makes the motto of the Orange-Nassau (the Dutch branch of the House of Nassau) his own, as a French variation on the German *stehen*: "Je maintiendrai." See no. 83, n. 3; no. 87, n. 10; and no. 123, n. 4.

94

Paris, 22 October 1962

My darling, while waiting for Your phone call, I must tell You right away that our son is well and that he is so glad to be home again! All his tenderness came out as soon as he found himself alone with me, he was moved, happy, sweet, and so nice. A real little loving soul, full of joy. I was touched by that welcome. He wasn't bored there and I think that they made a real effort to keep him occupied. His day in Versailles among the old carriages impressed him very much, and Mimi too, with whom he got along very well. But he surely missed me, in any case he says it a lot and with a tear in the corner of his eye. Jacqueline told me that he was very well behaved and obedient and very nice, sleeping well, and that everything went well. I am glad to have him back again. But you, my darling, this long week to get through far from you, knowing you are so unoccupied in Geneva, so alone, so alone with this terrible difficulty of living in this world that's become so hostile. May that pass quickly! May your return home be soon! May us both manage to get by as best as we can! These two days with you were very beautiful for me, I am thinking again of our walk together in Geneva, of our steps together in Nyon, in Saint-Cergue, I am thinking again of the crocus, of the rowans, of those marvelous colors. Of that stop for a moment among the larches, where, right beside me, you wrote that poem,[1] that poem so beautiful I reread it again just now when I put away my suitcase. It was so good for me to be with you, to feel you a little bit happy too that I was there. My love. We are not made to live for such a long time far from one another. If only you had been able to see a few new people. But everyone meets again! When will it be possible to get out of this infernal circle? Where can one find humans, cleanness, my God, my hopes are small, you know; luckily I still have love, very much alive, very much whole. I don't have more than that but I have what is most important. That is where I draw my strength, I know it well. I am waiting for you, my darling, I live in anticipation of our return, in anticipation of the moment when we will be together again. I resent myself often for knowing so poorly how to help you, for being so powerless in the face of everything that happens to you, I am completely disarmed, you know it well, but with the firm will to hold out, to hold out, because of our son and so that we may live for a long time together, all three of us. Of course we will have joys again, happy moments. We will fight together so that you can despite everything continue to write, even if you can't publish. So that you will be able to write to live, to help us to live and for your son.

Until soon, my darling, you will take the path to the station and you will go into the phone booth and we will be able to speak, you will know that Eric is well, that I have him again! That I have arrived, and I will know, won't I, that you bravely put the hours behind you, the days that separate us still.

Until always, until soon, my Love.

Gisèle

My darling, your second phone call just now. I was wrong, I resent myself for not having understood right away, I know that you understand more quickly and better than I do, I am thinking about it, I am thinking about it again, forgive me. You were calm but so unhappy. I am sad now, I irritated you, I left you even more alone after we spoke. My darling, forgive me. I was with Eric, with his joy, when you called again, he knew right away it was you. You hung up quickly, you could no longer put up with my incomprehension. I beg you, my love, to believe me: I will always be sure to really listen to you, to always try to understand. I believe you, my love, I believe you, I know that you see me, but the realities are often so hard that I don't always manage to admit them. With the Lalandes, I will be careful, I promise you. You are all alone this evening in Geneva, all alone, and I am all alone in Paris. Let's speak again before your return, right away, I beg you. If only I could call you, I am so worried. I feel far from you, unable to say a word to you, to hear your voice. My darling, I am calling to you, I am calling to you, do you hear me? I ask for your forgiveness, tell me that you hear me, that I can find you again and always. Oh! My darling, to be with you this evening! What I wouldn't give for that! This evening, it is very hard, after having hurt you, to be alone, to know you are alone. I was wrong, I understand. I regret it.

My love, forgive me!

Your wife

1. "Eine Stunde hinter" (An Hour Behind).

95

My Darling,

You are my wife—You are courageously the wife of a poet. I thank You for being that, so valiantly. You are, as well, the mother of my children,[1] You are the mother of Eric.

Thank You, my Darling, for being that so courageously. You are, You know it well, the wife of a poète maudit: doubly, triply "Jewish." Thank You, Gisèle de Lestrange, for taking on all that. Thank You, my Love, thank You Gisèle de Lestrange, for being my wife, so courageously. Thank You for being the mother of Eric.

At the end of the week—or at the beginning of next week—I will be back. Thank You for being the mother of our son. Thank You for being, despite everything, so courageous.

My writing[2]

[letter unfinished]

1. François, who died thirty hours after his birth, and Eric.
2. PC's handwriting at the end of this unfinished letter is very unclear.

96

[Geneva,] 24 October 1962

Thank You, my Love, for Your good letter! Certainly, I will hold out, we will hold out at our son's side!

I saw Demonsant yesterday—he will tell me today if I can leave Friday. But that seems to make him a bit uneasy, because ultimately it does not depend on him.

Yesterday, I saw Lydia again, whom I will see again, at her home, tomorrow for dinner. I was a bit talkative—as with Eberstark—but I am firmly resolved not to be like that tomorrow. This morning, telephone call from

Starobinski—I will see him perhaps, with Marc Slonim (Russian writer),[1] tomorrow evening, after Lydia.

There is, as You no doubt know, a rather worrying political tension in the world. Let war be avoided—I believe that it will be.[2]

The forwarded letters: they are not good.[3] For us, "literature" and what accompanies it continues to be hardly pleasing at all. Group 47 completes my repression.[4] In the *Spiegel*, the "national-communist" tendencies—*Der Ruf, Deutschland erwache*[5]...—[In the margin:] manifest themselves quite clearly. But we will hold out, calmly!

Paul

1. Hans-Josef Eberstark, a person also mentioned in PC's planner for 10 October 1962. Jean Starobinski, Swiss doctor, French language literary critic and essayist, at the time professor at the University of Geneva. Marc Slonim, writer, critic, and translator of Russian origin who had emigrated to the United States. It is probably upon the occasion of this meeting that Slonim, a friend of Marina Tsvetaeva's, dedicated his book *From Chekhov to the Revolution: Russian Literature 1900–1917* (New York: Oxford University Press, 1962) to PC: "A Paul Celan en souvenir d'une soirée à Genève / très cordialement / Marc Slonim."

2. Allusion to the Cuban Missile Crisis (23 October 1962).

This refers to copies of three letters that accompany the letter sent by GCL on 22 October 1962. PC probably means the request by H. Grössel (from 19 October 1962) concerning the republication of his translation of an essay by James Baldwin, "Everybody's Protest Novel," first published in German in *Perspektiven* no. 2 (1953), in an anthology of Baldwin's essays taken primarily from *Notes of a Native Son* and *Nobody Knows My Name*. In his copy of *Perspektiven*, PC underlined this latter title and added the comment: "Gibt es mich überhaupt?" (Do I exist at all?). PC will not grant his authorization for the publication of his translation in the volume *Schwarz und weiß, oder Was es heißt, ein Amerikaner zu sein* by Rowohlt (Reinbek, 1963), a publisher whom PC considered to be too close to Group 47.

3. Probably an allusion to the introduction to the *Almanach der Gruppe 47, 1947–1962* (ed. H. W. Richter with W. Mannzen; Reinbeck near Hamburg: Rowohlt, 1962), which includes five poems PC read in Niendorf in May 1952. In the introduction, Fritz J. Raddatz does not mention PC. PC is thinking of the repression of his poetry—often reduced by the majority of the Group 47 members to "poésie pure"—and of the seeming inability of the majority of writers and their public to see his poetry and thought as what they are: a memorial (Denkmal) to the victims of the Nazis and a form of resistance to the repression of history and forgetting.

4. "Der Ruf" means literally "the call"; "Deutschland erwache": nationalist slogan in reaction to the Treaty of Versailles (1919), used by the Nazis. PC is probably alluding as well to the fourth and last stanza of the Nazi song by Arno Pardun, "Volk, ans Gewehr!" (People, to arms!). With "Der Ruf," PC is referring to an article in the *Spiegel* in which its author, Rolf

Becker, describes the career of Hans Werner Richter, former member of the KPD (German Communist Party) between 1930–1933, Wehrmacht soldier, member of the editorial board of the review *Der Ruf* published by prisoners of war, then, in 1946, co-editor with Alfred Andersch of a review of the same name.

97

Moisville, 3 November 1962, 12:50

Dies ist der Augenblick,[1] da
die Werwölfe auf
der Strecke bleiben.
Kein
Scherge mehr
lebt.
Der Mensch, wahr und allein,
geht aufrecht inmitten
der Menschen.

3.XI.62, 12 Uhr 50, Moisville—

This is the instant, when
the werewolves fall
by the wayside.
Not
one henchman more
lives.
The human, true and alone,
walks upright among
humans.

1. See *NKGA*, p. 443.

98

I love You

   We will live, our son, You and me, together.
   And we will work.

                23.12.1962

                         [Unsigned]

99

                [Paris,] Monday, [1 January 1963]

My darling, my darling love,

   I am thinking of you ceaselessly, we need a lot of courage, both of us,[1] and we will have it, won't we?—We will have it, this courage, because we love each other, because we want to find each other again, to be together forever. We will hold out, we will win out, love will be stronger than everything. You often told me to pay attention to myself, to take care of myself. I promise I will and also to eat well, but you too, my Love, you must take care of yourself, like me, for our son, because we need each other.

   But I am well, be reassured, I will hold out, I feel strong because I am very close to you, every instant my thought is with you. Eric is doing well too, we will say good evening to you when we go to bed and you will hear us now, since you know that we love you, that we want you to come back to us very quickly. You have to take care of yourself, my darling, as I take care of myself by paying attention to myself because I know you desire that. I know that you need me, you know that I need you, you know that Eric needs us both.

   Courage, courage, my Love, it's very hard, but we will win out, and we will live all three of us together as always to love one another.

   I am waiting for you, I will always wait for you, as I've always done, calmly.

   Don't forget that I love you, that I will always love you, and that the only thing that matters is our love. It will live

                         Gisèle

1. At GCL's request, PC entered the private psychiatric clinic in Épinay-sur-Seine on 31 December 1962. A few days beforehand, in Valloire, PC had experienced his first crisis of delusion: hallucinations, threats accompanied by aggressive gestures toward GCL. PC accuses a passerby of being involved in the Goll Affair, telling him: "You too, You are playing the game!" During the early return trip, he violently tears the yellow scarf "like the yellow stars" from his wife's neck (Bertrand Badiou conversation with GCL). EC, just seven and a half years old, is a witness of these scenes.

100

[Épinay-sur-Seine,][1] 4 January 1963

Thank You, my Darling, for all Your letters! I am so reassured now that I know that You are well, both of you, You and our son.—Continue, please, to write to me every day:[2] it is from Your letters that my hope and my courage spring again.

Here, many things are reduced to their most simple expression (which is not, You know it well, the least rich), I take my meals regularly, I rest.

Today, it must have been Eric's first day back to school—I hope (and Your letters confirm it) that he has found again all his calm, all his courage (for he has it, in large quantities!).

You do not tell me what state You found the house in (paint, furniture, etc.), tell me something about that.

Thank You for paying attention to Yourself. That is, indeed, very important to me. Eric, he has great need of it—so, You will take care of Yourself, spoil Yourself, pamper Yourself.

Yesterday evening, I thought a lot about the moment when, arriving from Geneva, I found You on the station platform,[3] with Your brand-new coat that suited You so well. You were so beautiful—You are so beautiful!

And now, calmly, I am waiting for the hour when I will be with You again, You and our son.

I kiss You, my Beloved!

I kiss our son—kiss him!

Paul

1. See no. 99, n. 1.
2. Since his entry into the hospital, at the end of December, PC has received eight letters from GCL. The doctors have asked GCL not to visit.
3. PC's return from Geneva to Paris on 27 October 1962 (at Gare de Lyon).

101

[To Eric Celan]

[Épinay-sur-Seine,] 4 January 1963

My dear Eric, my dear son,

I think very much of you, of your work, of your courage, of your games and hobbies, of your life.

This vacation was not as we had hoped it to be. But we will make it up, surely.

Help mama a bit, be nice, particularly nice with her, wait for me with her. Until very soon, my dear Eric![1]

your Papa

1. PC's handwriting is very unclear.

102

[Épinay-sur-Seine,] 5 January 1962[1]

My very-beloved,

I got, today around noon, your letter from the fourth—thanks and thanks!

I am so happy that everything, at home, is finding its place again, that Eric is glad to take the path to his school again. Thanks for helping him, thanks for being so courageous!

As for me, there is surely a palpable improvement—it will be complete and irreversible when I will have rejoined you both.

You do not tell me anything about Moisville: water, trees, electricity—wouldn't it be useful to send a short letter to Madame Potier to have more details.

Doctor P.—for whom I waited a bit before writing you this letter—has not yet come to see me; he will probably come tomorrow. As for the attending physician, Doctor C., he comes by every day, and I am sure that he wishes us well.

Will you come to see me soon? In that case—you know that Épinay is quite far away—I think that the simplest thing would be to entrust Eric to Madame Virouleau[2] (and to come by *taxi*).

One or two books would certainly do me well, but everything is so scattered. Perhaps you will more easily find *La Pensée chinoise*[3] (in the studio or chambre de bonne), but that is of very limited importance.

The essential, my Darling, is that You are well, You and our son. You are without help at home—do not forget the restaurants.

What bothers me is my situation with respect to rue d'Ulm.[4] The New Year's greetings that were supposed to be sent from Valloire remained unsent—which is not too serious—but I wonder above all how to inform the École of this prolongation of my vacation. Perhaps you can telephone Prigent (number in the telephone book, under ENS, secretariat), perhaps Claude Fuzier (foreign languages instructor).[5]

I cannot wait to see you both again, but, before that, I have to start over (or rather to start being a bit hardier when it comes to secondary things). The doctors will decide about that.

My room—where I am alone—is very sober; bed, table, window overlooking a little garden that is still quite verdant and "monk-like." Since yesterday, they have been bringing me newspapers—you know that I had not read them for a while. The nurses have all found their smile again—it is true that the first two days I was hardly affable. But everything changes—soon we will be reunited again, to live, live, live.

Hug our Eric!

I kiss You

Paul

After this letter Doctor P. came to see me, I find him amiable.

---

1. This should be: *1963*.
2. A neighbor.
3. An essay by Marcel Granet (Paris: Éditions Albin Michel, 1960). During his hospitalization, PC will also read *Deutung biblischer Gestalten* by Margarete Susman (Stuttgart/Konstanz: Diana, 1960).

4. The ENS (located on rue d'Ulm and commonly referred to as "Ulm").

5. Jean Prigent was secretary-general of the ENS. Jean Fuzier was in charge of foreign language instruction at the ENS.

103

[Épinay-sur-Seine,] 10 January 1963

My Darling,

Just a few lines to thank You for Your two pneumatic letters and to tell You that, certainly, I am a bit disappointed not to see You today. But that means that You will come tomorrow, and so the wait for tomorrow has already begun.

I am happy to hear, once again, that You are well, You and our son. Everything is there. As for me, I will not hide from You that I am beginning to find the stay here a bit long; I will be very well when I am beside you two, in my house.

Moreover, the nurse, this morning, told me that nothing that serious was wrong with me—and it is true. But I admit that I am living in anticipation of my return and that the time spent here seems to me to be a bit empty.

It is ten thirty, I am leaving to deposit these lines at the office—that way You will perhaps still get them this evening.

Excuse me for not being more loquacious today. But You know well: I have chosen, I live toward You, with You, with our son.

I hug our son.

I kiss You.

Paul

104

[Épinay-sur-Seine] Saturday, 12 January 1963

My Darling,

These lines—which will not be numerous—are to tell You that I am thinking of You, of you two, of you, of our son. And that I think of coming home to find you both again, to live with you both.

Doctor C. came this morning, there was no question of leaving, but tomorrow, with Doctor P., I plan on insisting that I come back toward You, toward my life, toward our shared life. All that will happen, all that has to happen, as soon as possible.

I kiss You, my Very-Beloved, I kiss You and our son

Paul

105

Eine Handstunde hinter[1]
der Bussard-
schwinge, im Jura,
am Lärchenstein,

kam uns, auf
dem Unbeklommenen, wo wir
gingen,
etwas entgegen: das
Rohr, das
denkende.

Abschrift
19.3.63

A hand's hour behind
the buzzard's
wing, in the Jura,
at the Larch-Stone,

something came, on
the unanxious, where
we walked,
to meet us: the

reed, the
thinking one.

Copy
19.3.63²

1. See *NKGA*, p. 432.
2. Copy made the day of GCL's thirty-sixth birthday.

106

[Dedications and comments written by Paul Celan in two copies of *Die Niemandsrose*[1]]

For You, my Love,
on the Bridge of Years,[2]

Paul
Paris, 24 October 1963

[p. 10, beneath the poem "Das Wort vom Zur-Tiefe-Gehn":]

Wir sind es noch immer[3]

We are still what we are.

[p. 19, beneath the poem "Mit allen Gedanken":[4]]

Mit allen Gedanken ging ich	For You, my Love,
hinaus aus der Welt: da warst du,	this poem, again,
du meine Leise, du meine Offne,	which, it too,
und—	will help us to
du empfingst uns.	Resist.

Wer
Sagt, daß uns alles erstarb,   Paul
da uns das Aug brach? Paris,   26.4.1965
Alles erwachte, alles hob an.

Groß kam eine Sonne geschwommen, hell
standen ihr Seele und Seele entgegen, klar,
gebieterisch schwiegen sie ihr
ihre Bahn vor.

Leicht
tat sich dein Schoß auf, still
stieg ein Hauch in den Äther,
und was sich wölkte, wars nicht,
wars nicht Gestalt und von uns her,
wars nicht
so gut wie ein Name?

With all thoughts I went
out of the world: there you were,
you my soft, you my open, and—
you received us.

Who
says that all died away for us,
when our eye failed?
All awoke, all began.

Large a sun came swimming over, bright
stood a soul and a soul facing it, clear,
imperious they stilled
its path.

Lightly
your lap opened up, noiselessly
a breath rose in the ether,
and what clouded up, was it not,
was it not a form and from us,
was it not
as good as a name?[5]

[To Eric Celan]

For you, my beloved son,
upon seeing you again with mama,[6]

your Papa
Paris, 24 October 1963

1. *The No One's Rose*, (Frankfurt am Main: S. Fischer, 1963).
2. See no. 3, n. 2.
3. This is line four of "Das Wort vom Zur-Tiefe-Gehn" (*NKGA*, p. 129). See nos 63, 135, 136, 154, 186, 203.
4. See *NKGA*, p.134.
5. See "With All My Thoughts," *SPP*, p. 149.
6. PC just returned from a trip to Germany and Switzerland.

107

78 rue de Longchamp
Saturday, 21 December 1963

Thank You, my Darling, for Your two telephone calls. But yes, call me from time to time, I am glad to have Your news, to be able to participate a bit in Your stay in the mountains.

Here, all is calm. (Carmen,[1] currently, is busying herself discreetly in the kitchen.)

I read a bit: *Drei Frauen* by Musil, which I found the other day in an original edition at Gibert. A day of book purchases, in fact, that day: two

Michaux (*Que je fus* and *Voyage en Grande Garabagne*), for eleven thousand francs (a thousand francs less than anticipated), a Russian Babel[2] (two copies, one for the Wagenbachs).

Today, I expect to get back to work on the Sonnets.[3]

Yesterday evening, dinner at the Koroneoses', very friendly.[4] But I left quite early, well before eleven o'clock—and slept quite well.—I will not see P. until the 27th, but I expect to ask him to lower my doses, except for the sleeping pills.—Slowly, I will climb back up the hill and recover, again—we will climb back up together. So much energy invested in resistance—I will have to find the means to get past this stage, to *live again*, freely.

Monday it is our anniversary. You will find Your white lilacs upon Your return and that will be this very day. The bridge of years[5] endures and will endure.

I am sending You Eric's grades—I know how happy You are that he is working so well, and I am very happy about it too. Eric is carrying all our hopes, all of his—and I know them to be great.

Rest Yourself, ski well, sleep well. This year is also the year of our book.[6]

Hug Eric! I kiss You

Paul

---

1. Carmen Forcada Fernández, a cleaning lady who worked for the Celans.
2. Isaac Babel, *Конармия (рассказы)* (*Red Cavalry*) (Moscow-Leningrad, 1928; published by Flegon Press, 24 Chancery Lane, London).
3. Work on the typing-up of *Achtzehn Sonette* (Eighteen Sonnets) by Shakespeare for a program on the German radio station Norddeutscher Rundfunk, which will be aired in 1964, on the occasion of the poet's 400th birthday. These translations will also be published in summer 1964, in *Die neue Rundschau* (75th year, volume 2, pp. 204–13); sonnets 1–5, 43, 50, 57, 60, 65, 70, 71, 79, 105, 106, 115, 116, 119; see *GW* V, pp. 316–41, 344–348, 350–5, and 628f.
4. The Greek poet Kosmas Koronéos (or Koroneos) and his wife Louise lived at 53 boulevard Arago (13th arrondissement). K. Koronéos's mother having been German, he was also a German speaker.
5. See no. 3, n. 3. It is the Celans' eleventh wedding anniversary.
6. The future *Atemkristall*: Paul Celan, *Atemkristall, Radierungen von Gisèle Celan-Lestrange* (Vaduz: Brunidor, 1965). See Appendix, image 11.

108

78 rue de Longchamp, 23 December 1963

It is our anniversary, my Beloved. May it come again often, often, beside our son!

We must find all our strength again—we must!

It is past two o'clock, You were probably not able to call me. I am going down just to send these lines and then I will return to wait for You.

The Shakespeare sonnets are typed.

Your mother has again given us a present of five thousand new francs!

Hug our son. My heart hugs you both.

[Unsigned]

I am enclosing 4 Imménoctal,[1] You can take them in halves.

1. A barbiturate.

109

Majestic in Crans, 24 December 1963

Good evening, my darling,

A long long evening in front of me! They are very long in general, interrupted by the odious noise of this refrigerator cranking on! In Crans, it must begin soon—and in Paris? I am thinking of you. What will you find? They're odious, these holidays. They're detestable. But since they exist around one, it's even more trying for those who don't want to have them. Right? I would give very much to spend a few hours beside you this evening in our house.

The weather was ignoble, very cold, very cloudy, but above all this so tiring föhn, which paralyzes You and prevents You from doing anything. I have to admit to you that I quickly abandoned my plans to go to Plans-Mayens. I went for a walk with Eric in Crans, where he spent the aunt's money, then I brought him here with a Bûche de Noël. He played nicely the whole evening, but he talks all the time, and it's hard for me to read, or do anything. Let's hope for snow and for sun, so that he can enjoy it here as much as possible and so that we come home to you.

I hope every day that you will be able to work a little, that you will get a bit of joy from it. That your solitude will be fruitful, that the price to be paid for your poetry will not be too high. I also hope that you will find some comprehension with the Bollacks, to the extent that it's possible. I also hope that you can read, I was delighted that you made a few discoveries and also that you bought the Michaux books. You will reread them in that edition.

Maybe you will meet a few other people, have a few encounters that will be good for you. I hope that the mail is not bad. To know that you manage to live, not merely to kill time. This year will have been a very hard chapter in our life. May next year be different, while remaining our life! Let us hold out strongly united facing difficulties. Eleven years already! So short and so full, so painful, so difficult, but also with some joys, the unreplaceable, the true, life, with you, a son—and what a son!—you and me, and poetry, this is what, I think, is the most true, the most unreplaceable, the most unique, the most: life. All that you have taught me. All that I have been able to make my own, coming from you, the path travelled! My awakening to life, by you. My knowledge: yours. A very full life already. Thirty-six years! Only, already. Year-end—assessment—1964. The question-mark—the hope—the desire—new poems: new truths.

Eric told me yesterday: "I will be a scholar, but that's not all, I also want to be noble in love!"

Noble in love—yes, noble in love. I found that very beautiful. He is teaching me too.

It is hard for me to read, to think, to write. I will try to sleep. I hoped for your letter, but I don't have it—maybe tomorrow, but that's no doubt a day without mail. I will be able to speak to you on the phone, to hear your voice, to know how you are doing.

I kiss you, my darling, I love you

Gisèle

110

[Paris, 15 April 1964]

Good evening, my Darling,

I leave, You know it well, only to come back to You. Take care of Yourself, work well, for your exhibition, for our book.[1]

Hug our son.

I kiss You.

Paul

15.4.64

1. The future *Atemkristall*.

111

Rome, Friday, 17 April 1964

My Darling,

Just a note to tell You that I have arrived well, after a somewhat long trip, of course, but all things considered, not very tiring.

M. von Marschall and Iris Kaschnitz[1] were waiting for me at the train station, we had lunch at the Marschalls', then they drove me to the Hotel (Genio!), from where I ventured alone a bit into the neighborhood that surrounds it. Rome gives me a somewhat chaotic impression, one feels a bit aggressed by its stones.

This evening, with Iris and one of her writer friends, Ingrid Bachér[2] (who says she met me in Niendorf), at the home of a German Jew, Theile, who edits, on behalf of the ministry of Foreign Affairs in Bonn, a review or rather several richly illustrated reviews, of superculture, in Spanish, Portuguese, Arabic[3]...

Several hours with this man, luckily very talkative, for I did not really open my mouth.

This evening the reading, I will probably have a "German colony" audience[4] and will feel a bit lost. But anyway.

Tomorrow, it will be another Roman day, the last. Then Milan and Geneva[5]—and I will come back to You.

I kiss You, hug the son

Paul

1. Michael Freiherr Marschall von Bieberstein, director of the Goethe-Institut of Rome from 1964–5 is, together with his aunt, Marie Luise Kaschnitz, the reason for PC's invitation to Rome. Iris Kaschnitz is Marie Luise Kaschnitz's daughter. PC evokes his "two days in Rome" in "Mittags" (Midday); see *NKGA*, p. 191; *BIT*, p. 36.
2. A German writer, who lived in Rome. PC had met her at the Group 47 meeting in May 1952.
3. Alberto Theile, chief editor of the *Humboldt* review, which was published in Spanish and Portuguese editions, in which translations of PC's poems will be published in 1967. Theile also edited two other similar reviews published in Italian and Arabic.
4. The reading takes place at the Goethe-Institut.
5. In Milan, PC gives a reading at the Goethe-Institut, where he will meet the head of the translation division at the Mondadori publishing house, Cin Calabi, a friend of Jean Starobinski's. In Geneva, PC will see, primarily all for reasons having to do with his state of health, Jean Starobinski and his friend the psychiatrist Julián de Ajuriaguerra, who gives him his essay, co-written with François Jaeggi, on the poet Michaux and hallucinogenic drugs.

112

[Letter from Gisèle and Paul Celan to their son]

Hanover, Wednesday, 20 May 1964

My dear Eric,

We are thinking often of you and everyone asks us how you are doing. This evening Papa will read his poems.[1] I am, as you can well imagine, very glad to be able to be there—And tomorrow is the exhibition.[2] My etchings have finally arrived—on time. The director has arranged for me to come early with papa to see the people who will perhaps write something in the newspapers about it. I am very impressed, as long as everything goes well—

And you? I hope that the composition assignment will have gone well, that the cafeteria is good and that you will also spend a good day with Aunt Monique—

See you soon, my dear son

Mama kisses you

My dear Eric, in a little while I will read poems—who knows, one day you will do perhaps just as much, in your way. Or you will do something else, and this will still be like writing poems. I believe in you, I am thinking of you, I give you a big kiss. See you soon!

Your papa

1. Reading of thirty-six poems organized by the Literary Society of Hanover at the Wilhelm Raabe school.
2. Exhibition devoted to thirty-seven prints by GCL at the gallery of the Hanover Kestner Gesellschaft. See Appendix, image no. 8.

113

Moisville, 4 June 1964

Das Stundenglas, tief
im Päonienschatten vergraben:

wenn das Denken
den Pfingstweg herabkommt, endlich,
fällt ihm das Reich zu,
wo du versandend verhoffst.
Moisville, 4. 6. 1964
——

Das Stundenglas, tief
im Päonienschatten vergraben:

wenn das Denken die Pfingst-
schneise[1] herabkommt, endlich,
fällt ihm das Reich zu,
wo du versandend verhoffst.

The hour-glass, buried
deeply in peony-shadow:

when thought comes down
the Pentecostal path, finally,
to it falls the kingdom,
where you, being sanded over, hope against hope.[2]

1. In these two versions of "Das Stundenglass" (The Hour-Glass), the sole variation is between "Pfingst-/weg" and "Pfingst-/schneise." See *NKGA*, p. 192. PC cites, translates, and comments on this line in May 1966 (see no. 302, n. 2.)
2. See also "The Hourglass," *BIT*, p. 38.

114

[To Eric Celan]

[Deggendorf,] 7 July 1964

My dear son, here we are in the Bavarian Forest, very close to Bohemia, where we would like to go with you one day.[1] I hope that you are learning to swim and to ride horses, and that you are having a good time with your companions.—I give you a big hug—

Your Papa

1. PC will never go to Bohemia, despite his attachment to this formerly German-speaking region, the region of Rabbi Löw, of Rilke, and of Kafka, where his mother found refuge for three years during World War I, after the invasion of Czernowitz by Russian troops (see the photograph of Friederike Schrager and its caption written by PC, reproduced in the Appendix, image 1).

115

[To Eric Celan]

[Chaumont,] 20 July 1964[1]

My dear Eric, here we are, mama and me, in Switzerland since yesterday, above Lake Neuchâtel, at a thousand meters' altitude, with, if it were not so hot and the sky were less hazy, this view of the Alps.[2]—Friday we will be in Paris to be better able to wait for you. We give you a big hug

Papa

[Written by Gisèle Celan-Lestrange:] mama

1. The day before, PC and GCL were the guests of Friedrich and Lotti Dürrenmatt. The poem "Oberhalb Neuenburgs" (Above Neuchâtel), written on 2 August 1964, is dedicated to them. See *NKGA*, p. 449.
2. The postcard: "Chaumont. Vue sur les Alpes—Petit Hôtel Chaumont."

116

[To Eric Celan]

Aarberg, 23 July 1964

Here we are, mama and me, in a little Bernese market town, in a square with many flowers, after having gone over the little covered bridge that the card shows you.—We kiss you

Papa

[Written by Gisèle Celan-Lestrange:] mama

117

Kassel, 14 September 1964

Having hardly descended from the train, I run into, after carried having the suitcase to the luggage office in the train station itself, Madame de La Motte. And here we are, waiting for a blue trout, sitting at the table to have lunch. Thanks for the little note in the briefcase. I kiss You, my Darling, with our son.

Paul

118

[Cologne, 30 October 1964]

Your seven roses,[1]
Your husband

who loves You and
kisses You, with
Your son

Cologne, 30.X.64

1. See no. 68, n. 3, and no. 249.

119

HOTEL ALSTER-HOF
2 Hamburg 36—Esplanade 12
1 November [1964], 17:00

Hamburg, gray city. But my heart, when, in Cologne, it saw You leave, woke up, for You, entirely.

Certainly, it would be good for me to be able to live a bit in Germany, but if the language comes back to me, the faculty of concentration, of reading, of writing is still very far away. I register, intermittently, and I forget.[1]

Here, the hotel had a room only for one night and so I decided to go to Copenhagen tomorrow. How [long] will I stay there?

Even Cologne, which I still love for its echo of my first stroll with Böll[2]—destroyed Roman churches, one of which, I thought about it again yesterday, with a cross called "plague cross" (Pestkreuz),[3] arms in a V—even Cologne, with its possibilities too of seeing people in the city itself and nearby—I went, with Schallück, to see Ernst Meister, in Hagen, Kay Hoff in Bergisch-Gladbach,* Elisabeth Borchers** in Neuwied[4]—does not seem to be a place where I can work—

So I don't know. Vague receptivity to exterior things—poems will open themselves perhaps to that, thanks to that. But still the same impatience. Do I have to go back to Hamburg? In a little while I will see Karl Ludwig Schneider with his wife, I like them, perhaps that will give me ideas about Hamburg. Or I will return to Cologne—but essentially, above all, because

I want to hear what Böll, who will go to Berlin in the coming days to meet, with a view to an explanation, Graß and Richter,[5] will be able to tell me about the evolution of things in Germany, etc. I was, the other day, upon seeing him again, quite surprised to see that he did not like at all—or did not seem to like—the fuss made about Berlin, the neo-Prussianism, etc.[6]

Or I will go, after a day in Cologne—to buy, on discount, a typewriter—to Frankfurt or to Darmstadt...or to Allemann's.

You see, my darling, how much I migrate...and how badly I migrate.

Just a moment ago I thought that for my birthday I would like very much to be at home. But I will perhaps have to grant a bit of patience...to my impatience. Somewhere, unbeknownst to me, who knows, a new patience is preparing itself.

Tomorrow morning I will telephone You.

I hold You, very tightly, still and always.[7] Hug our son

Paul

---

1. Since January 1963, PC has been taking psychotropic medications (antidepressants and neuroleptics). Starting in 1964, he will constantly worry about his capacity for concentration and for memorization.

2. See no. 27.

3. PC sees this plague cross at the Sankt Maria im Kapitol church. This cross owes its name to the plague that struck Cologne in 1349 and which was followed by a pogrom, which led to the destruction of almost the entire Jewish community. The word "Pestkreuz" will appear in a poem written by PC about three weeks after this letter, in "Bei den Zusammengetretenen / Zeichen" (See NKGA, p. 201; BIT, p. 60). For PC, "Pest" evokes "die braune Pest," Nazism and anti-Semitism.

* Oh, lovely geography...[All annotations marked with asterisks were written by PC unless otherwise indicated. This particular note seems to be a commment not on Bergisch-Gladbach, but Neuwied, where Goll's publisher, Luchterhand, was located.]

** Great admirer of Nelly Sachs's, whose framed photo she keeps with the photo of her father in the uniform of a German officer...

4. Kay Hoff is the pseudonym of Adolf Max Hoff, German writer. Elisabeth Borchers, a German writer and translator, was, from 1960 to 1971, a reader at Luchterhand (in Neuwied), which had published an edition of poems by Yvan Goll at the initiative of Claire Goll.

5. Heinrich Böll will ultimately not go to Berlin in November 1964. The subject of the "explanation" was whether or not to support the SPD (the German Social Democratic Party) in the

Bundestag elections in 1965. While Böll had refused to participate in the meeting between the candidates and writers from Group 47 (April 1964), Günter Grass and H. W. Richter, as well as Siegfried Lenz and Walter Jens, supported Willy Brandt and the SPD.

6. PC was not fond of Berlin, symbol of the power and unity of the Reich; PC was, moreover, highly skeptical of German reunification, given the signs of a new German nationalism (see no. 96, n. 5).

7. Variation on "noch immer": see nos 63, 106, 135, 136, 154, 186, 203.

120

[Copenhagen,] Friday, [6 November 1964]

Hello, my Beloved, I hug You, with our son.

Copenhagen—very noble city, which I will have surveyed for three days. There was, in the Freedom Museum, a blue-white-red hat, worn as a sign of resistance against the Germans.[1] One day, I will bring You here, You will like it.

This evening, I will be in Hamburg, beside your letter

Paul

1. PC had just obtained *The Museum of the Danish Resistance Movement 1940–1945: A Short Guide by Aage Roussell* (Copenhagen: The National Museum of Copenhagen, 1964). Recalling his peregrinations around Copenhagen, PC will write, on 25 December 1964, the poem "Frihed" (see *NKGA*, pp. 204; *BIT*, p. 68); see also the poem "Welche Stimme hat, was du hast?" (Which voice has what you have?), *NKGA*, p. 452.

121

78 rue de Longchamp

[17–18 January 1965], Sunday evening

That really did something to me when You got on the train yesterday evening and when that train pulled away.[1] I had my heart in my throat, and heavy tears came up at the same time, from the depths of my being.

I am sitting here asking myself if I did the right thing by letting You leave, without a hotel booked, without friends, in this large foreign city. What kind of weather has received You? Have You been able to take a porter, make change, pay the chauffeur? But maybe one of the two girls who shared Your compartment was able to give You advice?

No, decidedly, we should, at least, have reserved a hotel room. Yesterday evening, while coming home, after a half-hour stop in a bistro at the corner of rue des S[ain]ts-Pères and b[oulevar]d S[ain]t-Germain, I almost telephoned the Ufers to ask them to pick You up at the train station. Then I told myself that, if You had left alone, it would be important to You to manage things Yourself, "like a grownup." But just now, I measured what Your departure was for me, and the uncertainty about Your accommodations. Was the Genio friendly, did they have any rooms? But what was for You this first Roman day, made of solitude—I almost said of "aloneness"?[2]

For me, You see, Your departure brought me one very big thing; all my love for You found again, without anything lost, my love completely whole, that of the first nights, that of the Empress of all my Bukovinas (there are only mine, the others, let us not speak of them, I have nothing at all to do with them), that of my Big Angelet Big, that of my Little Peach, that of Maïa.[3] (I brought the Yeats poems back from Moisville—You remember this book? You gave it to me on 16 July 1952, we had bought it at Brentano's, avenue de l'Opéra, You had indulged me:[4] I coveted this book for so many years, since I was sixteen years old, and here I was in Paris (where I *lived*!), had met Gisèle de Lestrange, who loved me and loved that which was poem, written and lived.) And the "green Berbers"[5] shined on us—they still shine on us and will shine on us. Oh, I will find again what I need to wrap You in my arms, put my arms around You and illuminate You, You, so clear already, so radiant.

I love You, my Love.

Short account of the day: Met the Silbermanns[6] at their hotel, then the 27 to Pont-Neuf, the rain, Notre-Dame, re-rain (cats and dogs), Madame not wanting to get wet (but it was pouring, truly), I take a taxi to bring them to my house (one does not eat lunch until two o'clock in Düsseldorf), thereupon, at Trocadéro, things calm down, we get out, the Eiffel Tower emerges and entices, then I explain the metro. Then at our house. A few phone calls to find, in Parîs [sic], the whole of Czernowitz; that works out, thanks to

Trichter and to Doctor Kraft. Finally two o'clock, I take them to have lunch on avenue d'Eylau; they must have grill, but tournedos is accepted, and boiled potatoes. Oh, how good the bread is in Paris! Then, people at a nearby table are reminiscent of Bucharest. And then, so that the metro may really exist in reality, I accompany them to the Jeu de Paume. There, Monet above all is admired. In the crowd, I recognize the face of a girl—but she worked for us, I tell myself, she recognizes me too, she is Austrian, impossible to remember her name[7] or when she was with us, I tell her that you have left, but that she should telephone us in three weeks, that way she will also see Eric again. But she tells me she does not know Eric. Now I do not understand anymore, I ask myself if she was at our house only for a trial period and if we showed her the door. I leave her with her friend.—At the end of the visit, she reappears, with her friend, and informs me that she was with the Dürrenmatts while we were there.[8] But of course. We recall the parrot, I learn that the old dog has just died. Then I leave, with the Silbermanns, but distressed by this confrontation with my failing memory. Yet it is not long ago, hardly a few months! I recognize the face, but do not find the name, and I am mistaken about the place, the context, etc. That made me quite unhappy, and it is the first time that something like that has happened to me.[9]

Silbermann, this morning, when asked about the death of poor Marcel Pohne, proves to be a man without a heart. He goes as far as to reproach Nadia for having written to a friend of Marcel's, who lives in Bucharest, "right away," and provoking in him a nervous shock[10]...

With the Bölls, it seems that the Silbermanns did anticommunism above all—they found the right audience.[11]

Anyway. From Jeu de Paume we went, by rue du F[au]b[our]g-S[ain]t-Honoré, to the Rond-Point des Champs-Élysées, here I couldn't take any more, it was windy too; I invited them to come for lunch on Tuesday, and I went home.

Will I be able to work in Your absence? I was able to write You these lines, these pages even.—But I feel deprived of my reviving powers today. I need You beside me. I need to know where You are, to know, all the time, that You are well, that everything protects You.—You will see, my Love, if You feel too lonely, do not hesitate to come back to France, first to the South, then to me.—What do I do? I wait for You. I wait Your telegram. (The concierge was not there during the day, I will go down in a moment to see. But she would certainly have brought it up to me.)

I feel like calling the Genio, but I am afraid of not making myself understood, I do not have the number, what's more I am afraid of not finding You there because, perhaps, You have gone out.

Yesterday evening, tried to call the aunt, "automatically": a gentleman, in pure English from England, answers—error. I ask for the number again through the ten-tone-zero-four: my aunt has gone out. I will telephone the Lalandes now, to speak a bit of You.

Telephoned the Lalandes, it is Lisou who answers (Jacques is at the theater, Jacqueline has gone out). She tells me that a telegram from Italy could take as long as a day and a half—that is long, it will not be as long as that, right?

Went down to the concierge—she is still not there. Went for a short walk in the street, toward Trocadéro, then went back up. My God, I have after all let You depart somehow into the unknown. Here, at our house, our lamps lit. It is hard. I need so much to know that You are well! Perhaps You will telephone me still this evening, even if it has not been arranged? We thought of so many things, not of that, the first thing we should have thought about.

I was just thinking of telephoning our son. But I have to be able to tell him how You are doing, I will wait for Your telegram. Will I be able to leave for Germany? There, I will face even more uncertainty.

It is 20:30, I will drop the Tops[12] a line. Telephoned Top, who is very nice. Spoke for around five minutes, felt my tears coming. How could I have let You go so far away, my love?

Strand, come back to me.

Some moments, these last years, I believed I had to live according to another law. But I am, very profoundly, deeply, Your husband.

I understand You, my love, I understand You. So much suffering, so much solitude, so much bitterness. But here, now, my heart is full of You. I feel Your mouth, I kiss You, we are at the train station, I'm telling You that I love You, and I say it from the depths of my soul, and You feel it.

Your eyes, my love, your eyes. Your soul, large, upright, without fault. Come, my light, be here.

Thought of telegraphing You, but they tell me that it is likely the telegram would not arrive until tomorrow, or if urgent, toward midnight. Asked, at directory assistance, for the number of the Genio.

You are certainly thinking of the son, of me. My love.

And, also, I need Your advice.

I have the number, but if I telephone You and You are out, You will be worried, when You return, when You hear that I called, whatever reassuring thing I can say (and that risks being poorly transmitted).

I can make You no reproach. And will not, anymore. Épinay—of course, You could not do otherwise. I well know it, well feel it. Clarity will install itself in us, for a long time, with our never-lost love.

Never, on my own trips, have I felt what I feel right now.

It is in You that my strength is reborn, thanks to You. Come. How could I have told You not to telephone me?

Call me, speak to me.

9:20: Called the Genio, with a call notice for Madame Antschel. Be there, my beloved, be there. (A half-hour waiting time was announced.)

The son is doing well, isn't he, he is skiing, he is amusing himself, he is working. Our dear Eric, our hope. Our son who was given to us living, who lives and who will live, a man, human. And strong and well protected, and from here, from Your home, from his home. And Jewish, humanly, humbly, proudly.

9:35: The telephone rings once, I pick up—no answer.

9:45: Re-telephone—"The telephone in Rome is off the hook."—I, stupidly telling myself that the hotel telephone was busy: "So cancel." Then, changing my mind, I ask again, but it is already another person, if the call notice has been accepted.—Hopefully You are not worried. Oh, I know, I am quite impatient, quite maladroit.

Without this campaign against me,[13] which is, as is more and more obvious, a vast attempt to repress, to exclude this poet, somehow from elsewhere, that I am: how serene our life would have been, full of love and of work, of our child's education. But we will not give up, we will hold out, all three of us, together, more and more united.

_____

Turned over the hourglass.

I have to calm myself. You are well, Your stay in Rome will be a success.

_____

Someone calls me: It was indeed the telephone in the Genio that was left off the hook, so that the call didn't go through.

_____

You are well, You are content.

Went back down to the concierge, who, this time, is there. No telegram, but that is basically normal. Tomorrow I will have Your news.—I turn over the hourglass again, everything continues. I will go take a Dominal,[14] then, thinking of You, thinking of our son, of both of your returns, I will go to bed.

I have to know how to leave You alone, tranquil, tranquilly.

But I would like for You to be here, like that, tranquil, near me, now.

_____

Monday, 7:15

Night with interruptions, rather insomniac, slightly nightmarish. But confidence upon awakening. I will have Your telegram at noon, I will send You one, I will post this letter.

A pack of Gauloises that you left here, opened. And your lighter. Have you bought another? Certainly, you smoked a cigarette at the train station. I ignite your lighter, I switch on, I illuminate.

I see You in Rome, sure of Yourself, strong, courageous, gathering what You need to work, Your eyes lucid, open to things. And things speak to You. Humans speak to You, receiving You, with friendliness, in the Italian way, with respect: they understand who You are, they understand it right away.

8 o'clock: Arrival of Carmen.

Opened the Yeats volume to page 62:

"The Lover Tells of the Rose in his Heart"

Before nine o'clock: Your telephone call. Do not stay longer than You feel like staying, my love. A week, if You can. Then drop by Your friend in Cabris and come back.

(In the morning mail, a letter from Mme Porena, the wife of the Roman composer, very nice, she worked on the two last volumes, also on the *Meridian*. I think that you should telephone her: 50-24-04. Address: via Bruzzesi 7. Seeing people, time will pass more easily.)—I will go to Würz-burg on Wednesday, for two days.

The lover tells of the *Rose* in his heart.

Paul

[In the margin:] The Tops, whom I telephoned yesterday, insist that you go see their friends, the Schaedels.

1. It was indeed PC who pressured GCL to go on this trip to Rome; PC himself had asked for this separation (PC's journal).
2. Celanian loan translation ("seuleté") of the German *Einsamkeit*.
3. See PC's terms of endearment in the letters from the 1950s (for example, nos 3, 4, 5, 8, 21, 25) and certain book dedications (for example, nos 81, 82).
4. *The Collected Poems of W.B. Yeats* (London: MacMillan and Co., Ltd., 1952). GCL noted on the flyleaf: "16 July 52. / Maya."
5. This invention, based on *réverbères*, or streetlights, comes from Eric Celan. PC occasionally wrote in the light from streetlights (see no. 202).
6. The day before, PC had reserved a hotel room for his friends Edith and Jakob Silberman, both from Czernowitz. They had emigrated to Germany, in part thanks to PC's connections, the previous year. On the relations between PC and Edith Horowitz Silbermann,, see Edith Silberman, *Begegnung mit Paul Celan* (Aachen: Rimbaud, 1993).
7. This person was named Ursula Teufel (literally: Ursula "Devil").
8. Around half a year before, in July 1964.
9. During this time, and subsequent to taking psychotropic medications, PC expresses his worry about memory loss in his autobiographical notes; see no. 119, n. 1.
10. Marcel Pohne, whose wife Nadia was expecting a child, had died in a car accident the previous month. The Pohnes were originally from Czernowitz.
11. Edith Silbermann had just moved to Cologne, to enter the literary milieu there as a translator from Romanian. Despite being sympathetic to West German Marxism and communism, Heinrich Böll could be very critical of certain applications of the doctrine, including in Eastern Europe. On this subject, see Böll, *Aufsätze, Kritiken, Reden* (Cologne: Kiepenheuer & Witsch, 1967); there are no reading marks in the copy in PC's library.

12. The German translators (of Beckett, in particular) Elmar Tophoven and his wife, Erika Schöningh.

13. The Goll Affair. See no. 4, n. 2.

14. This neuroleptic (prothipendyl) is used in the long-term treatment of schizophrenia and psychosis when agitation and hallucination are present; in weak doses, its effect is tranquilizing.

122

[Paris,] 19 January 1965

My beloved,

Your voice on the telephone this morning. Do not stay, if it seems long to You, do not look at it as an obligation or as any kind of task. Come back as soon as You feel like it, via Nice or directly.

Yesterday: mainly empty, wrote three letters: to DVA (Firgès, Group 47), to Oslo, (refusal to participate in the almanac published on the occasion of their Group 47 evening),[1] to Chr. Perels, student of Killy's and new reader at Fischer (banalities). Then sent "Hafen" to Bucharest, for their review, then a letter, very friendly, to the girl who asked for my collaboration.—At Claude David's, looked for 2 books on K. Kraus.[2] Present for M[onsieu]r and Madame: *Dans l'Entremonde*, watercolors by Klee.

Read, with an all too rapid glance, one of the books on Kraus: disgusting thing, unworthy of the Sorbonne, on a dubious man, a dubious oeuvre.[3]

This morning three letters from Eric that I attach to this one, with a stamped envelope so that he writes You, three others for his aunts.

I will leave tomorrow, it's a long trip, I arrive around seven in the evening. Why all that? A bit of manifested presence, nervousness, restlessness above all.

At one o'clock, the Silbermanns. He, a bit better, talking about Kraus. I say what I think. The unbelievable passage from *Merkur*,[4] which I show him, does not provoke any reaction. She: stupidity above all, the petite bourgeoise with sometimes high, sometimes low heels. They would have liked for me to take the metro in their place too.

I will write to Eric in a moment, will try, this evening, to call him on the telephone. Then a letter to write for Monluçon,[5] one to address to Michaux.[6]

In the mail this evening, a letter from Ruth K., announcing to me the delivery of *Merkur*,[7] another, hardly polite, from a Swiss writer editing, for Larese, a selection of Cassou, on which he would like me to collaborate. This smells, excuse me, a bit like blackmail.

My darling, no one to help us, to support us amidst all that. Let us face up to it, alone, always, together. Nothing will separate us.

I kiss You, my Beloved

Paul

---

1. PC responds to Kirsti Christensen, the representative of the Association of Norwegian Students, to decline the rights to publish translations of poems from *MG*, read at a literary event devoted to Group 47. In a letter to Felix Berner, in charge of legal affairs and rights at DVA, PC writes that he was never part of Group 47, in order to justify this refusal.

2. Works not identified. The program for the *agrégation* in 1965 included Karl Kraus (*Worte in Versen, 1916–1930*). Claude David, professor at the Sorbonne, taught courses on Kraus. The only book on Kraus preserved in PC's library is Caroline Kohn's doctoral thesis, *Karl Kraus* (Paris: Didier, 1962); the volume has numerous reading marks that have not been clearly identified.

3. Geneviève Roussel, one of PC's students this year, recalls: "Rue d'Ulm, 1965. In a very small room three students from Sèvres and one from the École normale, in a line in front of Paul Celan, hoped, beyond any preparation for the *agrégation*, for the mediation of the poet who, abandoning Stefan George [and *Der siebente Ring*, which figured in the exam program], had chosen to speak of Karl Kraus, the other poet in the program, and of his *Worte in Versen*. *Worte in Versen* was never considered, this volume of Kraus never opened. Immured in his tragic quest for a German language that, stripped of all ornamentation, would be truer, Paul Celan, speaking in monologue, gave a self-reflective reading of the pamphlet *Heine und die Folgen*. Imprecations of the emigrant poet against the feuilleton writer Karl Kraus, whose lesser abilities he identifies, uncovers pentameters and hexameters, warts of prose. Rehashing and amplification of Kraus's arguments against Heine, a poet, according to Kraus, of the hatred of Germany, and of the easiness imported from France, this country of the epigram, of cynicism, of flippancy. Perhaps the poet Paul Celan wanted to recreate, with the power of the word, a regenerative chaos, which is evoked by this bracketed and underlined phrase in his work copy of Kraus's text: 'Kunst bringt das Leben in Unordnung. Die Dichter der Menschheit stellen immer wieder das Chaos her; die Dichter der Gesellschaft singen und klagen, segnen und fluchten innerhalb der Weltordnung.' [Art brings life into disorder. The poets of humanity continually reestablish chaos; the poets of society sing and complain, bless and curse within the order of the world.] The ENS students from then, who loved Germany—Goethe and Heine—and France, have of these few hours an uncanny memory." This account, written in 1995, sent to Jean-Pierre Lefebvre (ENS), was published for the first time in the original French edition of these letters.

4. Reinhard Baumgart, "Unmenschlichkeit beschreiben. Weltkrieg und Faschismus in der Literatur" (Describing Inhumanity: World War and Fascism in Literature), *Merkur*, no.

202, January 1965, pp. 37–50. In this article, Baumgart writes of Celan's "Todesfuge": "The 'black milk in the morning,' death with the violin, 'a master from Germany,' all that composed in a refined score—did it not show too much pleasure in art, in despair that has become 'beautiful' again through art?" In the same issue of *Merkur*, Kurt Oppens criticizes Celan's "contentless form as mystery" and asks if his poetry represents an "occasionally emerging, despairing and radical aestheticism"; see "Blühen und Schreiben im Niemandsland" (To Bloom and to Write in No-Man's-Land).

5. Connected to EC's schoolwork. Monluçon is the director of the École communale in rue Hamelin (16th arrondissement).

6. PC, who is working intensively on his translations of poems by Michaux, has just received a letter from the latter accompanying "a short poem" (not identified) sent at his request. In this letter (date uncertain; dated by PC to 15 January 1965), Michaux recommends Doctor Pierre Mâle to him, the psychiatrist with whom PC will have psychotherapeutic meetings throughout the year.

7. Ruth Kraft, friend of PC's, born in Graz (Austria), raised in Czernowitz; emigrated to Bucharest, then to Israel, and back to Bucharest, before settling in Germany at the end of the 1950s, where she works as a radio presenter and journalist specializing in Romanian questions (Studio Welle, Cologne). During his relationship with Ruth Kraft, between 1940 and 1944, when she was an actor in the Yiddish theater of Czernowitz, PC gave or sent her many poems, including some written in a forced labor camp. In her letter from 17 January 1965, she announces the arrival of the "requested journals": two copies of the January issue of *Merkur*, which PC wished to share with those close to him.

123

via Zanardelli 28, Hotel Genio, [Rome,]

19 January 1965

My Darling, my Love, What joy to find on my return this evening (7 p.m.) your very long letter. It does one well, I assure you, when one is so alone, to feel all the same so loved and so much in the thoughts of the person one loves. For me too the departure of the train toward the unknown, leaving you on that sad station platform, that was very sad for me, very painful. The arrival in Rome was even worse, and this long first walk was exhausting, I could not walk anymore and I truly measured the miles separating us.

Yesterday was still nothing great, after your phone call I tried to reach the Ufers and Iris,[1] but like every foreigner, I was mistaken and pushed the button for too long so that I lost a few lire and above all the courage that I needed to attempt this operation. I gave it up until the evening, when I had the hotelier do it, who is very nice and speaks French. Ufer did not answer,

Iris's number was incomplete! But in the meantime I had all the same seen a little bit of Rome: piazza San Pedro, the church where I was admiring Michelangelo's *Pietà*, only to hear at that very moment a Spanish guide explaining that the original was in America for the moment and that this was a copy! Then, in the Vatican Museum, the Sistine Chapel with its very beautiful frescos by Michelangelo: *The Last Judgment* and *Creation of the World*. When I was 17 years old, that had made an immense impression on me, and, at 37, it's still magnificent. I stayed half an hour with my eyes wide open, but I went through the rest of the Vatican as fast as possible and with my eyes almost closed! And I came home quietly to the hotel without having lunch, around 2 p.m. At 3 p.m., I left again all the same, with the intention of continuing to see Rome since I'm here. I took the corso to piazza del Popolo, walked around in the quarter of galleries, luxury antique shops, then piazza di Spagna, which is marvelous. I went up this grand staircase, admired Rome from above, glanced over toward the Villa Medici, and I came back down through the piazza del Popolo, returned slowly toward the Genio via the attractive piazza Navona, and for dinner I had breaded veal and salad, a quarter-bottle of red wine and gorgonzola for 1000 lire. That was at 6:30 p.m., which shows that I have trouble filling my days, especially once night falls, I am so afraid of getting lost and am quite unable to take a tram.

It seems to rain every night here, but in the morning it's all right, and I can still walk without ever being cold. There are even people seated in cafés outside, but for me it's a bit too cold—.

This morning I had slept badly, but less badly than the night before and I had just gotten up when my phone rang. I resented myself for not being able to speak about anything with you. That device is paralyzing for me, maybe also the distance, the desire to occupy as best as possible the very short interval of time one feels one has.

To have at least told you not to worry, that everything is still going better, that I feel a little bit braver about asking for directions, that I am less glued to the map and am beginning to know my way around, in this neighborhood at least! But no, I was breathless from hearing you.

And today the third Roman day! Well begun with your phone call, well ended with your letter.

I visited the Pantheon, walked up the corso to drink a cappuccino on the p[iazza] del Popolo in what's called the intellectual café (few people for a rather expensive café), then a long walk in the Pincio and the Villa Borghese, where I got lost in no small measure, but where I spent two beautiful hours in the midst of magnificent trees, little palaces, temples, arenas, immense parasol pines, orange trees, cactuses, the good scent of damp earth and almost nobody. It was very pleasant. With you it would have been *marvelous.* I still found the Villa Giulia, not without difficulty, where I visited the Etruscan museum, very beautiful, but rich, rich, too rich for my ability to assimilate and retain, which is very weak. An hour all the same among the vases, statuettes, jewelry, magnificent sarcophagi presented remarkably. I remember above all a very beautiful *sarcofago degli sposi,* touching in its serenity, charm, love, which made me pray to be like that with you for eternity, knowing that it can be like that is a marvelous help. Having seen these two lovers united and serene, calm and so tender in death made me believe that we too, with our hard life, but beyond everything, full of love, would perhaps have a right, in a long time from now, to this fate of the two Etruscan lovers I saw, at the Villa Giulia, in Rome, this 19 January 1965, while thinking of you. (I have the reproduction, but it says nothing.)

Then, my stomach demanding its rights in the via Flaminia, past the People's Gate, I bought myself a quarter of a chicken, a salad, and a pear. It was past two p.m. Then I drank my tea in p[iazza] di Spagna in this quite amusing English tearoom,[2] in the midst of a few old Englishmen sitting alone and Italian waitresses speaking English, which is quite funny to hear.

Then the hair salon! Yes—and another walk on elegant streets with pretty window displays, much elegance (via del Tritone), to arrive at the very lively p[iazza] Colonna (businessman types), where I also remember that with Yolande we were accosted every instant by boys who offered to exchange money for you. That doesn't exist anymore, but I found *Le Figaro* there, and I went into the p[iazza] San Silvestro to read it, in front of the post office from where I had called you, and I drank a particularly good cappuccino, afterward.

Return to the hotel by taxi, because truly tired, around 7 p.m.

I forgot to tell you that I called the Ufers this morning (I figured out the quite simple trick of the public telephone!), but the old man had trouble understanding who I was! Heavens . . . but when he understood, he was very nice. His wife not being home, he took my number, and Mme Kraisky has just called me very kindly and will come to pick me up tomorrow evening at 9, after dinner, to go to their house. Iris Kaschnitz didn't respond to my letter, but it's still a bit early. I have also written to the address of Aunt Edith, just to pass a few hours, I ask her if she would receive me at some time (she was a great friend of mama's, very pious), she takes care of students, and even if, as I tell her, I am far past the age, I think I will ask her if she might have a place available in a group? to visit the Rome area a bit. So far, I have been unable to find the CIT[3] and I was surely just a few steps away several times.

You see that, despite my difficult start, I am trying not to get by too badly. Rome is all the same very seductive, there is so much to see, even if I am staying a long time, I will leave a good part for the next time with you. I must admit that I am all the same taken with the charm, the light, and the color that are so different from those of Paris. So many beautiful palaces, narrow old streets, the very rich but also the very very poor.

What wouldn't I give now to spend a long hour with you, here, in this rather sad and poorly lit room, in this little bed! . . . My love, I have a big "flood," right now, for you, Paul, my Love, my darling, yes, I am the empress of all *your* Bukovinas, but not others!

Don't worry about me, the bad hours of the beginning have passed all the same, I still feel like seeing Rome a bit, for it is very alluring, I won't stay if I become too tired of it, surely not. But since I am here, if I can, I want all the same to take advantage of it to hold out a bit. Even if I am very alone, even if I speak with almost no one.

At bottom, there is also a certain charm to being completely anonymous in a big city. Right now, I would prefer, I won't hide it from you, being here with you or having a least a few friends, which I don't, but I will try to overcome my solitude and to fill it with the Roman gardens, the Roman streets, a few museums. I absorb a little all the same. I think of etchings to come, vaguely. I unfortunately do not think I can work here (if only I had my new studio here!). But maybe when I return! Do you remember, after Amsterdam I had four or five etchings that came of themselves, including *Je maintiendrai*.[4] Thanks for all those beautiful titles.

I will quote you now for my joy and so that it be written again: "I will find again what I need to wrap You in my arms, put my arms around You and illuminate You, You, so clear already, so radiant. I love You, my Love."

Until soon, my Love, I will come back of course, and all three of us, we will hold out and we will fight, and we will win out.

For justice, truth: for Poetry: for Love.

Forward!

Gisèle

1. Iris Kaschnitz, daughter of the poet Marie Luise Kaschnitz.
2. Babington's.
3. Compagnia Italiana Turismo.
4. This print will be definitively entitled *Souvenir de Hollande—Erinnerung an Holland*, 1964. See Appendix, image 10. (The Celans had visited Holland from 23 to 26 May 1964. "Je maintiendrai" is the motto of the Orange-Nassau family, which for PC is a French variation on his "stehen." The Celans were particularly sensitive to the spirit of resistance inscribed in the history of Holland, the country of Spinoza, which rebelled against the persecution of the Jews (the general strike in February 1941). See no. 83, n. 1; no. 87, n. 10; and no. 93, n. 3. PC is the author of all the titles, mostly bilingual, of GCL's prints between 1954 and 1967.

124

[To Eric Celan]

[Paris,] 19 January 1965

My dear Eric,

Three letters this morning—that made me very happy.

Mama, as you know, is in Rome since Sunday, she seems to find that rather tiring, I think that she will not take her time to come home. Myself,

I leave tomorrow morning for Germany and will be back at the end of the week.

"The sun reigns over the azure. The night makes the snow sprout": it is very pretty, very clever; my dear Eric, I am very happy when you speak to us like that. But you have to make a big effort with your spelling—here, I count absolutely on you. The star that you will bring back for your skiing exploits will then sparkle twice as much.

Write right away to Mama, I am enclosing, for you, a stamped envelope with her Roman address. But do not take your time, since the mail, in Italy, is often slow.

Work well, ski well, amuse yourself well. For whatever has to do with skiing, I have no worries (but be careful as well!). As for your work and conduct, I am counting on your efforts and your progress!

I hug you

Your Papa

If, before the end of the week, you have anything urgent to ask, telephone Aunt Solange (Madame de Bourgies), Carnot 02-96. But most likely you will not have any need to call.

125

[Paris, 19 January 1965]

My Darling,

It is past nine in the evening, I managed, at eight o'clock, to get the son on the line, he seemed quite content, it is no doubt the skiing, then the skiing, and then, quite far away, the work. But he really needed to relax and to sparkle a bit on slopes other than that of spelling. I did not omit to remind him—I had already done so by letter—that I counted on him, of course for what concerned his second star, but also for his work and his conduct.

Long telephone call, around seven o'clock, with Solange, who will write you. Letters to Monluçon, to Michaux, sent.

Called the wake-up service for six in the morning; organized the drawer. I put all the keys in the drawer in the middle of the desk, and the key to this under the Sachs-Villatte.[1]

My Darling, I kiss You and kiss You.

See You soon

Paul

19.1.1965

I am going to water, copiously, the green plant in your studio.

1. PC frequently worked with his copies of two editions of this celebrated dictionary by Karl Sachs and Césaire Villatte, which display some underlinings and annotations: *Enzyklopädisches französisch-deutsches und deutsch-französiches Wörterbuch*, 2 vols., 29th edition (Berlin-Schöneberg: Langenscheidtsche Verlagsbuchhandlung, 1917), the first volume of which bears the note: "Paul Celan / Wien, Juni 1948" (Vienna, June 1948); and *Enzyklopädisches Wörterbuch der französischen und deutschen Sprache, Große Ausgabe*, 4 vols., 22nd edition (Berlin-Schöneberg: Langenscheidtsche Verlagsbuchhandlung, no date).

126

[Frankfurt am Main,] 20 January 1965, 15:30

My Darling, here I am disembarked in Frankfurt, where, in half an hour, I have a train for Würzburg. I asked myself, in looking at the map, if I should come home via Zurich, which will allow me to see Margarete Susman[1] and, possibly, Erwin Leiser.[2]

Take care of Yourself, I kiss You with all my heart

Paul

1. Margarete Susman, poet and essayist of German-Jewish background, author of numerous essays on Judaism, had emigrated to Switzerland in 1933.
2. Erwin Leiser, journalist and film director of German-Jewish background, had emigrated to Sweden in 1938. PC was in regular contact with the filmmaker behind the celebrated documentary about the Third Reich, *Mein Kampf* (1960).

127

[Würzburg,] 20 January 1965

From Würzburg, this fortress that You know[1]...Neske is here, but I will not see him until tomorrow after the inaugural lecture.[2]

I kiss You, I kiss You

Paul

1. Postcard: "Würzburg—Alte Mainbrücke und Festung Marienberg."
2. Beda Allemann has just been named professor at the University of Würzburg. Günther Neske, who had published Martin Heidegger, also edited poetry and a collection of recordings of writers reading their work, including PC and Ingeborg Bachmann.

128

[Würzburg,] 21 January 1965

Gathered, after having listened to Monsieur Allemann speak, at his inaugural lecture, of Intensity, gathered around a table, at the Residence, in a hall calling itself *"Seinsheim,"** that is to say "Foyer of Being," these "grouesses"[1]:

Brigitte Neske

Beda Allemann

Auf Wiedersehn am 10 Februar in Paris, Günther Neske. Dank![2]

Doris Allemann

* he was, but yes, a bishop...[Probably an allusion to Heidegger. Both Neske and Allemann were in close contact with Heidegger: the former as an editor, the latter as a scholar.]
1. Jocular francization of the spelling "Gruesse" (for *Grüße*), meaning: *greetings*.
2. "See you 10 February in Paris, Günther Neske. Thanks!"

129

[Zurich,] 23 January 1965

Happy Anniversary, my Beloved![1]

Zurich, after a Würzburg prolonged for the bank (currency exchange)—Allemann's speech, alas, dull, but I will talk to You about it again. No Leiser, but today, Margarete Susman[2] and Schlösser.—In order not to travel overnight, I will stop at Basel, from where, if I am lucky, I will reach You on the telephone. Tomorrow, in any case, I will be in Paris around one o'clock.

I kiss You, my Darling.

Paul

1. See no. 58.
2. Following this meeting with Margarete Susman, who is at this point ninety-three years old and half blind, PC will write the poem, "DER NEUNZIG- UND ÜBER- / jährigen Augen" (OF HER WHOSE EYES ARE NINETY YEARS OLD / and more), *NKGA*, p. 450.

130

78 rue de Longchamp
Monday, 25 January 1965

My Darling,

Having returned yesterday at one o'clock, from Basel, I had, beside Your so good and so beautiful letters, a very good afternoon, above all because I had had You on the telephone in Basel, completely content, visibly—"audibly"!—with Your sojourn, with Your walk in Naples planned for the next day. There was also a little letter from Eric, and at eight o'clock I spoke to him, as before my departure, on the telephone. His first words, like the other day: "Is it you, mama?" I had the impression, but maybe it had to do with the telephone, that he was not thrilled-thrilled, but that everything was all right anyhow. He had received a letter from you, had sent you one. Then, toward the end: "You know, I miss you." So I, touched, I told him that, of course, I missed him too and that we would see each other again soon.

Today, at eleven o'clock, Erwin Leiser, coming from London, going to Berlin. Many common points—is there hope for solidarity? He returns 4 February.

Then P.: very, very trying. He tells me that Mâle is an analyst.[1] I will go anyway, the 30th. But P. is terribly trying, and is the reason why this letter will end without giving you many details or true thoughts.

Telephoned Jean Bollack, back from Frankfurt: he has arranged his affairs; for what has to do with my problems, much more acute than his, he inundates me with empty platitudes, rendered affected by unnecessary intellectualisms. Oh yes. Did not even ask how you are doing.

Face up to it, anyway.

(In the mail, something from H. W. Richter and from H. Bender, the latter particularly disgusting.)

A letter from Françoise Bonaldi for You, a letter from the insurance agent . . .

This evening, Minder, Belaval. I will have to pull myself together.

This morning, and I will find it again in a moment, Your letter from the Villa Adriana, the leaves, the laurel, the card with the Ufers. Give them my best, as well as Kraisky. Oh yes, Madame Ufer has a Jewish face marked by what struck and continues to strike. But M. Ufer, he is not Jewish, but valiant, truly valiant.

You will surely see Iris and, possibly, her cousins, the Marschalls (von Biederstein, I think), who received me very kindly, who are truly kind. Pay them some compliments, from me too, they deserve it.

Ah yes! Yesterday evening, a telegram from Ruth: Nadia and son are well. Send a note to Nadia (Pohne, Schwalbengasse 2A, Köln), I sent, in the name of all of us, a telegram of congratulations. Will I be able to go, in eight days, to the Circumcision ("Brith"), as I had promised Marcel? That will be a Back-and-Forth, then, for the École will start. What can I buy (at the Châtelaine)?

I hug You very tightly

Paul

---

1. PC pursues, in private consultations, psychotherapeutic conversations with this psychiatrist, "P.," at the Sainte-Anne hospital. PC, who will never pursue a psychoanalytic cure, will also consult Mâle, a psychiatrist recommended to him by Henri Michaux, throughout 1965.

131

[To Eric Celan]

My dear Eric,

I was so glad the other day, upon coming home from my trip, to have you on the line. (I had only found, when I arrived, a short letter, for which I thank you.)

When you told me, at the end of our conversation, that you missed me, I was infinitely touched. Me too, I miss you too, my son, and mama misses you, we both miss you.

Mama tells me that she writes you often—you have no doubt received her letters. You have to respond to her, you have to write her often; here are, to this end, some envelopes with the complete address, and postmarked. I am enclosing as well some other envelopes, for me, and for the aunts, if you want to write them.

How is your work going, how is skiing going? I just saw, on rue Hamelin, M. Blazewski's bulletin, and I see that you all often take the ski lift. Are you getting used to it? If you have difficulties, don't you worry too much, it will come little by little. And then, there are so many slopes that you have climbed joyfully for a long time now, already, ahead of everyone. Mama was touched, too, by your "night that makes the snow sprout."

Soon we will be together. But before that you need to work well—I am counting on you for a "re-ascent" on this side too, to amuse yourself, to write us.

I hug you

Your Papa

Always write the date on your letters.

132

[Paris,] Thursday, [28 January 1965]

after having telephoned You:

Be well, my Beloved, be well! Take care of Yourself, stay, if You are doing well and You feel like it, but come home if You can, to have Yourself treated. But I hope that this will not be necessary.

No letter from You this morning, nor from Eric.

Yesterday, I went to look for the calling cards—here are a few, in case You would like to send flowers to Madame Ufer.

Write to me, speak to me, come back to me.

Paul

Followed Your advice and telephoned Jean. I will play tennis again tomorrow with him, Fusco, Fernandez.[1]

---

1. That is to say, with Jean Bollack, Mario Fusco (translator from Italian and academic), and the novelist Dominique Fernandez.

133

January 1965

Die ihn bestohlen hatten,
nannten ihn einen Dieb,
die ihn nachäfften,
verbreiteten, er sei ein Plagiator.

Diejenigen, die ihm Impulse verdankten,
fanden ihn nicht lebendig genug,
die er belebte, nicht nur mit Worten,
nannten ihn einen Toten.
Die Reklametüchtigen
ließen sich Bescheidenheit attestieren
und ihm Hybris.

Die Meuchler
nannten ihn feige.
Die sein Vertrauen mißbrauchten,
nannten ihn mißtrauisch,
die ihn beleidigten,
fanden ihn viel zu empfindlich.

Als er an
Solidarität appellierte,
bekundete man ihm Mitleid und Beileid.
Die gehetzt hatten gegen ihn,
verteidigten ihn,
"wie der Strick den Gehenkten."

Wem er heraufgeholfen hatte,
der ließ ihm hinunterhelfen.

Er wurde
zerkleinert
und neu verteilt.
Es waren
nicht wenig Freunde unter den Nutznießern.

Einer
wollte in die Arena steigen—
er bestieg
die Stufen einer Akademie,
derselben,
die denjenigen Preise verlieh,
die ihn verraten und verleugnet hatten.
Es stiegen noch mehrere
dorthin "empor."

Ehemalige Hitlerjungen
halfen ihm aus seinen Erlebnissen heraus
und hängten sie derjenigen über,
die sie nicht gehabt hatte
und sich willig ins neue Konzept
der Ehemaligen fügte.
Von der Ehemaligen gnaden
wurde sie zur
schlechthinnigen Jüdin.
Man nannte sie königlich—wovon
war ihr Purpur rot?
"Mag sein," verkündete sie,
"daß das Schicksal meines Volkes
an mir leuchtet."
Mag sein.
                      Doch wie?
Aber das
aus ihr selber Leuchtende
töteten sie.

Wer und was
trieb Nelly Sachs in den Wahnsinn?
Wer
brachte ihr
Verrat und Vermessenheit bei?

In Stockholm hört ich sie sagen:
"Die in Auschwitz
litten nicht das, was ich leide."
Das hörten auch andre, darunter
Lenke Rothmann.
Wer förderte das? Und welche Schuld
tobte dahinter?

im Jänner 65

They who had stolen from him[1]
called him a thief,
they who had aped him
spread the rumor that he is a plagiarizer.

The ones who owed him impulses
found him not lively enough,
they whom he animated, not only with words,
called him dead.[2]

The advertising experts
allowed their modesty to be attested
and his hubris.[3]

The assassins
called him cowardly.
They who abused his trust
called him mistrustful,
they who insulted him
found him far too sensitive.

When he
appealed for solidarity,
people expressed their sympathy and sent their condolences.[4]
They who had agitated against him
defended him,
"as the rope supports the hanged man."

The one whom he had helped to rise,
this person helped him to descend.

He was
picked apart
and redistributed.
There were
not a few friends among the beneficiaries.

One
of them wanted to enter the arena—
he climbed
the stairs of an academy,[5]
the same one,
which awarded prizes to those very ones
who had betrayed and repudiated him.
Even more people climbed
to that lofty "height."

Former Hitler Youths[6]
helped him out of his experiences
and draped them over the person
who did not have them
and who willfully embraced
the new concept of the former members.
By the grace of the former members
she became
the epitome of the Jewess.
One called her royal—what was it
that made her purple red?
"Could be," she proclaimed.
"that the fate of my people
shines on me."[7]
Could be.

But how?

But that
which shined out from her,
they killed it.

Who and what
drove Nelly Sachs into madness?
Who
taught her
betrayal and immoderation?

In Stockholm I heard her say:
"Those in Auschwitz
did not suffer what I suffer."[8]
Others heard this too, among them
Lenke Rothmann.[9]
Who instigated that? And which guilt
raged behind that?

in January 65

1. This text was very probably written after PC's reading of the critical articles by Reinhard Baumgart and Kurt Oppens, which were for PC reminiscent of the Goll Affair. See no. 141, n. 1. The following notes, a condensed version of the original French edition, also follow the outlines of Barbara Wiedemann's commentary in *GA*, no. 288.
2. Allusion to a phrase in Kurt Oppens's essay: "Celan entered his stage as a dead person."
3. Another allusion to a phrase from Kurt Oppens: "Celan too is economical, appeases his hubris, which is drunk with death."
4. This could refer to the declaration of support for PC signed by Günter Eich, Max Frisch, and Karl Krolow, among others, destined to appear in the German and Austrian press.
5. Werner Weber, writer and editor-in-chief of the *Neue Zürcher Zeitung*.
6. The persons meant here could not be identified with certainty. The commentary in *GA*, no. 288, mentions Hans Magnus Enzensberger and Peter Hamm, both admirers of Nelly Sachs.
7. Quotation from Nelly Sachs's *Eli. Ein Mysterienspiel vom Leiden Israels* (Eli: A Mystery-Play of the Suffering of Israel) (Frankfurt am Main: Suhrkamp, 1962), p. 75.
8. Recurring words uttered by Nelly Sachs during crises of paranoid delusion that PC evokes in his journal during his trip to Stockholm on 8 September 1960.
9. Friend of Nelly Sachs.

134

[Paris, 29 March 1965]

My Darling,

in Your copperplates I recognize my poems: they pass through them in order to be in them, still.

Paul

29 March 1965

135

[Paris,] Thursday evening
[15 April 1965], eight thirty

My beloved!

You have surely arrived at Francine's—give her my best—and here begin eight hours of calm and repose for You, and the games, the happiness for Eric, in the company of other children.

I have in front of me, beneath our lamp, your photo and our son's. And also, in a glass of water, the little birch sprig[1] from our home, from Mois-ville. Make sure You recover again, my beloved. All my love for You is here, in me, just as large as in the first moment. Nothing is lost of our love: *Wir sind es noch immer.*[2]

Hug our son—I hug You, with all my heart, firmly, faithfully

Paul

[In the margin:] I will not see the doctor until tomorrow, having arrived too late by car

---

1. PC felt a particular attachment to this tree, which evoked for him Eastern Europe and Russian poetry. Three birch sprigs (*bouleaux* in French) planted next to each other are the inspiration for the symbolic name of the house in Moisville, Les Trois Bouleaux, a name that will be in use between 1965 and 1966).
2. See nos. 63, 106, 136, 154, 186, 203.

136

[Dinard—Saint-Enogat,]

Saturday, 27 February[1] 1965

My darling,

I was delighted to feel you were a little less despairing today. I know that You love me, You know that I love You. Our love, in great difficulty, will be the stronger.

It will help us to find the way.

It will make us hold out.

It's very hard right now and we are not doing well, but we will climb back up. Let's keep our confidence.

We are so lost, far from one another, so lost also right now with one another. But that will change. Love will help us to find the way.

"Wir sind es noch immer."[2]

Your letter delighted me so much, touched me so much, encouraged me so much.

I am still tired, of course yesterday I rested in the sun, I even tanned, but I still don't look well and still have awful dark rings under my eyes. It is gray and rainy today but it is not cold. I just spent two hours in my room, with the window wide open, trying to rest. Eric was on the beach with the other children and I saw him with his shovel and his bucket, in the hope of catching sand eels in the sand. He is very content, is doing very well, and is very nice.

It's low tide.

Lots of rocks, seagulls, and in the distance the buoys sounding their sad signal at regular intervals. The villas on the beach are horrible, but the view of the sea is very beautiful. We will leave soon to take a walk all together and tomorrow I will go maybe by speedboat to Saint-Malo, which is ten minutes from here. It's a town surrounded by ramparts, and I think that will please Eric.

Henri is finally less odious, and I feel free to stay here or to go for a walk by myself, or with Eric.

I'll call you tomorrow and every day. Courage, my Love, and until soon

Gisèle

1. Actually Saturday, 17 April.
2. See nos 63, 106, 135, 154, 186, 203.

137

[Paris,] Tuesday, [20 April 1965]

Just a line, my Beloved, just this *Wir-sind-es-noch-immer*, to welcome You home, in Moisville, in our house, You with our son.

It is hard, but we will climb up again,[1] we will help Eric to live.

The evening of my return from Dreux, here, I thought that I was from here, too, that I found myself within my walls, that I will not move, will not leave France—the country where I found my wife, where I found You, You my Very-Limpid, my Very-True, my Very-Upright-and-very-Faithful.

Hug our Eric. Say hello to the House. Say hello to our Poplars, our Roses, our flowers and our verdure.

I hug You

Paul

1. One week later, in the same climate of anxiety, PC will re-dedicate, to GCL, a copy of the poem "Mit allen Gedanken" (see no. 106).

138

78 rue de Longchamp, [5? May 1965]

My Beloved,

All that I do, I do it, believe it, for our son, for You, for the three of us.

I will go to have myself treated,[1] You will take back Eric, You will make sure he works, You will await my return together, then we will live and work, all three of us, happy.

Paul

Everything will go well. We will find our friends again too. And all that we love.

1. Regarding his state of health, PC wrote this unsent letter to Jean Starobinski, with the heading "78 rue de Longchamp" and dated "Paris, 3 May 1965": "Dear Friend, / I was so touched when You told us—I take it as addressed to the three of us—in a moment so difficult for You, that You count us among this Jewish community that is not that of ritual, but that of the heart [see no. 198, n. 3]. We are that, believe me, we are that, all three of us: Eric, Gisèle, myself. / But things have become very, very hard again for me: the doctor who is treating me, on the recommendation of Michaux, Doctor Mâle, does not have my confidence. I sense and know well that I was wrong to take this step, on the advice of a writer fundamentally foreign to all that I am, all that I think, all that I feel. / Tomorrow, I have to stop my work at the École: I am too tired and, after publications in Germany (in 'Die Zeit,' 'Merkur,' with my own publisher—a book that appeared under the title '1945—Ein Jahr in Dichtung in [sic] Bericht' and has an epigraph with some lines pulled out of one of my poems—it is a love poem—which could lead to the belief that I endorse this book, which is nothing other than a nationalist mishmash)—so I am very tired. / Gisèle, very tired, insists that I go to a clinic—Doctor Mâle proposes one for me at Sèvres ('Bellevue'), but I do not trust it. / Could You, very rapidly, help us, by recommending to me a *Jewish* doctor (Professor Leibovici perhaps?). Do it, by telegram if possible. You can save all three of our lives, who will remain eternally grateful to You. / I cannot easily leave Paris, as Gisèle is worried. But in our little apartment, in the presence of Eric above all, everything is so difficult. / What to do? There has to be a way out, once again, made by human solidarity. For what is Judaism if not a form of the Human, what is Poetry if not a form of this same Human. / Act, please, help us. (Perhaps through Ajuria?) / I am very troubled—they have done so much to trouble me! But I am not lacking entirely in lucidity. / Help my son, help my wife, help me. / Our affectionate thoughts go to you all! Live under a serene sky, among upright and sincere humans, among true friends! Let Your help for us all arrive in time! Thanks, with all my heart / Paul Celan."

   The doctor mentioned is Professor Serge Lebovici: psychiatrist and psychoanalyst; son of a doctor from Romania who immigrated to France at the beginning of the twentieth century and who died in Auschwitz; member of the French Communist Party 1945–9; anti-Lacanian; cofounder, with Julian de Ajuriaguerra, of the review *La Psychiatrie de l'enfant* (1958).

   The work mentioned, which had just been published, is actually entitled *1945—Ein Jahr in Dichtung und Bericht*, ed. Hans Rauschning (Frankfurt am Main: S. Fischer, 1965); the "love poem" mentioned is "Mit allen Gedanken."

139

[To Eric Celan]

78 rue de Longchamp, [5? May 1965]

My dear Eric,

you know that I am not doing very well right now—I have to have myself treated.

You will stay a few days with Aunt Monique, then Mama will come get you, you will come home to our house, you will work well, you will grow, you will wait with Mama for me to come back to live with you, work with you and for you. Nothing, you know it well, can separate us. Be nice to Mama.

I hug you very tight, my son Eric!

See you soon! Bye!

You Father

140

[Paris, 6? May 1965]

[Dedication and note written by Paul Celan in the second edition of *Die Niemandsrose*]

For You, my Beloved, while
thinking of Eric, whom soon
all three of us will find again
to raise him, to see
him work and grow
next to us, in our
house, in working ourselves,
for him.
On the Bridge of Years, in Paris,
May sixth 1965

Paul

[p. 53, as the last stanza of the poem "Die hellen Steine":]

Und unser Sohn Eric
lebt mit uns,
froh,
wächst auf,
während wir für ihn
arbeiten
und
da sind.

And our son Eric
lives with us,
joyous,
grows up,
while we work
for him
and
are there.

141

[Paris, 7? May 1965]

For You, my Love,
For You, Alix-Marie-Gisèle
de Lestrange, spouse of Antschel
For You, my Very-Noble,
For You, the Mother of my Son

[Unsigned]

Ein Dröhnen: es ist
die Wahrheit[1] selbst
unter die Menschen getreten, mitten
ins Metapherngestöber.[2]

7. Mai 1965

A roaring: it is
the truth itself
which has entered among the humans, into the midst
of the whirlwind of metaphors.
7 May 1965[3]

1. The notion of "Wahrheit" (truth) should be read in the context of the Goll Affair. On November 7, 1962, in a gesture of incantation and of resistance, PC will write this tercet: "Es muß Wahrheit geschehen / und / Liebe." (Truth must happen / and / Love.) See also no. 184, n. 3 and *GA*, no. 289.
2. This version of this poem is the only one dated 7 May 1965; the others are dated 6 May 1965. For the final version of this poem, see *NKGA*, p. 210;
3. See "A Roar," *BIT*, p. 86 and "A Roaring," *CSP*, p. 127.

142

[To Eric Celan]

78 rue de Longchamp, [7 May 1965?]

My dear Eric, we will hold out!

You are well, Mama is well, I will be well. We will live in our house and will work, happy, free. Here on rue de Longchamp. Nothing can separate us. I hug you, with Mama, we will remain together, bye and see you soon!

Your Father

143

[To Eric Celan]

[Paris, 8 May 1965?]

Goodbye, Eric. Be strong, work well, I love you. I will come back.

Your Father

144

78 rue de Longchamp, Saturday, 8 May 1965

My darling, my Love,

It was very hard to part from one another,[1] and I am thinking of you without cease. I am back in our house. I reread your letter, I reread your poem,[2] and then I called our son. He is well, he is very well, he is having fun, he is content, of course he asked me for your news right away, and I told him that you had to rest for some time near Paris, but that it would not be long and that soon, very soon, all three of us would be together again.

He will help me to wait for you, as I will help him to wait for you.

All will be well, my Love, and we will win out, together. Courage, my darling. You will come back to us stronger, and we will begin again, as always, to live, to fight.

I will rest too, I will spoil myself, as you desire, and Monday, I will call Mme Magder so that she helps me to recover.

Don't worry about us. Rest as much as possible, we need you so.

Tomorrow, I will drop off this letter so that you have my news very quickly. And Monday, after having seen the son and had lunch with him at home, I will go to bring you another letter. And then I hope to be able to come to stay with you for a while. You are so close to Paris. I want so much to see you.

Until soon, my darling Love.

I love You and kiss You

Gisèle

Write to me if you can.

---

1. PC has just decided, at GCL's encouragement, to be treated in a clinic recommended by Dr. Pierre Mâle four days earlier.
2. "Ein Dröhnen: es ist" (no. 141).

145

Le Vésinet,[1] Sunday, 9 May 1965

My Darling,

I had a good night, the morning too was good, a few moments ago—it is almost noon—a brief visit from Doctor L., then from Doctor Mâle. What was worrying me is fading away, has already almost faded away, I am myself surprised at the rapidity with which this occurred.

I asked Doctors L. and Mâle to allow You to come see me as often as possible—You will be able to. And You can write to me as often as You feel like it.

Tomorrow, I will have a note from You. I cannot wait to know how You are doing, how the son is doing.

I read a bit, leaf through the books I brought,[2] which give me, from time to time, my own idea.[3] There too I have to climb back up.

I look at You, for a long time, I hug You and tell You to hug our son.

Paul

[In the margin:] Bring me, please, some fruit—I consumed quite a lot of it at home, as You know, and now I miss it.

---

1. PC, having two nights earlier suffered once again from "Beziehungswahn" ("madness of relation," the technical term he uses, in quotation marks, in his journal dated 8 May 1965), has decided, upon GCL's encouragement, to have himself treated at the Villa des Pages, a private psychiatric clinic in Vésinet (Seine-et-Oise, today Yvelines), which had been recommended to him by Dr. Pierre Mâle several days earlier.
2. These works, often underlined during these days of reading in the clinic, include Shakespeare's *Hamlet, Troilus and Cressida, King Lear, Othello, Macbeth, Antony and Cleopatra, Cymbeline,* and *Coriolanus* (in L. L. Schücking's bilingual edition: *Shakespaeares Werke* [Berlin-Darmstadt: Tempel Klassiker, 1955]); G. Chr. Lichtenberg's *Die Bittschrift der Wahnsinnigen* (The Petition of the Mad); see Lichtenberg, *Gesammelte Werke,* 2 vols., ed. Wilhelm Grenzmann (Frankfurt am Main: Holle, 1949); Franz Kafka's *Erzählungen* (Frankfurt am Main: S. Fischer, 1961), in particular "Elf Söhne" (Eleven Sons) and "In der Strafkolonie" (In the Penal Colony); Henri Bergson, *L'Évolution créatrice*; Laozi, *Die Bahn und der rechte Weg* (The Path and the Right Way), trans. Alexander Ulav (Leipzig: Insel, 1912).
3. Notations of this sort are most often preceded by the sign: "i" for "idée." See no. 34, n. 3.

146

Le Vésinet, Monday, 10 May 1965

My Darling,

Thanks for your so good letter. It arrived yesterday after my nap—before this nap I had written You one. In the morning it seemed to me I saw a blue Major[1] pass, very slowly, in front of the gate—was that You, had You just dropped off Your letter?

It is twelve thirty, it is the hour when You go to pick up Eric at school to take him home—ours. I am so content with this idea, You know well why, for how many reasons!

You can come to see me every two or three days—will I see You in little while already? Or tomorrow?

I try to read, I take notes,[2] I even wrote a poem (preceded by an almost-poem).[3]

Hug our son—I put my arms around you both, I hug you, I am with you.

Paul

---

1. A Renault Major, the Celans' car.
2. PC has just read Kafka ("Eleven Sons") and Lichtenberg, or rather the long introduction by the editor, Wilhelm Grenzmann; PC underlines and makes many notes in the margin of this latter text in particular (see no. 155, n. 3). Among the passages marked or underlined are: "Ich bin eigentlich nach England gegangen, um deutsch schreiben zu lernen" (I actually went to England in order to learn how to write German). "Man muß sich seine Lehrtätigkeit denken, wie seine Notizbücher aussahen, und wie er seine Briefe schrieb: überladen mit Witz und Einfällen, mit Geist und Tiefe, aber er war immer in Gefahr, den roten Faden des Gedankens zu verlieren." (One must think about his teaching activity, what his notebooks looked like, and how he wrote his letters: filled with wit and insights, with spirit and depth, but he was always in danger of losing the red thread of his thought.). "Er hatte die Gewohnheit, alles zum Zeichen zu nehmen, zog aus jeder Sache eine Vorbedeutung, machte täglich gleichgültige Dinge zum Orakel. Jedes Kriechen eines Insekts gab ihm Antworten auf Fragen über sein Schicksal; ging ihm die Kerze aus, so nahm er es als ungünstige Vorbedeutung und änderte weitreichende Pläne. Er machte sich zwar vor, daß er mit dem Aberglauben spiele, aber er war sich auch darüber klar, daß der Aberglaube sein Spiel mit ihm trieb. 'Ich glaube nicht an diese Dinge, aber es ist mir doch angenehm, wenn sie nicht widrig ausfallen.'" (He had the habit of taking everything as a sign, took from everything an omen, daily made indifferent things into oracles. Every creeping insect gave him answers to questions about his fate; if his candle went out, he took it as an unfavorable omen and changed wide-ranging plans. He told himself that he was just playing with superstition, but it was also clear to him that supersti-

tion played its game with him. "I don't believe in these things, but it is still pleasant for me when they do not turn out adversely.") (p. 53). "Kinderzeugen und Bäumenpflanzen sind ihm wichtiger als Bücherschreiben" (Making children and planting trees are more important to him than writing books) (p. 60); cf. no. 208, n. 3.

3. PC had written, the evening before, the first version of the poem "Lichtenbergs zwölf" (Lichtenberg's Twelve), see no. 148; and "Irrennäpfe" (Bowls of the Deranged), see no. 151.

147

Le Vésinet, 11 May 1965

My Darling,

Thanks for Your second letter, thanks for Eric's. It was a great joy to have it: I had been waiting for You a bit, then, around four o'clock, when I thought that something had prevented You from coming, I ran into the small dark-haired nurse who smilingly held it out to me.

Yesterday evening, I had a quite long conversation with one of the doctors from here, Doctor G. I just learned that it was with him that You had spoken on the telephone yesterday evening; I will probably know this evening if You are coming tomorrow. I very much hope so.

The days, certainly, are a bit long, the morning today was broken up by a film projection—voyage on the Nile, rock temples—made, with much skill and a good sense of timing, by Mme. L.[1]

My big diversion this afternoon will be to go—all by myself, like a grownup—to the local hairdresser.

I read, or rather: I try to read. It is nice out, before me I see oak trees with long trunks, which I had taken for ash trees (and which made their way into the poem of which I spoke to you yesterday—and which will remain there).[2]

Thank Eric for his letter. I am so glad that he is doing well. And take care of Yourself, spoil Yourself.

Doctor L. told me just now that he expects to keep me for fifteen days. That is long and not too long. So it will be for the 23rd, for the anniversary day.[3]

I kiss You on Your mouth and tell You to kiss our son on his forehead and on his two cheeks.

Paul

1. Psychiatrist.
2. See no. 151, line 3 of the poem "Irrennäpfe, vergammelte."
3. See no. 58, n. 2.

148

Le Vésinet, 10 May 1965, 18:00

"Erinnerung an D."[1]

Lichtenbergs zwölf mit dem Tischtuch
ererbte Mundtücher—ein
Planetengruß an
die Sprachtürme rings
in der totzuschweigenden Zeichen-
Zone.

Sein
—kein Himmel ist, keine
Erde, und beider
Gedächtnis gelöscht
bis auf den einen
eschengläubigen Blauspecht—
sein vom Stadtwall gepflückter
weißer Komet.

Eine Stimmritze, ihn
zu bewahren,
im All.

Das Rotverlorene eines
Gedanken-
fadens.
Die lautgewordenen
Klagen darüber, die Klage
darunter—wessen

Laut?

Damit—frag nicht
wo—
wär ich fast—
sag nicht, wo, wieder.

———

Endgültige Fassung
Le Vésinet, 10 May 1965. 18 Uhr.

"Memory of D."

Lichtenberg's twelve napkins
inherited with the tablecloth—a
planet's greeting to
the language-towers all around
in the sign-zone to be silenced
to death.

His
—it is no sky, no
earth, and the memory
of both extinguished
except for the one
blue tit who believes in the ash tree—
his white comet plucked
from the city wall.

A glottis, to
keep it,
in space.

The red-lost of a
thought-

thread.
The lamentations about it
which have become spoken sounds, the lamentations
beneath it—whose
sound!

With that—do not ask
where—
I would almost be—
do not say, where, again.

———

Final version
Le Vésinet, 10 May 1965, 18:00[2]

1. For the published version, see *NKGA*, p. 211.
2. See "Lichtenberg's Twelve," *BIT*, p. 88.

149

[Le Vésinet,] Wednesday
[12 May 1965,] four thirty

Thank You my Beloved, for coming, thank You for being there, always, for holding out.

You have given me strength—I will hold out, too, beside You, beside our son.

With all my heart I hug You

Paul

[To Eric Celan]

[Le Vésinet,] 12 May 1965

My dear Eric,

I was very happy with the letter that you wrote me after your return from the Mill,[1] very content to hear, from Mama, and this time in person, how you are doing.

I know that you are in the midst of improving at school—I congratulate you on that, I am, as you know well, very proud of that.

Tomorrow, you will bring us new songs.

Work well, amuse yourself, my son!

See you soon! Bye!

Your Papa

---

1. During the days before his father's hospitalization, EC was staying with his aunt in Rochefort-en-Yvelines.

150

Le Vésinet, 13 May 1965

My Darling,

I got Your letter from yesterday evening, this morning, just after breakfast, and after having had a very good night. (I fell asleep around nine thirty and woke up at seven, with a brief interruption, but without needing to take pills again.)

Yourself, You can rest and spoil Yourself a bit today, and the son has marvelous weather for his scouting exploits. This evening, he will come back all content to the house, with new songs.

Just a moment ago, Mme L.[1] came by, for her visit—decidedly, it has been her above all since yesterday—she was above all glad to hear that I had had a good night. I spoke to her especially of my memory—she is optimistic.

So let us be optimistic, us too. We will continue, all three of us, to fight, to live.

I kiss You for a long moment. Kiss our Eric.

Paul

---

1. A psychiatrist.

151

"Give the Word"[1]

Ins Hirn gehaun—halb, zu drei Vierteln?—,
gibst du, genächtet, die Parolen—diese:
"Tatarenpfeile," "Kunstbrei," "Atem."

Es kommen alle, keiner fehlt und keine.
(Sipheten und Probyllen sind dabei.)

Es kommt ein Mensch.

Weltapfelgroß die Träne neben dir,
durchrauscht, durchfahren
von Antwort,
Antwort,
Antwort.
Durcheist—von wem?

"Passiert," sagst du,
"passiert,
passiert, passiert."

Der stille Aussatz löst sich dir vom Gaumen
und fächelt deiner Zunge Licht zu, Licht.
—

Le Vésinet, 14.5.1965.
Endgültige Fassung[2]

Cut to the brains—halfway, three quarters?—,
you, benighted, give the passwords—these:
"Tatar arrows," "Art mush," "Breath."

They all come, no man is missing and no woman.
(Siphets and probyls are there.)

A human comes.

As large as the world-apple the tear next to you
murmured-through, traversed
by answer,
answer,
answer.
iced over—by whom?

"Pass," you say,
"pass,
pass, pass."

The silent leprosy detaches itself from your palate
and fans your tongue with light, light.
—

Le Vésinet, 14 May 1965
Final version.[3]

Irrennäpfe, vergammelte
Tiefen.

Wär ich die Esche draußen,
ich wüßte, wohin
mit soviel bitterem
Grau
und dem eng-
gezogenen Denkkreis
um solche
Bilder.

—

Le Vésinet, 9 May 1965[4]

Bowls of the deranged, rotten
depths.

If I were the ash tree outside,
I would know what to do
with so much bitter
gray
and with the circle of thought
tightly drawn
around such
images.[5]

—

Le Vésinet, 9 May 1965

1. Poem written 13–14 May 1965, inspired by reading *King Lear*. In his copy of volume 4 of the Schücking edition of Shakespeare (see above, no. 145, n. 2), PC underlined almost every expression from Shakespeare at the root of this poem, including: "LEAR. Natur ist hierin mächtiger als die Kunst. [...] O schön geflogen, Vogel. Ins Schwarze, ins Schwarze! Hui!—Gebt die Parole! / EDGAR. Süßer Majoran.— / LEAR. Passiert" (LEAR. Nature's above art in that respect [...] O! well flown, bird; i'the clout, i'the clout: hewgh! Give the word. / EDGAR. Sweet majoram.— / LEAR. Pass.") (4.6).

The other passage from this scene to which the poem makes reference does not have any underlining: "LEAR. Wie, kein Entsatz? Gefangen? Bin ich doch / Der wahre Narr des Glücks. Verpflegt mich wohl, / Ich geb' euch Lösegeld. Schafft mir 'nen Wundarzt, / *Ich bin ins Hirn gehaun*" (LEAR. No rescue? What, a prisoner? I am even / The natural fool of Fortune. Use me well; / You shall have ransom. Let me have surgeons; / *I am cut to th'brains.*), *ibid.*, p. 518; the italics are the editor's.

PC also underlined and marked numerous other passages from *King Lear* during the month of May. In *Othello* (in the same edition of Shakespeare's complete works), PC marked a few exchanges whose connection to "Give the Word" also seems clear: "OTHELLO. 'Tis true: there's magic in the web of it: / A sibyl, that had number'd in the world / The sun to course two hundred compasses, / In her prophetic fury sew'd the work; / The worms were hallow'd that did breed the silk; / And it was dyed in mummy which the skillful / Conserved of maidens' hearts" (3.4, p. 61). "IAGO. Why, by making him uncapable of Othello's place; knocking out his brains" (4.2, p. 79).

2. See the final version in *NKGA*, p. 212.

3. See "Give the Word," *BIT*, p. 93.
4. See the final version in *NKGA*, p. 211.
5. See "Lunatic-Bowls," *BIT*, p. 88.

152

78 rue de Longchamp, Friday, 14 May 1965

My darling,

Keep patience, keep courage, keep hope, keep confidence and all will go well. I know that it's not pleasant for you to be at Le Vésinet, and I know that the days must be long, difficult to fill. I understand Your solitude, my Beloved, I truly understand it.

It was a pleasure to see You, to know that You continue to try to read, that you are writing and that You know, that's not nothing. The poem from today is among the most beautiful, I think.

Upon my return, with ice cream, I was welcomed by our son, content also to have Your news. Content to think of being able to leave for Moisville.

Altmann called, very nice, and I told him that, very tired, you had left to rest in the countryside near Paris, that I would bring you the proofs on Monday, we will telephone again on Wednesday evening to make an appointment with Fequet and Baudier. But he thinks it's not urgent. He has read the proofs and seems to believe that there is just one error with a capital letter. Otherwise, the paper and format of the proofs seem completely normal to him. Other proofs with the page layout in the true format will need to be done.

I am so delighted that this book is taking shape. For me, it is, you know, a true joy to be able to accompany your poems with my etchings, also a great honor, and I hope that it will be a beautiful book. Our book, for our son.

I write You this note in the hope that you will thus hear from me by Monday morning, I will come, as expected, Monday around 3:15.

I kiss You, my darling.

Until soon

Gisèle

153

My Darling,

Your two letters that arrived a moment ago—what a surprise, what a wonderful surprise!

Patience, courage, hope: yes, that I still have and I will do everything to preserve them, to consolidate them, to augment them. Yes, it is hard. But, certainly, we will hold out.[1]

This afternoon, You will go to Moisville with Eric, I would have wanted to be waiting for You there, with a letter at least, but according to my calculation, it would not have arrived in time.

So here are these lines to say hello to You on Monday, on rue de Longchamp, where we are at home, just like in Moisville.

I am glad about the telephone call from Altmann. But yes, it is our book, it is being made, it will be there soon, and we will make still others, rest assured of that.

It is ten thirty, the doctor has not come yet, I will ask him if I may go post this letter myself so that it reaches You in time.

It is very hot. Yesterday evening, taking some air outside, the little lady, reader of *An English Murder*, spoke to me. We spoke about the weather and the dinner (it was almost the hour). "It is the triumph of tepidness," she tells me (regarding the weather or the dinner?). Then: "You live in France, Monsieur?"—"Yes, Madame, I live in Paris." She leaves tomorrow and informs me that stays here are usually for fifteen days.

How did You find the house in Moisville? It is pretty. We will keep it. And we will plant many trees.

I kiss You and kiss You. And ask you to kiss our Eric.

Paul

[In the margin:] For the correction of the proofs, can You also bring me an eraser? And a regular pencil? Thanks.

---

1. See no. 83, n. 1; no. 87, n. 10; no. 93, n. 3; and no. 123, n. 4.

154

Le Vésinet, Tuesday, 18 May 1965

My Darling,

A note, to begin the day, to be near You, to tell You how much these three hours that we spent together yesterday did me well.

When I returned,[1] I had another visit from a doctor (G.), then I read—all of a novella by Camus,[2] which I *followed*—I had dinner, I read more. And I had, without taking Mérinax again, a very good night.

Few words, few things—and yet it is a lot of progress. This is strength found again to fight, together, for and with our son. And Poetry, too, will come to help us. We still are what we are, we are still in what we are.[3]

Kiss Eric. I kiss You and kiss You again.

See You tomorrow!

Paul

1. From a walk around the hospital's park with GCL.
2. Albert Camus, *L'Exil et le royaume* (Paris: Gallimard, 1957). PC had just borrowed, from the hospital library, this volume, which contains six novellas, the others being *La Femme adultère, Les Muets, L'Hôte, Jonas, La Pierre qui pousse*.
3. Reference to his line, "Wir sind es noch immer." See nos 63, 106, 135, 136, 154, 186, 203.

155

[Le Vésinet,] Tuesday
18 [May 1965], five thirty

My Beloved,

I got, when I returned from a short walk, Your letter from Moisville. Your flowers-and-trees letter, written beside Eric while he was reading.

May things, for us, take a different turn—that of flowers, of trees, of birds, of truly human humans!

Tomorrow You will be here and we will organize my departure from here. It will be, You know, the beginning of a new battle to fight. We will need effective, real help. We will find it.

I was able to read all of a play by Shakespeare—*Coriolanus*[1]—without losing the thread.[2] "Das Rotverlorene"[3]—you remember? Well, we will find it again, this "lost red," desperately red, desperately alive.

With all my strength, Yours and the son's.

Long live Moisville! Long live Paris!

We will hold out.[4]

Paul

1. The play shows reading marks from acts III to V. PC noted the date of his reading at the end of the play: "18 May 65 / Le Vésinet." The highlighted phrases include: "CORIOLANUS. To hear my nothings monster'd" (2.2); "CORIOLANUS. [...] There is a world elsewhere" (3.3); "VOLUMNIA. Anger's my meat; I sup upon myself, / And so shall starve with feeding." (4.3); "VOLSCE. [...] but your favour is well appeared by your tongue." (4.3); "CORIOLANUS. [...] O world, thy slippery turns! Friends now fast sworn, / Whose double bosoms seems to wear one heart." (4.4); "AUFIDIUS. [...] One fire drives out one fire; one nail, one nail; / Rights by right founder, strengths by strengths do fail" (1.7). "COMINIUS. [...] He was a kind of nothing, titleless, / Till he had forg'd himself a name o' the fire / Of burning Rome" (5.1);

2. On PC's worries about his memory, see no. 119, n. 1.

3. "Das Rotverlorene" is the result of the combination of two idiomatic German expressions: "der rote Faden" (the red thread), an expression invented by Goethe in *Elective Affinities*, and "den Faden verlieren" (to lose the thread); this is among the phrases marked by Celan in Grenzmann's introduction to Lichtenberg (see no. 146 n. 2). PC alludes to the third stanza of "Erinnerung an D" (which will be called "Lichtenbergs Zwölf" in the final version); see no. 148.

4. See no. 83, n. 1; no. 87, n. 10; no. 93, n. 3; and no. 123, n. 4.

156

Le Vésinet, Thursday, 20 May 1965

My Darling! My Beloved!

It is two o'clock in the afternoon, I have just, after having lain down (without sleeping) for an hour and a half, opened the door which leads to the terrace and the garden; a blackbird[1] is walking on the lawn, it is nice out, there is sun, a tranquility comes to me—I write to You.

Today is the day before my return, I have been thinking about it all the time since this morning. Tomorrow, around this time, You will come to Le Vésinet, You will settle what there is to settle in the clinic office, then You will come to get me and with You I will see again the House, the one on rue de Longchamp, and the one in Moisville, these two Houses where You have waited for me with Eric.

Thank You, my Beloved, thank You again and again for all that You are, for all that You do!

There are, as I know well, many things still which remain to be surmounted. We will surmount them.

The son is there, the ordeals, happily, have not been shared with him, he has his joys, he is full of gifts, he will flourish and will continue to flourish, to grow up, to become a man. Our hearts, burdened still, little by little will open up to all that comes to us from Eric, calmly we will breathe beside him.

And we will take up our work again. I have seen your etchings born beside my poems, born from these poems themselves, and You know well that *Atemkristall*, which, again, opened the paths of Poetry for me, is born of Your etchings.—So how could we not find again, in our most inner selves, that which, in its way, has helped us and will help us to accompany Eric? Of course, we will find all that is ours, we will find again our strength and our joys.

I hope that You will have these lines tomorrow morning, to begin the day.

Hug our son Eric, hug him very tightly, very tenderly. I put my arms around you both, I am with You, I kiss You

Paul

---

1. PC will write, later, in the evening, a poem entitled "Vom Anblick der Amseln" (Of the Sight of Blackbirds); see *NKGA*, p. 213, as well as *BIT*, p. 94. This last poem of the fourth cycle of *AW* corresponds to a caesura in PC's life: his departure from the hospital. PC liked to highlight the etymological link between Antschel (his family name), *Amsel* (German for blackbird), and the name Amschel evoked by Kafka in his journal, on 25 December 1911: Amschel is Kafka's Hebrew name, which he shared with his mother's maternal grandfather.

157

[Paris,] 28 July 1965

My Darling,

Six o'clock—the hour when You are driving toward La Messuguière, when you arrive perhaps. I hope that all went well, without any trouble at all.

For my part, I went, a bit late—there was a telephone call from Altmann at the moment I was preparing to leave—to the dentist. It was, as You had guessed, going picking,[1] doubly, without an injection, but with cold anesthesia (a jet of cold water, I guess). Rid of it despite everything, at the moment when, on the inside, I am recuperating mordantly.

No mail from Eric this morning, or, at least so far, this evening. (Regarding the mail in general, leaflets.)

I wrote, at quite some length, to Erich von Kahler.[2] It says quite a few things, it is not too badly formulated—I am enclosing a copy here for you. (Brief note: the Spartacists—the Spartakusbund— around Karl Liebknecht and Rosa Luxemburg were, just after the war of 1914–1918, the revolutionary German communists.[3]—Rosa L. was Jewish, born, like Mandelstamm, in Warsaw.—"Gleichschaltung": that is the Nazi "standardization." I oppose to it "Gleichheit," true Equality.)

Telephoned Aunt Berta,[4] who is well and sends you "grouesses."

All my best to this poor and so courageous Françoise.

I hug You

Paul

[To Erich von Kahler]

Dear Mr. von Kahler,

returned from England, where I visited with my family a sister of my father's who emigrated there from Vienna, and just before a trip to Germany, I found the two offprints, in which You speak of me with such reverent words, which You had the amiability to accompany with such comforting words.[5]—I thank You for that, dear Mr. von Kahler.

I have often, since Your departure and for various reasons, thought of the conversations that I was able to have with You in Paris. Thought also—allow me to say it directly—with the regret that much of what occupies me, primarily what has to do with what is Jewish, that much that is highlighted and given by what is poetry, that much that finds its home in what is German remained undiscussed.

Many frightening things are happening, even at this moment, in the world—I do not lose sight of it. As I do not lose sight of what is happening in Germany, precisely there, where still yesterday, from afar, I was still with some hope.—Leftist nationalism, leftist nationalism too, I detest it, as well as leftist anti-Semitism. As long as we, we who are Jews, attempt to be and to remain Jews, are not recognized as born equal and of equal status, everything remains the way it was in the past. There, dear Mr. von Kahler, it seems to want to remain, with all the power drawn and reanimated—also from the "new ones," the younger ones—from proto- and para-Nazism.

Equality—: yes, always. Equalization and standardization—: never!

Perhaps You remember that I, back then, in Darmstadt, recalled Gustav Landauer[6]—which was silenced to death (I almost want to say: silenced alive) not only by the press, but also even, on the spot—You are astonished! Do not be astonished!—by the microphones of the highly perfected loudspeaker system.[7]

Not that it was not clear to me that Landauer—even our good Margarete Susman says it[8]—committed the most tragic, yes, most childish (or most childlike?) [mistakes] and put them into the world, also the world of literature. But, You see, in the middle of the war, a thought of Landauer's came into my mind, again and again, which he, I believe, recorded in his journal from World War I: the thought of the newly moved. From that, dear Erich von Kahler, I lived in those years, and with that, when I was able to, I went to Germany, to a country that I am only now, only today, beginning to recognize a little.

Certainly, how could it have been otherwise? Who wants, while being astonished, to be able to distinguish between three-quarter- and four-fifths-truths, even after the first (and "second") experiences, to distinguish between newborn evil and evil passed down many times, between brown-red

and red-brown, between self-invented anti-Semitism and the kind that is
(sometimes by self-hating Jews) bestowed (or at least co-nourished)?

Now, dear Erich von Kahler, I am telling You nothing new—I am only
telling it in a new way, another (how many-eth?) time. Yes, I know the
song about "Jewish" Kapos. And one—the same one—of the...metaphor
of the concentration camp-methods in the German literature of today.[9]

Yet...be that as it may be. In me lives on, not without pain, yet strongly,
that thing that comes from Landauer, also mixed with a bit of the Spart-
acist "Despite everything." It lives there—may I say it?—together with
older things, with what is Jewish, a bit isolated, but not cut off from the
sources, not without hope for a human today and tomorrow—it lives, not
without contact with the poetical, not without its interrogation and its
being put into question, not without all the words of reassurance that
come from there.

Allow me to greet You warmly and, just as warmly, to wish You all my
best.

Your Paul Celan[10]

1. That is to say, removing teeth. The term used by PC, "la cueillette" belongs to the figurative language used by dentists, cited not without humor by PC. See no. 256, n. 1.

2. American literary scholar, historian, and philosopher who wrote in German and English, member of the Institute for Advanced Study at Princeton, born to a Jewish family in Prague, and a former member of the conservative George-Kreis.

3. On these two revolutionary communists assassinated in 1919, see "Du liegst" (You lie) (*NKGA*, p. 485) and the study of this poem by Péter Szondi, "Eden," in Szondi, *Celan Studies*, trans. Susan Bernofsky with Harvey Mendelsohn (Stanford: Stanford University Press, 2003).

4. Berta Antschel. See no. 21, n. 2.

5. Erich von Kahler had sent PC offprints of two of his articles: "Deutsche und Juden" (in *Aufgespaltenem Pfad* [Darmstadt: Erato-Presse, 1964], a volume edited by Manfred Schlösser for Margarete Susman's ninetieth birthday), with the dedication: "Für Paul Celan herzlich und nah [For Paul Celan in cordial closeness] / EK"; as well as "Form und Entformung" (*Merkur*, April-May 1965, nos 205–6), with the dedication: "Paul Celan in Freundschaft und / Bewunderung [For Paul Celan in friendship and / admiration] / EK."

6. See *The Meridian: Final Version—Drafts—Materials*, ed. Bernard Böschenstein and Heino Schmull, trans. Pierre Joris (Stanford: Stanford University Press, 2011; hereafter *Meridian*).

7. No other eyewitness account of this "technical" incident has been found.

8. See Margarete Susman's essay, "Gustav Landauer" (1919), re-edited, revised, and lengthened,

in *Vom Geheimnis der Freiheit. Gesammelte Aufsätze 1914–1964*, ed. Manfred Schlösser (Darmstadt & Zurich: Agora, 1965), pp. 255–70.
9. Alluding above all to the review of *NR* by Hans Egon Holthusen. See no. 36, n. 3.
10. Original German-language letter to Erich von Kahler attached to PC's letter to GCL not included here.

158

[Paris,] Thursday, 29 July 1965

My Darling,

Thanks for the telegram. I am glad that all is well, for Eric and for You. I think that calm—as I said to You citing Madame L., boredom—is even healing. You know that I was much lower than You were then, and yet I revive. You revive and will revive, like me, and You will do new, beautiful, very beautiful things.

I went over to Fequet and Baudier this afternoon, which gave me the chance to see our book again, without your etchings of course, but both of them, Monsieur and Mademoiselle (Fequet? Baudier?) told me that they find them beautiful. Saw the sample, the canvas sample that Fequet kept—except for a few details, it is the same thing as Duval's. You will see.

Mail from this morning: letter from Dumitriu, correct. Letter, also, from the insurer—I am enclosing the insurance certificate. This evening: 1. *Mercure*, latest issue. 2. J. Bollack, *Empédocle I*, with the following dedication accompanying it (in pencil): "To Paul and Gisèle Celan / 'And never do They cease to exchange their paths...'[1] Aux Barreyroux, 27 July 1965 / J.B."

It is on frothy alfa-paper... and, at least concerning the dedication, alfa paper that froths and froths, that is to say that froths with self-praise.

You need a little of everything, as they say, to make a half-world (of academics).

That's that.—Allemann is different.

I am enclosing for you the copy of a letter to Petre Solomon. There again, I have to show a bit of rigor.*

After the visit to Fequet's, was in the Latin Quarter, took two books for the École.

I hug You

Paul

1. Jean Bollack, *Empédocle I. Introduction à l'ancienne physique* (Paris: Les Éditions de Minuit, 1965). Bollack cites his own translation, to which he adds an ellipsis, of line six of Empedocles's fragment 31 (following the numeration of his edition).
* [In the margin:] In recopying it, I find this letter too harsh, and too explicit—I will keep it.

159

[Paris,] Saturday, 31 July 1965

My Darling,

Just a few lines to thank You for Your—very beautiful, very ascending and reascending letters, for Your card that arrived this morning.

Too bad that it is so hot. But very certainly this stay will do You good. Send my regards to Françoise. I conceive her disappointment, her fatigue after so much courage so badly invested. These doctors over there, are they good? She has to see the best and we have to help her do so if necessary.

I have not thanked You yet for Your telephone call—excuse me. From Eric, I only have the lines that You transcribed for me. What is this story of the strap missing from his backpack? Could You send him one? Or should I?

My days here are very calm and without any events other than the mail, that is to say Your letters and the epistles which I receive thanks to my "profession." On this side, there is a clear "improvement," with just one exception: that of the editor of the review *Die Hören*, who—there must have been a leak on Fischer's side, to conclude from Dumitriu's note (circular)—offers me, illustrating well the sado-masochistic alternation of these Linksnibelungen evolving in the "magnetic" field of Group 47, apologies reeking of lies.[1]

Apart from that, the National Library of Vienna asks me, with "k.u.k." politeness, for a photo.[2] Another request for a photo, and even for a portrait (in oil paint or in pencil...), a reproduction of course, from Kröner, for one of their glossaries.

This morning, at the same time as Your card from La Messuguière, a large illustrated card from Würzburg, with the signatures of Allemann's students.—Letter from DVA, very polite: the new edition of *Mohn und Gedächtnis*.

Otherwise, not much to tell you. A bit of reading. The other day, several letters written, then only one sent: to the Würzburg book store, about the Bessarabian carpet.[3] I am enclosing a copy for you. (The line in Russian comes from a song that You have often heard me sing; Tatar-Bunar is the name of a place where there was, in the twenties, a communist revolt, repressed by the Romanians.)

Tomorrow, I will get to work seriously.[4] Yesterday, tennis with Heinz Wismann and his fiancée. Rain—torrential downpours yesterday evening, a real deluge, so much so that I am not sure if we will be able to play again this evening. Tomorrow, if it is nice out.

I have become a regular at the Cinémathèque (since the Ranelagh is closed).

Yesterday evening, *Grapes of Wrath*,[5] quite beautiful.

We revive, my Darling, and we will prevail, with our son.

—Work well, read well, rest well!

Give all my best to Françoise

Paul

Telephoned Jacqueline the other day: she was absent. Just a moment ago, Lisou, whom I was able to reach, told me that it was going very poorly for Jacqueline's father.

[To Edith Hübner]

Paris, 29 July 1965

Dear and respected Madam,

Your gift, the Bessarabian carpet, is now here—has crossed, without being questioned, this border too. ("Never did I know the countries.") And it will travel on in a few weeks, to Normandy, where it will have a roof over its head, for a long time.

Bessarabia—what is that for me? Much, because of humans, because of what is human.[6] Names. Some that are familiar to You and some that could be familiar to You, belatedly: because I have taken them with me, like You, dear Madam, have taken the carpet.

One day, perhaps if You, on the way to Brittany, stop in Paris or in Moisville—that is the name of the place in Normandy where Your gift, der Bessarabian carpet, will be and will wait—I will enumerate and recount the names and attempt to bring them to life.

Его за вечер в степи молдованской—[7]

—a song, a "tune" (by Vertinsky?) and yet not one, with the "Molda-vanka"[8] in it, wafted over from Odessa, from Babel's Red Cavalry,[9] *from the son of the rabbi, from Tatar-Bunar.*

And not only from that. Brought to life by Your carpet, which has tra-versed—how awful!—the "Warthegau."[10] (We, at home in Bukovina, we, who did not like what was "Romanian," also because it forbade us—the Jews—our language, the German language, also the language, we called it "Kotzen."[11])

Only today, dear Madam, because of You, and because so much awak-ens to presence with it and in it, do I learn to love it, do I teach others to love it.

It was a good time in Würzburg—I thank You, also for that, warmly. And Your brother-in-law. And Fräulein Reder.

Your Paul Celan[12]

1. This refers to a letter of apology from Kurt Morawietz with regard to the publication of Claire Goll's "Orpheus mit der Gitarre" and PC's "Matière de Bretagne" on the same page (*Die Hören*, no. 2, 1965, p. 11). The word "Linksnibelungen" (left-wing Nibelungen) is a synonym, for PC, for "left-wing anti-Semites." The expression "in the 'magnetic' field" refers to André Breton and Phillipe Soupault's *Les champs magnétiques* (1920).

2. This request came from the General Director of the Austrian National Library (letterhead in Gothic characters). The old-fashioned salutation used, "Euer Hochwohlgeboren," is reminis-cent of the protocol and stiff forms of address of the "kaiserliche und königliche Monarchie."

3. As a souvenir of, and as thanks for, his reading in Würzburg on 22 July 1965, Edith Hübner,

who ran a library, had sent to PC a little rug woven in Bessarabia, a region split today between Moldova and the Ukraine and which, like Bukovina, was part of Romania between the wars (it was ceded to the USSR in June 1940, before becoming part of Romania again the following year).

4. PC is probably referring above all to the work of revising his translations of Michaux and of preparing his courses at the ENS.

5. *Grapes of Wrath* by John Ford (1940), the movie adaptation of the novel by John Steinbeck (1939).

6. Between July and August 1941, thousands of Jews from Bessarabia fell victim to persecutions and waves of deportation on the orders of the Romanian authorities (see Raul Hilberg, *The Destruction of the European Jews*, Vol. II [New Haven: Yale University Press, 2003].

7. "He, in the evening, on the Moldovan steppe."

8. The name of the old Jewish quarter of Odessa, where Isaac Babel was born.

9. On Babel's *Red Cavalry*, see nos 107 and 457.

10. After the invasion of Poland by Germany in 1939, the Wartheland became the Reichsgau, a territory integrated into the "Großdeutsche Reich."

11. Der Kotzen (or die Kotze): in Austria and in Bavaria, the word designated a sort of rough wool covering; PC plays with the word's homologue, the verb kotzen, which means "to puke."

12. Original German-language letter to Edith Hübner enclosed with PC's letter to GCL not included here.

160

[Paris,] Tuesday, 3 August 1965

My Darling,

This morning, like yesterday, two of Your beautiful letters—yes: *beautiful*—and the card from Cabris. Thanks, thanks, thanks. This morning too, the letter from Eric that I am enclosing with this one: he is doing well, that is the essential thing, but his spelling, co-essential, is not quite glorious. There is work, still, waiting for You.

I am sorry about Your tooth, my Darling. What to say? Attacked, shaken, again and again, for years and years, we have, despite everything, held up. But we are marked, You as well as I. Nevertheless we climb back up, already, and we will climb back up still.

If You see the dentist, ask him if he can save the root for You to make You a *pivot tooth*. (That is what they made for Solange. For me, a man without roots, no pivot.)

But yes, I also noticed, the day of Your departure, that Your white hairs were a bit more numerous. I resolve, full of trust, to attach to these lines a letter written the other day and which I had kept—here it is. Upright, we continue, without blushing from what has marked us—let those who are responsible for it blush!—without flinching.

Remember Your return ticket, my Darling. Do not stay too long, nor for too short a time. I am waiting for You, always, every day.

I hug You

Paul

Greetings to Françoise.

Yesterday, I started the Michaux—until then, I had been reading Novalis[1]— that went very well, and am sending, at the same time as this letter, five proofread chapters to Dumitriu.[2]

[Paris,] 29 July 1965

Late at night, I think of You, my Love.

I see You.

I see Your eyes. Deiner Augen Gestalt und Adel.[3]

I see Your hair too, and Your white hairs, more numerous of late. Carry them, my Darling, in these artificial times, carry them proudly: they make my love younger. And my love will make You younger.

---

1. Friedrich Novalis, *Heinrich von Ofterdingen* (PC was probably reading the edition by Ewald Wasmuth—*Werke, Briefe, Dokumente*, 4. vols. (Heidelberg: Lambert Schneider, 1953–57), v. 1. The passages marked by a line in the margin of PC's book include material from the appendix of the text: "Heinrich wird im Wahnsinn Stein—'Blume' Klingender Baum—goldner Widder—Heinrich errät den Sinn der Welt. Sein freiwilliger Wahnsinn. Es ist das Rätsel, was ihm aufgegeben wird" (Heinrich becomes stone in his madness—tree that sounds like 'Flower'— golden ram—Heinrich guesses the meaning of the world. His voluntary madness. It is the mystery that is posed to him), p. 221.

2. PC, editor of the first volume of Michaux's works scheduled to appear in 1966 with S. Fischer, is sending his corrections and revisions of the translations of his collaborator, Kurt Leonhard.

3. "The form and the nobility of your eye." Allusion to line 10 of "Ich hörte sagen"; see no. 19.

161

My Darling,

Thank You for Your telephone call from yesterday, Your card (Re-Messuguière, very pretty, very "marquise de Cabris," so very Mirabelle...) from today.[1] It arrived at the same time as a card from Katja Arendt, from Prague,[2] reminding me about the charms of this city, telling me as well that Eric Arendt was in Neuwied, at Luchterhand... We have such solidary friends![3]

Put into motion by Your question, I wrote, yesterday evening, in the Fontaine de Jade,[4] while meditating upon the Chinese mushrooms and the bamboo shoots—there was some chicken, too[5]—then, at my table, where nothing grows—this poem.[6] It is, as You can see, insurrectional and glacial at once. A placard revolt, redder than red, under the—surprised?—eyes of seals. A revolt of other things too, of geologies, of scriptural things, of the heart.—But no commentaries! Poetry first (France, Germany, etc. afterward)!

I kiss You, my Darling!

Paul

Dunstbänder-, Spruchbänder-Aufstand,
röter als rot,
während der großen
Frostschübe, auf
schlitternden Eisbuckeln vor
Robbenvölkern.

Der durch dich hindurch-
gehämmerte Strahl,
der hier schreibt,
röter als rot.

Mit seinen Worten
dich aus der Hirnschale schälen, hier,
verscharrter Oktober.

Mit ihm das Gold prägen, jetzt,
wenns herausstirbt.

Mit ihm den Bändern beistehn.

Mit ihm das glasharte Flugblatt vertäuen
am lesenden Blutpoller, den
die Erde durch diesen
Stiefpol hinausstieß.

Paris, 4.VIII.1965

Vapor-bands-, banners-revolt
redder than red,
during the great
frost-snaps, on
sliding ice-hills, in front of
seal-peoples.

The ray hammered
through you,
which writes here,
redder than red.

With its words
to peel you out of your brain-shell, here,
buried October.

With it to stamp the gold, now,
when it dies outwards.

With it to stand with the banners.

With it to fasten the glass-hard flysheet
to the reading blood-bollard, which
the earth expelled through
this illegitimate pole.[7]

1. The description on the postcard that GCL sent on 3 August 1965 reads: "Cabris (A.M.), alt. 550 m. La Messuguière. Charming Provençal village. Above Cannes and Iles de Lérins. Wonderful view over the coast of Cap-Ferrat of the foothills of Toulon. Corsica is visible in clear weather. Its origins go back to AD 400. Decimated by the plague and completely abandoned, it was reconstructed around 1496. Ruins of its Feudal Castle (from around the year 1000), where lived, at the beginning of the eighteenth century, the Marquise of Cabris, sister of Mirabeau." We should recall here that GCL is the daughter of the marquis and the marquise de Lestrange. On the word "Mirabelle," see also no. 73.
2. See the poem "In Prag" (In Prague) written 12 October 1965 (*NKGA*, p. 198; *BIT*, p. 52). PC will, however, never return behind the iron curtain to visit this city.
3. Luchterhand was for PC above all the publisher of Yvan Goll's poems in the edition procured by Claire Goll; anything associated with this publishing house was suspicious for PC.
4. Chinese restaurant, 54 avenue Bosquet (7th arrondissement).
5. In English in the original ("there was some chicken, too").
6. *NKGA*, p. 216; for the list of translated words, see no. 163.
7. See "Vaporband-, Banderole-Uprising," *BIT*, p. 102.

162

[To Eric Celan]

[Paris,] 4 August 1965

My dear Eric,

Thanks for your letter, which I really enjoyed. (I sent it right away to Mama, whom it also made happy.)

That campfire in the company of all the packs from the area must have been an amazing thing, and one which you will certainly not forget. So tell me a little more about the place where you all are, about the Pyrenees— these mountains that I do not know yet and which I count on knowing a bit thanks to your stories.

I only stayed in Germany for a week, first in Würzburg, where I read poems at the University—there were a lot of people, who truly listened— and where I saw the Allemanns again—greetings to you from them, as well as from Urs (pronounced as "ours"[1]), then in Frankfurt, where my editor reserved a room for me on the eighteenth floor of a skyscraper.

Several times, I recounted your cannibal stories—with much success.

The eighth, in four days, I will be there, in Paris, for your return. I think that a little Fontaine de Jade wouldn't hurt us.

I hug you,

Your Papa

[In the margin:] It would be nice of you if you wrote me another letter—here is a stamped envelope.

1. That is to say, like the French word for "bear."

163

[Paris,] 6[1] August 1965

My Darling,

I just noticed that the words I explained, which I wanted to attach to the poem sent yesterday, stayed behind on my table—so here they are today.[2]

I am also sending You a clipping from *Combat* on "German Europe."[3] (I have trouble understanding myself as "European," as I have never known how to be "Western." There are humans everywhere in the world, aren't there?) That does not seem to me too far removed from what I believe I am observing, for some time now, in the evolution of things German.

No letter from You this morning—Did You have a good day at the Bourboulons'? I hope so, ardently.—No letter from Eric either—I wrote him yesterday, without thinking that he will only get this letter the night before his return.

This morning, telephone call from Jacques, from Vitry-le-François: old Lévy seems to be dying. (I had telephoned yesterday, they were still registered as absent subscribers, they told me that they were in Vitry.) Jean-Pierre is down there too, Lisou left for Hungary.

No mail this morning, only printed matter (Anthology by Hartung).—Life, here too, is slow.

I kiss You, my Darling

Paul

Band, ¨er—bande, ruban / Dunst—vapeurs / Spruchband—transparent, pancarte dans les manifestations (révolutionnaires) / Aufstand, ¨e—insurrection / Schub, ¨e—poussée / Frost, ¨e—gel / schlittern—glisser, patiner / Buckel—bosse / Robbe, -n—phoque / Volk, ¨er—peuple / hämmern—marteler / Strahl, -en—rayon, jet / der durch dich hindurchgehämmerte Strahl—le rayon / jet martelé à travers toi / Hirn—cerveau / Schale—bol, écorce / Hirnschale—boîte crânienne / schälen—peler, décortiquer / verscharren—enfouir, enterrer / prägen—empreindre (un chiffre sur une médaille), graver; frapper, battre monnaie; estamper, monnayer / sterben—mourir / "hinaussterben" (mot à moi)—mourir vers l'extérieur, apparaître en mourant, de par la mort / beistehen—secourir / glashart—dur comme verre / Flugblatt—manifeste / vertäuen—amarrer / Poller (mot rare, de marine)—pivot (en bois ou métal) pour amarrer les bateaux / Blut—sang / Pol—pôle / Stief—(n'existe pas seul, tu le connais dans Stiefmutter—belle-mère, marâtre; Stiefsohn—beau-fils, fils d'un autre lit; le dictionnaire comporte aussi "Stiefkönig"—roi illégitime ou d'emprunt) / stoßen—pousser

---

1. Actually the 5th.
2. See no. 161.
3. In his article, Andersen cites Walter Ulbricht's appeal to West Germany (the BRD) to cooperate economically with East Germany (the GDR): "Big industry in Germany is on the best path to bringing about the reunification of Europe, into which the GDR would see itself integrated little by little. At the rate things are going, this German-Slavic Europe will have achieved the stage of reality in the not too distant future when Europe, from the Atlantic to the Urals, will be at nothing more than its nebulous phase." The article by Georges Andersen attached to the letter, "L'Europe allemande et M. Ulbricht," had been published in *Combat* on 4 August 1965.

164

[Paris,] 6 August 1965

My Darling,

Just a note: to tell You how glad I was to talk with You on the telephone yesterday evening and to hear that You are starting to relax. That is relaxing, for me too.

And to forward You Eric's letter and M. Blabla's[1]—unexpected—letter. (I allowed myself to open it.)—What is this "indisposition" of Eric's during my stay at the clinic, of which You did not want to speak to me?

I hug You

Paul

I do not think it is necessary to respond to Bl., anyway not immediately.

---

1. Monsieur Blazewski, EC's teacher at the elementary school on rue Hamelin (16th arrondissement).

165

La Messuguière,[1] [Cabris,]
Friday, 6 August 1965

My darling,

I am rereading your beautiful letters, which are also poems, and the poem, and I feel very spoiled. Alone in a corner of the garden with a semblance of coolness beneath the olive trees, I am thinking of You, of all these riches You give me. I do not feel alone, I even feel particularly indulged and close to You.

I am rereading Your words of hope, of encouragement, I make them mine, I repeat them to myself and I find my courage again, my strength, little by little. The calm of this place, the beauty of the region, the possibilities of speaking with Françoise, with others too, help me. I'm not doing much, but in our great solitude, it feels good all the same to be able to exchange a few words from time to time, even when they are not essential words. That distracts me, maybe a bit like when you go to the movies, because I have nothing better, it's often a bit trivial, a bit carefree, the influence of the sun too, of the heat overwhelming everyone here.

I am resting very much. The long deck chair, the library cool and always empty, or almost, and very quiet. The tall linden tree with its little table. The singing of cicadas. All that helps me and I feel that I am climbing up again. I am a bit carefree, at bottom even quite at ease. I feel like a member of the house, the kitchen is open to me. I drink a pastis there from time to time with simple and decent people (not everyone has this privilege), and then this little group, Nicole Belmont, the young and carefree Englishman, this good guy who is handicapped physically but so simple and open who is resting from his tours as traveling librarian. It's not much, but I feel that I can once again laugh a little again (despite the tooth, accepted and forgotten) and make others laugh too—make others reflect too a little bit. And then there's Françoise, nice, simple, poor, but so rich and humble in her convictions. I just read her the little passage from your letter where you said that you understood her disappointment in so much energy invested for nothing, I don't have it in front of me, you say it much better, of course. She was so touched: "Yes, that's exactly it, I didn't realize it." I feel in her an understanding, such a receptiveness, such an openness toward the other, toward the person who is suffering, seeking, struggling. I truly hope that you will know her one day, I think that you would really get along with her. But I come back to the poem, I had stumbled a little, as you might expect, especially over "Blutpoller" and "vertäuen," now with all your explanations, thanks for this great patience that you have with me, it is becoming clearer and I see again the true you, true revolutionary so distant from the communists, always in the true and the pure—and then, the poet, this is so close in you, so bound to these discoveries that are so much your own, so beautiful, so mysterious and simple at the same time. I like this "Robbenvölker," this "röter als rot," this frost snap, these ice hills, and also

Mit seinen Worten
dich aus der Hirnschale schälen, hier,
verscharrter Oktober.

I feel the true life, which rises up again in You, the possibility of finding Your richness still so close and which seems to You so far away—often.

Try not to give too much importance to the Fischer events. I know how difficult it is to work in an environment of lies and incomprehension, of treachery (I am thinking especially of Musulin), of sluggishness and half-lies and promises that never pan out. I know, I understand. But I also try to think of other realities. Of that group of students, for example, who you told me were so quiet in order to listen to you. Those who, beyond the possibility of hearing you transmit your poetry by reciting it, were also able to hear you speak of poetry. You know how rare human exchanges and moments of comprehension are, one must know they are rare, and know that they are "second moments" just as you speak of "second states."

You are so rich, you discern (with a true discernment), you also have knowledge, all that is so rare and was given to you so generously, and you have also known how not only to maintain it but to make it bear fruit and to share it. It's beautiful, you know. I repeat that often to myself. You know that I am all the same one of your greatest admirers! No? Then know that.

I feel that, when I return, we will work, I believe that I will all the same bring back a bit of strength in me, it's still fragile, and discouragement, my great enemy, is often lying in wait for me. But we will manage, to find our spiritual youth and our strength together. You will help me still, as your letters help me, and then I will try too with my feeble means.

Maybe after dinner I will go to post this letter in Cabris. The evenings are cool and so pleasant and relaxing, but at night I worry all the same and I often wake up with a start, not very calm, even anxious. It's not always easy to be far from one's beloved and one's son.

All the same, I think that I'm lucky to be here. I am relaxing a lot among the old people and now things have been rejuvenated a bit and tomorrow two more little young men, that's to say, around thirty years old, should arrive.

I can still, at bottom, move among the thirty-somethings. Maybe even better than among the old people, who are touching but not very fortifying and a bit depressing.

Until soon, my love.

I kiss You

Gisèle

166

[Paris,] 10 August 1965

Thanks for Your letters, my Darling, thanks for Your good, Your beautiful letters. Thanks-thanks.

You are doing better, I am sure of it.

Yesterday, it was Eric's day. And the day of Your telephone call. And of Your letter from Friday the sixth, posted, departed from Cabris yesterday morning.

Eric's day above all.

He is doing well (even if, I think, he does not have an extraordinarily good look about him). Surely, from the point of view of independence— imagine, he had even washed his shirts—that did him much good. There are, as I told you, new songs—above all, he sings in tune.

At eight fifteen, after a telephone call, I went up to Mme Rieul's. I had to finish a card game—families—with Bernard (or Bertrand?) Rieul. At home, a bath. Put the things to be washed in the backpack. Your telephone call. Invited Marie-Thérèse to Fontaine de Jade. Ordered, there, the "House specialties": Peking duck, Szechuan lamb (or vice versa), then, for dessert, donuts with apples flambés. Marie-Thérèse, content, having left us for an hour for a business meeting (rue de Bourgogne, apartment), we went on foot toward Alma and coming across, on the way, on avenue Bosquet, a toy store displaying a little plane that can be launched with an elastic band and that was not very expensive, we went in to buy it for Antoine. Upon this, the idea occurred to me to ask the proprietress—a bit from another time—if she had puzzles. She had some, and there were two, of which one, simpler, is for the cousin, another, without images, very English but made in France,[1] for our son.—To the Musée Galliera, the 63 to the Trocadéro. Until then, real conversation with Eric—I am glad to hear myself recount things to my son, without losing the thread (as happened so many times during these last years). Clear impression that Eric is content to see me again—what is more, this morning already, he had told me that he has missed us—later, when, around three thirty, Monique and Robert, whom we are waiting for in front of the house, come to pick him up, I even have the impression that Eric is a bit sad not to be able to stay with me.

I go back up to work, then, around six o'clock, I go down to send the corrected manuscripts to Dumitriu (who, so far, has not yet confirmed the receipt of the first manuscripts sent).[2]

And now, since the Cinémathèque is closed Mondays, I head, like a true ambler, toward Étoile, then I descend, thinking vaguely of finding a film, glued, more and more, to the shop windows—in search of a scarf for You, a simple tie for me—take avenue Franklin-Roosevelt, find myself at rue du Faubourg-S[ain]t-Honoré, turn there to look for a scarf, find, unfortunately, not one that is pretty—everything is, decidedly, more and more sophisticated—wind up, finally, at the Palais-Royal and decide—the day is gastronomic—to offer myself a dinner at Pied de Cochon. What was made: artichoke bottoms, tournedos à la Béarnaise, all of this washed down with a half-bottle of S[ain]t-Amour.

There it is.

Today: A letter from You. At noon, telephoned to the Mill. Eric, content, tells me that the Rabette[3] has left its bed.

Worked—advancing quite slowly. Your letter from Sunday evening that—the concierge is not there, the mail distribution leaves something to be desired—was sticking out a bit of the slit in the mailbox.

Do not forget to take care of Your return ticket, my Darling. Have good, very relaxing days! All my best to Françoise.

I kiss You, kiss

Paul

---

1. "Very English" and "made in France" in English in original.
2. PC had just sent Dumitriu six "chapters" of Michaux translations.
3. River on which the Mill, property of Monique Gessain, was built.

[Paris,] Wednesday, 11 August 1965

My Darling,

Just a few lines so that there may be lines on your table that come from mine.

Good day yesterday, with, after a rather slow morning, a bit of Cinémathèque around six thirty—after sending my letter—*Que Viva Mexico*, by Eisenstein, but silent, too ethnological for my taste, which made me leave after three quarters of an hour and a good dozen of giant cactuses cut down with a knife or—if I understood correctly—*sucked out* by means of a sort of calabash-siphon by very wrinkly peasants, who had come from far away, with kinds of barrels hanging from the flanks of their mules, into which the cactus milk flowed, in meager streams.—Or maybe it was something else and I understood nothing. There were also processions, with the Virgin, virgins, and revirgins, veils and smiles. Then misery, copiously recorded—in Mexico of course and not in Russia, where, at the time, there was an enormous amount, caramba!

After the dinner, Michaux until three thirty in the morning. (A propos: Mme Viénot is indeed the daughter of Mme Mayrisch S[ain]t-Hubert, to whom Michaux dedicated his "Ecce Homo"—in *Epreuves, Exorcismes*—which was translated, into the (Austro-?)German language by the under-signed.)[1] That is advancing, slowly.

This morning, letter from Dumitriu, confirming his receipt of the first manuscript, telling me that Leonhard is ready for the meeting planned for the end of the month, in Frankfurt. I will not be able to not go, but that will have the advantage of finishing the work.

This dear Swiss, Walter, does not respond—too bad for him and his Gruyères (left-wing and neo-Catholic!).[2]

Tennis for an hour—rather good performance.

Re-Michaux. Telephone call from the Institut autrichien, then from an emissary of Viennese culture, in Paris to contact "culturophores" (that is how I decided to translate, into franco-Celanian, the Teutonic "Kulturträger."[3]

Tomorrow this gentleman, of an absolute linen-decency, and who would like, with Your husband, to contemplate who in the landscape of German letters could write, for this very-courageous review that he publishes, at the expense of these very republican princesses, baronesses, and other esses,[4] who, with the benediction of richly mothballed Austro-Marxism, make flow together, for we are, in Vienna, not very far from our beautiful Passa-u, where everything converges, converges, converges, who make converge, I am saying, the Occident and the Orient with their very fresh and even a bit sweet waters,[5]—tomorrow this gentleman-of-quality(-ies) will come to reflect together with me about who, for the above-mentioned review, could write an article about me.[6] That will be at the coffee-hour.

And on this I will silence my loquacity

and kiss You

Paul

1. *Epreuves, exorcismes 1940–1944* (Paris: Gallimard, 1945), pp. 44–57. This translation of "Ecce homo," which appeared in S. Fischer's *Almanach* (1963, no. 77, pp. 125–129; *GW* IV, pp. 598–607), was not republished in the second volume of Michaux's works, published in homage to PC. Kurt Leonhard will publish his own translation of this in *Dichtungen, Schriften II* (Frankfurt am Main: S. Fischer, 1971), pp. 23–29.
2. PC had written to Otto F. Walter, head of the eponymous Swiss-German publishing house, on 20 July 1965, about a possible meeting in Paris. Walter, who in 1961 had published PC's translation of Jean Cayrol, *Im Bereich einer Nacht—L'Espace d'une nuit*, was aware of PC's difficulties with S. Fischer, and proposed to PC to become his publisher. The meeting will not take place until 4 July 1966.
3. Professor Dr Karl Kogler, deputy director of the Austrian Cultural Institute in Paris, had mentioned to PC a telephone call from Otto Breicha, representative of the Österreichische Gesellschaft für Literatur, who wished to meet writers and artists of Austrian origin living in Paris.
4. The review is *Wort in der Zeit*, published by the Österreichische Gesellschaft für Literatur (Palais Wilczek, Herrengasse, Vienna).
5. PC recalls here his visit with GCL to this German city, mentioned in the *Nibelungenlied*, and the postcard they wrote to Péter Szondi from there on 11 July 1964: "From Passa-u, from Passa-u, where that flows together, where that flows together." In Passau, on the German-Austrian border, the Inn and Ilz rivers converge with the Danube. Because the two phonemes have "converged" in French, PC insists on the pronunciation of the diphthong, perhaps also in connection to a German lesson, during which he may have drawn GCL's attention to the German pronunciation of his first name, "Pa-ul."
6. Wieland Schmied and Max Hölzer are envisioned at first for this task. The former, who has already published articles on *MG* and *SG* in *Wort in der Zeit* (in 1955 and 1959) will recuse himself, because he does not have the time to devote himself to this work; PC will not manage to reach the latter. This project will not be completed.

168

[Paris,] Friday, [13 August 1965]

My Darling,

excuse me for the very annoying telephone call from yesterday evening: I was in shock at the news of Jacques's car accident.[1] So everything that seemed to me to prolong Your trip by car was unbearable for me.

Maybe this return in three steps that I proposed to You is really too long. Do the best you can do, as seems best to You. But please avoid unnecessary risks. One is never sure of one's neighbor, as You well know. On the way home from vacation, people are often irritated, even more careless than usual.

Have Your tires checked, etc. If You send the car by freight train, take a *very good* spot for You in the train, a *sleeping car* if possible.

I received, this morning, Your letter from Tuesday: thanks.

Take care of Yourself, think of Yourself, think of us.

I kiss You

Paul

---

1. PC noted in the family planner, for 12 August 1965, at 10:30 a.m.: "Telephone call from Jaqueline: Jacques's serious accident." The day before, GCL had informed PC that their neighbor and friend, Jacques Lalande, had a car accident on his way to Vitry-le-François (Marne) to be at his dying father-in-law's bedside.

169

[Saint-Paul-de-Vence, 17 August 1965]

Returned here,[1] above all to see this magnificent Giacometti room in a unique setting.

We have to come back here together.[2] You will like it very much. It's very terrible, it's unforgiving, it's cruel and glacial at times, it's hell, perhaps not. But it's very true. That's what convinced me and moved me very much.

A revelation, as rarely.

I kiss you

Gisèle

1. The museum of the Maeght Foundation.
2. PC will go alone in October 1968.

170

[Paris, 20 August 1965]

My Darling,

I am writing to You less—by which You can see that I have lost my momentum a little. But I was able to speak with You, yesterday, on the telephone. This morning, telephone call from Solange and Eric—he is content, amuses himself, plays ping-pong (or rather: tries to play), regrets the absence, in Toisley, of a "flipper." That, as I had already noticed in Paris, seems to be his new passion.[1] One of our walks was, actually, toward the "Bowling" on the avenue Victor Hugo, closed, luckily. But, the car having stopped at Dreux, "Aunt Solange" wanted to indulge this penchant of her nephew's.

The day before yesterday I wrote this poem, below.[2] It is quite decent, it seems to me, maybe not opaque enough,[3] not "there" enough. Nevertheless, at the end it recuperates—it recuperates *itself*.

Otherwise, nothing new. No mail this morning, no response from Walter,[4] none from Insel, to whom I sent, on the sixth and by certified letter, the papers for the taxes.

I am playing tennis this evening, with Mayotte's two brothers and Heinz Wismann. Yesterday evening, I treated myself to a Russian *Othello* at the Cinémathèque, rather "kitschoide" with its beautiful overlocal colors—or local overcolors—and its declamations.[5] But Russian is such a beautiful language and Shakespeare—for me, there is nothing more beautiful and more grand than Shakespeare. As for the characters, above all for what has to do with Iago, it has to be said that they remain, keeping everything in perspective and keeping all handkerchiefs, very current. That cannot disappear, the traitors[6]... We know some of them, don't we?

In the German gazettes and in others, the commentaries on the Frankfurt trial. We could not have expected anything else. That will nourish the hypocrisies and dissimulations some more for a few light-months[7]...

Good, I will come to an end. One would perhaps have to advance on spindly legs, like these Giacometti men of whom you speak so well in your letter, but there again, don't you think, one ends up in the foundations.

So, with an arm that is not too long, not too filiform, I surround you, then with the other I close the circuit.

Paul

Friday, 19[8] August 1965, in Panam.[9]

Ruh aus in deinen Wunden,
durchblubbert und umpaust.

Das Runde, klein, das Feste:
aus den Blicknischen kommts
gerollt, nahebei,
in keinerlei Tuch.

(Das hat
—Perle, so schwer
wars durch dich—,
das hat sich den Salzstrauch ertaucht,
drüben, im Zweimeer.)

Ohne Licht rollts, ohne
Farbe—du
stich die Elfenbeinnadel hindurch
—wer weiß nicht,
daß der getigerte Stein, der dich ansprang,
an ihr zerklang?—,
und so—wohin fiel die Erde?—
laß es sich drehen zeitauf,
mit zehn Nagelmonden im Schlepptau,
in Schlangennähe, bei Gelbflut,
quasistellar.

durchblubbert—"transglouglouté" / umpaust—entouré d'intervalles / "Das Runde...Tuch.": *c'est la larme* (dont parle le poème) / Elfenbein—ivoire / zeitauf—"en amont du temps" (en remontant le temps) / Nagelmond—lunules (des ongles) / Schlepptau—câble de remorque (ins Schlepptau nehmen—prendre en remorque) / quasistellar—quasistellaire [*sic*]...

Paris,
18 August 1965

Relax in your wounds,
traversed by gurgling and surrounded by pauses.

Round, small, and firm:
out of the looking-niches it comes
rolled, nearby,
into no handkerchief.

(That
—pearl, so heavy
it was because of you—,
that dove down and won the salt-shrub,
on the other side, in the double-sea.)

Without light it rolls, without
color—you
stick the ivory needle through
—who does not know,
that the tigered stone that pounced on you
sounded its last against it—,
and so—where did the earth fall to?—
let it turn itself against the stream of time,
with ten lunulae in tow,

close to snakes, at yellow tide.
quasi-stellar.

Paris, 18 August 1965[10]

1. PC does not let on that he, too, liked to play pinball, in the early 1950s, including while waiting for his friends (Bertrand Badiou conversation with I. Chiva).
2. "Ruh aus in deinen Wunden," *NKGA*, p. 217.
3. On this important aspect of PC's poetics, see *Meridian*, p. 7.
4. The editor Otto F. Walter; see no. 167, n. 2.
5. Soviet film by Sergei Yutkevich (1956).
6. Allusion to the Goll Affair (see no. 4, n. 2) and to the journal *Merkur* (see no. 122, n. 4).
7. The verdict of the Frankfurt Auschwitz Trials was delivered the day before, 19 August 1965, after more than a year and a half of investigation and 182 days of court hearings: out of the twenty Nazi criminals charged (members of the Gestapo, doctors, SS-Führers, including Wilhelm Boger), only six were sentenced to life in prison, and three were acquitted.
8. Actually the 20th.
9. Argot for Paris.
10. See "Rest In Your Wounds," *BIT*, p. 104.

171

[Paris, 21 August 1965]

My Darling,

Just this very little note to accompany Marianne's letter, found yesterday evening under the door, upon my return from tennis.

I am happy that You will come home soon.

I kiss You

[Unsigned]

Friday,[1] 21 August 1965

1. This should read "Saturday."

172

[Paris,] Sunday, 21¹ August [1965,]
seven in the evening

My Darling,

Not a spectacular day yesterday, despite Your beautiful letter from Thursday and your telephone call.

Decidedly, this publishing house that sends me, without an accompanying letter, *opened* letters, which are addressed to me personally—no, that is not all right.² My question, albeit "protocolled" (protokolliert) by Dumitriu, regarding these "two major American publishing houses interested in my works" (postcard from New York, written by this dear Tutti two or three years ago): still without response.³

They needed, these bastards, a German-language writer, who is known and who, moreover, could start their "Lyrik" series—so, with the help of this very-literary bastard, Hirsch, they set the trap for me—and I walked right in,⁴ counselled by my "friends" Ingeborg, Lenz, Schallück.

Anyway.

This afternoon, Cinémathèque again: *October,* or rather *Ten Days That Shook the World* (based on the book by John Reed that I gave you a few years ago), directed by Eisenstein.⁵ The USSR brought it out of its archives, this film from before Stalin's terror, it is from 1928, and in the opening credits, before the images, you could read that it was dedicated to the proletariat of "Piter"—that is Petersburg's popular name:

*Питерскому Пролетариату*⁶

so I, you know me, I applauded.

—*Pssh!* No reaction!

That is what I received as an answer, imposing itself in a hall where no one came to support my applauding. Yet there were readers of the *Observateur*...But the *Observateur*, it is "Leftism," it is the admirers of the Série noire, pederasts, the Idhec,⁷ yea-yea Marxism, etc., etc.

So, alone, I saw Petersburg, the workers, the sailors of the Aurora. It was very moving,[8] calling to mind sometimes *The Battleship*,[9] reminding me of the thoughts and dreams of my youth, my thoughts of today and of always,[10] always-true-always-loyal-Poetry, I saw my placards, in large numbers, those that, not that long ago, I evoked in the poem I sent you—"Vapor-bands, *Banner-Revolt*";[11] I saw the October Revolution, its men, its flags, I saw Hope always on the way, brother of Poetry, I saw...

Then, at a certain moment, at the moment when the insurgents enter the Winter Palace, it begins to leave Poetry behind and to become Cinema, film shot, tendentious and over-the-top, the intertitles turn into propaganda—everything that was History and its Characters was elsewhere, from the beginning, that which was less convincing, the role of the Social-Revolutionaries of the Left was made to disappear totally—so the heart unclenched itself, searched its silences (won, lost, regained), surrounded itself with that and took me out of there, alone, as I had entered, passing by the hedge of young cinephiles and young girls "mit tupierter Frisur," wearing too much makeup, in pants, kind of left-wingish youth from the 16th,[12] feeble and irresolute.—But there were, surely, a few who knew, accepting, here too, the terrible eclipses.

Long live the Sailors of Kronstadt!

Long live the Revolution! Long live Love!

Long live Petersburg! Long live Paris!

Long live Poetry!

Paul

---

1. Actually the 22nd.

2. PC notes in his correspondence notebook, which also serves as a journal: "Freitag, 20 August 1965 / Brief bzw. Umschlag S. Fischer, Poststempel Frankfurt 19 August 65, enthaltend einen geöffneten Brief von J. Laughlin, New Directions an mich, N[ew] York, July 6, 1965, adressiert an P.C., 178 rue de Longchamp und als unbestellbar zurückgegangen. [Friday, 20 August 1965 / Letter, or rather, envelope from S. Fischer, post-stamped Frankfurt 19 August 65, containing an opened letter from J. Laughlin, New Directions, to me, N[ew] York, 6 July 1965, addressed to P.C., 178 rue de Longchamp and returned to sender—addressee not at address.] After a telephone call with Dumitriu, the latter attributes the opened letter to the "tactlessness of a secretary."

3. On 31 August 1965, Dumitriu will communicate to PC the names of these two New York publishing houses: New Directions and Farrar, Straus & Giroux.

4. PC had left DVA in 1958 and published *SG* the following year with S. Fischer, relations with whom, particularly with their former director, Rudolf Hirsch, degraded as a result of the Goll Affair.
5. *October* (1927), Soviet film by Sergei Mikhailovich Eisenstein, based on John Reed's *Ten Days That Shook the World* (1919). PC had given the French translation of this work to GCL over ten years earlier, in 1954.
6. "To the Proletariat of Piter."
7. *France Observateur* (today *Le Nouvel observateur*): weekly magazine founded in 1949, edited by Claude Bourdet and Gilles Martinet, at the time close to the Parti socialiste unitaire (PSU). The Série noire is a well-known series of detective novels published by Gallimard, which continues to be published today. When PC was not well, he expressed intolerance towards homosexuality, unable to get beyond the precepts of the Book of Leviticus. The IDHEC (Institut des hautes études cinématographiques) is the film school in Paris at the time.
8. See the third stanza of "In eins," written 24 May 1962: *SPP*, p. 188.
9. *Battleship Potemkin* (1925), Soviet film by Sergei Mikhailovich Eisenstein, filmed in Odessa.
10. Regarding PC's thoughts about revolutionary movements and about the "Social-Revolutionaries of the Left" evoked in the following paragraph, see *Meridian*, p. 3, and the text of the radio program *The Poetry of Osip Mandelstam* (in *Meridian*, pp. 217–21), as well as no. 157 and the letter to Erich von Kahler.
11. See no. 161.
12. Wealthy neighborhood in Paris.

173

[Paris,] Tuesday, 24 August 1965

My Darling,

Here is a letter from Lisou, which arrived this morning, I allowed myself to open it.

Telephoned Jacques, who tells me he is doing better. I will go to see him at the clinic tomorrow at four o'clock. Jacqueline is with her father.

No news from Eric, but it is nice out, he must be having fun, he is having fun surely.

I am waiting for You. Have a good trip! Have a good Arrival!

Paul

174

Paris, Gare de l'Est, 1 September 1965

Hello, my Darling, hello and goodbye and see You soon!

Hello, my dear Eric, see you soon!

Relax, amuse yourselves, work a little.

I kiss you.

Auf Wiedersehen!

Paul

My best to Jean-Pierre. Freundschaft!

175

Frankfurt am Main (as it is not or hardly),[1]
Mainpromenade
2 September 1965

My Darling, here I am in Frankfurt, after a good trip.—Dumitriu was sleeping, he only works in the afternoon. In the city. Bought little notebooks.[2] Bookstore: found, in the series "Der Dom" (collection of Mysticism published in the twenties by Insel), the Writings of Ruisbroeck, whom Michaux calls, with Lautréamont, his "ingenious friend."[3]—Telephone calls: Dr. Lotsch, whom I will see tomorrow at noon. Unseld, who invited me to dinner Monday evening. Mme Kaschnitz away until Monday. It is ten thirty, I will go over to Insel about the tax matter.

I hug You with Eric

Paul

---

1. The postcard shows Frankfurt seen from the left bank of the Main, from a peaceful, almost idyllic perspective, hardly allowing the modern city to be glimpsed.

2. PC liked to have, in the interior left pocket of his jacket—near the heart—one of these notebooks, which he always chose with a black cover and lined paper (the brand: Grosse, "Im Haus Schwan"). Particularly from 1963 on, he had the habit of writing down sketches of poems, often preceded by a small "-i-" in these notebooks (in addition to practical or bibliographic information, autobiographical notes, and thoughts).

3. A quotation from the end of Michaux's poem "Amours," in *La Nuit remue* (Paris: Gallimard, 1935), p. 186, translated by Celan in Michaux, *Dichtungen, Schriften*, vol. 1 (Frankfurt am Main: S. Fischer, 1966), pp. 176–81.

176

My Darling,

just a note.

I hope that You are well, You and Eric.

Here, the work with Leonhard went well yesterday and the day before yesterday. I hope to finish this evening or tomorrow. What's more, Leonhard has to return home tomorrow evening, since his wife had an operation, a few days ago, on her gallbladder.

Dumitriu went to Vienna, where Musulin already was, apparently for the Historians' Convention.

Monday, I will have to resolve the details for the printing of the first volume of Michaux, then I will dictate some pages translated by me.

Monday evening, I will see Unseld, at his house. At Insel,* the details for the taxes are resolved, I have the paper, valid through 1967, which is valid for Fischer too.

Telephoned Krolow, telephoned Mme Kaschnitz, who returns Monday.

Will I go to Italy (or rather to Vicenza)? Maybe, I feel a little like it.

We hold out. We will hold out.

I hug You, with Eric.

Paul

Strange paper. isn't it? It is completely "intercontinental."[1]

---

* they were perfectly courteous

1. The very thin, almost transparent paper, looks like wrinkled paper. The address of the hotel is printed vertically in the right-hand margin.

177

Monday, 6 September 1965

My Beloved,

Your two first letters—so beautiful—this morning: thanks. Thanks. Thanks for You, for Eric, for everything.

"Komm o Sonne."[1]

I am doing well. This morning, even, I am in a little poetic trance, a sort of effervescence: I wrote a little poem that I will copy for You this evening or tomorrow, and that I will comment on for You.[2]

The work with Leonhard went well. This morning, he went back to Eßlingen: his wife's gallbladder was operated on there the day before his arrival. He will come back on Thursday, and we will have work left for two good days. Will I go to Italy? I don't know at all. To tell the truth, I did not intend to go anymore, but since, in Your letters, You encourage me to do so...

This evening, at dinner, I will go to the Unselds'.

Very soon—it is two in the afternoon—to Fischer Verlag.

This morning, tried again to call You in Moisville: nothing to be done, "busy lines" for around two hours. But I was able to get, from Jacques, Your news.

Tell Jacqueline and her mother that I am thinking of them. I heard from Jacques that old Lévy died two days ago. I think of old Lévy.

Work well, my Beloved. We climb back up, we are in the midst of climbing back up. And Eric climbs with us, close to us. Hug him.

I hug You

[Unsigned]

Freundschaft to Jean-Pierre.

---

1. Reference to a German phrase which EC has recently learned ("Come, oh sun"), and to which GCL made reference in a letter from 2 September 1965.
2. PC does not seem to have sent this poem to GCL during this month. PC is referring here to "Frankfurt, September" (written 5–6 September 1965), in which the figures of Freud and Kafka

appear (*NKGA*, p. 225; *BIT*, p. 110). PC wrote the first version of this poem, entitled "Frankfurt; Ajin, September" and dated 5 September 1965, in a notebook in which he kept his journal during this period; he further specified the date of additions and corrections made the day this letter was written: "Frankfurt, / 6 September 65," "? 6 September 65."

178

Les Trois Bouleaux, [Moisville,]
9 September 1965

My darling, I wrote to You Yesterday already, then I tore up the letter, not knowing where to send it. Will You still be in Frankfurt tomorrow? No doubt, but the Moisville mail will not be able to reach You, and where will You be after that? Oh well, I do need to chat with You, perhaps I'll have an address to send You my daily reports.

Today: work day. The shafts of burnt Estérel pines came back to me strongly, I tried to make something of it, and then Giacometti's figures appeared to me.[1] I saw a clear relation between the two. I drew, several sheets with more or less precise experiments. After some time, I thought, that's it, that my etching would be born, that I had the right, the opportunity to leave behind paper for copper, but something else came, more imperious every time.

Finally, I decide, a beautiful copperplate, very clean, well polished, I begin. Hours of work ahead for a first acid biting. I think it's good, the acid biting I wanted—successful. And now, indecision again. I thought I would continue. I still had at least a big day of work ahead in two stages. What should I do? If only you were here. Do I continue all the way to the end of my project? Or I stop. For I think that's it, that the essential is there and all the rest, many things were supposed to come, would be superfluous.

So here I am very alone with my solitary figures.

For the moment, it could be called *Movement*. At first, it was, almost bizarrely, *Hommage to Giacometti and to the Burnt Pines of Estérel*! Do I stick with *Movement* or do I push toward Giacometti and the pines? Not, of course that it will be this title!![2]

Maybe I will wait until your return to make an etching! Maybe I must stop and make a different etching in the first direction. I don't know, I don't know. The temptation!!

I worked the whole morning—I have to tell you that Eric, on his own, brought me this morning, in bed, a very warm coffee, toasted and buttered bread!—the whole morning and the whole evening. Tomorrow I hope to work more.

The weather was quite good and the children played outside!

I can't wait to know what will be the result of your week, from your work with Leonhard as well as from your encounters with editors and writers. So many relations so difficult to establish as true ones!

My weak point: the irregular nights scattered with anxious awakenings and nightmares, I extend them until around nine, not managing to wake up completely. The eye I open with difficulty remains sleepy for a long time.

Yesterday I reread the poems of *Von Schwelle zu Schwelle*, I liked them very much. I also read Du Bellay and Ronsard in an anthology, but all I can read, apart from yours, are those by Michaux and Supervielle. I leafed through the French poetry shelves in our so beautiful library for a long time, but I always return to the same ones.

I am waiting for the poem you announce to me and am delighted about your "poetic trances"! You are doing so well right now, you are working, you are completely new. Only more poems will come this winter! Only more etchings too!

With Eric: "Wie schön ist es im Herbst!"
"Das Laub wird gelb, rot und braun."[3]

It's going well, we read, he understands, he is opening up and I don't insist too much on vocabulary or on memorizing; he guesses, correctly. He realizes it and is very happy. Monday I will go to Paris in the late morning with the children, we will have lunch at Jacqueline's, Jean-Pierre will go to see Jacques and I will see the director with Eric. We will return to Moisville in the evening and to Paris definitively on Saturday the 18th, in the afternoon I think. The first day of school is the 20th.

And you, where will you be until then? If only I could reach you on the phone! But when?

I hope, if everything is organized with the cafeteria as planned for Eric, to be able to go to the studio more often, three days a week maybe. And to visit galleries again. I hope for a good year of work for both of us. A little like our first year on rue de Longchamp![4] I wonder what you will do, if you will translate something beautiful. I am delighted when you make plans like the other day with Altmann!

Friday the 10th. The weather is good, we are going to Dreux, I am sending the letter! . . . Didn't hear from you this morning.

Where are you?

I kiss you where you are

Gisèle

1. Alberto Giacometti's sculptures seen in the Maeght Foundation (see no. 169).
2. Final title: *Hommage à G.* (October 1965)
3. "How pretty it is in the fall!" / "The leaves become yellow, red, and brown."
4. In 1958.

179

[Handwritten telegram]

[Frankfurt am Main, 10 September 1965]

The Michaux is finished[1] I am going to Italy tomorrow via Innsbruck hug You with Eric

Paul

1. The first volume of the bilingual edition of a selection of poems by Michaux will be published the following year: *Dichtungen, Schriften*, vol. 1 (Frankfurt am Main: S. Fischer, 1966). The book is "edited by Paul Celan based on the selection made by Henri Michaux in collaboration with Christoph Schwerin, in translations by Kurt Leonhard and himself." The day before, PC and Kurt Leonhard had written a poem to celebrate the end of their work: "Ein- und Ausfahrt freihalten! Gedicht!" (Allow entry and exit! Poem!), *NKGA*, p. 477.

180

My Beloved,

You received my telegram—I am going, indeed, to Italy, to Verona, then, from Verona, to Vicenza, tomorrow morning, but not via Austria, the passes into Italy are flooded, but through Switzerland. The train is direct, via Basel to Milan, where I will be tomorrow evening at 17:32.

No stop in Basel. But in Milan I will take advantage of the occasion to speak with Mondadori (Mlle Calabi). After Milan, Verona. Then Vicenza. Padua, Parma, Ferrara? Maybe. On the way back, a brief stay in Ticino, to see Robert Neumann. Then return to my home, Your home, our son's home, in Paris, in Moisville.

Bravo my son, you are swimming! Congratulations. I am proud of you.

Michaux (I) is finished.—This evening, another visit to Unseld, in the presence of Martin Walser, then discussion. Nothing definitive. But propositions that were rather correct.[1]

I love You. Long live our love. Long live our son Eric. Long live Poetry. Long live Truth. Long live the Jews.

Always Yours

Paul

Thanks for Your letters, Your so beautiful letters. Thanks. Until soon. Forever.

---

1. Siegfried Unseld, who was aware of PC's difficulties with S. Fischer, proposed to PC to publish his next volume of poetry with Suhrkamp. PC will not take up his offer until December 1966.

181

[Handwritten telegram]

[Paris, 11 September 1965]

I am back[1] all is well call me I am calling You and hug You with Eric

Paul

1. For unknown reasons PC did not go on his planned trip to Italy.

182

78 rue de Longchamp, [19 September 1965]

My Darling, my Beloved,

You will emerge quickly from this trial,[1] You will emerge grown, healed, enriched, You live and You will live, with me beside our son Eric, You will live numerous happy years, years of love, of work, of happiness, together we will lead this life, yes together we will lead it, You while making, also, etchings, paintings too if You feel like it,[2] You will see beautiful things, they will come to You, with simplicity, in large numbers, You will carry, like me and our son Eric, *Judaism in Your heart,*[3] the true one, You will see, with me, Eric progress in his studies, enter the University, exercise a beautiful profession, get married, to a woman worthy of him, You will see, with me, Eric and his wife, our grandchildren, boys and girls, yes, You will experience all of that and all that is true and beautiful.

Paul

19.9.1965

1. Since his return from Frankfurt on 11 September 1965, PC has been experiencing a profound crisis. Paul and Gisèle Celan, who have extremely tense relations, reflect on the necessity of separating, at least temporarily, above all to protect their son. Celan rejects the idea of separation, affirms the permanence of the ties that bind him to his family, and explains his state by qualifying his return from Frankfurt as a "return of a warrior—of a Jewish warrior."

2. PC's extreme sensitivity to colors and tendency to excessively interpret certain ones (brown, for example—see no. 71, n. 5) led GCL to periodically abandon painting, and even to not wear colorful clothing; at these times she privileged black, white, and gray, the colors of her prints. See also no. 184, lines 4–9; on colors perceived as benevolent, see e.g. no. 189, n. 2, and no. 414, n. 8.

3. See no. 138, n. 1 and no. 198, n. 3.

183

[To Eric Celan]

78 rue de Longchamp, [19 September 1965]

My son Eric, you live, you will live, you grow, you will grow, you will be an upright, courageous man, you learn and you will learn, you write and you will write, you sing and you will sing, you love and you will love, you are loved and you will be loved, you will have a wife worthy of you, intelligent and beautiful, you will have children, boys and girls, you will have a beautiful profession, you will have loyal and frank friends, you will be just and charitable, you will love poetry and you will make it, you will have religion and you will respect that of others, you will be a good Jew, you will be in good health always, in good health for a long time, a true man.

Your father

19.9.1965

184

[Paris,] 24 September 1965[1]

Gezinkt der Zufall,[2] und zerweht die Zeichen
Gezinkter Zufall, doch zerwehte Zeichen

Luftdurchstoßen Irr- und Abersinn

Farbenbelagerte, zahlenbelagerte
Liebe
Farbenbelagerte, zahlenbelagerte
Wahrheit

Farbenbelagerter, zahlenbelagerter
Mensch:
mit Hilfe von oben
wirst Du frei, mit Liebe und Wahrheit,[3]

Eric, du wächst, groß und gesund

Marked is chance, and breath-scattered the signs
Marked chance, yet breath-scattered signs

air-pierced unreason and irrationality

Love
Besieged by colors, besieged by numbers[4]
Truth
Besieged by colors, besieged by numbers
Human
Besieged by colors, besieged by numbers:
with help from above
you will be free, with love and truth,

Eric, you grow, big and healthy[5]

---

1. The poem is dated at the top right, like a letter.
2. See *NKGA*, p. 226.
3. See no. 141, n. 1.
4. PC, who had an extensive acquaintance with the symbolism of numbers and colors (see below, no. 255, n. 1), could spend a long time counting off things—for example, the cars passing by on rue de Longchamp—and interpreting the results of these enumerations;associating colors, numbers, dates, and speculating on their relations (Bertrand Badiou, conversation with GCL).
5. See also "Chance, Marked," *BIT*, p. 112.

185

78 rue de Longchamp, [10 October 1965]

My Darling,

Soon we will have been married for thirteen years; we have lived together for fourteen years. We have lost two children;[1] we have Eric, who must grow up beside us, whom we must raise.

To separate from each other would be the victory of our enemies. I do not accept this separation.[2] I do not accept leaving this house, my house. Here, I will battle, still and always.[3] Here, You will find Your strength again, Your work, Your love, Your understanding, and You will help me in my battle.

Here, my son Eric will live and will grow up, he our joy and our Pride. Here, Poetry will live. Here, our Love will live, indestructible.

Paul

10 October 1965

1. PC refers to the death of their son, François, the day after his birth, in October 1953, and to a miscarriage of GCL's, probably in 1952.
2. See 182, n. 1.
3. See nos 63, 106, 135, 136, 154, 186, 203.

186

[Paris, 15 October 1965]

Weißt du, wir sind es noch immer.[1]

15.10.1965

[Unsigned]

[You know, we are still what we are.]

1. See nos 63, 106, 135, 136, 154, 203.

187

[To Eric Celan]

[Saint-Jean-de-Luz,] 22 October 1965

My dear Eric, here is, for your collection, a very pretty view of the port of S[ain]t-Jean-de-Luz, just as I was able to see it this morning, while disembarking from the train.[1] There was, in front of the station, an immense Basque, calling himself the Jumping Man,[2] and all green: it was a bus (which I will take perhaps to go to Ascain). Then, smaller and under (Basque) berets[3] ...Basques. Tuna and re-tuna,[4] a rather beautiful beach, dominated by sumptuous and closed hotels. The city is stylish and summery.

Work well, amuse yourself, be nice to Mama and hug her for me.

I hug you

Your Father

---

1. After weeks of extreme tension, PC decided the day before writing this postcard to go away on a trip (PC's journal). During this solitary journey across France, he will write six poems and take notes for two others, which will be part of the first cycle of *Fadensonnen* (*Threadsuns*; hereafter *FS*. See no. 189, n. 3; no. 191, n. 1; and no. 193, n. 1.
2. Le Basque Bondissant is the name of a regional transportation agency in San Juan de Luz.
3. PC himself liked to wear Basque berets (see no. 470).
4. The postcard's inscription: "St-Jean-de-Luz (Basses-Pyr.)—The Port, the unloading of Tuna on the Dock, at the back, the House of the Infante."

188

[To Eric Celan]

[Ascain,] 22 October 1965

My dear Eric,

Your father, already so Basque, embasques himself more: here he is, at three in the afternoon, thanks to the "Jumping Man," in Ascain, a "typically Basque" village, as the guide puts it. Very white houses, licked clean, wearing tile hats, with well-painted shutters, green or red. All that well arranged, well tidied around the void of the off-season.—

The yoke that you see, I just came across it: he probably was just leaving the barber's, his wig re-clipped.[1]—Hug mama!

I hug you

Your Papa

1. The postcard's inscription: "Basque Country—Basque farm and yoke." The yoke placed on the heads of the oxen is covered in a kind of ornamental rug made of heavy wool.

189

[To Eric Celan]

[Hendaye,] 22 October 1965

My dear Eric,

Same day, a bit farther away, in Hendaye. I took the road that runs along the Corniche[1] to get there—it is 14 kilometers from S[ain]t-Jean-de-Luz; I had the Ocean on my right, calm, blue; once, in the distance, a wave, very white, came to play, for me, the fish with no name.[2]—Here, I went up to the border, it is a bridge,[3] on the other side I glimpsed the city of Irún.

I like this card very much, which, with so little on it, says it all.

Hug Mama—I hug you.

Your Father

1. The postcard's inscription: "Hendaye (Basses-Pyrénées)—La Corniche toward Hendaye, behind, Spain and the Spanish Mountains." See Appendix, image 15.
2. PC interprets the appearance of, "on [his] right," the "Ocean," "calm, blue" and the "wave, very white," and these two colors as benevolent signs (see also no. 184, no. 414).
3. The bridge (note the numerous references to bridges in these letters) crosses the Bidassoa, a river in Basque country that forms a natural border between France and Spain. On this bus ride to Hendaye, PC writes "Hendaye" (NKGA, p. 230; BIT, p. 124).

190

Pau, Hôtel Beaumont, place Royale

23 October 1965

My Darling, my Very-Beloved,

Happy anniversary again! In two months, it will be our big anniversary[1]

—let us have many more still, in full possession of our strength, of *all* our strength found again, while raising Eric!

I wrap You in my arms
I hold You, I kiss
You

Paul

1. PC had called GCL on this "little anniversary" (on the notions of "little anniversary" and "big anniversary," see no. 58, n. 2.

191

[To Eric Celan]

Pau, 23 October 1965

My dear Eric, I just visited the Castle, with its French ceilings (visible joists and sunken panels), its furniture (Gothic, Renaissance, and Louis XIII, etc.), its Gobelin rugs and Flemish tapestries, its canopy beds, its clocks, its chimneys.

Here is the carapace (or shell) of the tortoise in which the good king Henri was cradled.[1]—But many have been cradled "outside the tortoise," including you and me.

I hug you both, Mama and you.

Your Father

1. The postcard's inscription: "Pau (B.-P.)—The Castle—Cradle of Henri IV." The short poem "Pau, nachts," of which PC has just written the first version, is inspired by this visit to Pau Castle. See *NKGA*, p. 230; *BIT*, p. 124).

192

[To Eric Celan]

[Pau,] 23 October 1965

My dear Eric, the sun that, according to the newspapers, ate, the day before yesterday, a big piece of the comet with the Japanese name[1] that dared to approach it, this sun endures above this good city of Pau, where I spent the night, in a hotel on the place Royale, where stands the statue of Henri IV, "lou nouste Henric" in Béarnese, as you well know: it is he who gave France to Béarn, the chicken to the pot, and his name to a tournedos that I tasted last night, washing it down with a good wine from the region.

I hug your mother, and hug you

Your Papa

2. The comet Ikeya-Seki.

193

[To Eric Celan]

[Tarbes,] 23 October 1965

My dear Eric, it is nice out and I went, to see it but also to send you a new card, to Tarbes, the capital of the former country of Bigorre. This is the *Hautes*-Pyrénées, but I have not smelled the freshness of the altitude. The city is frankly ugly. On the train, there were quite a few people going to Lourdes, which was on the way. In some places, the mountain showed itself. I wrote a little poem.[1]

I hug you both, Mama and you.

Papa

1. "Der Hengst" (The Stallion), *NKGA*, p. 231; *BIT*, p. 126.

194

[To Eric Celan]

Pau, 24 October 1965

Eric, my dear son! It is Sunday, I hope that you are having a good time with your friends. Mama no doubt went to see her friend from Reims—she will be there this evening and you will have so many things to tell her about!

Yesterday evening, while coming back from Tarbes, I wrote two poems,[1] then I thought for a long time, and intensely, of you and of Mama.

I hug you both, you and her.

Your Papa

Good school, good classes! See you!

---

1. "Pau, nachts" (Pau at Night) and "Pau, später" (Pau, Later) (*NKGA*, p. 230; *BIT*, pp. 124 and 126).

195

Toulouse, Monday, 25 October 1965

My Darling,

I am thinking of You, I am thinking of our son, of our love.

I would like for You to know how much I believe in our love. My strength—it has to come back, and yours too will come back. Eric is strong and courageous, intelligent—his difficulties are only temporary.

Pau, facing the Pyrenees, was calm. Here, under a somewhat troubled[1] sky, it is noisy, very noisy. I will take the train, in a little while, for Montpellier. Before that, I will try to telephone You.

Then, gradually, I will come get up.

I see You, I look at You.

I kiss You, my Beloved, I hold You and hold you up, I surround You with the future

Paul

---

1. The perhaps Franco-Celanian word employed, "chabouillé," is not lexicalized, but might call to mind the verb "chambouler" meaning "to upset, to shake up."

196

[To Eric Celan]

[Toulouse,] 25 October 1965

Lieber Eric! Ich schicke Dir einen Gruß aus Toulouse.[1] Toulouse, "red" or "rose" city, called that because of its numerous brick buildings. The Basilica is the oldest Roman church in the south of France, and its beauty is much more sober and more imposing than it is in the photo.[2]

Otherwise, the place du Capitole, in the center, between one and two o'clock, was quite Boul' Mich',[3] with its students in the cafés. It doesn't lack for noise, quite the contrary.—Good health! See you soon. I hug you both, Mama and you.

Papa

1. (Dear Eric! I am sending you a greeting from Toulouse.)
2. The postcard's inscription: "Toulouse—City of Art, Town of Violets—The Insignia of the Basilica Saint-Serinin (eleventh to thirteenth century)—Masterpiece of Roman art."
3. Boulevard Saint-Michel.

197

[To Eric Celan]

[Montpellier,] 26 October 1965

My dear Eric, here is your daily card, from Montpellier[1] this time, where I spent the night.

The sea is not far away, but I will not go play the fish. I feel like some altitudes and ascents.—Work well!

I hug your mother and I hug you.

Your Father

1. The postcard's inscription: "Montpellier (Hérault)—General view and Towers of the Saint-Pierre Cathedral."

198

Avignon, 26 October 1965

My Darling,

Here I am in the Café de la Gare, in Avignon, the fortified city, in front of two rows of plane trees,[1] full of leaves, forming a vault of crowns.

I will come back here with You and with our love found again, renewed.

Here is another little poem written last night in Montpellier.[2]

I kiss You, yes,

Paul

Die Unze Wahrheit tief im Wahn,

an ihr
kommen die Teller der Waage
vorübergerollt,
beide zugleich, im Gespräch,

das kämpfend in Herz-
höhe gestemmte Gesetz,
Sohn, siegt.[3]

———

Montpellier
25.10.1965

The ounce of truth deep in madness,

up to it
come the plates of the scale
rolling over,
both together, in conversation,

struggling, raised
to heart-level, the law,
son, will win.[4]

228

1. Avignon was the first stop on PC and GCL's honeymoon in Provence, in late December 1952. For PC, plane trees had a benevolent symbolic value tied, also, to that honeymoon trip. PC and GCL will never return to Avignon.
2. During this week in October, PC seems to have addressed only this poem, "Die Unze Wahrheit," to GCL (see *NKGA*, pp. 231–2).
3. In a letter dated 29 March 1965, Jean Starobinski had written to PC: "My father was a Jew according to the law of the heart (and not according to ritual); You belong to this same community, and I feel myself more strongly attached to it today." See above, no. 138, n. 1. See also Jeremiah 31:33 and Ezekiel 36:26–27.
4. See also "The Ounce of Truth," *BIT*, p. 128.

199

L'Isle-sur-Sorgue, 26 October 1965

My Darling,

Avignon, our nuptial city—I am looking at my ring—what could I have done without You? I just said this to You: I will come back here with You, with our love found again.

The idea occurred to me to go see René Char. Also to get away from cities a little bit, taking advantage of the buses. Then, in the direction of Fontaine-de-Vaucluse—you remember: "...Und wir sangen die Warschowjanka. / Mit verschilften Lippen, Petrarca";[1] that was, turned toward the Siberia of Exiles, toward Poetry, Exile and Land of the Pride of Man, toward this "Judenlocke, wirst nicht grau,"[2] that was, surrounding us, with Eric, our tenacious raison d'être—it is still that—so, no touristy fountain, no Poet-Terminus, no Laure-Hostelry.[3]

Took the Saumane Road, found Char's house—he was not there. It is better that way.

I went a few kilometers on foot and I saw this Provençal landscape again that I do not at all know how to love without You.

I am waiting for a bus. (And, also, for something beyond the Why and Wherefore, giving me back some aplomb.)

You see: I speak to You, still and always.[4]

Paul

1. Penultimate stanza of "Hinausgekrönt," a poem in the fourth and last cycle of *NR* (see *NKGA*, p. 158; *SPP*, p. 190).
2. Line eight of "Mandorla," a poem in the second cycle of *NR* (*NKGA*, p. 146; *SPP*, p. 172).
3. Fontaine-de-Vaucluse, known for its spring, which is the source of the Sorgue river, was the place of Petrarch's exile. Petrarch retired there at the age of thirty-three, after meeting Laura in an Avignon church on 6 April 1327.
4. See nos 63, 106, 135, 136, 186, 203.

200

[To Eric Celan]

[L'Isle-sur-la-Sorgue, 26 October 1965]

Hello from here, hello from everywhere, for everywhere!

See you soon! Bye!

Papa

201

[To Eric Celan]

[Avignon,] 26 October 1965

We will come here, all three of us, Mama, you, and me, and we will dance, with joy.[1] But in Paris, there are also bridges, and there too, in our way, we will dance.

See you soon

Papa

1. Postcard caption: "Reminder of Avignon." The postcard presents views of the Palais des Papes, the Bridge of Avignon, and fortifications. PC's reference is to the famous children's song "Sur le pont d'Avignon."

202

My Darling,

Valence—God, how could I have thought it was pretty! It seems pretty lousy to me.

A poem,[1] for You, my Beloved, accompanies these poor lines, written by the bad traveler that I am. It was our "green Berbers"[2] who, from afar, from so close, had me write it.

I hurt You profoundly, I know it well. But my return from Frankfurt was, in some way, the return of a warrior—of a Jewish warrior.

My Jewess, I hug You. Hug our son, Jewish, who, with us, struggles.[3]

Paul

In den Geräuschen, wie unser Anfang,
in der Schlucht,
wo du mir zufielst
—es war eine Schlucht—,
zieh ich die Spieldose auf, wieder,
du weißt:
die unsichtbare,
die
unhörbare.

———

Endgültige Fassung

Spieldose—boîte à musique
aufziehen—remonter

In the noises, like our beginning,
in the ravine,
where you fell to me
—it was a ravine—,
I wind up the music box, again,
you know:

the invisible,
the
inaudible.[4]

1. "In den Geräuschen," *NKGA*, p. 232.
2. See no. 121.
3. See the last stanza of "The Ounce of Truth" (no. 198).
4. See *BIT*, p. 128.

203

[Paris, 21 November 1965]

To find our love again

Paul

21 November 1965

Das Wort vom Zur-Tiefe-Gehn,[1]
das wir gelesen haben.
Die Jahre, wortlos, seither.
Wir sind es noch immer.[2]

Weißt du, der Raum ist unendlich.
Weißt du, sie fliegen nicht weit.
Weißt du,
nur was ich dir zuschwieg,
hebt uns hinweg in die Tiefe

The word of Going-to-the-Depth,
that we read.
The years, wordless, since then.
We are still what we are.

You know, space is endless.
You know, they do not fly far away.
You know,
only what my silence confided in you
lifts us away into the depths.[3]

1. See *NKGA*, p. 129.
2. See no. 63, 106, 135, 136, 154, 186.
3. See also *SPP*, p. 137.

204

[To Monique Gessain]

78 rue de Longchamp, 27 November 1965

My dear Monique,

Here is a note for Gisèle[1]—I only heard from her through Solange, and by telephone.

Please understand me: Gisèle needs to return with Eric, Eric needs to be in his home, he needs to take up his work again.

Me, I am ready for a calm dialogue—my trouble comes only from this separation, to which, certainly, I contributed by my departure for England.

I thank You, Monique, for all that You do. Send me a note.

Paul

78 rue de Longchamp, 26 November 1965

My Darling, quickly, give me a sign of life, written by You, Eric's news, written by him.

I am waiting—do not delay responding to me.

I hug You, with Eric.

Paul

Quickly, my Darling, we need to do everything for Eric, and we will help him to live as best as we can.

1. After a brief trip to Switzerland (Basel and Neuchâtel, 21–23 November 1965), PC returns to Paris, the day of his forty-fifth birthday, in a state of extreme despair and exaltation. During the night of 23 to 24 November 1965, PC attacks GCL and attempts to kill her with a knife. GCL and EC flee and take refuge with their neighbors, the Lalandes. On 25 November 1965, PC, having planned to go to Rome, decides to leave for London, where his aunt, Berta Antschel, lives. But he returns to Paris the following day. When he arrives at rue de Longchamp on 26 November 1965, PC, in the midst of a crisis of delusion, leaves in search of his absent son. GCL hurries to pick up EC at the end of his judo class to find refuge with her sister, Monique Gessain. PC, in search of his family, goes to the home of Monique and Robert Gessain, who conceal from him the presence of GCL and EC. The following day, deciding that it is necessary to leave Paris, GCL goes with EC to Cormeilles-en-Parisis (Val-d'Oise), to stay with a childhood friend, Ileana de Vogüé. On 28 November 1965, at the request of GCL and PC's doctors, nurses of the psychiatric hospital of Garches (Hauts-de-Seine) come to get PC. They place him in a straitjacket (PC will write, on 1 March 1967, "DIE LIEBE, zwangsjackenschön" (Love, Straitjacket-pretty), *NKGA*, p. 245; *BIT*, p. 167. On 3 December 1965, it is decided to transfer PC to the psychiatric clinic of Suresnes. On 4 December 1965, GCL goes to Garches. On 5 December 1965, PC is transferred to Suresnes. GCL refers to all these events in her planner.

205

[Paris,] Tuesday, 30 November 1965

Paul, Paul,

What can I say? I came home with Eric yesterday evening, he courageously went back to school, I am trying to get up again, Madame Magder will help me.

So there's no need to worry about us.

But you need to be cared for, you need to find yourself again. Since your return from Germany in September, you haven't been doing well. Please, let yourself be cared for, it is necessary, and don't lose courage. Paul, Paul, please!

Gisèle

206

[Suresnes, 6? December 1965]

I am, as You no doubt know, in the Hospital of the Suresnes Castle—I would also ask You to give me, as often as possible, news, Eric's and Yours, written by him.

What to say?

I need pyjama pants—wool pyjamas would be best.

Help Eric—he will help You in turn. I am thinking of You and hug my son.

Paul

Could You send me the *Choix de Poèmes* by Éluard?[1]—I forgot to ask if it was possible, but You could perhaps find out by calling.

---

1. *Choix de poèmes 1914–1941* (Paris: Gallimard, 1942).

207

78 rue de Longchamp
Tuesday, 7 December 1965

Paul, there is no need to worry about us. Eric is doing very well, he was, as you know, unhappy about all that happened at home, but now he has started again, found his strength again, work is going better, he is nice and well behaved and tries hard. He surely needs a vacation, calm, very much, but all is well for him, he is still just as happy with the boy scouts, with judo, and he likes school too, he is working hard.

I, as you can imagine, have suffered a lot these days. I have become skinnier, slept little, and my blood pressure has fallen. Madame Magder gave me the same treatment as the other time, and that will help me to recover.

But you, Paul, you have to take care of yourself, you have to recover, you were doing so badly for over two months. You waited too long, now you have to, you absolutely have to find your calm again, the true you. The true you is so far from images, from signs that carried you along further than you thought: all the way to putting in doubt my loyalty and making it impossible for me to come home.

I am thinking of you ceaselessly. I know how unhappy you are, I know how everything is difficult. But have courage, you must beat the illness, you must live, write, find yourself again in the true.

In this hope

Gisèle

208

Château de Suresnes, 10 rue Gallieni,[1]

9 September[2] 1965

Gisèle, I am sending You these lines, after having received, a while ago, Yours from 7 December. (You will find a letter for You in the folder of letters from the month of November, above the radiator.)

But of course, I am glad to know that You are doing better and that our son is well. It was, as You know well, very hard for me to find myself, upon my return from London, before such a terrible choice.[3] I have done everything to, as you say, *find myself again* in the true.

I have to beat the illness, you tell me. Certainly, but here, at the Suresnes Castle, they simply communicated to me, in person, that I was *interned*.* Do you realize what that means?[4] You have to do everything so that I can leave Suresnes and get into a clinic subsidized by the Ministry of National Education.** Do it quickly. You will have done it not only for me, but also for Eric and you, and, since you tell me that I have to write—writing is, for me, making poems—for poetry. According to an old habit, which you know from me, I take you at your word: *In this hope!* Hug Eric and thank him for me for his letter. Write to me quickly!

Paul

I cannot remain removed for too long from my milieu, from my activities, from things.

[In the margin:] Thanks for the pyjamas and the shirt.

---

1. Actually "quai Gallieni." The clinic was in a castle in the middle of a park bordering on the Seine.
2. Actually: December (the correct month was added by GCL).
3. Is this "choice" the same as the one expressed in one of his last letters to GCL, on 14 January 1970—"Before the choice between my poems and our son, I have chosen: our son"? (See below, no. 463). In his reading of Lichtenberg in the clinic at Le Vésinet the previous May, PC had underlined, in the preface: "Kinderzeugen und Bäumepflanzen sind ihm wichtiger als Bücherschreiben" (Making children and planting trees are more important to him than writing books). In Jean-Paul Sartre's preface to Mallarmé's poems, PC underlines: "Pas un jour ne s'est
* No time frame was specified to me.

écoulé sans qu'il ne fût tenté de se tuer et, s'il a vécu, c'est pour sa fille" (Not a single day passed without his being tempted to kill himself and, if he lived, it was for his daughter); see no. 146, n. 2.

4. The law of 30 June 1838 (Public Health Code in France) allows for two modes of internment: "voluntary internment" (*placement volontaire*) and "compulsory internment" (*placement d'office*) decided upon by the administrative authority, the prefect of the relevant region. PC is in "compulsory internment." According to the law of 30 June 1838, the sick person cannot leave the place in which they have been interned until a new decree is issued by the prefecture, based on a "medical certificate from the doctor of the establishment indicating that the sick person has been healed or has improved"; see *Manuel de psychiatrie*, ed. Bernard Ey (Paris: Brosse Masson et Companie, 1963); and see no. 220.

** La Verrière⁵ would be one.

5. Name of the commune of Yvelines (to the southwest of Paris, today integrated in the new town of Saint-Quentin-en-Yvelines) where the psychiatric clinic of the Mutuelle Générale des enseignants was located. PC will never be hospitalized in La Verrière.

209

[Suresnes,] 14 December 1965

My dear Gisèle, I thank You very much for Your good letter from the twelfth, which reached me yesterday evening.

Thanks for giving me Your news, and Eric's news. I am glad about what You tell me about his work at school, glad about what he told me about it himself; it is, don't You think, reassuring. May the vacation, close already, strengthen him, may it procure for him lots of joy!

You too, this little change will do You good—I wish that for You.

I have not yet thanked You for sending me Éluard's Poems.¹ There is something very springlike in these poems.

You tell me to find myself again—certainly, I ask for no more and I am doing, as you see, everything possible. Be thanked in advance for all that you are doing for me in this sense.

Thanks for wishing me courage. I am thinking of you.

Paul

I am writing to Eric, and will enclose the letter that I am addressing to him with this one.

[To Eric Celan]

My dear Eric,

Thanks for your good letters—I am very glad to know that you started work at school again; I am proud of your results, and very glad also to know that you are having fun.

Soon it will be vacation, you will go skiing—don't forget that there too you have to know how to have fun—you will see plenty of beautiful things.

As for the trimester's grades, I would like to see them too—but the essential thing is of course that you make true progress in all the subjects.

Thanks for thinking of me, Eric. I am thinking of you, as you well know.

I hug you

Your father

1. See no. 211, n. 1.

210

Suresnes, 20 December 1965

My dear Gisèle,

Thanks first of all for Your long letter and for the news it brings me. I am, as you can easily guess, happy and proud of Eric's results at his school. I did not yet receive the letter from him that You mentioned, but it cannot be long in arriving.

Your vacation is soon—but I hope these lines will reach You still before You leave for Montana. I also hope that You will be content with your accommodations there. I will ask of You, for Eric just as much as for Yourself, a bit of caution. Write to me regularly—I will try to do the same thing. To start, tell me which day You are leaving and when You will be back.

About myself what can I say? The days are long. I am subjected to an antidepressant treatment, by injection. Believe me: I am doing my best. You tell me that You know how difficult it is—I thank You for this understanding. As I thank You for wishing me courage. Tell Eric that I am thinking of him and that I am waiting for his news.

Paul

Thanks for the pyjamas and the shirts.

211

Suresnes, 23 December 1965

Thanks, Gisèle, for the two letters. The first, which arrived yesterday morning, was, with its commentary on Eric's grades, a bit dry, but the second—the one from 21 December—which arrived in the afternoon, and which I did not at all expect, was able to produce something like astonishment.

Yes, the days here are long. I did not ask you for any books except for the Poems of Éluard:[1] first of all because, when leaving for Vésinet,[2] I had brought some,[3] and then because I had trouble reading. They bring me, every evening, *Le Monde*.

Concerning treatments, I have consented to them since my arrival here. Last night, I had a bit of a fever (38?),[4] this morning too, so because of that I have to take pills for three days.

I would like for Eric and you to feel well in Montana. It has rained here, so I tell myself that up there a good snow, very soft and copious, is covering your slopes. Have a good vacation! Tell Eric that I am proud of him and that I hug him.

Paul

1. The evening before writing this letter, PC had underlined and dated, in Éluard's *Choix de poèmes: Musicien (Les Nécessités de la vie*, 1921), the distich without a title in *L'Amour, la poésie*, 1929); among those non-dated: "Couronnée de mes yeux" (*La Rose publique*, 1934).
2. PC means Garches; PC had been hospitalized at Le Vésinet in May of the same year.
3. Including Goethe, *Spruchweisheit in Vers und Prosa*, vol. 3 of *Sämtliche Werke* (Leipzig: Tempel, no date).
4. Or 100.4° Fahrenheit.

212

Suresnes, Tuesday, 28 December 1965

Thanks, Gisèle, for your two letters, the one written the day before your departure and after your meeting with Doctor R., and the second, which arrived last night, bringing me the first impressions of Montana. At the same time I received Eric's wishes—I am delighted to see him so relaxed, so much at ease with colors.[1]

To judge from the place it occupies in the newspapers, Crans seems to be even worse than You described it to me two years ago and I am very glad that You were able to choose Montana.

Too bad that the hotel is a bit noisy—which side of the skating rink is it on?—but in a place like Montana, one quite quickly gets used to this kind of background noise.

Nourish Yourselves well, offer, to Eric and to Yourself, little extras—the Relais de la Poste occurs to me, with the meals we took there and which were not at all expensive.

You ask me to speak of myself. Here You are: the treatment with injections, about which the doctors (Dr. R. and Dr. Fon.) told me that it was equivalent to what they had envisioned administering orally, proves to be less effective anyway; they propose the other one to me again, with Moditen,[2] for a duration of three weeks to start—and I am, I admit, still hesitant and am granting myself time to reflect.

Apart from that, the days are what they can be. My little temperature has disappeared completely, and that is better too, since, to track down all these little reactivated banalities, it is really better to choose one's setting.—I asked if, upon your return, you could come see me—but Dr. R. is clearly opposed to that.

I wish you as well as Marie-Thérèse beautiful days in Montana, I wish you a very happy new year

Paul

P.S. Do you remember the blue-lined notebooks I brought back from Montana? Can you bring me back a few of those?

[To Eric Celan]

My dear Eric,

Your New Year's Wishes with the mountains so well populated by pine trees—but also these famous ski slopes that one can imagine there, as famous as they are powdery—with the sky so clearly revealed, so benevolent—thanks for all that!

I know that you found your form very quickly—keep it, develop it. How proud I am of your prowess in school; I am equally proud of yours as a skier. (A bit of caution, still, right?)

I wish you a happy new year
and hug you

Your father

1. On PC's relation to colors, see nos 71, 182, 184, 189, 414.
2. A neuroleptic, or antipsychotic, drug (fluphenazine).

213

Suresesnes, 30 December 1965

My dear Gisèle,

Thanks for the two illustrated cards, the one from your arrival and the one from the 27th, confirming receipt of my letter. Everything you tell me breathes contentment, it is almost contagious, and I am indeed content, every time that I think of Eric and you in Montana.

Today, I also received your package of chocolates and your letter from the 28th—things really do not delay in coming.

My flu is completely gone, I don't have any temperature. I had thought I would be able to write to you today that I had begun the oral antidepressant treatment, but the drugs have not yet arrived and it will probably be tomorrow that I take my first pill.

Everything you tell me toward the end of your letter is truly nice and it is very touching for me. I will probably ask you, when you return in a few days, to take a few steps (regarding Verrière too).

You have already found Yourself again—and You will continue. I am happy that Eric is well—tell him that. And tell him that I hug him.

Paul

214

Suresnes, Monday, 3 January 1965[1]

My dear Gisèle,

Here is a note to greet you upon your return to rue de Longchamp. May this new year be good to You, good with You! May You continue to help Eric and to work for Yourself.

I don't have much news to share with You about me. On Christmas Eve, I started the Moditen treatment. The treatment with injections (the name of which I do not know) continues.

Like You, I think that the transfer to La Verrière is desirable and must be done in the shortest time frame: I ask You to act to this end, energetically.

A note addressed to Eric accompanies these lines.

I am thinking of You

Paul

[To Eric Celan]

[Suresnes,] 3 January 1965

My dear Eric,

Thanks for your card from 30 December, with its so pretty view over the Rhône Valley and the mountains, with, above all, the good news about your form in general and the form of skiers in particular. Everything seems to be going well, and I congratulate myself for that as I congratulate you. Same also goes, moreover, for your palette, given you by your aunts. I suppose that here too there is considerable progress—with your participation of course. (It doesn't work all by itself, a palette, right?)

But here you are now at home, with, all around you, a big new year completely open, and, from a school standpoint, you will have to apply yourself.

Happy New Year, Eric! Things open themselves to you, come toward you, wait for you to come toward them.

Happy and Good New Year!

Your father

1. Actually: 1966.

215

Suresnes, Wednesday, 5 December 1966

My dear Gisèle,

You must have returned yesterday with Eric, I was expecting to hear from You today at the latest, and it is because I have not that I address this note to You, concerned.

But Thursday, with Eric's return to school, is, certainly, very busy for You.

I hope to hear from You, by mail or by a note left at the castle, by tomorrow.

I am thinking of Eric, I am thinking of you.

Paul

216

[Suresnes,] Wednesday
6 January [1966], after lunch

My dear Gisèle,

Doctor Fon. came by a little while ago for his visit and told me that You had telephoned yesterday afternoon at three—so here I am reassured about You.

I hope that Eric has found his return to school easy.

As for me, I will, calmly, continue to swallow my Moditen pills: Doctor R. finds that that is going well.

Yesterday I remembered the two readings that I accepted for mid-February: Geneva and Zurich. I cannot give that up.

I gaze at You and think of You

Paul

[In the margin:] If You come by, could You leave me one of my *wool* pyjamas? Thanks in advance.—Maybe You can sort the mail a little?

217

Paris, Friday, 7 January 1966

My dear Paul,

I received your two letters when I went to the office before seeing the doctor. I had telephoned the day before yesterday, but could not be seen until today, at the same time I left a letter for you as well as the notebooks and writing paper that I brought back from Montana. I thought that if I had sent them by mail you wouldn't have heard from me earlier.

I spoke to the doctor about La Verrière, but he told me that for the moment it is impossible administratively and that we would have to wait still before taking steps in that direction. Despite that I will get back in touch with Doctor Lé. You will probably also mention it Sunday to the doctor who will come to see you. I hope that you know that I am doing and will do everything possible so that you are well taken care of and in the least tedious conditions.

You ask me if I am sorting your mail, I am organizing it simply by putting the date of arrival on the envelopes. It is accumulating, lots of books and publications, letters too, and, I think, one from Böschenstein. I don't know what you want me to do. If you want, I can send all of that to you at Suresnes, I don't know if you feel up to dealing with letters from Fischer and others right now. You'll tell me what you want me to do.

There have not been many phone calls, but Walter called asking for confirmation of a planned discussion.[1] He called back fifteen days later. I told him that you had to leave Paris and that I didn't know when you would be back. The Austrian Institute also called about the anthology, since they heard that you had refused the rights.[2] The director hopes that you will change your mind, attaching great importance to your participation and considering the presence of your poems in this anthology to be essential. I told him that in your absence and without hearing from you he could only respect and adhere to your decision. He asked if he could call again this January. The secretary general of the École called twice to ask very kindly how you are and conveyed his wishes for your prompt recovery. Claude Davide too, who was sorry to hear that you had to leave to rest.

Tell me if I can do something and what you want me to say on the phone. Just before, a Monsieur Blokh, a Russian, I think, requested books of Russian poems he needs which he lent you two or three years ago. I asked him to write and told him you were absent from Paris, since I could neither retain nor understand the names of the Russian poets in question.

Eric has started working on Latin, me too, but I don't feel very good at that. A composition coming up, in German: we prepare it a little every day. Yesterday he went to play with his Bourgies cousins at their house, where I had left him before coming to Suresnes. He was very glad.

Answer me, about the mail and the phone calls.

Know that I do not forget you and will do everything for you to be treated in the best conditions, but that doesn't depend entirely on me, on the contrary.

I am thinking of you, you know it

Gisèle

---

1. See no. 167, n. 2.

2. The anthology in question is *Poésies autrichiennes 1900–1965*, trans. Maurice Bouchet et al. (Vienna: Berland, 1966). On André Thérive, see no. 220, n. 4.

218

My dear Gisèle,

Thanks for your nice letter. It was given to me just before dinner, with the notebooks and the superb writing paper, and I was very happy with it. I often reread You.

Doctor R. came yesterday evening also, he kind of just blew in, announcing to me that Dr. Fon., with whom he saw You yesterday, during today's visit, will give me the details of Your meeting from yesterday.

It's been done: Doctor Fon. just stopped by—I learned, first of all, that the doctors think that the two readings, in Geneva and in Zurich,* come a bit early.—I had, myself, thought that it would be precisely a good way to resume contact—and I believe that still. But I do not have the dates—very close together—in mind—isn't it toward February twentieth? In any case, it would be difficult to postpone. We must insist.

Then, Doctor Fon. spoke to me about La Verrière as . . . a very exclusive establishment ("They are playing with a closed box office, it's all booked" etc.). Doctor Fon. also tells me that at La Verrière they expect the sick person to follow a strict regimen if they are to take him.—You see that there's good reason to complete the picture that You have of it.—I think it would be best for me to submit here to the treatment begun that, in principle, should be finished by January twentieth.

Then the mail. Here, you can see, there is no opposition to that (which amazes me a bit). So put it all in a big envelope and drop it off for me . . . and be kind enough to drop it off: I do not like it when mail is readdressed etc. Then, do the following: drop off little packages of letters, with a little note from you inside.

I am delighted about Eric's success—you do not even know how happy I am when I reread what You tell me about it. I am thinking of Eric, I am thinking of You

Paul

1. Actually: January.

*I planned to bring You, if You felt like it

219

Thanks, my Darling, for all that. I will not keep the books, they're too cumbersome.

Thanks again. Till soon

Paul

I sent You a rather long letter this morning.

220

[Suresnes] Sunday, 9 January 1966

My dear Gisèle,

Thanks for Your good letters—Your letters so copiously good. I reread them often.

I will try to respond to their two essential points.

First of all Eric: I am proud and happy about his results—tell him that.

My stay here, my transfer to La Verrière, respectively:

This morning, I had a visit—accompanied by the two doctors from here—from a doctor from the Prefecture, Dr. Du., who explained to me that I was in a state of administrative internment, by virtue of a law from 1838.[1]—I had already had to face that during a prior visit by the same doctor and the two doctors from here.—This time Dr. Du. (or Dou.?) told me that it was a de facto situation that I had the right to refuse. That is what, obviously, I did. That opens the Verrière perspective again and I ask you to contact Dr. Lé. and to explain the situation to him. It is essential. And, allow me the pun that, here, is not one: existential. Be sure that I appreciate your help. (Would it be necessary to consult a lawyer? Where to find one? On the advice of the associate of Seghers?)

My readings in Geneva and Zurich (mid-February): the doctors are against it, it's too soon.

My mail: I don't really know, certain things could, possibly, distract me. Send it to me or rather drop it off for me in an envelope once a week.

Walter: I will write him, but I do not have his address—yes, I have it.

Blokh: he is the father of the couple who invited us over once on rue du Bac. (She: dreadful painter, he: novelist.) I don't know where the book is, but I will search for it.[2]

But yes, tell people that I am not in Paris and that I am resting (in the country).

We will strive to get up again, to overcome.

I do not need any books—from time to time I open the Éluard volume, to find a line there—otherwise I read your letters and those of the son.

Perhaps we should take steps to see each other a few moments.[3] *Speak to me a bit of You.*

Gazing at you, thinking of you

Paul

For the packages of books that have arrived: open them, date the books, send me if possible a list of the authors and titles, chronological, with the names of the senders.

[In the margin:] P.S. For the Austrian anthology: I refuse to appear—as I have already made known to Fischer—in an anthology done by the collaborator A. Thérive.[4]

[In the margin:]* Tell the doctor from La Verrière that I want neither deep sleep nor electroshock therapy.[5]

1. See no. 208, n. 4.

The Celans had been invited to dine with Alexandre and Nadia Blokh on 13 February 1963. Blokh is the pseudonym of the novelist and translator Jean Blot, who translated Osip Mandelstam's "About an Interlocutor," in *L'Éphémère* (no. 4, September 1967, pp. 66–73), and is the author of a monograph on Mandelstam, in which he evokes his conversations with PC about the Russian poet (Paris: Seghers, 1972, p. 115).

2. Given the seriousness of what has happened, the doctors still refuse to allow PC and GCL to see each other.

3. André Thérive was not the editor but one of the translators of the anthology. The president of the Association of Literary Critics of the *Flambeau*, an organ of the Croix-de-Feu, Thérive worked at the *Petit Parisien* and at *Nouveaux Temps* starting in 1940; in 1942, he participated in the Weimar Book Week. Upon the liberation of France, he was sentenced to eight months

in prison. After the war, he published numerous essays of literary criticism in *Revue des deux mondes* and *Les Nouvelles littéraires*. He was an officer of the Légion d'honneur.

4. PC seems never to have been given either deep sleep or electroshock therapy.

221

[Suresnes,] Tuesday, [11 January 1966]

My dear Gisèle,

Just a note about the mail: there is not much of any importance, aside from a few rare letters, New Year's wishes, quite numerous, then various banalities.

But when You came by here, with all that, I felt it, simply, grandly. So tell me what You are doing!

You have to tell *Starobinski* where I am. Personally, I would have liked to be able to speak with him—but that will be for another time. Tell him that I would like for the February reading to be postponed to later—April, May, for example—You have to write to Zurich—in the folder for August or September You will find the corresponding letter ("Radio Zurich").

It has snowed.

Where are my loved ones? They are here, I am looking at them, I am thinking of them—of You. Think of Yourself, You must.—I hug Eric.

Paul

Will You come by one day?

Do You want me to ask to see You?

[In the margin:] Do not come by too often, if that tires You out.[1] But if You come by, would You be so kind as to bring me my long cotton boxer shorts?

1. GCL spends almost every day at Suresnes in order to meet with the doctors, and to drop off and pick up the mail for PC.

222

[Suresnes, 21 January 1966]

My Darling,

I love You. All, in me, would like to tell you that.
Stand firm. Thanks for taking care of Eric.
I kiss You

Paul

Friday evening

223

Suresnes, 25 January 1965[1]

My dear Gisèle,

Here is a note to find You, during these very hard days for You, for me
as well.

With Doctor R. we make new resolutions, we envision a solution.

Will You not come to Suresnes for a short visit? I hope so

I am thinking of you

Paul

1. Actually: 1966.

224

78 rue de Longchamp, 26 January 1966

My dear Paul,

I know how difficult everything is for you, and this thought does not
leave me. Be assured that I am constantly in touch with the doctors taking
care of you, directly or indirectly. They alone, as you know, can help you
right now.

Of course I will come to see you, but Doctor Fon., whom I just called,
asks me to wait a few more days.

You speak to me so little in your letters. We saw each other last time in such a dramatic moment.[1] All my wishes, all my desires, go toward your cure, and I know that this is the aim of the doctors who are trying to help you. Patience, Paul, you need to find yourself again, to get back all your ability to concentrate, in order to do your work, to write, your memory too, you need to find calm again.

All that will come back, I know that it is a long time for you, believe me, I understand the extent of your suffering.

Eric is doing very well, school, judo, cub scouts, everything is going well.

See you soon, and don't lose your courage. You will find yourself again

Gisèle

1. Reference to PC's internment on 28 November 1965. See above, no. 204.

225

Suresnes, Monday, 31 January 1966

My dear Gisèle,

I've owed you a letter for a long time, and I several times worked up the momentum to write you one.

But what to say? With the known and the unknown...I embroider...I embroider on the right side, I would say, on the protected side too.

Where is Eric? Where are You? My two fundamental questions with, of course, a where am I? that merits being emphasized.

Little elevation with [text missing], you see. Let speak, whom? You two, my son and my wife.

I do not read at all—it's lamentable. May You avoid this phase ("phase"[1])!

I am taking—virtuously—a tour around my room—vast and virtuous in turn, but also very loud regarding the unarticulated or para-articulated. (God! Don't end with that!)

If You have a letter from Eric, copy it and give it to me.

I stop—I look at You

Paul

[On the back of the envelope:] They just brought me your letter from the 27th.

1. PC alludes to his use of this word in the context of the Goll Affair, which unfolded in three "phases": Phase I—1949–52, Phase II—1953–9, Phase III—1960–2.

226

78 rue de Longchamp
Tuesday, 1 February 1966

My dear Paul,

I just received your letter from yesterday. First of all, I must reassure you on one point: Eric and I are in Paris, rue de Longchamp. You ask me, if I have a letter from Eric, to copy it for you and send it to you. But he is with me. He is at school right now and must even be in the midst of composing his Latin to French translation. Yesterday evening and this morning (on Tuesdays, he goes at 9:30), we reviewed the vocabulary list and the use of cases together, he knew it well, and for the moment, it requires of course a major effort of memory, but he understands and manages very well. I think he even likes Latin now. Don't worry at all about him, he's still got the remnants of a cold but he's feeling very good. I help him with his work every evening. After dinner we read together, which he likes doing, and I try to hide my worries from him. He is calm and serene. This evening I will tell him to write to you. He doesn't do it often since, as you know, he has a lot to do for school and has only one desire, once he has finished, which is to play a bit and relax.

As for me, what can I say? You know Paul, I think of you ceaselessly, you cannot doubt it. To hold out, to help me to hold up in the midst of this drama of your health and also to be able to continue taking care of the son as well as I can, I have gone back to etching. From time to time I go to Lacourière, where the working atmosphere helps me a little and brings me out of a too great solitude. At home I work too.

I have gone back to working with my press, right now, every day, I make prints of my etchings. I also printed twenty copies of *Au lieu d'une inscription, En chemin, Les Filets encore*,[1] on a beautiful Japanese paper that I bought from Madame Chassepot at the same time as the press.

Soon I will start to create prints of *Noir-Argent*, the one that is in your room, and *Les Dunes toutes proches*.[2] I think I told you that I asked Frélaut to print ten copies of recent etchings, which I made last year, which are too big to do myself: first of all that would be tiring and then I am not set up to do it in good conditions and I don't manage to print them evenly enough when they are so large. This way, I give myself the possibility to show them and if necessary to leave prints in a gallery, also to sell them if the opportunity presents itself. I did not have any copies other than those that I need to keep with me.

I told you that the Point Cardinal gallery[3] has bought seven or eight of them, I think I'll be able to "deliver" them in eight days. Monsieur Hughes truly liked them, I think. He gave me good advice for trying to sell them among his colleagues, and I hope that will lead to something. As soon as I have the etchings printed by Frélaut, I think I will go to see the Maeght gallery,[4] to show them new ones—I hardly go out, I read little. My blood pressure has surely gone back up, but despite everything I am quite tired and I will probably go to see Madame Magder one of these days.

From day to day, I live a difficult destiny, a difficult life, as you know. My thoughts go to you, and I understand, believe me, your drama and your suffering. I will do all I can to help you, you know how hard it is.

It is not easy knowing you are at Suresnes, and I understand how frightful it is. I am eager to know that you are doing better and that we can envision a transfer to La Verrière, which would be a step toward a more normal life for you.

I am thinking, I am thinking of you ceaselessly.

All is so difficult, unjust in this world, for you, for many. Despite everything, it's necessary to hold out, to envision better days.

I received a note from Böschenstein, who had heard that you were ill and could not come to Geneva, he sincerely regrets that, sends his wishes for your prompt recovery and tells me that he lives with your poems and often encounters among his students young people who love and who are profoundly touched by your poetry.

Never forget that, even if you don't feel it all the time, know, Paul, that many live with your poetry, through your poetry.

I leave you now. I have to tidy up the house a bit, but there too, nothing to worry about, Carmen comes less often, but Eric and me, that doesn't make for too much work, and I manage very well, without doing too much.

I have not found steady work yet and maybe I will not manage to, it's not urgent, but I'm still looking. I will keep you posted.

Write to me, Paul, if you can. Don't lose confidence. You will find your calm again, your true self, your memory, your possibility for work.

I am thinking of you

Gisèle

1. *Au lieu d'une inscription—Statt einer Inschrift*, 1964; *En chemin—Unterwegs*, 1964; *Les filets encore—Die Netze wieder*, 1963.
2. *Noir-Argent—Silberschwarz*, 1963; *Les dunes toutes proches—Dunnennähe*, 1963. On the bilingual titles of GCL's prints, see above, no. 123, n. 4.
3. With the recommendation of René Char and André du Bouchet, GCL will present *Atemkristall* to Jean Hughes, head of the Galerie Le Point Cardinal (3 rue Cardinale, 6th arrondissement).
4. Galerie Adrien Maeght, 42 rue du Bac, 7th arrondissement.

227

[Suresnes] Thursday, 3 February 1966

My dear Gisèle,

Thanks for your letter, from yesterday, thanks for *your* letters, numerous and helpful, this whole time.—Eric wrote me too—I will thank him too, he deserves it so much.

Thanks for the package of letters: there is one that you likely saw: it announced to me the death of Margarete Susman, which happened on 16 January, in Zurich.[1] You know it well: it is a true loss.

I am enclosing with this page the letter from Radio Zurich,[2] with a letter that I ask you to post.* It is really time that I cancel—God knows I was happy to go to Zurich, for me a serene and welcoming city, with and also thanks to Margarete Susman. May my feather become a bit more agile again, and a bit closer to things that happen beyond my horizon-walls.

I am glad that your work is organizing itself around what, in art, you make live and you put into relief. Now, in etching, you realize yourself, in freedom.

For me, there were intestinal difficulties recently, but since yesterday it's over. (It was a lot of constipation, very painful.)—Now, a few secondary phenomena still have to disappear. Then—but when, this then?—we'll see.

Hug our son.

I speak to you. I look at you

Paul

P.S. You wrote to Böschenstein to cancel for me, right?

[Suresnes,] 4 February 1966

My dear Gisèle,

Another note to propose again that you come pay me a little visit here, one afternoon. (Doctor R. tells me that this does not pose, from their point of view, any problems.)—So come when you want, the earlier the better, after two in the afternoon, you will just need to present yourself to Doctor R. or his replacement, and they no doubt will bring you toward the pavilion where I am.

One more *urgent* thing: I am enclosing the letter from Radio Zurich—you have to tell them right away that I am tired and resting in the country, and thus will be prevented from coming to Zurich, as I had planned. Convey to them my sincere regrets and my hope of being able, on an occasion in the near future, to do a program of poems.—Write to them in French, in your name, from me. Their address is, it seems to me, Bernese—copy it from the envelope or the letterhead. Indeed, I wonder if it would not be simpler to telegraph ...

So—I am waiting for You. I hope that you come, simply. But if that is difficult for you, I ask you, I ask you, to say so simply, as always.

Paul

After reflection: Yes, send a telegram to Dr. Kurt Weibel Redakt[ion] Radio und Fernsehen[,] Schwarztorstraße 21[,] Bern: "Bedaure aufrichtig Lesung Zurich krankheitshalber absagen zu muessen mit den besten Gruessen Paul Celan."[3]

1. In a letter dated 27 January 1966, which most likely accompanied the announcement of the death of Margarete Susman at the age of ninety-four, Manfred Schlösser (director of Agora Verlag in Darmstadt and Zurich) proposes to PC to read to him, on the occasion of his stay in Zurich, the last "moving words of this wonderful woman."
2. In a letter dated 18 January 1966, Kurt Weibel, editor in chief of programs at the Swiss Radio and Television Society, asks PC for a photograph for publication in Radio Zurich's program; the recording of the reading had been scheduled for 20 February 1966.
3. "Sincerely regret having to cancel Zurich reading because of illness with best greetings."
 * I will wait until tomorrow to write it.

228

Clinique de la Faculté de Médecine
1 rue Cabanis, Paris, 14th [arrondissement]
Monday, 7 February 1966

My dear Gisèle,

Here is a note, with the new address, to keep you up to date. Furthermore, in Suresnes, they told me they kept you up to date.

So much so that yesterday, Sunday, visiting day here, I thought a little that You would come. The second visit is Thursday. I ask You to come.

Until then, I ask You to drop off for me (My name, here,* is Paul *Antschel*) two towels, a brush, a toothbrush, two washcloths, a pad of letter paper the same dimensions as this one, envelopes, two Bic pens. What else to say? I am doing my best.

Hug our son for me. Write to me, I need that, as I need letters from Eric

Paul

P.S. Please put the things I am asking you for in a *little* suitcase, which I will keep

Visits: Sunday and Thursday, one to three thirty

* Best is: Paul Antschel-Celan—that way they'll get used to both names.

229

[Paris,] Wednesday, 9 February 1966

My dear Gisèle,

I just received your letter and, at the same time, the visit from Doctor O. (whom I already saw once, the day before yesterday).

Yes, so come to see me tomorrow—I am looking forward to it. Everything is handled flexibly here; that is a quality I appreciate.

Ask, upon arriving, to be guided a bit toward the building where I am (University Clinic (director: Prof. Delay[1])).

Can you bring me a few oranges and a package of Lu butter biscuits? And also a little money, 30 new francs will suffice for me.

Hug Eric and congratulate him for me for his work at school.

I am waiting for you

Paul

1. Jean Delay, head of department of the University Clinic at the Sainte-Anne hospital, Chair of the Clinic for Mental Illnesses and the Brain at the Faculté de médecine in Paris.

230

[Paris,] Friday, [11 February 1966]

My Darling,

Thanks for coming yesterday, that gives me hope for us all.

This morning, I was seen by Professor Delay, then by his office neighbor, Professor Pi., whom we met at the Austrian Institute, and who recognized me immediately, then immediately, on the request of Professor Delay, saw me for an interview. Hug our son, I hug You

Paul

231

Paul, my darling,

Don't forget that I live very close to you, that I am thinking of you ceaselessly, and that nothing that happens to you can be foreign to me.

We have always had a difficult life. You may have believed, I know, that I kept my distance from you, it's only that I couldn't take any more because of your illness. But you will get away from all that. You will be able to find yourself again truly. You must trust in that. You are surrounded by the best doctors, who know who you are, who want to help you. I know that all that is very hard for you right now and has been for a long time, I think about it often.

Then, you will see, your strength will come back, and your memory and concentration and inner calm, through work too you will live again. That's what I am trying to do myself. It's the only thing I can do to hold out, to continue to help Eric become a man to, also to be.

Until soon, Paul, trust the doctors, there will be better days, I am waiting for you confidently too.

Until soon, until very soon.

Beside your son who loves you too,

who is waiting for you too

> Gisèle.

232

78 rue de Longchamp, 14 February 1966

Paul, my darling,

I thought of You this morning on my way to Cochin for that radiography. As soon as You know the result, tell me. I was able to reach Doctor O. and spoke to him, as you had asked me, about your intestinal problems, about the food and also your teeth. As soon as you have seen a dentist and an eye doctor, tell me how things look.

I think often of you, of all the courage that's necessary to have yourself treated and to get out of this bad state. Let's not lose confidence, Paul, let's believe in better days.

Madame Zucman, that doctor I had met at La Messuguière, came today and bought two etchings from me, *Gris et noir*, you know, it's the one in your room and that you like, and also *Petite composition*,[1] which is now sold out, all we have left are the first three numbers that belong to us and which I keep from every published etching for the three of us. So today I made another 20,000 old francs.

When I come back, do you want me to bring you the latest etchings I've made these days, to show them to you? I'm not so sure if they're good. I draw a lot but I don't always attain a result.

I am beginning a new series of etchings in the same format as the book—maybe we can do something with it. Every time that I make one, I am conscious of your enormous contribution to them. Not one of my etchings would be there without you. You know it. And when you told me that in my copperplates you recognized your poems, you could not have told me anything more beautiful or more grand for me.

Until soon, Paul, until very soon, beside you,

with your son

Gisèle

Tomorrow I will go to the studio until Eric's return, when French to Latin and German as well as Latin and German to French translations await me. But I can still cope with the sixth grade level, except for math, where the time zones are completely beyond me. Eric's scientific knowledge is already expansive, but knowledge of the Meridian and of meridian-like things will come to him too, I am sure of it.

---

1. *Gris et Noir—Grau und Schwarz* (1958), *Petite composition—Kleine Komposition* (1958).

233

[Paris,] Tuesday, 15 February 1966

Thanks, my Beloved, for your letter from the 13th: it illuminates my heart, as well as the one, very breezy, very much at ease at the same time, from our Eric.

Here, everything moves along and yesterday was the bronchial exam I told you about. Result: nothing with the bronchi to worry about.

On the way back here, I run into Ho.,[1] doing his rounds, who tells me that you have to organize your visits after I have seen him about this. He also spoke to me about a meeting with me, but I don't have, today, any news. That will come, I can wait.

You don't know—well yes, you know very well what your letter constitutes for me. You too, you need rest—but the knowledge that I am safe from relapses is there, isn't it, to wrap you in the kind of thoughts that we know—always—how to make rise and last in us.

I hug you, and I hug Eric

Paul

[In the margin:] Imagine that: in the X-ray department, I ran into Doctor Mâle[2].

1. It was in fact Dr. O.
2. See no. 138, n. 1.

234

[Paris, 16 February 1966]

My Darling,

I got Your letter from the 14th around noon, —it is yet again, like the preceding ones, "soulful,"[1] it is a joy.

Saw, after the doctors' visit, Doctor Ho. (is that written correctly?),[2] who told me, among other things, that you can call him and see him whenever you want. I told him how much gestures like this can touch me. Then certain "themes" of the campaign against me[3]—he understands all that.

About your visits, he thinks that they would have to be spread out, but I wrested an—elastic—*every ten days* from him.

What to do about next Sunday, scheduled with You? I would say, come that Sunday, and then we will see.

Say a word to Eric excusing me for not writing to him—but I will write to him soon—other than through you.

I look at you and hug you. Hug our son.

Paul

1. Celan's invented word, "âmeux," is a literal translation into Franco-Celanian of the German word "Seelisches," a substantivized adjective, derived from the adjective "seelisch" (soulful, of the soul), derived from the noun "Seele" (soul).
2. Dr. O.
3. See no. 75, n. 1.

235

[Paris,] Wednesday, 16 February 1966

My Darling,

I realize that I did not respond to your question about your etchings.

I would very much like to see all of them, but I worry that the conditions here are not very accommodating for this kind of exhibition. So bring the ones that are not too big, that you can fit into a portfolio.

Concision of this letter—you know that too has to get better. This past summer, when You were in Provence, I found, among other things, my epistolary strength again.[1] Once more I will find it.

I kiss you, come Sunday,

I kiss You again,

Paul

1. See the letters from summer 1965.

236

[Paris,] Thursday, 17 February 1966

My Darling,

Yes, come this Sunday* and bring a few of your etchings, the ones that are not too big: You know where I am, with its possibilities.

I saw O. yesterday, he seems content with the evolution of my state. (The encephalogram did not show anything, he tells me.)

The bronchial exam was a bit tiring, but the results, there too, are good.—Dr. O. told me that you can come see him or call him any time—I thanked him warmly for that.

But boredom digs itself a little place—I hope that the treatment will offer a solution.

Hug Eric, I hug You

Paul

P.S. Mademoiselle Arrietta (I don't know if I am writing her name correctly)[1] expects you Saturday, to organize the insurance paperwork. She has a good head and awaits you, with this head, Saturday afternoon.

For me, do not forget, please, the two cups made of plastic.

---

* but let Doctor O. know in advance
1. Reine *Arrieta* was the social worker at the University Clinic.

237

[Paris,] Wednesday, 23 February 1966

My Darling,

The good news: there's nothing wrong with my eyes, but I will have to wear glasses.

No treatment yet: they are waiting for the X-rays of my lung (right), for a stain that they did not manage to locate, to decipher. But the radiologist and the doctors from bronchology were loud and clear: there is nothing that can be a cause for worry.

So that's that. This morning, I went to the ophthalmologist, around eleven o'clock, a nurse comes to get me: it is Delay who receives me with O. and another (an internist probably).—A bit less affable, but all the same very nice. He has my file shown to him, the X-rays, O. comments on all that. Let this man act as I hope he can!

We also spoke about La Verrière, which he did not seem exceedingly fond of.

And You? Your etchings are very beautiful. You know it well. And my poetry will always enjoy being in its glimmers, lights, in its ravines, and guided by its asperities.[1]

Hug Eric.

I hug You

Paul

P.S. Can you bring me, on Sunday, two clean pairs of underwear? Don't forget to ask O. for permission to see me.

1. See no. 134.

238

[Paris,] Wednesday, 2 March 1966

My Darling,

Doctor D., who called me today, around noon, told me that he had received a call from you and that you reproached yourself for not coming back until March 10th, or Thursday in eight days.

I thank you, my Darling, for this act, thanks for helping me to learn what waiting is.[1]

As for my treatment here, nothing definitive—tomorrow, after the "Big visit," that's to say the visit from Professor Deniker,[2] the doctors will meet to establish my treatment.

My teeth: I will have to see the Hospital stomatologist. So, please drop off the Insadol for Dr. D., they will have it brought to him.

(Please drop off for me a *metal* teaspoon (*not* silver!).)

Hug our Eric, please spoil him. And tell me what we, Eric and me, can give you for my birthday.

I wrap you in my arms, I hug you

Paul

[In the margin:] Dr. D. told me that you already have (or will soon have) the glasses—thanks!

---

1. The doctors had just asked GCL to suspend her visits.
2. Weekly visit by the head of department, accompanied by the entire medical team: the head of the clinic, the internal and external physicians, the head social worker, the chief supervisor, and the nurses.

239

[Paris,] Wednesday,[1] 3 March 1966, noon

My Darling, a quick note to tell you that my glasses, so much awaited, are sitting, all golden, even very strongly golden, on my nose and are helping me to write this letter. For reading, it's a truly effective aid, but my glass hardly lends itself to being looked through all day (for now?).

Tomorrow, the day after the Big Visit, or one of these days, my cure will be established with Deniker—before then, a stop at the stomatologist of the neighborhood.

I would like for you to come Thursday, 10 March, but if that doesn't work, come on 18 March—unless you can only make yourself free on Sunday.

The exhibition at the Goethe-Institut presenting the book and your etchings—when does it have to be scheduled? Will I still be here? I hope not, I really want to be there, with you beside me. Easter falls on April 10th, maybe I will be in good shape by then—to tell the truth I already am to some degree—try to see, if you call or when you come to see the docs.

I just saw Mademoiselle Arrieta: she wants to call you (gave her the telephone number).

Frankly, I see what I write, and that delights me, for *reading* is an integral part of my life.

I thank you, I kiss you and ask you to hug my son for me

Paul

1. Actually, Thursday.

240

[Paris,] Wednesday, 3 March 1966

Just a word, my Darling, to tell you that the glasses "work." I just looked at myself in a mirror: these lenses are copiously fastened. A bit too much so, if You will permit me this critical remark (addressed to the optician of avenue Kléber).

My treatment, as I told You, will begin one of these days.

I will do everything, my Darling. Please hug Eric and congratulate him on his big achievements.

Will You come eight days from today, or will You come this Sunday, I don't know at all, but I am sure that I will wait for you

Paul

241

[To Eric Celan]

[Paris,] 4 March 1966

My dear Eric,

Thanks, above all, for your letters and for the pretty drawing you sent me. I am very glad about your progress, which Mama tells me about when she comes to see me or when she writes to me.

Now, you will have less trouble finding, correcting your handwriting and bringing home good grades in orthography; I am persuaded of that.

You ask me how I am doing; well, I am doing decidedly better and hope to find myself again, with you and Mama, in our house.

Do you know that it's Mama's birthday the 19th of March? You have no doubt already thought of that—perhaps you can tell me what Mama would like. I will then be able to send you the money you need to buy it. I will tell Mama to give you, from me, the money you lent me once and that I have not yet paid you back.

But there will be one other thing: two little poems, in German,[1] which I send you in this same envelope.

Hug Mama for me.

I hug you

Your father

Um dein Gesicht die Tiefen,
die Tiefen blau und grau,
viel Singendes, Gereiftes—
du weiß, du ungenau.

Der ungestufte Abgrund,
er tut sich selber auf,
es kommt das Gehn-und-Gehen
und erst zuletzt der Lauf.

Die Adlerschnäbel brechen
dich von dir selber frei—
Geräusche ihr, kaukasisch,
im Großen Einerlei.

Around your face the depths,
the depths blue and gray,
much that sings, has ripened—
you white, you cloudy.

The unterraced abyss,
itself open gapes,
there comes the walk-and-walk
and at last the race.

The eagle-beaks break
you from yourself free—
Noises, you, Caucasian,
in the Great Monotony.[2]

Flüssiges Gold, in den Erdwunden erkennbar,
und du, außen und innen
verrenkt zur Warnung
vor Sinn- und Wahrspruch.
Der Unbotmäßige kaut
mit an den reifen, voranschreitenden
Schoten der Lippen-
blütler.

(28.2.1966)

Molten gold, recognizable in the earth-wounds,
and you, outside and inside
wrenched as a warning
against sayings and verdicts.
The unruly one chews
along on the ripe, advancing
pods of labiated
flowers.

---

1. The manuscripts of the poems "Um dein Gesicht" and "Flüssiges Gold" were put by PC in
the *Eingedunkelt* (hereafter *ED* file), probably in summer 1966. See *NKGA*, p. 410 and 460.
2. See also "Around Your Face," *FB*, p. 279.

242

78 rue de Longchamp, Friday, 5[1] March 1966

My darling, I received Your two letters: one before and the other after the glasses. You like them? You don't say if the frame suits you. In reality even if the optician is good, there was not that large of a choice in gold. But in any case you can change them later.

About the lenses, it will take, I imagine, some time to get used to them, but they will surely help.

Maybe you would like me to bring you a book, let me know. I will come, of course, to see you this coming Thursday, in the meantime I hope to hear from you often.

I called Henri Michaux. He has not received the second set of proofs.[2] He asked me to bring him etchings and received me for a long time, looking at them for a long time. I was touched as he bought six from me, including two large ones, so I made a hundred thousand (old) francs.[3] I was very surprised by his choices. Those that have a tormented or nervous or a bit black dimension he did not want to have in his home, he found them too troubling. He chose almost all among the old ones, and indeed a pretty choice, I think, *Traces, Aujourd'hui, Rencontre* (which I think is one of the most beautiful, I know that you like it a lot too). Curiously, he also chose *Aquatinte* (which we had always found a bit too Chinese, a bit too facile), and then *Noir-Argent* (the little one in your room).[4] Also a large one that is still waiting for a title and dates from the return from Hanover (little reliefs technique like in *Atemkristall*).[5] That's all. You know that he is reserved and doesn't say much, despite that I was rather touched that he looked at my etchings, that he kept so many, and after all I had the impression that he didn't find them that bad.

Yesterday evening, I reflected on the portfolio for a long time, it's not easy. I have a few ideas, I drew and searched until very late in the night and this evening maybe I will manage to see something a little more precise emerge. What I really need to do is a small cycle, for which, I hope, you will find me a title.

Eric was very content that you ask me to spoil him, but don't worry, I am not bullying him! If only there were not so much work for him! I think that the series of compositions is finished; still some results to wait for. French and Latin will not be marvelous, but German, math, history, and geography will be very good.

So tomorrow I will go to Moisville. I think, given the rain we had this winter, I will find a house that is a bit damp and that will need to be aired out and a garden that is very green but overrun by weeds.

I will put the water back on, as Eric really needs rest and relaxation after a week of school and he would really like to go back to spending his weekends in the country.

Tomorrow I will send the spoon in the mail. I hope you will receive it quickly. If I can bring anything Thursday, let me know.

Also, tell me what decisions the doctors have made about the treatment.

I kiss you

Gisèle

1. Actually the 4th.
2. On this volume of translations, see no. 179, n. 1.
3. Or around 200 USD in March 1966.
4. *Traces—Spuren*, 1957; *Aujourd'hui—Heute*, 1958; *Rencontre—Begegnung*, 1958; *Aquatinte—Aquatinta*, 1958; *Noir-Argent—Silberschwarz*, 1963.
5. Most likely the etching that will be entitled *Oben—Là-haut*, 1964.

243

[Paris,] 7 March 1966

A line, my Darling, to thank you. Your etchings have taken the Great Path, which they ended up opening.

I am eager for the exhibition at the Goethe-Institut:[1] will I have returned then, or will I be able to return for a few hours?

Thanks and bravo to Eric. Tell him that it is particularly touching for me that he is so strong in German.

My glasses are useful to me, already. I will tell you about that Thursday.

Now I hug you, while telling you to hug Eric

Paul

1. In the Paris Goethe-Institut's invitation to the opening, on Monday, 18 April 1966, one reads: "Paul Celan—Atemkristall," twenty-one unpublished poems with eight etchings by Gisèle Celan-Lestrange / Etchings by Gisèle Celan-Lestrange." See Appendix, image 11.

244

[Paris,] 8 March 1966

These lines only:

I hope with all my heart, with all my being that we will see each other again in little time.

Hug Eric, I hug You

Paul

245

[Paris,] Monday, 14 March 1966

My Darling, in a few days it's your birthday, it is true, we will see each other beforehand, on Thursday, but I see that nothing really "birthday-like" is planned, so the idea occurs to me to ask for a leave of absence for this day. To tell the truth, it is Doctor O., to whom we confided the news about the opening for your etchings—Doctor O. told me that he would not like to send me or resend me on leave without having already done so for one day. Anyway, we will see Thursday or a bit later—I know the opinion of the doctors, it is necessary to hear the others—

The stomatologist, moreover, counts on pulling out two to four front teeth, which will be replaced, after the healing period of around one month, by teeth made of resin, discreet.

My Darling, my Beloved, I ask you for one more thing: the Anthology of Russian Poetry, edited by Elsa Triolet[1] (for my files) and the Mallarmé prefaced by Sartre in the new Gallimard series ("Poésie").[2]

You are, with your work, knock on wood, in a good phase.

May it last, and it will help you, it too, to find yourself again.

Hug Eric, I hug you, with him.

Paul

1. *La Poésie russe*, bilingual Russian-French edition, an anthology edited under the direction of Elsa Triolet (Paris: Seghers, 1965).

2. *Poésies: Poésies, Choix de vers de circonstance, Poèmes d'enfance et de jeunesse*, preface by Jean-Paul Sartre (Paris: Gallimard, 1966). PC noted the date "17 March 1966." His copy of this volume contains numerous reading marks, in Sartre's preface as well as in Mallarmé's text, including the following phrases in the preface: "Le suicide est un acte parce qu'il détruit effectivement un être et parce qu'il fait hanter le monde par une absence. Si l'être est dispersion, l'homme en perdant son être gagne une incorruptible unité; [...]! [exclamation point PC] l'absence resserre les choses, les pénètre de son unité secrete. C'est le mouvement même du suicide qu'il faut reproduire dans le poème. [...] Considérée du point de vue de la mort, la poésie sera, comme le dit fort bien Blanchot, 'ce language dont toute la force est de n'être pas, toute la gloire d'évoquer, en sa propre absence, l'absence de tout.'" (Suicide is an act because it effectively destroys a being and because it makes the world haunted by an absence. If being is dispersion, man, in losing his being gains an incorruptible unity; [...]! [exclamation point PC] absence tightens things up, penetrates them with its secret unity. It is the movement of suicide itself that must be reproduced in the poem. [...] Considered from a point of view of death, poetry will be, as Blanchot puts it so well, "this language whose power is in not being, its glory in evoking, with its own absence, the absence of everything"), p. 10. "Pas un jour s'est écoulé sans qu'il ne fût tenté de se tuer et, s'il a vécu, c'est pour sa fille" (Not one day passed without his being tempted to kill himself and, if he lived, it was for his daughter), p. 14.

246

[Paris, 15 March 1966]

Your letter from Monday, before me, read and reread.

Here is your soul, up high, a navigating sail, for me.

(Here, thought again for you, about the memory of Saint-John Perse and of his "Chant de l'Alienne").[1]

You will come Thursday, that's not far away at all.

Your son, my son, is with you and battles.

Let him gather in the fruits of his labor in their truth, again and again.

I hug You

Paul

[In the margin:] Perhaps telephone the Goethe-Institut to know what they think about the *date* of the exhibition. I might be able to have leave for this day.

1. PC alludes in particular to the last verse of the first part of the "Poème à l'étrangère" (which calls to mind the family name of GCL, de Lestrange), which carries the epigraph, "Alien Registration Act" (a United States federal statute from 1940): (*Exil, suivi de Poème à l'étrangère, Pluies, Neiges* (Paris: Librairie Gallimard, 1945), p. 37). PC's copy includes numerous reading marks and translation drafts. PC had likely read this poem to GCL.

247

[Paris, Wednesday, 16 March 1966]

My Darling,

I just spoke with Doctor O.: he is not very fond of the idea of my leaving for the exhibition for our book. And just as little fond of the idea of what, for us, is essential: contact with the literary, artistic world. But perhaps we will manage despite everything to be granted this (these) time(s) away...

In any event, try, if this letter reaches you before Thursday, to find out what would be the time frame for the Goethe-Institut.

Excuse me for being brief, we will be able to see better, tomorrow, together.

I hug Eric and I hug you

Paul

I had just finished writing this letter when I was called to see Doctor Delay.—Long conversation with him, here is what is essential: he asks you to telephone him as soon as you can, in the morning before 9:30. Do it, my Darling, here is his number: Élysée 77-07. He wants you to come see him.

I hug You again

Paul

248

[17 March 1966]

Angefochtener Stein,
grüngrau, entlassen
ins Enge.

Enthökerte Glutmonde
leuchten ein Kleinstück Welt aus:

das also warst du
auch.

In den Gedächtnislücken
stehen die eigenmächtigen Kerzen
und sprechen Gewalt zu.

17.3.1966
An Gisèle, zum 19 März 1966[1]

Assailed stone,
gray-green, released
into the narrow.

Haggled-away moon-embers
light up a little piece of world:

so you were that
too.

In the memory-holes
the imperious candles stand
and bestow power.

17.3.1966
To Gisèle, for 19 March 1966[2]

---

1. The manuscript of "Angefochtener" was put by PC in the *ED* file. This copy was made for GCL for her thirty-ninth birthday. Another version of the poem carries the note: "An Gisèle, für den 19 März 1966 / am 17 März 1966." See *NKGA*, p. 271.
2. See "Contested Stone," *BIT*, p. 230, "Disputed Stone," *FB*, p. 267, and "Stone, Cast into Doubt," *CSP*, p. 161.

249

[Paris,] 18 March 1966

It's your birthday tomorrow, my Darling—so happy birthday!

My Beloved, we have to continue, don't we?

May the seven roses be present in a new form, for You and for our son.

Paul

Was with D. this morning, but there were assistants, students who had done extensive studies; I was not able to speak of myself. (We spoke of *Nadja*[1] when I was there.) I will see Dr. D. again soon.

But we spoke briefly about your exhibition—in order to say [that] I can be there, they need to know, here, the date. So call them when You have set it.

I composed—that is the word, this time—a new poem, a hard but true poem, and therefore helpful. I will send it to you tomorrow.

I hug you, with Eric,

Paul

1. A new edition of *Nadja* by André Breton had been published three years earlier (Paris: Gallimard, 1963). Breton's novel attacks psychiatry and denounces the treatments the ill were made to undergo "in the Vaucluse asylum" (p. 159) where Nadja was brought and where PC will be placed in November 1968. Breton critiques in particular the practices of the doctors of Sainte-Anne hospital, including a certain Professor Claude: "It is necessary never to have gone into an asylum in order not to know that they *make* the mad just as in the houses of correction they make bandits" (p. 161).

250

[Paris,] 18 March 1966

My beloved, these words, quickly, to thank you for having written me upon your return. I am glad that André du Bouchet responded as you say.

But I need to give this note to the nurses, so that you have it tomorrow.

I hug you, see you Sunday.

Paul

251

Die Atemlosigkeiten des Denkens,
auch auf den Gletscherwiesen,
ohne Beweis.

Über den Großen Steinschild
stürzt ein Morgiger heim.

"Ihr Tiefgesenke
mit euren Trögen aus Lehm,
unterwegs."

Rauhbrüchiges schabt
an Namen und Stimmen herum,
eine unverlierbare Nothand
brennt Sterniges ab.

Der durch nichts zu trübende Blick.

Einen Tod mehr als du
bin ich gestorben,
ja, einen mehr.

An Gisèle, am 20.3.1966[1]

The breathlessnesses of thought,
on glacier meadows too,
without proof.

Over the Great Stone-Shield
A being from tomorrow collapses home.

"You deep hollows
with your troughs made of clay,
*on the way."*²

Rawness-and-brittleness grates
around on names and voices,
an unlosable hand of rescue
burns starriness away.

The gaze that nothing can cloud.

One more death than you
have I died,
yes, one more.

To Gisèle, on 20 March 1966

1. The manuscript of "Die Atemlosigkeiten des Denkens" was given to GCL on the occasion of her visit on Sunday, 20 March 1966 (PC's journal), then put by PC in the *ED* file. See *NKGA*, pp. 460–1.
2. Quotation not identified.

252

[Paris,] 21 March 1966

My Darling,

Thanks for *Ulysses*—it's a book I've loved for a long time, which I reread often.¹

I hope that all is well, that all will go well. (Regarding my teeth, it was crowded today and after a good hour of waiting, they came to tell us that we will be admitted next Monday.)

I wrote another poem—here it is.² (Not too many unknown words, with the exception of "*krauchen,*" which is a—more expressive—synonym of "kriechen."|

I hug you, with Eric

Paul

Kantige, schief-
gesichtige Sippe,
mit hellem Holz erspäht.
Dahergekraucht kommt sie,
durch Königsstaub.
Hier wohnen wir nicht.

Umdrängt jetzt
von Unverlierbarem,
groß und unverschwiegen: du.

Hör dich ein, sieh dich ein,
sprich dich ein.

———

21.3.1966
An Gisèle

Angular, sharp-
faced tribe,
espied with bright wood.
It comes crawling over,
through king's dust.

Here we do not live.

Thronged now
by the unlosable,
large and outspoken: you.

Listen your way in, look your way in,
speak your way in.

21.3.1966
To Gisèle

One can thus imagine that not all of the reading marks in *Ulysses* date from March-April 1966. His copy is the authorized translation (in two volumes) by Georg Goyert, 5th edition (Zurich: Rhein, 1952). The two volumes have numerous reading marks and underlinings, and, at the end of the second part (volume 2, p. 196), the date "12 April 1966." PC does not seem to have read the novel in the original English. Among the many marked passages is the following (the English edition cited is that edited by Danis Rose [London: Picador, 1998]): "STEPHEN. (Stringendo.) [...] Ein Stern, ein Morgenstern, ein Komet ging auf bei seiner Geburt. Er leuchtete bei Tag allein am Himmel, heller als die Venus während der Nacht, und bei Nacht schien er über dem Delta der Cassiopeia, der sich zurücklehnenden Konstellation, welche die Signatur seines Anfangs unter den Sternen ist. Seine Augen beobachteten ihn, wie er tief unten am Horizont, östlich vom Bären stand, während er um mitternacht durch die verschlafenen Sommerfelder ging, wenn er von Shottery und aus ihren Armen zurückkehrte," vol. 1, p. 255 (STEPHEN (stringendo)—[...] A star, a daystar, a firedrake, rose at his birth. It shone by day in the heavens alone, brighter than Venus in the night, and by night it shone over Delta in Cassiopeia, the recumbent constellation which is the signature of his initial among the stars. His eyes watched it, low-lying on the horizon, eastward of the Bear, as he walked by the slumberous summer fields at midnight, returning from Shottery and from her arms [p. 200]). For PC, this passage likely echoes memories associated with GCL, who had helped him to deepen his knowledge of "things of the sky," to identify certain constellations, and in particular Cassiopeia, while PC had helped her to learn about "things of the earth," to observe plants and stones, and to call them by their names (Bertand Badiou conversation with GCL). Among three highlighted passages concerned with Stephen Dedalus's mother is the following: "DIE MUTTER (Ihr Gesicht kommt immer näher, sie atmet Aschenatem.) Hüte dich! (Sie hebt langsam ihren geschwärzten, verdorrten rechten Arm auf Stephans Brust, streckt die Finger aus.) Hüte dich Gottes Hand!" vol. 2, p. 177 (THE MOTHER (her face drawing nearer and nearer, sending out an ashen breath)—Beware! (She raises her blackened withered right arm slowly with outstretched finger towards Stephen's breast.) Beware God's hand! [p. 508]).

3. See *NKGA*, p. 461.

253

[Paris,] Saturday, 26 March 1966

My Darling, You are coming tomorrow, the son is leaving on vacation—I'm the only one whose situation doesn't change.

My fountain pen gone, I wrote with a ballpoint pen, round and polyglot, which the nurses gave me.[1]

I am enclosing for you this poem,[2] to be, still, in Your poetic and French vicinity.[3]

I look forward to seeing You again.

Hug Eric,

I hug You

Paul

    Fischer Bücherei,
    Jahnn, *Perrudja*[4]
    A. Adler, *Menschenkenntnis*[5]
    Die neue Rundschau[6]
    Akzente[7]

Can I ask You to bring me the aforementioned books and reviews?

I thank You in advance

Paul

    Unterhöhlt,
    vom flutenden Schmerz,
    seelenbitter,

    inmitten der Worthörigkeit
    steilgestellt, frei.

    Die Schwingungen, die sich
    noch einmal bei uns

    melden

    26.3.66

Hollowed out,
by the flooding pain,
soul-bitter,

in the midst of word dependency
raised up, free.

The vibrations, which
once again with us

announce themselves

1. PC refers to the thick pen with four colors often used by nurses.
2. See the final version of the poem, *NKGA*, pp. 461–2. In his journal, PC mentions his plan to send "Unterhöhlt" to GCL.
3. Enigmatic reference, since none of the poems written around 26 March 1966 is accompanied by a list of translated words.
4. Hans Henry Jahn, *Perrudja* (Frankfurt am Main & Hamburg: S. Fischer, 1966). There are numerous reading marks in this volume, including the following: "Er war das einsame Ich, das an sich selber unfruchtbar geworden, das ergebnislos. Er konstruierte die Bekanntschaft mit einer Frau! [exclamation point PC] Wonnesame Augenblicke sog er ein. [...] O morsche Lust! Zuviel hat sie versprochen. / Ein Fremder droht nun ihren Schoß zu brechen." (He was the solitary I, which had become sterile by itself, resultless. He constructed an acquaintance with a woman! [exclamation point PC] He sucked in delightful moments. [...] Oh, rotten lust! She promised too much. / A foreigner now threatens to break her lap.)
5. Alfred Adler, *Menschenkenntnis* (Frankfurt am Main/Hamburg: S. Fischer, 1966).
6. *Die neue Rundschau* 1, 1966.
7. *Akzente* 1/2, March 1966. PC checked the name "Céline" in the table of contents, and read and annotated an article by Fritz J. Raddatz about Céline ("Zwischen Wahrheit und Wirklichkeit. Ein Versuch über Louis-Ferdinand Céline").

254

[26 March 1966]

Vor Scham, vor Verzweiflung,
vor Selbst-
ekel fügst du dich ein,

sprachfern,
kommt das Unirdische, kippt
in sich zurück,

beim erdig Umher-
liegenden, bei
den Ulmenwurzeln
hebt es ein neues Gelaß aus,
ohne Geträum,

einmal, immer

An Gisèle
Samstag, 26 März 1966[1]

Out of shame, out of despair,
out of self-
disgust you engraft yourself,

far from speech,
the unearthly comes, tips
back into itself,

near the earthy one lying
around there, near
the elm roots
it digs out a new little room,
without dreams.

once, always

To Gisèle
Saturday, 26 March 1966

1. The manuscript of "Vor Scham" was given to GCL on 27 March 1966, the day of her visit (PC's journal). See *NKGA*, p. 462.

255

[Paris,] Sunday, 27 March 1966

My Darling! My Beloved!

Thanks for having come, thanks for having wanted to speak with me about my problems (which are and which remain yours, without many exceptions).

Ich warte—I am waiting.

May You find the tickets for the Railroad, and beyond the departure, the return, both in the comfort that Your state demands.

To my right, to my left:[1] you. And we walk, and Eric joins us. Hug him.

I hug You

Paul

1. PC regularly interpreted and ascribed significance to, right and left, as well as to numbers and colors. See no. 87, n. 8.

256

[Paris,] Monday, 28 March 1966

This note, my Darling, upon my return from the dentist: they removed my two loose bottom teeth. It was, as with the first extractions, going picking.[1] What was a bit disappointing for me is that the prostheses will not be fixed. Another disappointment: my next appointment is set for May 4th.

I reflected on everything we told each other yesterday.

See you Thursday,

I kiss you

Paul

1. In French, "la cueillette" belongs to the figurative language employed by dentists, reproduced, not without humor, by PC.

257

[Paris,] 28 March 1966

My Darling,

Here I am again, with two poems that have ripened between the day before yesterday and today.[1] Take them as a hello thrown by a heart.

I love You.

Paul

> Über die Köpfe
> hinweggewuchtet
> das Zeichen, traumstark entbrannt
> am Ort, den es nannte.

> Jetzt:
> Mit dem Sandblatt winken,
> bis der Himmel
> raucht.
> 28.3.1966

> *Swung high over*
> *the heads*
> *the sign, ignited with the strength of dreams*
> *at the place that it named.*

> *Now:*
> *Give a signal with the sand leaf,*
> *until the sky*
> *is smoking.*[2]

> Wirfst du den beschrifteten
> Ankerstein aus?

> Mich hält hier nichts,

nicht die Nacht der Lebendigen,
nicht die Nacht der Unbändigen,
nicht die Nacht der Vielhändigen.

Komm wälz mit mir den Türstein
vors Unbezwungene Zelt.

28.3.1966

Do you cast the inscribed
anchor-stone?[3]

Nothing holds me here,

not the night of the living,
not the night of the indomitable,
not the night of the many-handed.

Come roll the door-stone with me
in front of the Unbowed Tabernacle.[4]

The manuscripts of "Über die Köpfe" and "Wirfst" (one of the first versions of this poem is dated "27 March 1966 (Sunday)"). Cf. *NKGA*, p. 270. The day before writing both poems, PC had read Book Nine of Homer's *Odyssey*, translated into German by Wolfgang Schadewaldt (Hamburg: Rowolt Klassiker, 1958): "Und auf ihr ist ein Hafen, gut anzulaufen, wo kein Haltetau nötig ist und auch nicht nötig, Ankersteine auszuwerfen [...]. Doch am Kopf des Hafens fließt helles Wasser, eine Quelle, hervor aus seiner Grotte, und Pappeln wachsen darum. Dort liefen wir an—und es ging ein Gott vor uns her—während der dunklen Nacht, und da zeigte sich nichts, das man sehen konnte," p. 112; "Doch er trieb das fette Vieh in die welte Höhle, alles Stück für Stück, soviel er melken wollte, das männliche aber ließ er vor die Türe, die Widder und die Böcke, draußen in dem tiefen Hofe. Und setzte alsbald einen großen Türstein davor, den er hoch aufhob, einen gewaltigen. Den hätten nicht zweiundzwanzig Wagen, tüchtige, vierrädrige, wegwuchten können von dem Boden: einen so großen schoffen Stein setzte er vor die Türe," p. 114 (The island cove is landlocked, so you need / no hawsers out astern, bow-stones or mooring [...] You'll find good water flowing from a cavern / though dusky poplars into the upper bay. / Here we made harbor. Some god guided us / that night, for we could barely see our bows / in the dense fog around us"; "Then over the broad cavern floor he ushered / the ewes he meant to milk. He left his rams / and he-goats in the yard outside, and swung / high overheard a slab of solid rock / to close the cave. Two dozen four-wheeled wagons, / with heaving wagon teams, could not have stirred / the tonnage of that rock from where he wedged it / over the doorsill. [Homer, *The Odyssey*, trans. Robert Fitzgerald (New York: Doubleday/Anchor, 1963), pp. 149, 152]). The word "Türstein," associated with the biblical word "Zelt," evokes Jewish tombs with rolling stones (for example, see Mark 16:2–4).

2. See "Heaved Far Over," *BIT*, p. 228, "Catapulted," *FB*, p. 263, and "Over the Heads," *CSP*, p. 157.

3. For "Anchor-stone" and, in the previous poem, "lifted," see PC's underlinings in Book Nine of Homer's *Odyssey*: "Ankersteine," "Türstein"; "wegwuchten."

4. See "Do You Throw," *BIT*, p. 228, " Do You Exhume," *FB*, p. 265, and "Will You Throw," *CSP*, p. 159.

258

78 rue de Longchamp
Monday evening [28 March 1966]

Just a note this evening, Paul, my darling. I thought of you today, it's not easy for me either, you know. Going, coming, working, preparing this exhibition, with the decisions to be made, and knowing you are, all this time, where you are, with your teeth and the problems they cause you, with the treatments and time that you have to be treated so long, to wait, and try despite everything to work. I know I don't need to tell you all that. I found your two letters this evening on my return and I know well, without your telling me, that it is hard for you that Eric is going to the mountains, that I am going to the south, and that you are staying there. I know, I know, I understand, believe me.

But don't lose courage, you are getting back your strength and finding yourself again. You're finding yourself again, aren't you, if you realize now, as you told me on Sunday, that you had gone too far with Eric and that it wasn't good for him. Your real you is still in you, he waits for you, he calls and you hear him already.

You will find again your confidence in me, in others, in yourself above all and despite the meanness of the world, all the injustice, you will be able to live again and hold out and help your son, your wife, others too.

We loved each other, we hurt each other and arrived at a despairing impossibility of dialogue. Now it will be necessary to reconstruct again, begin again. I know that is your desire, that you do everything for this and in this hope. That supports me already. We must hope. We will try, we are already trying.

Aren't we already taking some steps in that direction? Of course, Paul, and you feel it, don't you, like me.

See you Sunday, my darling, I kiss you

Gisèle

259

[Paris,] Tuesday, 29 March 1966

My Beloved,

Here, in all its nudity, a poem to pass the time—no, here is a true poem[1]—der Ungebändigte is the person who cannot be dominated (bändigen meaning to dominate, tame)—to attach ourselves to that a little and to hear ourselves live.

Till Thursday.
Hug Eric if you write him,
every time, always
Paul

Der Ungebändigte, dreimal
überschüttet mit Gaben,
deutlich, weithin,

die Ulmwurzel
entläßt die Liebenden aus
der Umklammerung,

Schwerzüngiges, alt und am Sterben,
wird abermals laut, Beglänztes
rückt näher,

über der Tafel
schweben die doppelt geohrten
Becher aus Gold. Keiner
der wild gegeneinander Gestoßnen
war dem Ungebändigten
jemals so nah.

29.3.66

The indomitable, three times
showered with gifts,
distinct, from far away,

the elm root
releases the lovers
from the clutch.

The heavy-tongued, old and in the agony of deathrattle,
becomes loud again, refulgence
draws closer,

above the table
float the two-eared
goblets made of gold. None
among those shoved wildly against one another
was ever so close
to the indomitable.[2]

---

1. The manuscript of "Der Ungebändigte, dreimal." Cf. "Deutlich," the final version of the poem, *NKGA*, pp. 269–70. Another version of the poem contains the note: "29 March 66 / An Gisèle (Abschrift brieflich an G. [copy sent to G.])."
2. See "Explicit," *BIT*, p. 226, and "Plain to see," *FB*, p. 259.

260

[Paris,] Wednesday, 30 March 1966

My Darling, I just received your letter from Monday—thank you for everything you tell me there. I am giving you, in response, a little poem written just now: "Nach dem Lichtverzicht" ("After Having Renounced the Light"*).

I transcribe this poem[1] for you—

At the end of your letter there is an error: you tell me *till Sunday*, but I had noted that you will come *Thursday*, so *tomorrow*. I am counting on it, my Beloved.

[Unsigned]

[In the margin:] Can you bring me a notebook, quite big, but with unlined paper?[2] Thanks in advance.

Nach dem Lichtverzicht:
der vom Botengang helle,
hallende Tag.

Die blühselige Botschaft,
schriller und schriller,
findet zum blutenden Ohr.

30 March 1966

After the renunciation of light,
the day bright, ringing
with the steps of messengers.

The beatific-blooming message,
shriller and shriller,
finds the bleeding ear.[3]

 * or: "After the Renunciation of the Light"
1. The manuscript of "Nach dem Lichtverzicht." See *NKGA*, p. 269.
2. In a school exercise notebook labeled "Gedichte -i-," PC copied the group of poems written in the "clinic of Prof. Delay" (Sainte-Anne) between the beginning of March and the beginning of May 1966. It is from this group that he will later take the cycle of poems published in 1968 under the title *Eingedunkelt*.
3. See "After the Lightwaiver," *BIT*, p. 225, "Having Renounced the Light," *FB*, p. 257, and "After Renouncing Light," *CSP*, p. 153.

261

[Paris, 31? March 1966[1]]

Hello, my Darling, here is the "daily" poem[2]—let's hope that lasts.

Rest, draw, take notes, write to Eric and to his father.

Have a good vacation, good tomorrow

Paul

Einbruch des Ungeschiedenen
in deine Sprache,
Nachtglast,

Sperrzauber, gegen-
wirkend.

Von fremdem, hohem
Flutgang unterwaschen
dieses
Leben.

An Dich, Gisèle, heute und immer

Effraction of the unseparated
into your language,
night-glist,

Anti-charm, counter-
acting.

By the strange, high
current washed out
this
life.

To you Gisèle, today and always[3]

1. Conjectural date proposed by the editor, 31 March 1966, corresponding to the date of composition of the poem "Einbruch."
2. GCL noted in pencil PC's translation of the first verse of "Einbruch des Ungeschiedenen" in the upper margin: "Infraction du non-séparé." Cf. "Einbruch," the final version of this poem from *ED, NKGA*, p. 272.
3. See "Irruption," *BIT*, p. 233, "Irruption," *FB*, p. 273, and "Invasion," *CSP*, p. 167.

262

[Paris,] 1 April 1966

My Darling,

I am here, with the books, I am reading (not very well, but well enough anyway).[1]

Did You have a good trip?

You have fifteen days in front of You—I hope that the weather is as good, over there, where you are, as here.

Excuse me for having sent You, without commentary, the poem "Einbruch des Ungeschiedenen" ("Infraction[2] du non-séparé"). Here still some words explained: Glast—"luisance," "Sperrzauber"—anticharme (charme-barrière), Flutgang—(dé)marche du Flot (l'océan).

Tell me how You and Eric are doing.

I hug You

Paul

1. Aside from Joyce's *Ulysses*, PC read the following books (the influence of these readings is noticeable in the poems written in the Delay Clinic, which were published in *ED*, and among the unpublished poems from this period): Thomas Wolfe, *Von Zeit und Strom. Eine Legende vom Hunger der Menschen in der Jugend (Of Time and the River)*, 1935, 2 vols., translated by Hans Schiebelhuth (Berlin: Rowohlt, 1936). Both volumes show numerous reading marks; at the end of the second volume, PC noted the date 25 March 1966; Joseph Conrad, *Der Geheimrat (The Secret Agent)*, 1935, translated by G. Danehl (Frankfurt am Main: S. Fischer, 1963). The volume has numerous reading marks and, at the end, the date noted by PC: 6 April 1966; Homer, *Die Odysee*, translated by Wolfgang Schadewaldt (Hamburg: Rowohlt, 1958); the volume is marked with the date of its acquisition ("Frankfurt am Main / 20 March 1959") and has many reading marks. PC noted his date of reading on page 84 and 93, at the end of books six and seven, 30 March 1966; p. 123 at the end of Book Nine, 27 March 1966 (see above, no. 257, n. 1); p. 138, at the end of Book 10, 28 March 1966; p. 191, at the end of Book 14, 24 April 1966; and, p. 296, at the end of Book 22, 29 March and 13 April 1966.
2. PC uses "infraction" according to its etymology, whereas a more conventional French translation would be "effraction," "entée par effraction," or "irruption."

263

[Antibes,] Friday, 2[1] April 1966, noon

My darling,

I just arrived in Antibes, a bit late, with little sleep, a real headache, and still no coffee in my stomach. The sun is hot, the sea stupidly blue and the coast, as always, noisy and full of cars.

It was not much fun yesterday evening to leave all alone among the crowd of vacationers more numerous than ever. I finally managed to find a taxi and reach the train station without too much difficulty. Impossible to have a sleeping car, but in my compartment where everything was reserved I was ultimately alone and I was able to lie down and sleep a bit, choosing either to suffocate or to freeze, according to whether I opened or closed the window, choosing also to make of my coat either a cover or a pillow. Finally, I have arrived, now in front of a coffee and toast, outside, in the sun.

My courage is not immense, I see the port, palm trees, also cars. I will wander a bit in the city, but not for a long time. Then I will go get my suitcase at the left-luggage office and a taxi to Cap d'Antibes, since I need to wash up a bit and rest.

I am thinking of you, I am thinking of you very much, Paul, you know it. Everything that happens to you, understand, affects me in the deepest part of myself and your wounds, your drama, your fate, I live through them too, without saying too much about it, completely alone, but very intensely. You said to me: It's a mystery: how do you hold up? There is no mystery, and I have often said it, You were everything for me, often that collapsed, but you remain everything for me. In the drama and the solitude of the suffering that I live through, Eric and his presence and his age and his need of life, of joy, of calm, help me to start again, as well as work, as well as your courage to accept this harsh trial of medical treatment, which is your lot right now.

While I see people, while I manage, on the outside, to not manage things too badly, that does not mean that there are not other difficult hours, or this physical and moral exhaustion that often gets the best of me and takes the upper hand. I hope to benefit from the sun, from the air, from nature, it is a source of strength for me that I would like so much for you to have again like before.

A pebble, a blade of grass, the line of a hill, witnesses of the perpetual drama of nature, are realities for me, which can help me. Not to understand but perhaps to know.[2]—I hope to find hours of reflection, of silence, I know well that there is no answer to all of my questions, and that ultimately everything remains a mystery, but in the knowledge of the mystery one can perhaps go deeper into things, without finding there an explanation, perhaps all the same a bit of serenity.

My revolt against the injustice of life, and the difficulty of being, I cannot remove them from myself for an instant, but a calmer knowledge of life, I wish for that.

But I am tired and I am unable to tell you what I feel the way I would like to. I will write to you again soon, don't leave me without your news. That you may soon walk again, with me, in the sun, free.

Let us not despair, my darling.

I kiss You

Gisèle

chez Madame Marraud
Villa Pampero
rue Notre-Dame
Cap d'Antibes, Alpes-Maritimes

1. Actually 1 April.
2. PC marked with two lines in the margin the passage from "A pebble..." to "Not to understand but perhaps to know."

264

[Paris,] Saturday, 2 April 1966

My Darling, I just received your two letters, the one from before your departure and the one from Antibes.

You are frank—You know how much I need, just like You, to know that the returned strength manifests itself already.

You write: *Not to understand but perhaps to know.* May Reality, evoked in this way, be there, remain there, may it accompany You.

It is good that this exhibition will take place soon,[1] in this return to better spirits.

Thanks for the little images.[2]

My Darling, what should be done in order to send the medicines to Sperber? You have the address book, so look in there for Margul-Sperber or just Sperber, and send him, by airmail, a few lines to ask him what the name of the medicine is—then you can send it from Antibes.[3]

—

Do you know how Eric is doing? I think so, You do. So tell me. I like hearing You "re-tell."

I hug You

Paul

1. See no. 275, n. 2.
2. PC's discreet and jesting manner of confirming receipt of the money sent by GCL on 31 March 1966.
3. GCL had already sent the requested codeine for Alfred Margul-Sperber, who is gravely ill at this time, in Bucharest.

265

[Paris, 2 April 1966]

"Das Narbenwahre" ("Le Vrai-cicatrice") *["The True-As-A-Scar"]*, here is the result of my various cogitations.[1]

Today, I hug you, before I get back to you, with the (necessary!) words

Paul

2.4.66

das Äußerste—l'extrême
nicht zu Entwirrende—[translation missing]

Das Narbenwahre, verhakt
ins Äußerste, nicht zu
Entwirrende,

Längst
ist der Schautanz getanzt,
der schwergemünzte,
hier in der Einfahrt,
wo alles noch einmal geschieht,

endlich,
heftig,
längst.

———

2.4.66
An Gisèle

The true-as-a-scar, hung up
into the extreme, not to
be extricated,

Since a long time ago
has the show-dance been danced,
the heavily coined medallion,
here in the driveway,
where everything happens again,

finally,
violently,
since a long time ago.

2.4.66
To Gisèle

1. The manuscript of "Das Narbenwahre, verhakt." Cf. *NKGA*, p. 463.

266

[Paris, 3? April 1966]

Für Gisèle

Die Narbe—la cicatrice / narbenwahr—vrai comme une cicatrice / vrai"
cicatricement" / verhakt—accroché / der Haken—le crochet / das Äußerste
—l'Extrême / entwirren: antonyme de verwirren—brouiller [*sic*], / das
nicht zu Entwirrende—impossible à dévider, à sortir de la confusion /
längst—il y a bien longtemps / der Schautanz—la danse-"show" [*sic*], / die
Schaumünze—la médaille (enfin: démonstrative) / münzen—frapper mon-
naie / die Einfahrt—l'entrée (pour automobilistes?) / heftig—avec violence

267

My Darling, here is the poem from yesterday—Today, I just finished it, that is to say I think I will not make any further corrections.[1]

I like liberating myself from my poems, as you know.

Do you know how Eric is doing?

Too nervous, still, to send You a list of words—that will come too.

I love You and wish You a good time of repose (in work)

Paul

Bedenkenlos,
den Vernebelungen zuwider,[2]
glüht sich der hängende Leuchter
nach unten, zu uns,

Vielarmiger Brand
sucht jetzt sein Eisen, hört,
woher, aus Menschenhautnähe,
ein Zischen—

findet
verliert

Schroff,
so liest sich, minutenlang
die schwere,
schimmernde
Weisung.

4.4.1966
Endg[ültige] Fassung

Without hesitation,
against the obnubilations,
the hanging candelabra glimmers itself
downward, to us,

Many-armed fire
seeks now its iron, hears,
from where, from the nearness of human skin,
a whistling—

finds
loses

Brutally,
so reads, for whole minutes
the heavy,
shimmering
order.

Final version[3]

---

1. The manuscript of "Bedenkenlos." Cf. *NKGA*, p. 269.

2. In no. 268, PC draws GCL's attention to the spelling of the preposition *zuwider*, which means "contrary to," "against," "in defiance of," in order to avoid possible confusion with *wieder*, meaning "again."

3. See "Unscrupulously," *BIT*, p. 225, as well as "Thoughtless," *FB*, p. 255, and "With No Second Thoughts," *CSP*, p. 151.

268

[Paris, 5? April 1966]

"Bedenkenlos"

Bedenken haben—avoir des scrupules, des hésitations / Vernebelung—obnubilation / zuwider—contre / sich nach unten glühen—lueurs en bas, de-

scendre incandescent / vielarmig—aux bras multiples / Brand—incendie /
Eisen—fer (Brandeisen—tisonnier) / aus Menschenhautnähe: Nähe—prox-
imité / Menschenhaut—peau d'homme / Zischen—sifflement / schroff—dur
comme pierre, brutal / die Weisung—l'ordre, [*sic*—no full stop]

269

[Paris,] Wednesday, 6 April 1966

My Darling, I have received, until now, only a single letter: the one from
2 April.

O. is absent—so no news from him, or from Doctor Deniker, who is
traveling.

I am sending you another poem[1]—with some words.

Write to me, tell me how you and Eric are doing.

Paul

Das Seil, zwischen zwei hoch-
wohlgeborene Köpfe gespannt, oben,
langt, auch mit deinen Händen
nach dem Ewigen Draußen,

das Seil
soll singen—es singt,

Ein Ton
reißt an den Siegeln,
die du befremdet erbrichst.

Endg[ültige] Fassung
6.4.1966

———

Das Seil—la corde / hochwohlgeboren—de haute lignée / spannen—tendre / draußen—dehors (ici substantivé): Le dehors / an etwas reißen—essayer d'ouvrir par la force / Siegel—sceau / erbrechen—ouvrir par la force, arracher / befremdet—étonné

The rope, stretched between two
high-born heads, above,
reaches, also with your hands,
for the Eternal Outside,

the rope
shall sing—it sings,

A tone[2]
tears at the seals,
which, astonished, you break open.

Final version
6 April 1966

---

1. "Das Seil, zwischen zwei hoch-." Cf. *NKGA*, p. 463 for the truly final version of this poem, which PC revised subsequently and would send to GCL on 16 April 1966 (no. 276).
2. See Thomas Connolly's translation of this version of the poem (*Paul Celan's Unfinished Poetics*, Oxford: Legenda, 2018, pp. 43, 51).

270

[Paris,] Wednesday,[1] 7 April 1966

My Darling, I hope to have news from You in a little while. In the meantime I have transcribed a poem that came this morning, with little hesitation on either side, its or mine.[2] Here it is, without commentary (except: "*Sehklumpen*"; a compound word made of "sehen," *voir* [to see], and "Klumpen," *motte* [clump] (—of soil, etc.), so *motte œilletée*[3] etc.)

It has already been a week since You left—think of giving me your news, as well as Eric's.

I hug You

Paul

Mit dem rotierenden
Sehklumpen stößt du zusammen
bei Eisfeuerschein:

Erblickt, erblickt!—Durchstoßen—

du kennst den Schrei,
weißt, daß geschrien wird, auch
an deiner Statt,

mehr als das steht dir nicht zu,
das Spiel geht ohnehin weiter,

es wälzt sich
durch die erste beste
Buchstabenöffnung

und meldet ungehört
Gewinn und Verlust

——

7.4.1966
Endgültige Fassung

With the rotating
clump of sight you collide
in the light of ice-fire:

Glimpsed, glimpsed!—Forced through—

you know the scream,
know that people scream, in
your place too,

more than that is not your due,
the game will go on anyway,

it rolls itself
through the first and best
opening in a letter of the alphabet

and unheard announces
the profit and loss

7.4.1966
Final version

1. Actually Thursday.
2. Cf. *NKGA*, p. 461 for the final version of the poem.
3. Franco-Celanian neologism ("eyed clumps").

271

[Paris, 7 April 1966]

"Vom Hochseil"

Hochseil—corde raide / herabzwingen—forcer q[uelqu'u]n de descendre /
ermessen—évaluer / Gabe—don, cadeau / käsig—"fromageux" / über j[eman]
d|en] herfallen—tomber dessus, attaquer / Zeiger—aiguille de la montre /
nach Menschenart—à la manière des humains / herauserkennen—que tu
reconnais dans la foule / unbußfertig—qui n'est pas prêt de dire sa coulpe,
qui n'est pas prêt à dire (apporter) son repentir / die Buße—le repentir,
l'amende / unbotmäßig—qui ne se plie pas, n'est pas serf / Botmäßigkeit—
servitude

Here is another poem,[1] young as can be, for You.
I kiss You.

Paul

Vom Hochseil herab-
gezwungen, ermißt du,
was zu gewärtigen ist
von soviel Gaben,

Käsig-weißes Gesicht
dessen, der über uns herfällt,

Setz die Leuchtzeiger ein, die Leucht-
ziffern,

Sogleich, nach Menschenart,
mischt sich das Dunkel hinzu,
das du herauserkennst

aus all diesen
unbußfertigen, unbotmäßigen
Spielen.

Forced down from the
tightrope, you measure
what is to be expected
from so many gifts.

Pasty-white face[2]
of he who falls upon us,

Set the luminous hands in, the luminous
ciphers.[3]

Right away, in the way of humans,
the dark mixes itself in,
which you discern

among all these
unrepentant, unbowed
games.[4]

1. Cf. *NKGA*, p. 270.
2. Celan's source for this image is *Der Geheimagent* (Berlin: S. Fischer, 1963), G. Danehl's German translation of Joseph Conrad's *The Secret Agent*; see *NKGA*, p. 972. As Thomas Connolly observes, "the face of Verloc's overweight accomplice, Michaelis, is described as a 'käsiges Mondgesicht' (in the German translation) or 'pasty moon face' that 'drooped under the weight of melancholy assent.'" (Thomas Connolly, *Paul Celan's Unfinished Poetics*, p. 172).
3. See Thomas Connolly's discussion of the "menetekel" motif from the book of Daniel in this poem, in which he argues that the "Leuchtziffern" are not a clock dial but rather literally "luminous ciphers," and continues: "Contrary to Menasseh's interpretation, the biblical account suggests that the reason no one could assist Belshazzar in reading the writing was that he is the only one able to see it. Even Daniel, who reads the writing and gives its interpretation, does not see the writing, such is his ability to read and interpret what he has not seen." (*Paul Celan's Unfinished Poetics*, p. 175).
4. See Joris, Fairley, and Gillespie's translations as, respectively, "Forced Off," *BIT*, p. 22; "Forced Down," *FB*, p. 261; and "From the Highwire," *CSP*, p. 155; as well as Thomas Connolly's translation in *Paul Celan's Unfinished Poetics*, pp. 171–2.

272

[Paris, 8 April 1966]

… Oder es kommt
der türkische Flieder gegangen
und erfragt sich
mehr als nur Duft.

———

8.4.66

... Or maybe
the Turkish lilac comes along
and gleans
more than just perfume.

This is a fragment from a too "rich" poem[1]—I just excavated it and completed it. And here is a French version:

... Ou bien s'en vient*
le lilas à la turque,
questionnant, il obtient
plus que du parfum.

I received Your letters—thanks, that helps me, you know it well.
   kiss you

Paul

1. This refers to "Das Narbenwahre, verhakt" (see no. 265); "Oder es kommt" was initially the last stanza of this poem. See the last version of this poem in *NKGA*, p. 463.
* Ou bien s'en vient
  le lilas à la turque
  ses questions, à la ronde,
  glanent plus que du seul parfum
  (cueillant plus que du parfum
  (odeur etc.)).

273

[Paris,] Friday,[1] [9 April 1966]

This—"daily"—poem,[2] quite black, but of the "standing up" and "despite everything" variety, hard, harsh, coarse.

You will not at all (or hardly) lack in vocabulary, in any case here are some "explained words":

stachlig < Stachel: dard, pointe
Hartlaubgebüsch: maquis, garrigue.

Hug Eric, I hug You. Have a good trip home! See You soon
                                        Paul

9.4.1966

Notgesang der Gedanken,
von einem Gefühl her,

das hat
der wachgesungenen
Namen nicht viele,

stachlig,
so, unverkennbar,
aus dem Hartlaubgebüsch,[3]
steht es mit ihnen hervor, dir
entgegen,

stachlig.

Es geht ein kleines Sterben
umher, umher

9.4.66

Distress song of thoughts,
from a feeling,

it has
not many names
awakened by song,

thorny,
like this, unrecognizable,

from out of the maquis,
it stands up with them, in
your way,

thorny.

A small death goes about
around here, around here

1. Actually Saturday.
2. Cf. *NKGA*, p. 464.
3. In the right margin, "der Macchia," probably added after sending the poem, as a variant of "dem Hartlaubgebüsch."

274

[To Eric Celan]

[Paris, 12 April 1966]

My dear Eric,

Here you are again in our good house—I write you to tell you my joy in seeing you making progress in school, my joy in seeing you succeed, as well, in so many games and sports.

Me too, I have worked a bit and I am not at all displeased. As you know: Poetry is something very high, very harsh. I counted the poems written since the *Niemandsrose* (*La Rose de personne* or *La Rose nulle*)[1] and I realize that I have finished a new cycle of Poems and, thanks to that, a new book is finished.[2] Never have I written so much; in publishing a book, I've never known so much *work*. But you will see—soon—when you will have made progress in German, we will start, or rather: we will continue to see, together, what I do, what you do. Mama will have helped you so much—hug her, for that too.

I hug you.

Your father

1. See no. 106, n. 1.

2. PC has probably "counted" the eighty poems of the future *AW* (from September 1963–September 1965) and the twenty-two poems that will constitute the first cycle of *FS* (September 1965–November 1965), as well as the eleven poems written at the "clinic of Prof. Delay" (March–April 1966) of which he has just made a selection; that is, in total, 113 poems to which four poems must be added that were excluded from the final versions of *AW* and *FS* (see *Die Gedichte aus dem Nachlaß*, ed. Bertrand Badiou, Jean-Claude Rambach, and Barbara Wiedemann (Frankfurt am Main: Suhrkamp, 1997; hereafter *GN*), respectively pp. 95–98, 392, and pp. 111, 399. PC left no trace of a plan for such a volume, which would have been the longest in his oeuvre. Ultimately, PC will not publish this "new cycle of Poems" in the context of *AW* or *FS* and will later opt for its separate publication under the title *Eingedunkelt*, in *Aus aufgegebenen Werken*, ed. Siegfried Unseld (Frankfurt am Main: Suhrkamp, 1968), which brings together "abandoned works" by Samuel Beckett, Karl Krolow, Wolfgang Koeppen, Hans Erich Nossack, Peter Weiss, Uwe Johnson, Wolfgang Hildesheimer, Nelly Sachs, and Martin Walser; see *NKGA*, pp. 267–72.

275

[Paris,] Thursday evening, [14 April 1966]

Paul, my darling,

Just a short note before going to bed to tell you that after leaving you we went, as planned, to the Goethe-Institut, Eric and me. I liked the poster and I think that it is really good. There, everyone was very content, Raczynski as much as Hock, the librarian who gave us a hand in the room, and Monsieur Schmitt (? I don't know his exact name),[1] the former head of the Goethe-Institut. They have begun to distribute it all over Paris. I am sending you the program and the invitations.[2] You had told me not to do it, but you see, it's discreet and takes up so little room that I am doing it all the same. It's after all our book, I wanted to make you participate as early as possible in the exhibition. We worked for a long time and Eric, happy as can be, helped us.

Most of the etchings are already framed and it looks good. Also, the long table that will present the book is almost completely finished, it is still missing the cloth that will cover it and which I will go to buy tomorrow in Montmartre with the librarian, at the Marché Saint-Pierre. We all want the cloth to be very simple, like what is in my studio upstairs[3] and close in color to that of *Atemkristall*. I think all will be well. They had thought of another cloth they had, but it did not seem very pretty to me, and right away they agreed to buy a different one.

There is a lot to do still, but it is already coming together well and there are still four days to go.

I am thinking of you. I would have liked of course to prepare all that with you, as you can imagine.

Eric was glad to bring the etchings, to transport the frames along the wall and to give me his opinion. We left late and I had nothing at home, so we decided to have dinner on avenue Victor Hugo, in a little restaurant where he had been with Marie-Thérèse a long time ago. He was very proud to bring me there.

We came home early—the backpack courageously prepared—and quickly to bed. He has been sleeping for a long time already. Tomorrow he goes back to school.

I leave you now, I have to sleep, long day again tomorrow. The fabric, the copperplates of the book that will be shown have to be picked up at the Frélauts'. The pages of the book have to be put in their frames. Eric and his work in the evening.

I don't forget you, I am thinking of you.

I kiss you, my darling

Gisèle

Write to me whenever you can.

You'll see, at number 22 of the catalogue, I changed the title *Je maintiendrai* to *Souvenir de Hollande* as you had asked me to.[4]

1. Christian Schmitt had been head of the Goethe-Institut of Paris from 1962 to 1965.
2. Attached to the letter: a flyer and little catalogue of the exhibition at the Goethe-Institut (17 avenue d'Iéna, 16th arrondissement; from 19 April to 6 May 1966), with a description of *Atemkristall* as well as the bilingual titles of the thirty-nine etchings presented; and an invitation to the opening, on Monday, 18 April 1966, which reads: "Paul Celan—'Atemkristall,' vingt et un poèmes inédits avec huit eaux-fortes de Gisèle Celan-Lestrange / Eaux-fortes de Gisèle Celan-Lestrange" (Paul Celan—"Atemkristall," Twenty-one unpublished poems with eight etchings by Gisèle Celan-Lestrange).

3. In the chambre de bonne, which served as a studio at 78 rue de Longchamp.
4. A sole copy of this etching has the original title, written in PC's handwriting, followed by the date "21.XI.1964." See Appendix, image 10.

276

[Paris,] Saturday, [16 April 1966]

My Darling,

the leaflet mentions the date of 19 April as the date of the exhibition opening, while the invitation card mentions the date of 18 April.[1]

I hope that someone will have realized that, in time.* But yes, someone has realized that, in time.**

Keep our hope, always.

I ask You to hug Eric

and hug You

Paul

Das Seil, zwischen zwei
Köpfe gespannt, hoch oben,
langt, auch mit deinen Händen,
nach dem Ewigen Draußen,
das Seil
soll jetzt singen—es singt.

Ein Ton
reißt an den Siegeln,
die du erbrichst.

Endg[ültige] F[a]ss[un]g
17. 4. 1966[2]

The rope, stretched between
two heads, high above,
reaches, also with your hands,

for the Eternal Outside,
the rope
shall sing now—it sings.

A tone
tears at the seals,
which you break open.

Final Version
17. 4. 1966

1. PC confuses the exhibition opening date (18 April) with the date of the first day of the exhibition at the Goethe-Institut (19 April).
 * Or, which is probable, try to reach [phrase unfinished]
 ** The exhibition opening is the priority so to speak, *all will go well.*
2. GCL noted in pencil the date of the poem accompanying this note in parenthesis above "Saturday": "(17.IV.1966)." PC had already sent GCL a version of the poem *Das Seil* on 6 April 1966 (see no. 269). Cf. *NKGA*, p. 463.

277

Paris, 16 April 1966

[To Eric Celan]

Mit uns[1]

Avec nous autres,
les cahotés et néanmoins
du voyage,

l'un et l'autre
intacte [*sic*],
point "usurpable,"—
le chagrin

insurgé

———

A Eric, en l'embrassant
Son Père
Paris, 16.4.1966

Mit uns

With us others,
The ones who've been jolted and nevertheless
are traveling,

the one as well as the other
intact,
not "usurpable,"—
the sorrow
insurgent

To Eric, with a hug
His Father
Paris, 16.4.1966

1. PC provides the title of the poem in its original language (*NKGA*, p. 272).

278

[Paris,] 21 April 1966

Just a note, Paul, my darling, to tell you about my joy at having found you full of hope, full of courage for this step toward healing that this new treatment represents. My joy also at having been able to allow you to share, a bit, the exhibition of *Atemkristall* and the etchings. Thanks for having trusted me to organize that all on my own. I am also glad that you like the poster.

I am sending with this letter a catalogue of the exhibition to D. and Deniker.

After leaving you, I went to the Goethe-Institut. The room was so calm, there was nobody and, like a child, I looked again at each of my etchings and, for a long time, the book. I saw in the guest book that Henri Michaux had come and that touched me very much. His was the last signature: maybe he had just left. I learned that a very young girl, probably German, had come and had copied out each poem. This gesture alone already justifies the entire exhibition. I hope that it will touch you as it did me. When the lady at reception told me that just now, I had tears in my eyes and she also seemed happy to tell me that.

During these three weeks, there will no doubt be a few people there, who will be helped and transformed a bit by the chance to read the poems in the calm of this very beautiful room. All that is good and I am delighted to tell you that.

Eric is coming home now, and in order that he too may one day read *Atemkristall*, we will do German together.

Until Thursday, my darling, I kiss You, as You know that I love You

Gisèle

279

[Paris,] Friday, 22 April 1966

Here, my Darling, is the most recent of the daily poems.[1] It would like to tell You, too, how much, in everything I set out to do, I am close to You, still and ever.

They just took my blood—in view of what? I do not know, the word "glycemia"?—was that it? I don't know at all. It is to prepare the therapy,[2] probably. Someone just told me that I will be on the radio around ten o'clock.

I am proud of this book that we made, it's an upright[3] book, hardly a pause in its steps—our steps, with our son.

Hug Eric,

I hug You

Paul

P.S. Think about which day You want to show me the exhibition, so that I can ask for leave.

Wildnisse, den Tagen um uns einverwoben.

Alleingängerisch, wieder
und wieder, rauscht,
über die Meldetürme hinweg,
eines großen weißen Vogels
rechte Schwinge
hinzu.

22.4.1966

Wildernesses, woven into the days around us.

Like a lone wanderer, again
and again,
beyond the message towers,
a big white bird's
right wing
rustles in.

1. See *NKGA*, p. 467.
2. Sakel therapy or insulin shock therapy: one of the treatments for schizophrenia, abandoned today, which consisted in provoking shock, PC underwent a different form of insulin treatment but probably did not undergo Sakel therapy.
3. See no. 83, n. 1; no. 87, n. 10; no. 93, n. 3; and no. 123, n. 4.

280

[Paris,] Friday evening, 22 April 1966

My darling, my darling Paul,

I wanted to tell you this evening that I am thinking of you in the solitude of my nights, in the solitude of my days. I hold out for my son, for you, and your courage and your hope, when you shared that with me last Thursday, you helped me, you strengthened me. Keep the courage to fight to heal, as I keep the courage to work, to be there waiting for you. So that finally we will be together forever again.

I love you Paul, even when I can't tell you. I love you, Paul, forever, know that.

With all my heart

Gisèle

281

[Paris,] 23 April 1966

My Darling,

Tomorrow, probably, the insulin treatment will start and I am writing You to tell You that I've been, since yesterday, a little anxious. I even thought, this morning—after a not very good night—of going to find the doctors to speak to them. But I will not do it. "There is no retreat," says René Char, on the stone that he gave us, "but a millennial patience."[1]

There are many leaves of absence around me, and I notice, of course, all these departures. (Monsieur Sébille, who is leaving too, will bring this letter to the post office.)

Anyway, I am trying, still. But I need to live again among humans, with You and our son.

Hug Eric for me.

I hug You

Paul

---

1. René Char most likely gave this stone to the Celans between 1955 and 1956.

282

2nd letter, [Paris,] Saturday, 23 April 1966

My Darling,

Your letter from the 21st arrived—I do not know how to thank you.

Yes, I am on the way to recovery.

All that you say about the Exhibition makes me happy. And I "grandly" feel our hearts that speak calmly to "each other," speak with one another.

You nourish me with light, with light, I feel it very strongly and I live on that. See you Thursday!

Paul

[Paris,] Saturday afternoon, 23 April 1966

My Darling,

A little while after your visit, your letter from Friday evening was brought up to me.

How can I thank you for it?

Yes, there is our love. And the courage of our love. And Eric, this Greatness of love.

I love you, my Darling, forever.

I live, I await, I live on this awaiting.

With all my heart

Paul

I saw, after your visit, Doctor D.—very encouraging too.

[Paris,] Saturday evening, 23 April 1966

My love, my Light, Geliebte,

Your letter, entirely equal to you, fills up my heart—I let it travel around and toward all my shores,[1] I inundate the world with it, yours and mine, I rejoice, painfully, in truth.

How could I have been blinded, when so close to me, your love, again and again, gave radiant proof of her to whom my own heart, on the way, coming from far away, remains committed. *I see you, my Darling.*

I write you here a few lines[2] that have come from a world, ours, *our* own:

Schreib dich nicht
zwischen die Welten,

vertrau der Tränenspur
und lerne leben.

Don't write yourself
between the worlds

trust the streak of tears
and learn to live.[3]

Paul

[Paris,] Saturday, 23 April 1966

My Darling,

I have to make a correction: my treatment will not begin, as I thought I had understood, Monday, 25 April, but only on Friday the 29th. The reason for that is that I need to have an electrocardiogram ahead of time and the cardiologist only comes on Fridays.

So I will see You—won't I?—*Thursday the 28th.*

I wrap you in my arms, I kiss you

Paul

1. PC's formulation recalls this passage in his Bremen speech: "Das Gedicht kann [...] eine Flaschenpost sein, aufgegeben in dem—gewiß nicht immer hoffnungsstarken—Glauben, sie könnte irgendwo und irgendwann an Land gespült warden, an Herzland vielleicht" (A poem [...] can be a message in a bottle, sent out in the—not always greatly hopeful—belief that somewhere and sometime it could wash up on land, on heartland perhaps.); *GW* III, p. 186, and *SPP*, p. 397.
2. Cf. the final version of the poem, *NKGA*, p. 467.
3. See also "Don't You Write," *FB*, p. 283.

283

Gisèle, mein Licht und mein Leben,

hab Dank für den *Herzbrief*,[1] hab von Herzen Dank. Umarme unsern Sohn, denk an uns drei.

Paul

24.4.66, am späten Nachmittag

Gisèle, my light and my life,

My thanks to you for your *heart letter*, thanks with all my heart. Hug our son, think of the three of us.

Paul

24. 4. 66, in the late afternoon

1. On the envelope of GCL's letter from 22 April 1966 (no. 280), PC had written in pencil: "der Herzbrief (the heart letter) / 23 April 1966."

284

[Paris,] Monday morning, 25 April 1966

My Beloved,

I should have asked for a leave of absence, I would surely have received it, but all is still possible this week, my treatment will not begin until next Monday. I think Friday or Saturday would be the dates to ask for. That way, I would have your opinion first, on Thursday. Furthermore, it is precisely Thursday that one requests leaves of absence, during the doctors' Big Visit. Let me know by letter what you think about that.

Hug our son, I hug you

Paul

285

[Paris,] Monday evening [25 April 1966]

Paul, I cannot tell you with what emotion I read, I reread, I keep in me the poem "Schreib dich nicht" and the letters that arrived this evening from you. You call me your Light, your Light and your life—you see me, you recognize me.

So much suffering, such a long separation, a difficult path in the hope of a new encounter. And now the breach in the wall that separated us opens, opens.

A living glow sets alight millions of stars that are sparkling now. Millions of stars that I look at, that I see. A whole world that is reborn. In you, in me, from which our son will be able to live.

It's incredibly beautiful.

Thanks

Gisèle

286

[Paris, 27 April 1966]

Weihe—initiation / gießen—verser / Guß—versement / Weihguß—"offrande liquide" / spenden—dispenser, faire don de / spalten—fendre / Abgott—idole, faux dieu / huldigen—rendre hommage

My Darling, a little poem[1] and some words—I hope that you will like it.

I wait for you to wait for you, to remain, to live with you, with the son, and...a few people.

See you tomorrow!

Paul

Weihgüsse, zur Nacht,
aus der Tiefe
lehmiger Hände gespendet.

Unterm abgespaltenen Licht:
der für immer entstiegene,
flüchtig aufscheinende
Abgott,
dem ein Teil deiner selbst
huldigen kommt
in der Pause.

Endg[ültige] F[a]ss[un]g
An Gisèle: 27.4.66

Liquid votives, offered at night,
from the depths
of clay-covered hands

Under the split-apart light:
the forever-emerged,
fleetingly appearing
false god,
to whom a part of yourself
comes to pay homage
in the pause.

Final version
To Gisèle: 27. 4. 66

1. Cf. *NKGA*, p. 467.

287

[Paris,] 27 April 1966

My Darling,

Here is the good news: Doctor D. has accorded me a "leave" for the day after tomorrow, Friday.

So You will come to get me in the morning, let's say around ten o'clock (or rather nine o'clock, if that is not too early for You), and I will spend the day with You and Eric, which will end around six o'clock, the hour of the evening meal, or—I need to look into it—toward eight o'clock.

Hug Eric, I hug you.

Paul

P.S. Tomorrow, when You are here, you will have to go see, with M. Duval, which clothes are mine—myself, I do not know if I have shoes here.—That will be quickly done.

288

[Paris,] Sunday, 1 May 1966

My Darling, it is profoundly Sunday—Monday is slow in coming, because, above all, of an error, this one: today they did not stop the medicine treatments, as is meant to happen before the Sakel therapy.[1]—So I do not know if my treatment will start tomorrow or later.

I am thinking of this depth of us two, of us three—of the teardrop[2] so barely viscous, which unites us—in anticipation of what joys? There will be some, soon. For today, the attached poem: "Zerstörungen" (Dévastations)[3]...

I hug you both, You and Eric

Paul

Die Zerstörungen?—Nein, weniger
als das, mehr
als das.

Es sind die Versäumnisse
mit den schwatzenden Ringel-
tauben an ihrem Rand,

Blick und Aug, zusammengewachsen,
erklettern die Kanzel
über der weithin in Streifen
zerschnittenen Grafschaft,

Eine Sprache
gebiert sich selbst,
mit jedem aus
den Automaten[4] gespienen
Gedicht oder dessen
Teilen.

1 Mai 1966 / An Gisèle

The devastations?—No, less
than that, more
than that.

It is the omissions
with the chattering ring-
doves on their edge,

Gaze and eye, coalesced,
scale the pulpit
over the county cut up
into long strips,

A language
gives birth to itself,
with every
poem spit out by the machines
or with each of its
parts.

1 May 1966 / To Gisèle

1. See no. 279, n. 2.
2. See "Give the Word," lines 7–12 (no. 151) and "Ruh aus in deinen Wunden" (no. 170).
3. The manuscript of "Die Zerstörungen" was put by PC in the *ED* file. Cf. the last version of this poem, *NKGA*, p. 468.
4. This could be a reference to the story by R. C. Phelan, "Gibt es mich überhaupt? Eine Erzählung" (Do I exist at all? A Story), published in *Der Monat* (no. 147), which Celan read in December 1960.. It recounts the success of a Texas farmer who, starting from nothing, becomes a famous writer. He is in fact an impostor, whose writings are the product of an "automatic typewriter" capable of producing literary texts in any genre and of the highest level: no one (Niemand) is thus the cause of the oeuvre or of the author's success; or rather, the creator is an impostor. At the end, the story itself turns out to be the product of the automatic typewriter. Celan sees in this fable the reversal of his own poetics, a provocation in the wake of the Goll Affair, and interprets the name of its author as a malicious allusion to his own name. PC's impression was reinforced by the publication of a letter by Franz Koebner to the editor of *Der Monat* (published in no. 149, February 1961), which begins: "Sehr geehrter Herr Phelan! / Seien Sie mir nicht böse. Ich weiß, daß Sie kein Plagiator sind. Es kommt eben vor, daß man, ohne es zu ahnen, seinen 'Vordenker' hat" (Very esteemed Mr. Phelan! / Do not be angry at me. I know that You are no plagiarizer. But it happens that one, without suspecting it, has his "precursors"). Péter Szondi, after taking steps with the editorial board of the review, later informs Celan of the real existence of R. C. Phelan, a scientist in New York writing under his real name (see *GA*, no. 120).

289

[Paris,] 1 May 1966

Paul, my darling,

Eric sold lily of the valley this morning, and he even came up with two other cub scouts, worried that I wouldn't find it in the neighborhood, so it is on a very calm Sunday that I am writing to you with the beautiful lilac and the lily of the valley in the room. In a little while I will go drink a coffee at the Lalandes', then pick up Madame de la Motte at the train station. I reserved her a room in the hotel, as you had advised me (at place de Mexico, above the tobacco shop).[1] I find it after all quite touching that she has come so far despite her age to see *Atemkristall* and the etchings.[2] Of course, it is also a bit much, but let's not forget the solitude of this poor woman who essentially has no family left and has been miserable for a long time. I don't have much patience for people right now, but for such a short amount of time I can accept her presence.

A very nice call from Elisabeth, who has been to the exhibition, to tell me how beautiful the book is, as well as the etchings. She is delighted that you came to the house, that you are now close to your return.

Eric just got a 16 for his German composition, it's a very good grade, he thinks he is 5th in his class, and that makes me happy, as for him, he is delighted. He needs encouragements like this. He seems to have gotten off to a good start again since his return from the mountains. I am glad you saw him doing so well, before that trip he was really very very tired.

People must all have left for the country, it is so nice out, the street is so calm and the shutters closed due to the sun, I hear the turtledoves cooing, not a single car, it's marvelous. I worked a little on the portfolio today, it will be necessary to find a title for it, or will the poem also be the title of everything?

Next week I think I will return to the studio as I have several etchings underway.

I am thinking of you, I am thinking very much of you, I see you again here at the house, with your courage, your calm, your hope. I hope that Moisville in July will help you to find your strength again and also to feel better.

See You Thursday, Paul, my darling, I kiss You.

Gisèle

1. On Hildegard de la Motte, see no. 48, n. 4.
2. On the exhibition at the Goethe-Institut, see no. 275, n. 2.

290

[Paris,] Monday, 2 May 1966

My Darling,

thanks for your beautiful letter. I have to correct my letter from yesterday: in fact, my treatment began today.[1]

I am delighted that I will see You Thursday, I thank you for coming. Hug Eric.

I hug You

Paul

1. See no. 279, n. 2.

291

[Paris, 2 May 1966]

Herbeigewehte mit dem voll
ausgefächerten Strandhafer-Gruß,
ich werde nicht da sein,
wenn du das Rad der Beglückung schlägst, unterm Himmel,
das himmelnde Rad,
dem ich aus unausdenkbarer Ferne
in die Naben greif,
ein Einsamer, schreibend.

——

Endg[ültige] F[a]ss[un]g
An Gisèle
2. Mai 1966[1]

Blown over with the fully
fanned out beach-grass greeting,
I will not be there,
when you do a cartwheel of good fortune, under the sky,

the wheel rising skyward,
that from an unthinkable distance
I grip by the hub,
a solitary person, writing.

Final Version
To Gisèle
4 May 1966

I kiss You

                              Paul

1. "Herbeigewehte"; cf. the final version of the poem, *NKGA*, p. 468.

292

                              [Paris,] Monday, 2 May 1966

My Darling,

   Four lines,[1] in the evening, here they are, with
   feuilles de tilleul faisant évanouissement, le gardant.
   Le tout, pour les précipités vers le haut,
   est un psaume, dans un bruit de métal.

   linden leaves that make you swoon, keeping it.
   It's all, for those precipitated upwards,
   a psalm, amid a din of metal.

One needs to have the courage to accept such short poems.
   I hug You
                              Paul

Hug our son.

Do not forget, for Thursday, two light undershirts, light pyjamas, the Uni-prix slippers.

Lindenblättrige Ohnmacht, der
Hinaufgestürzten
klirrender
Psalm.

─────

Endg[ültige] F[a]ss[un]g

Linden-leafy swoon, the
clinking psalm
of those made to fall
upwards[2]

Final Version

1. These four lines paraphrase the manuscript of the enclosed poem, "Lindenblättrige Ohnmacht"; cf. *NKGA*, p. 469. One thinks here of the coma provoked by the insulin injection during Sakel therapy. See no. 279, n. 2.
2. See also Thomas Connolly's translation of these lines (*Celan's Unfinished Poetics: Readings in the Sous-Oeuvre*, pp. 20–21).

293

[Paris,] 4 May 1966

My love so profoundly hurt,
  My invulnerable love,
  with all my heart I speak to You, I wrap You in words of silence, I wrap You in my arms, I reunite us around our son, we are here all three of us

Paul

294

[Paris,] Thursday, 6¹ May 1966

Paul my darling,

I have told you this, I am writing it to you now. Keep your confidence, your courage, your hope. This insulin treatment is done only with the aim of stimulating your memory and helping you to be able to concentrate before your departure, as well as to prolong the improvements already seen with the preceding treatment.² Then in three or four weeks, you will begin to go out, to get used to life, also to movement, to the tiring rhythm, little by little, and then we will go to Moisville, we will go back together to Moisville, first the two of us, in the calm of our countryside, of our house, then with Eric.

It won't be easy, it can't be easy, but we will manage. You will be careful and, little by little, your strength will return. That will be the moment for you, calmly, to begin work on the manuscripts again, to type them up, to organize them.³

Maybe you will also be able to translate a few new Éluard poems.⁴ And then we will walk, in the little woods, or on the roads with the wheat, the poppies, and the cornflowers. The big oxeye daisies that you like will be in bloom along the wall, there will be roses, geraniums, grass, birds.

Maybe, if you aren't too tired in August, we can spend a few days in Amsterdam.⁵ Or in September a few days with Eric on the coast. We'll see how you're doing. If that isn't tiring. Maybe André du Bouchet can come with his children in September for a weekend and the Lucases for a few days, if you feel like it. Lots of plans are possible. You know it.

So, Paul, that bad night discouraged you, and you are tired of it all, and that is understandable. Illnesses are an ordeal, I realize that, and even before you told me that, I knew it. Tomorrow morning I will call D. It is important that the treatment is completed, there was maybe a little wavering, but I am sure that you will sleep well this evening already.

Until Sunday! Courage, my darling,

I love You and kiss You

Gisèle

1. Actually the 5th.
2. "Antidepressive treatment, by injection," according to PC's letter from 20 December 1965 (no. 210).
3. PC will not decide the title of a selection of poems from those written during his hospitalization (*Eingedunkelt*) until 17 July 1967. This cycle will appear in a volume of "abandoned works" no. 274, n. 2).
4. PC published only one translation of an Éluard poem, "Nous avons fait la nuit je tiens ta main je veille," in 1959. During his years in Bucharest (1945–7), he had translated the cycle of eleven poems entitled *Les petits justes* (*Die kleinen Gerechten*; typescript in the DLA Celan collection), as well as a few other poems from *Capital de la douleur*.
5. PC and GCL will take a trip to Holland in September 1966.

295

[Paris, 7? May 1966]

My Darling,

Your good letter—how do you do it?

I slept a little last night, with Chloral then Imménoctal.[1] But it was insufficient.

Doctor D., very nice, came this morning, then Co.

I will have Théralène tonight.

You are full of good plans—yes, I will see your roses, your daisies. Our son. Friends.

I am a bit sick of it, but I will hold up.

Excuse my handwriting.

D. was at avenue d'Iéna,[2] he must have spoken to you about it. Very nice.

But where is my strength?

I love you with all my heart, with your son

Paul

Come Sunday
Bring stamps.

1. Sleeping aids.
2. At the Goethe-Institut, to see GCL's exhibition.

296

[Paris,] Monday [9 May 1966]

My very beloved,

I took a nap, it's the afternoon, three thirty.

This morning, the injection, which left me a little clammy. Increase to seventy[1] tomorrow. My hand quite uncertain, as you see.

Bring me butter, please, lots of compote, lots of sweet oranges.

I will stop. I hug you, with Eric

Paul

1. PC is referring to an increase in the dosage of his insulin shots, in International Units. See no. 279, n. 2.

297

[Paris,] Wednesday, 18 May 1966

It's a rest day today, little insulin,[1] and I take up the pen, a bit tardily, I know it well, to tell You that I am thinking of You, of all that You are, of all that You do.

Yesterday, day of strikes and vacation—You probably have returned to the house, titmice, roses, and daisies, the calm and stable presence of our house. I take a tour with You and I notice the trees, the goat's leaf, the interior sober and elegant.

Tomorrow You will come back and we will speak with each other of the future. I am waiting for You and hug you, with Eric.

Paul

2. See no. 279, n. 2.

298

A note this evening before going to bed, my darling, to wish You a good night.

A bit discouraged by my etchings, which don't respond, or rather the copperplates, which don't respond, which don't accept, which remain closed to me and want nothing from me right now. Unless I am the one who can't find them right now. In any case, the dialogue copper-Gisèle is not establishing itself and I am having trouble, trouble. You know how hard it is. All the more so as I spend hours on it, and these hours, with the house, Eric's work, I don't know what else, but I have little time, and it's hard for me to find these hours.

Tomorrow I am going to Moisville. I worked so much today, from 10 to 5 with only a ten-minute break for a coffee, sandwich! And then, nothing, nothing! Tomorrow I will bring neither copperplates nor paper. I will sleep and get the garden ready for your arrival. If only I could stick the fig tree[1] back in and make it emerge from the grass!

Hard life, hard life, too often, for too long. Sometimes that weighs so heavily. Maybe one day I will once again be able to rest on your calm and your strength. I am waiting for that. Now you will give me that. Won't you?

A few beautiful years of calm. Long years of calm! Looking at the grass, the leaves, looking with you.

Ah! Yes! That will happen, won't it, once again. You remember, one winter, on the balcony at rue de Longchamp, you had called me to watch the first snow of the year with you! Before the first snow of the year, you will call me to watch it with you.[2]

I kiss you

Gisèle

1. GCL means the mulberry tree.
2. See no. 58, n. 6.

299

My Beloved,

It's Sunday afternoon, almost five o'clock, You are in Moisville, with Eric, outside probably, in front of the house, in a deck chair, walking Your eye along the wall and its ivy, inspected with Your gaze the peonies having anticipotted[1] their Pentecost, replanting already, the mulberry tree, and, perhaps, a few other trees. Eric is not far from You, and You are having a good Sunday.

Here, it is humid, the visits numerous, I am still a little disappointed not to have received a letter yesterday. (But I will no doubt have one tomorrow.)

The treatment[2] is taking its course, without any problems—except for my neighbor, who had a quite spectacular crisis of convulsions yesterday, at the very beginning, so much so that they immediately re-sugared him, without having been able to avoid that the poor man bit his tongue. But I am only at my sixteenth injection (or "piquouse," as they say here), and thanks to Pentecost, I will have to chew on a good chunk of the month of June. But I will wait patiently.

I thought of the books and reviews (Walser and *Monat*[3]) that I asked You for, and no doubt it is a bit complicated for You to procure them. I have another idea, easier to accomplish, inspired by an article I read in the *NRF*.[4] Bring me *La Peau de chagrin* by Balzac in German translation. You will find it in the chambre de bonne—take out the last volume (the tenth, I believe), You will find there the index of the different novels by volume— the novel, in German, is called *Das Chagrinleder*.[5] Then take, among the last volumes, a random second one, and bring me both.

To tell the truth, I still have a good portion of *Ventre de Paris*,[6] but I find the charcuterie, foie gras, galantines, pork chops with pickles, etc., etc., far too abundant.—Maybe You can choose for me as the second Balzac a collection of shorter stories.[7]

Take care of Yourself, eat a little more, vegetables, fruit. Work well and have Eric work.

Till Thursday.

I hug You with all my heart with Eric

Paul

I need two clean pairs of underwear, also pyjamas.

Bring me some papers, including *Le Figaro littéraire* and the *Quinzaine littéraire*.

1. This appears to be an invented portmanteau word composed of *anticiper* and *empoter*. On the peonies, see "Das Stundenglas, tief" at no. 113.
2. See no. 279, n. 2.
3. *Der Monat*, no. 212, May 1966; Martin Walser, *Halbzeit* (Frankfurt am Main: Suhrkamp, 1960).
4. An article by André Pieyre de Mandiargues on Balzac's *La Peau de chagrin*, "Le Supplice de la peau" in *NRF*, no. 161, 1 May 1966, pp. 930–7.
5. *Das Chagrinleder*, translated by Hedwig Lachmann, in *Cäsar Birotteau, Kleine Erzählungen, Das Chagrinleder, Die Menschliche Komödie, Deutsche Ausgabe in 10 Bd.*, vol. 7 (Leipzig: Insel, 1925). Three times between 1961 and 1963, PC had given to his students at the ENS, in the context of a course devoted to oral French-to-German translation, an extract from the first chapter of *La Peau de chagrin*, "Le Talisman," which has to do with suicide (from "Il existe je ne sais quoi de grand et d'épouvantable dans le suicide" [There is something great and terrible in suicide] to "une femme s'est jetée dans la Seine du haut du pont des Arts" [a woman threw herself into the Seine from the pont des Arts]).
6. Émile Zola, *Le Ventre de Paris* (1873). It has not been possible to identify the edition PC read here; perhaps PC borrowed it from the hospital library.
7. Perhaps *Die Geschichte des Dreizehn*, translated by Ernst Hardt (Leipzig: Insel, 1909).

300

[Paris,] Monday, 23 May [1966], two o'clock

My Darling,

The joy, this morning when, toward ten thirty, Your two letters arrived, the one from Thursday and the one from Friday. It was still my insulin "session," it was reaching the end, and I was able to read, calmly, what You told me.

Do not worry about Your dialogues with the copper; nothing can be put in question there; it is too strongly anchored, it is truly rooted, a necessity for the material just as for the spirit. Indeed, I think that if I were there, I would manage quite quickly to demonstrate to You that what, for You, is in question, is, for the most part probably, realization in a still unknown area.

When I am there, and that will be, I hope, soon, I will try to be as You desire. (Only one problem probably: my teeth, but that too I will try to overcome.)

I am so content with Eric's success, despite all the tempests that he could not avoid hearing rumble. But he has known me to be hardworking and strong, he sees You work, act, he senses Your big presence, he knows that nothing would be able to disunite us, he has, finally, thanks to all that and with all that is there in terms of jolts, an idea, I believe quite clear, of our love that englobes him and that holds him and will hold him always.

Thanks for the efforts with Top.[1] If it's not too complicated, bring me, Thursday, the thick book by Walser. And the two Balzacs of which I spoke to You yesterday.

With all my heart, I hug You. Hug Eric for me.

Paul

I will soon need stamps—bring me some, as well as some envelopes.—All my best to the Bourboulons and the Veyracs.

1. Elmar Tophoven.

301

My Darling,

Tuesday—two more days before Your visit.

It is two o'clock, I am in my room, my neighbor is playing his transistor radio, it's a more or less "beatle"[1] program, the two others, stretched out in their beds, sleep despite the noise.

My treatment,[2] this morning, went normally—toward ten thirty, after drowsiness and sweating and, this time, without the accompaniment of "divagations"—I cite the report of the nurse, M. Mann (like Thomas)—I was re-sugared and standing. For my neighbor it took longer and, again, it was quite difficult to see. They gave him "the comatic shock," while for me it is the "moist shock." (I am learning, you see.) They re-sugared him intravenously to bring him back from "paradise." (Sorry for this cruel language.)[3]

My Darling, I am waiting for Thursday. Excuse me for being, once again, a bit demanding, but I need the following: 1 pair of pyjamas, 3 pairs of underwear, 3 pairs of socks, long underwear, "Florilège" eau de cologne, from Panthène. Thanks for taking care of this.

I look at You, You and our son, soon it is Your holiday,[4] I do not forget it, I hug You

Paul

Bring me envelopes too please

1. In English in the original, as in the Beatles.
2. See no. 279, n. 2.
3. Entire parenthetical remark in English in the original text.
4. Mother's Day this year fell on June 5th, the day before EC's eleventh birthday.

302

[Paris,] Thursday, 26 May 1966

My Beloved,

This letter, written shortly after Your departure from here, to wish You, You and our son—as well as his guest[1]—a good stay this Pentecost weekend.

"Wenn das Denken den Pfingstweg heraufkommt"—"When thought climbs up the Pentecost path," I wrote, two years ago I believe, in front of the peonies[2] gathered in large groups in the bamboo. Well, thought climbs back up—for all of us, it passes, with these lines, close to the chickadees, it takes a tour of the garden, it is called back, in front of the door of the Three Birches, to orient itself by the forty buds of climbing roses.[3]

I wish you two, you all[4] a good stay.

I hug You

Paul

Thanks for all that You do.

1. Sabine Bollack, the daughter of Mayotte and Jean Bollack.
2. PC cites from memory lines four and five of the first version of "Das Stundenglas (no. 113), reinventing, probably unintentionally, his own text: "Wenn das Denken / den Pfingstweg *herab*kommt" (When thought / *de*scends the Pentecostal / path) [editor's emphasis].
3. PC alludes to a phrase in a letter from GCL from 23 May 1966, devoted in part to the garden in Moisville: "There are more than forty rose buds ready to blossom on the climbing rose near the door."
4. In the above-cited letter, GCL evokes the visit, in Paris, of Romanian acquaintances of PC's, including the poet Maria Banus.

303

[Paris,] Friday, 27 May [1966], four o'clock

My Darling,

Will these lines reach You tomorrow, Saturday, before Your departure? In this case, they wish You, first of all, a good trip and a good stay. Or if not You will find them upon Your return on Tuesday—then I wish You a good return to our home in Paris!

I thought again about the telephone call from Moret and his proposal that I teach a class in June. This opportunity should not be missed, and it is, moreover, so I think at least, completely feasible, between June 10th and 20th for example, since my insulin treatment is supposed to be finished in around twelve days, and since the doctor has spoken to You about *leaves of absence* that are supposed to precede my definitive return. I *can very well teach a class in French-German translation*[1] during such a leave of absence, on the condition that I obtain two days of leave, an afternoon to prepare my class, the following morning for the rue d'Ulm; in the evening of the second day I will return to the clinic. So call Doctor D. and speak to him about it.

Then, with Moret and Tophoven, we can set, with the agreement of the students, the date of the class. The best thing would be for You to *write* to D.

I read around a hundred pages of the book by Walser:[2] it has a great mastery, too great for the story of a business traveler, it is garnished with bourgeois people, and it is of a great uselessness, including its—artificial —creaking. Walser is one of Germany's best beasts of the pen and, with

Enzensberger, one of the master-pillars of Suhrkamp.—I was able to read, as well, three little stories by Balzac.[3]

Wait for the letter to Otto Walter: I will write him some lines and Thursday You will take them to put them in the mail.

I hug You, You and our son,

we will hold out[4]

Paul

1. Preparation for the oral exam in French-to-German translation that is part of the *agrégation*—the highest teaching certificate in France, necessary for teaching in German in secondary and higher education institutions. See no. 13, n. 7.
2. See no. 299, n. 3.
3. See no. 299, n. 5.
4. See no. 83, no. 1; no. 87, n. 10; no. 93, n. 3; and no. 123, n. 4.

304

78 rue de Longchamp

[27 May 1966,] Friday evening

My darling, From ten this morning to seven this evening, I conversed with the copper, three plates are already prepared, I think. It was a bit feverish up there, a lot of people, but everyone worked seriously and it was a good atmosphere.

From my table to the acid tray, from the varnish to the printing press, I did not cease working.

I met Eric only after judo. He is glad that I'm working and is interested in it, proud too that I can count on him and that I find, on my return, his work done, and done well.

He is sleeping now nearby, calm. And I drew a bit more and, before writing to you, filled a sheet with little squares, which I am sending you here. It's not much, I know, but it relates a little to the etchings I made today. Oh the relation is very distant! And then, pen and paper have nothing to do with printing ink on copper worked on with acid.

But I am tired, a bath and then I will go to bed. Tomorrow I am leaving for our house in Moisville. I hope for beautiful, calm evenings after working in the garden. You know, it's often like that, after the wind and the clouds of the day there comes a great calm with the transparency of the air there that is so precious to me, in the evening, and that light heavy only with calm.

Soon we will see that together, we will know it together, we will experience it together.

Eric had a phone call from Henri Michaux. But I was not able to reach him when I returned. I will try tomorrow morning. He has asked so loyally for your news for six months!

Good night to you too. I am thinking of you.

I kiss you

Gisèle.

305

[Paris,] Saturday, 28 May [1966], two o'clock

My Darling,

Thanks for Your letter from Saturday—I am very glad that we had, at the same time, the same idea regarding the class to be taught at rue d'Ulm. If my treatment[1] is finished in around ten days, I will be able to have, who knows, before my definitive departure, several leaves of absence in June and to teach two or three classes—which would be convenient for us financially.

I will surely be able to, it needs to happen before the publication of the results of the written exam of the agrégation.

I started to make some notes for the poem to accompany Your etchings.[2] For the moment it is only a quite vague idea, but present. But look perhaps at the poems of the second collection—the one after *Atemgänge*—and choose a poem that You like.[3]

I added a few sentences to the letter to be sent to Walter, which is very good. Keep the draft as a copy and write a new letter, with the completed text. Thanks for everything.

I hug You, with Eric

Paul

1. See no. 279, n. 2.
2. This will be published the following year: GCL's *Portfolio VI*, ed. Robert Altmann (Vaduz: Brunidor, 1967); it includes the poem "Diese / freie, / grambeschleunigte Faust" (*NKGA*, p. 221); see Appendix, image 12.
3. PC refers here to the twenty-two poems written between 19 September and 23 November 1965, in part during his trip through the south of France (*NKGA*, pp. 221–34). A number of these poems, which will constitute the first cycle of *FS*, are evoked or cited in this correspondence or sent to GCL: see nos 184, 198, and 202. PC has not yet written any other poem from the future *FS*. *Atemgänge* (Breath Gaits)—or, in the singular, *Atemgang*—is one of the titles envisioned for the collection of poems that will ultimately be entitled *Atemwende* (*Breath-turn*); see below, no. 380, n. 1. The poem ultimately chosen, "Diese freie, grambeschleunigte Faust," is dated "Paris, 29 June 1965" and, it seems, was never part of *FS*.

306

[Paris,] Friday, 3 June 1966

My Darling,

This note for Your return.

I saw Doctor Co. just before and I spoke to him about the class to be given at the École before the publication of the written exam of the agrégation; I asked him to speak about it with Doctor D. and I reminded him that the latter, fifteen days ago, had told me that he would have me called to see him; Co. told me that he will speak to D. of all that. I hope that I will be able to give these classes. Regarding this, I will need the typewriter, remember it please. Remember as well to look for the Burns[1] at Delatte.

I hope that *Retour Amont*, which is also, according to the newspaper You brought me, an homage to Giacometti,[2] is a beautiful book. The days to come promise to be nice, I see You in the evening serenity in Moisville.

I hug You

Paul

1. Robert Burns: *Burns*, trans. Richard de La Madelaine (Rouen: E. Cagniard, 1874). PC also possessed an edition of the poems in the original English: Robert Burns, *Poems and Songs*, ed. James Barke (London and Glasgow: Collins, 1960).
2. See the poem by René Char entitled "Célebrer Giacometti" in *Retour amont*. (Paris: Gallimard, 1966). Inside, in PC's hand, the date 5 June 1966. The second copy in PC's library has the dedication "To Paul Celan / his friend / René Char;" PC inserted his unpublished translation of the poem "Dernière marche" (Letzte Stufe) at page 44.

[Paris,] Monday, 6 June 1966

My Darling,

It's our son's birthday: happy birthday to him and to you. I hope the two letters sent to Moisville arrived in time.

I received Your letters, two on Saturday, the one from the third this morning. Thanks for the French Burns[1]—it is, alas, nothing but a little literary curiosity, but we couldn't have known.

Thanks for the little etching—I find it very beautiful, perhaps we will make it, with a little poem, into a greeting card for the New Year (and new day).[2]

Doctor D. came Friday evening and told me what I already knew regarding the École, but also that it is possible that I will leave definitively the thirteenth.[3] To tell the truth, I did not understand if it was the thirteenth that the École wanted me to teach my class. But the decision has not been made, it is also possible that we will choose the solution of leaves of absence.

Doctor D. expected Your telephone call on Monday, I informed him that, since You are in the country, You will not be able to reach him. So You will have news on Wednesday, and I, from You, on Thursday. Personally, I prefer, of course, to leave definitively and to prepare well the classes that I have to teach (several if possible).

From time to time, I add a few lines to the poem ("Opaque")[4] that is to accompany Your new etchings.[5]

Do not miss the Villon exhibition at Nouvel Essor, rue des S[ain]ts-Pères (forty, I believe), and that of Matta at Iolas, B[oulevar]d S[ain]t-Germain.[6]

I hug You, with Eric

Paul

Please bring me two pairs of underwear, some writing paper, a tube of toothpaste.

---

1. See no. 306, n. 1.
2. See no. 308, n. 1.

3. In fact, PC will leave the hospital on 11 June 1966. The 13th corresponds to the date of the writing of "Schlafbrocken" (Chunks of Sleep); see *FS, NKGA*, p. 235; and no. 308.

4. The poem evoked here could not be identified, nor is it clear if "Opaque" refers to the title of the poem. PC does not seem to have written poems between 3 May 1966 and 13 June 1966, when he wrote "Schlafbrocken." On opacity, an essential quality of poetry for PC, see no. 170, n. 3.

5. On the future *Portfolio VI*, see no. 305, n. 2.

6. Exhibitions of the work of Jacques Villon and Roberto Matta, respectively.

308

Paris, 13 June 1966

Schlafbrocken, Keile,
ins Nirgends getrieben:
wir bleiben uns gleich,
der herum-
getröstete Rundstern
pflichtet uns bei

Paris, 13. Juni 1966[1]
Für Gisèle

Chunks of sleep, wedges,
driven into nowhere:
we remain equal to ourselves,
the round star consoled
all around
approves us with its light[2]

Paris, 13 June 1966
For Gisèle[3]

1. 13 June 1966 had initially been envisioned by the doctors as the date of PC's definitive departure from the hospital. This poem—the first that PC wrote in rue de Longchamp after six months of hospitalization and the first of the second cycle of *FS*, together with the print sent

by GCL to PC on 2 June 1966, comprised a collector's edition (Vaduz: Brunidor, December 1966) given to the Celans' friends and acquaintances with their New Year's greetings.

2. The translator has followed Bertrand Badiou's French translation of this line.

3. The manuscript of "Schlafbrocken, Keile" was framed with a draft by the artist of the print that inspired it (private collection, EC). Cf. "Schlafbrocken," *NKGA*, p. 235. See also "Sleep-morsels," *BIT*, p. 136, and "Debris of Sleep," *FB*, p. 77.

309

[Paris, 1966?]

Good evening, my Darling, rest, spend good days here, in Paris, in two houses, with our son.

I take Your hand, I kiss You,

I hug our son

Paul

310

[Paris or Moisville, summer or fall? 1966]

I found that you were very very well today, in great shape—teeming with ideas.[1]

Don't lose courage, your rich possibilities are there very close by, even if they remain a bit hidden.

See you soon. I kiss you

Gisèle

1. Between June and October 1966, PC wrote seventeen of the twenty-three poems making up the second cycle of *FS*.

311

[To Eric Celan]

[Conches-en-Ouche,] 12 July 1966

From Conches,[1] where we met up, after having visited the charming Vallée du Roulir, with our friends Luca and Micheline, after supplying ourselves with something to garnish and wash down our four trouts, an affectionate thought including you in our feast,

your Papa

1. Postcard caption: "In an airplane above ... Conches-en-Ouche (Eure)—the church"

312

[To Eric Celan]

[Breteuil-sur-Iton, 18 July 1966]

My dear Eric, incredible but true: we are in Breteuil.[1] From where we send a gaze toward you and the Pyrenees, where, we hope, the sun is shining.

I hug you

Papa

1. Postcard caption: "Breteuil-sur-Iton (Eure)—the public park."

313

[To Eric Celan]

[Dreux,] 18 July 1966

My dear Eric, as you see, we are in Dreux, in the shade of the belfry.[1] It is to accompany Luca and Micheline, who are going home to Paris. Next Saturday, we will come home in turn, to wait for you.

I hug you

Papa

1. Postcard caption: "Dreux (Eure-et-Loir)—The belfry built under François I."

314

[To Eric Celan]

[Damville,] 20 July 1966

My dear Eric, we are in Damville to buy paper.[1] I will in fact, finish typing up a volume of poems.[2] I am delighted about your approaching return, I hug you,

Papa

1. Postcard caption: "Damville (Eure)—Puiseaux et Lavoir sur l'Iton."
2. These poems, written between September 1963 and September 1965, will be published the following year under the title *Atemwende*. PC had already evoked this collection in a letter to his son on 12 April 1966 (no. 274).

315

[To Eric Celan]

[Leiden, 12 September 1966]

My dear Eric, as you can see, we are still wandering around, our nomadic souls are very much awoken, Leiden,[1] hardly reached, will be left right away, for the Hague.—With Mama, I hug you

Papa

1. Postcard caption: "Leiden Universiteit."

316

[To Eric Celan]

[Gand,] 14 September 1966

My dear Eric, after a visit to Bruges and, today, to Gand, we have reached the end of our journey. Tomorrow, Thursday the 15th, we will return to Paris to wait for you there.—I hug you

Papa

317

rue du Château d'Eau
Saint-Cézaire-sur-Siagne, Alpes-Maritimes
22 December 1966

Paul my darling,

If only you knew how blue the sky is and how good it is to lie around in the sun. I am on a path, sitting on a large stone, the hill descends in terraces, and the olive trees are shining, the bushes are dense and thorny: "vegetal hardness."[1] There is no one, not a house, only boulders, stones, trees, shrubs, and then I hear the Siagne, flowing in the background: that's all.

I listen: a bird, a blade of grass stirring, a passing insect, and all that is really alive for me too.

The path that descends turns, turns without end according to the whims of the hills as though it were looking for the heart of mystery.

Having gone to sleep very late last night, I had continued to make attempts on paper, I spent the morning in my room, with the window wide open, I read poems by Emily Dickinson, which Françoise had put in my room, it's wonderful to have free time. Then I worked. Maybe even a gouache came out of it a little. But it's not very new. Well, maybe it's necessary to have the courage or the humility to repeat oneself.

In my so great disorientation with myself as well as with my etchings, I don't always see clearly and am not so sure where I'm going. I listen to you and tell myself that one needs to know how to wait, I listen to you and tell myself that one needs to know how to wait [sic]. I don't know why the price of this empty waiting, for only a few weeks, seems so dear to me.

Tomorrow is December 23rd. Day of lilacs, day of pre-mimosas, day.

I am thinking of you, I am thinking that perhaps you are working at your table, all alone, I am thinking of the poems that will be born, I hope.

I kiss you, my darling

Gisèle

1. Allusion to a planned title for a print from March 1965, definitively entitled *En guise d'une présence—Statt einer Gegenwart.*

318

[Paris,] Friday, 23 December 1966

Happy anniversary!

My Darling,

Thank for your letter: I am glad that You were welcomed nicely. A thousand thank yous to Françoise. May the winter be clement.

Two evenings ago I accompanied Eric to the train station; at eleven-twenty, during boarding, little Luc was not there as arranged, and I think that Eric was quite disappointed, even if he said nothing.

Yesterday, for me: two dentist's sessions, of almost two hours each. I have, in front, a temporary bridge. This morning, re-dentist, and in a little while re-re-dentist.

Yesterday, regarding the poem-etching,[1] very nice phone call (from Berlin!) from Péter Szondi.[2] The day before yesterday, thanks over the phone from Pierre Bertaux[3] (he is going, with his son, his daughter-in-law, and his granddaughter, to Draguignan (La Martinière, route de Grasse) and told me that if you feel like seeing him, a note by telegram would suffice).—Thanks from Minder: "Thanks for Your wishes and the magnificent etching!" Perhaps you can pay them, after having called ahead, a little visit.

This morning, an Austrian review, *Literatur und Kritik*, with some ignominies and infamies regarding my collaboration on Michaux (I).[4]—Dear Austria... And, also, a letter from J.-C. Schneider that I transcribe for you[5]—tell me what you think of it.—

I hug You

Paul

1. See no. 308, n. 1.
2. Péter Szondi was, since summer 1965, Professor of General and Comparative Literature at the Freie Universität Berlin.

3. French Germanist, professor at the Sorbonne. A member of the "Ordre de la Libération" and a former high-ranking civil servant, Pierre Bertaux had used his influence to support PC in various situations.

4. In a review of the volume of translations of Henri Michaux, *Dichtungen, Schriften I* (see no. 179, n. 1) signed by Hans Jürgen Fröhlich and published in *Literatur und Kritik* (review published by Otto Müller, Salzburg, December 1966, 9/10, pp. 113–5), the reviewer claims that the majority of the translation work was done by Kurt Leonhard and that the publisher "probably expects a promotional effect from the name 'Celan.'" In reality, as numerous typescripts preserved in the Deutsches Literaturarchiv Marbach demonstrate, PC had also reread, often corrected, and reworked the translations by Kurt Leonhard.

5. The handwritten copy of the letter from the Germanist, translator, and poet Jean-Claude Schneider, which is no longer attached to PC's letter, was classified with the original in one of the chronological correspondence files.

319

rue du Château d'Eau
Saint-Cézaire-sur-Siagne, Alpes-Maritimes
25 December 1966

It is past midnight, my darling, I have stopped painting to write to You. Maybe You are still with our warm friends the Lucases! Maybe you have already come home.

When I think of Your patience with the dentist, You have all my admiration, and I am ashamed during this time to be so peacefully in the sun in this so beautiful countryside. But, you know, in winter, it is quite severe, and these very somber mountain faces also give one a bit of vertigo. It is very steep here, and since there are no houses or humans visible, it has much severity and grandeur; it's not exactly pretty, it's even sometimes so wild, so arid that it has a mysterious and sometimes a bit disquieting beauty.

I thought again with joy of the poem you told me you wrote, I hope you will send it to me.[1] Excuse me but in this inn the telephone was in the hallway, patrons were passing by, the innkeeper was constantly coming to check the hourglass and I didn't feel quite capable, in the midst of the noise and people walking by, of truly listening to you. I was already, after all these attempts, very content to have you on the line despite the place being so ill-suited to a true dialogue.

I am also thinking again about that critique of the Michaux, it's saddening. I don't see how you could have the courage to take on again, under the current conditions, a second volume. I still hope it will be possible to translate Michaux again but to translate him alone.

I showed and gave Françoise the *NRF*.[2] She really likes the little she knows of your poems and remembers the few lines that I translated for her a year and a half ago.

One word, one phrase to live with, she asks of me. But, you know, she doesn't like the translations very much and her little German allows her to grasp more with a literal translation than she can through J.-C. Schneider. She is still glad to have this help.

The Christmas parties seem to be over, which pleases me, I like so little this holiday atmosphere. Yesterday evening I left Françoise very early and, after a long walk, I painted, painted a lot and I began to find a little freedom again. Let's hope that it's not too bad, I painted late yesterday, this morning, in the evening again, but I don't have any idea.

I am groping my way along a bit with colors and mixes that seem to me to become a bit richer but remain poor; that happens a lot, maybe that's what is necessary after this major disorientation, after those very different etchings.

It's odd that infinitely numerous colors seem less rich in possibilities to me than the infinity that goes from black to white. My colors repeat and the form remains less rigorous than in etchings. And then I don't know where I'm going, when I start, it's the big worry, that I am drowning there, that I am throwing myself in. The last one always seems to be the best, but then it goes off to join the pile that seems so mediocre.

Despite everything I am working, even quite a bit, at least four hours a day.

The gray of boulders, the reds of the earth, the grays and greens of the trees, and the russet of the oaks meet the blue of the sky. All that is a bit jumbled together. Last night I continued the theme of my New Year's greetings etching, *Presque des Iles—Ile aux enfants morts*—which I spoke to you about before leaving. It has become something else but you will recognize it.

What I am doing right now is unthinkable without my walks, without what I see, but it has nothing to do with that, and I don't really know what it is. It's even troubling. I don't know where I want to get to, nor where that goes, nor what comes of it. I don't know at all, but I do it spiritedly and with fervor, and that imposes itself on me without so much reflection. Do you think it's possible to work like this? Tell me!

I don't understand these gouaches very much, I wouldn't know what to say about them, they are not entirely foreign to me but not entirely present either.

It's hard, you know, all the more so as my life here is composed of moments of great solitude.

Françoise is of course always there, but her presence is such a presence that I cannot put up with it all too much, nor indeed all these encounters with difficult fates, with shattered beings, with suffering, with which she is surrounded. But she is so good, so much of another world, so rare. But it's a bit too much for me.

She continues to suffer in her stomach or the bottom of her lungs, or pleura, I beg her to see a doctor, but I must admit that I am a bit afraid of what she has in store; in two days she will see one.

I think that tomorrow I will have your letter and I am delighted, but write to me often often [sic] long letters with much about you. I really need it. From Eric I don't hope for many letters, but if you have any, send them to me.

My room isn't so bad, luckily; I don't understand so well how I manage to live there since the heating is scanty, but I am never cold. The only unpleasant thing is the freezing staircase. It's quite amusing to live in a room on the third floor of an empty house, I have the key to it and I am completely at home. You could come spend a few days here, if you felt like it, there is a big bed to receive you and me with you, Françoise would be delighted, but aside from that only the severity of a village numbed with winter, very nice little old men, little old ladies and cold, draughty streets, but a stone's throw away, the hills, different on each side, and beautiful, so beautiful.

Yesterday I could not fall asleep before 2 in the morning, I never go to bed early but sleep late and begin to emerge a little around 10:30 in the morning. I would like to recuperate a little before my return, I am less tired, I think, but it's still not great.

Write to me, my darling, at length. I kiss you

Gisèle

---

1. GCL is probably referring to "Wenn ich nicht weiß, nicht weiß," written 23 December 1966.
2. The *NRF* (1 December 1966) contained Jean-Claude Schneider's French translations of nine of PC's poems.

320

[Paris,] 27 December 1966

My Darling,

First of all thank you and thank you for Your wishes and the etching. Here it is across from her sister: the coppers, rewritten in Your hand, exchange their messages, "lestrangely."[1]

I hope that my express letter did not worry You. I have recovered since then, and yesterday, with D., I found, regarding all these subjects, vigorously articulated thought.

Yesterday, visit from Hugo Huppert: translator of Mayakovsky and, I did not completely realize it until after reading the books he gave me, an incorrigible Stalinist.[2] He left me three of my books[3] to sign; but I will take them to his hotel tomorrow, unsigned, and accompanied by a letter that is very polite but reminds him of Mandelstamm and Marina Tsvetaeva, and, also, my anti-Stalinist position.[4]—Dear Austria, again. And what's more, alas, doubts about Erich Einhorn, who gave Huppert my telephone number and a photo that, upon his request, I had sent him a few years ago.[5]

This morning, disappointment: the attached letter, from the gallery of Mme Unseld. It is hardly polite and promises strictly nothing. I ask myself—already!—if the fact of your having written in French to Mme Unseld doesn't have something to do with it. What to say, what to say? (Poetry, an affair of abysses.)

Yesterday with the Lucas: friends.

Tomorrow, I am having lunch with André du Bouchet: a friend.

I am enclosing for you a friendly letter from J.-C. Hémery, arrived this morning.[6]

I wrote a hard, difficult to translate poem, among other lines, this one: "Die Jüdin Pallas Athene"[7]—

I had hoped for a phone call—did Eric write to You? I have no news at all.—Give my best to Françoise.

Happy New Year! I hug you

Paul

1. PC alludes of course to the name of his spouse, De Lestrange (that is to say, *de l'étranger*: of abroad, or of the foreign), which originally referred to someone who had been "foreign" in a land, as it happens, in Palestine (GCL emphasized with bitter irony that her ancestors had participated in the Crusades and, therefore, in the persecution of the Jews), but above all to *l'étrangeté* (strangeness or foreignness), a necessary quality, according to PC, for poetry as for printmaking. On this topic, PC notes, in 1968, this reflection of Paul Valéry's: "Any view of things that is not strange [étrange] is false" (see *SP. Historisch-kritische Ausgabe*, 10.2., p. 143). On the notion of *fremd* (foreign, strange) associated with *Dunkelheit* (obscurity), see *Meridian*, in particular pp. 7–9.

2. Hugo Huppert, a member of the Austrian Communist Party in 1927, emigrated to the USSR in 1928 and worked at the Marx-Engels Institute in Moscow, before returning to Austria in 1951. Celan refers to the following books: Wladimir Majakowski, *Politische Poesie, Nachdichtung von Hugo Huppert* (Frankfurt am Main: Suhrkamp, 1966); Hugo Huppert, *Erinnerungen an Majakowski* (Frankfurt am Main: Suhrkamp, 1966) (this volume contains the dedication "In aller Herzlichkeit für Paul Celan—Hugo Huppert, Paris, Weihnachten 1966." (Cordially, for Paul Celan—Hugo Huppert, Paris, Christmas 1966); *Wladimir Majakowski in Selbstzeugnissen und Bilddokumenten, dargestellt von Hugo Huppert* (Reinbek near Hamburg: Rowohlt, 1965); this volume contains the remark written by PC: "Von Hugo Huppert, / Paris, 26.XII.66 / vgl. S. 160"; on p. 160, PC marked Huppert's quotation of Joseph Stalin in the chapter that brings together testimonies (Zeugnisse) from diverse artists and writers. See *FREN*, pp. 321–4.

3. Of these, only *NR* has been identified.

4. In his letter to Huppert, PC writes, "I would have gladly replied to this dedication—I cannot: You defend in Your monograph and also in Your 'Memories', explicitly and implicitly, Stalinist positions. You know that one of my poetry volumes that I was supposed to sign, on your cordially expressed wish, is dedicated to the memory of Ossip Mandelstamm and that it also recalls Marina Tsvetaeva; beyond that it attempts, like the poems and translations that preceded it, to stand against everything Stalinist, *also* against everything Stalinist."

5. Einhorn had asked for a photo of PC and his family in his letter from 11 June 1962 (see Paul Celan-Erich Einhorn, "Briefe" 3, *op. cit.*; see also here, no. 87, n. 3).

6. PC and GCL had met Jean-Claude Hémery, a writer and translator from German (among others, of Nietzsche and Thomas Bernhard) in September–October 1954.

7. PC cites freely lines 12–14 of "Wenn ich nicht weiß, nicht weiß" (When I Don't Know, Don't Know), written 23 December 1966. (Cf. *NKGA*, p. 241.)

321

[Paris,] Thursday, 29 December 1966

My Darling,

Your phone call and, and hour later, your letter from Wednesday. Thank you, my love, thank you.

This stay in Provence, I feel it, does you good in a profound way, even if you don't realize it immediately, you will feel it in the weeks and the months to come.

A little sad that Eric writes so little. But confident, despite everything, in the beneficial effects of skiing.

Armand Robin: yes, I know him a little. We have translations, by him, of Block, Yesenin, Pasternak, and of—I forget[1] (*Quatre Poètes Russes*[2])— sometimes "over the top," "artistic" translations, but always carried by the spirit of Poetry. Someone, recently, had told me that Robin had been a member of the Fédération Anarchiste—who? Was it Frénaud?[3] I don't remember.

Tell Françoise that I hope that everything can contribute to support her, to keep her going, to carry her in her so courageous, so ardent existence.

You, my Darling, I kiss you, ever and forever on the Bridge of Years.[4]

Happy New Year! Happy Years!

Paul

[In the margin:] This is written on the "Three Candlesticks"[5] from Aunt Berta, who has just very kindly written us.

1. The poet whose name PC forgets is Vladimir Mayakovsky, a poet favored by Hugo Huppert, from whom PC has just distanced himself for serious reasons; see above, no. 320, n. 2 and n. 4.

2. *Quatre poètes russes: V. Maïakovsky, B. Pasternak, A. Blok, S. Essénine*, trans. and ed. Armand Robin (Paris: Éditions du Seuil, 1949).

3. The Celans had recently received the poet André Frénaud together with Petre Solomon at rue de Longchamp, on 28 November 1966 (GCL's diary).

4. See no. 3, n. 2.

5. "THE THREE CANDLESTICKS—1649": PC very much liked this English stationery given to him by his aunt, Berta Antschel, on which three candlesticks are represented in filigree. Several poems recopied in this correspondence were written on this stationery, as well as a complete copy of *Schneepart* (Frankfurt am Main: Suhrkamp, 1971; hereafter *SP*), intended for GCL and EC. The logo of the brand is represented on the inside of the envelopes. On 4 August 1969, PC will put his wedding ring in a sealed envelope representing "The Three Candlesticks," with the following note: "Ring 4 / August 1969."

322

[Paris, 4 January 1967]

My Darling,

Thanks for having telephoned, again. Eric and I, we are waiting for you. It's pleasant here.

I avow that I am rather bothered today by my shingles: itches and little burns, not painful, but let's say, a bit stronger than yesterday, the thing is there. What's more, Mme de Montaigu, allergic to the penicillin that she administers to her patients, received me all covered (her face and hands) by eczema—not contagious, but all the same.—I wrote a new hard and harsh poem.[1]

I hug you

Paul

[In the margin:] Your BLEU train departs Nice at 20:20 and arrives at Paris-Lyon at 8:54.

1. "Gewieherte Tumbagebete" (*NKGA*, p. 243; see "Braying Tumba Players," *FB*, p. 116.)

323

[To Eric Celan]

[Paris, 8 February 1967]

Mein Sohn Eric, ich grüße Dich. Ich grüße Euch, Menschen.

My son Eric, I greet you. I greet you, humans.

Paul Celan

8.2.1967[1]

1. Note written in the Boucicaut hospital (78 rue de la Convention, 15th arrondissement), where PC was urgently hospitalized after a suicide attempt, in order to be operated on there. On 30 January 1967, after locking himself in the chambre de bonne that he was using as an office, PC had attempted to plunge a knife—probably a paper knife—into his heart. The knife had passed very close to the vital organ, gravely damaging his left lung. GCL only managed to save PC *in extremis*, after having forced open the door. PC will write a few months later, on 8 September 1967: "DAS WILDHERZ, verhäuslicht / vom halbblinden Stich / in die Lunge" (THE WILD HEART, domesticated / by the half-blind stab / in the lung); *NKGA*, p. 292; see also *BIT*, p. 272; it is the last poem of the third cycle of *Lichtzwang* (*Light Duress*; hereafter *LZ*). In his planner, GCL noted her visits to PC on 31 January and 1, 3, 6, 7, and 13 February 1967.

324

78 rue de Longchamp
Friday, 18[1] February 1967

My darling,

In asking how you are doing, as every day,[2] I learn that you are worried about Eric. He is well, is continuing his normal activities, school, work at home, boy scouts. He had very very good results on his first compositions of the trimester and is once again in a period of compositions, with a lot of work.

If you need something, write to me or have it told to me.

I am thinking of you without cease, of all your difficulties. You were doing so well in January! Courage, Paul, you must live, find yourself again, calmly.

If I have to do something with your mail, you'll tell me.

I hope that a new dialogue will be possible between us.

See you soon

Gisèle

<hr>

1. Actually the 17th.
2. PC was transferred from Hôpital Boucicaut to Sainte-Anne (under the direction of Jean Delay). The doctors asked GCL to limit or avoid visits at first.

325

[Paris,] Tuesday, 28 February 1967

My dear Gisèle, I received, this morning, your letter from yesterday, then, toward noon, the letter from Eric, the list of mail, the fruit. Thanks for everything.

Your letter dismayed me: I understand your preoccupations, and I think I understand a certain number of things beyond these. If you feel too tired for Thursday, don't come until Sunday.

I saw Doctor D. just before and spoke to him of the problems that we discussed the other day: replying to my mail, the reading and sending of the manuscript of new poems,[1] sessions with the dentist. In everything, Doctor D. has shown himself to be very affable. Regarding the dentist, you need to get in touch with him so that he tells you the number and the duration of sessions envisioned, so that I can obtain the necessary leaves; then let the doctor and me know his answer.

Regarding the mail, there are, I believe, relatively few letters from editors—but they are probably important.[2] (Bring, please, the others also, that will distract me.)

For the manuscript, try to find and bring the copy, as well as some sheets of white paper (for the summary, etc.). Perhaps you will be able to bring also the staples and the little machine to affix them; and some folders to put the manuscript in.

And now, so that I don't tire you out, I will finish this letter. Not without recalling the first letter that you sent me here, with the words with which it begins. You told me there Until soon. I say it again, here.

Paul

1. *AW.*
2. Among these letters, two from Siegfried Unseld: in the first, the head of Suhrkamp and Insel acknowledges receipt of the manuscript of the translation of Shakespeare's sonnets and speaks of various problems and editorial projects tied to PC's rupture with his former publisher, S. Fischer. In the second letter, Unseld informs PC of DVA's refusal to cede the rights to *MG* and *VS* to Suhrkamp for the purpose of publishing a *Gesamtausgabe* (complete edition) of PC's poems.

326

[Paris,] Wednesday [8 March 1967]

My dear Gisèle,

I was just seen by Dr. D., who is up to date, moreover, about my dental problems thanks to you. I had, for my part, asked for an appointment beginning the day before yesterday, when the upper bridge became completely detached.

Doctor D. tells me that he will get in touch immediately with Mlle Arrieta to arrange the sessions I need with my dentist. So I probably will have leaves of absence, and I will need, for that, my clothing: overcoat, pants, shirt, underwear, tie, socks, shoes—It is again you who has to assume the transportation of all that, thanks in advance.

How are you both, you and Eric? I wish for you to find your calm and the taste for work again. For Eric, success at school and a vacation, close at hand and joyous.

I worked, yesterday and the day before yesterday, on the manuscript of *Atemwende*. It is really the densest thing I have written so far, the most sweeping. At certain turning points in the text, I felt, I admit, pride.—I ultimately divided the manuscript into cycles—it had to be aired out—unequal in expanse, but "in sich geschlossen," as one says in German. For the end, preceded by a blank page, alone and a cycle at the same time, the "EINMAL."[1]

Otherwise, I read the letters—there is one among them, from a young Berlin composer, which touches me immensely: a true, beautiful letter.[2] And I read the brochure with the essay on my poems: there again, it is a step forward with regard to what there has been so far.[3]—Currently, I am reading the Shestov, I am only at the introductory notes by Benjamin Fondane,[4] but—I can follow, I do not lose the thread![5] Ah, to be able to read like before!

I will spend this afternoon establishing the table of contents for the manuscript.

Will I see you again before Sunday, when you bring the clothing? Would it be useful to call Mlle Arrieta the day after tomorrow, for example? Time is a little short—vacation is approaching—and the dentist needs to set the date of the appointment.

Until Sunday at the latest! All my wishes!

Hug Eric.

Paul

1. "Einmal," poem written in September 1965; *AW, NKGA*, p. 218. "In sich geschlossen": literally, "closed in itself," that is to say, forming a whole.

2. Tilo Müller-Medek (born in Jena in 1940), whom Erich Arendt had introduced to PC's poetry and who lived in East Berlin, had written to PC twice, the previous year, about setting "Todesfuge" to music. In the brief letter PC alludes to here, the "young Berlin composer," who had heard PC read his Alexander Blok translations on the radio, writes about his project of setting these poems to music, before expressing his admiration for PC.

3. Peter Paul Schwarz had sent PC his essay "Totengedächtnis und dialogische Polarität in der Lyrik Paul Celans" (Memory of the dead and dialogical polarity in the poetry of Paul Celan), which had just appeared in the review *Wirkendes Wort* (Düsseldorf: Schwann).

4. Lev Shestov, *Le Pouvoir des clefs (Potestas clavium)*, translated by Boris de Schloezer with a preface, "Rencontre avec Léon Chestov," by Benjamin Fondane (Paris: Flammarion, 1967). The volume has numerous reading marks by PC, for example on p. 10 (*Rencontres avec L. Chestov*), where the phrase from Spinoza that PC had already recopied at the beginning of the 1960s appears: "Non ridere, non lugere, neque detestari, sed intelligere" (Do not laugh, do not mourn, do not hate, but understand)—PC noted the date "7. 2 [in error, instead of 3?] 67"; on p. 26, PC marked and underlined "elle [a certain Mrs. Bespalov, the author of a study entitled *Chestov devant Nietzsche*] y dit que pendant que l'homme est tombé à l'eau, Chestov est sur la rive, qui lui ordonne: 'Ne te noie pas; tu le peux'" (she says there that while the man has fallen into the water, Shestov is on the bank, and says: "Do not drown, it can happen to you"). PC also marks the second epigraph of the first chapter of Shestov's work ("Mille et une nuits [en guise de preface]," p. 37: "Qu'on ne nous reproche donc plus le manqué de clarté, puisque

nous en faisons profession. / PASCAL" (Let us no longer be reproached for lack of clarity, since we make our profession from it), and adds the comment: "Meridian-Zitat" (quotation from *Meridian*). PC had already marked this phrase, in September or October 1959, in a different edition of *Pouvoir des clefs* (Paris: J. Schiffrin, 1928), with this thought of Pascal's—cited from memory by Shestov—reflecting for PC an essential aspect of his poetry.

5. On "not losing the thread" see above, no. 155, n. 3. On PC worrying about his ability to concentrate and remember, see above no. 119, n. 1.

327

[Paris,] Wednesday, 8 March 1967[1]

Dear Paul,

I cannot take Paris anymore, in this apartment with the phone calls, with this whole drama we are living through. I will not be able to come Sunday, I am leaving tomorrow evening,[2] before my nerves go completely, which would not help with anything.

I hope to quickly shut myself away, in total rest.

Courage. Much courage.

Gisèle

I sent you this morning what, I think, you asked me for, Eric is staying in Paris and will continue going to school.

He is very well, don't worry.

[On the back of the envelope:] Your letter just arrived. Thanks. The suitcase with your things will be left with Mademoiselle Arrieta this evening.

1. Letter dated by PC.
2. Underlined by PC, who adds in the margin "Thursday!"

328

[Paris,] Thursday, 9 March 1967

Thanks, my dear Gisèle, for the two packages of books[1] that arrived this morning. So many beautiful things to read! I began the Lévi-Strauss,[2] read in it, so far around twenty pages, it is approachable, but it is too soon to form an idea of the work's tenor and reach.

Yesterday, I finished rereading *Atemwende* and I created the table of contents. It is now a manuscript of 93 pages, and I ask myself if the Canson paper that is to cover it should not be folded twice on the side of the back of the manuscript. Once the stapler is brought here, we will be able to prepare everything to be sent.

Don't forget the pen. And note, for the letter to Unseld,[3] *your* bank account number as well as *mine*.

Hug Eric, who, I hope from the bottom of my heart, is climbing up all the slopes again.—You too, climb up them again.

Until Sunday

Paul

[In the margin:] The appointments at the dentist's will probably begin Monday or Tuesday; Professor Deniker just assented to it.

---

1. Most of them have been identified because PC dated them; several have many reading marks:
—The fifth volume of Shakespeare's works, which contains *Cymbeline* (see above, no. 145, n. 2); this play has numerous reading marks, see below, no. 331, n. 2; at the end, the date of reading: "13 March 67 / Cli[nique du] Pr[ofesseur] D[elay]."
—Lev Shestov, *Athènes et Jérusalem. Un essai de philosophie réligieuse*, translated by Boris de Schloezer, with a preface, "L'Obstination de Chestov," by Yves Bonnefoy (Paris: Flammarion, 1967); PC mentions several dates of reading: 17 March 1967, at the end of Bonnefoy's text (p. 16); 19 March 1967, at the end of the Shestov preface (p. 38); at the end of the volume, PC inserted the sketch and the clean copy of "Die abgewrackten Tabus," a poem written 18 March 1967; see final version *NKGA*, p. 246.
—*Große deutsche Verse von Schiller bis Fontane*, edited and with an introduction by Hans Mayer (Frankfurt am Main: Insel, 1967); the date of reading: 20 March 1967.
—Thomas Bernhard, *Verstörung* (Frankfurt am Main: Insel, 1967). The volume, which contains numerous reading marks, annotations, and "i" marks, is dated "20 March 67 / C[linique du] P[rofesseur] D[elay]," and, at the end, the date of reading: "23 March 67 / C[linique du] P[rofesseur] D[elay]." PC underlines and marks with a line in the margin, for example, p. 183: "Tödliche Selbstgesprächigkeit. Wahnsinn durch sich selbst als Wahnsinn der Welt, der Natur" (Deadly monologue. Madness from oneself as madness of the world, of nature); at the end of the volume, PC notes, in relation to his reading of p. 107: "-i- / Die Schwermut aufs neue geduldet, / pendelt sich ein" (Melancholy put up with again, / finds its rhythm); cf. "Unverwahrt," dated 8 April 1967, *NKGA*, p. 249.

—Bartholomé de Las Casas, *Kurzgefaßter Bericht von der Verwüstung der Westindischen Länder*, ed. Hans Magnus Enzensberger (Frankfurt am Main: Insel, 1966). The volume, which has numerous underlinings and often critical remarks on the footnotes, includes the note "20.3.67. Cl[inique du] P[rofesseur] D[elay]" and, at the end of the text, the date of reading, 25 March 1967.

—Edmond Jabès, *Le Livre des questions* (Paris: Gallimard, 1963). The volume is dedicated "To Paul Celan / With the very strong sympathy and the admiration of / E. Jabès / (…after a long conversation in Geneva / with Jean Starobinski / where the subject was often / You)"; PC noted the date of reading: 30 March 1967.

—Edmond Jabès, *Le Livre des questions II. Le Livre de Yukel* (Paris: Gallimard, 1964). The book carries the dedication: "To Paul Celan / In all sympathy / and very cordially / E. J."; date of reading: "31 March 67" and "31 March 67 / C[linique du / P[rofesseur] D[elay]"

—Edmond Jabès, *Le Livre des questions III. Le Retour du livre* (Paris: Gallimard, 1965). The book is dedicated: "To Paul Celan / in all esteem / E.J." Date of reading: 1 April 1967.

—Sigmund Freud, *Gesammelte Werke*. vol. 13 (Frankfurt am Main: S. Fischer, 1963). The poems "…AUCH KEINERLEI / Friede" and "Wirf das Sonnenjahr" (7 May and 11 May 1967; *FS, NKGA*, pp. 257 and 258) are closely tied to the reading of two essays in particular published in this volume: "Jenseits des Lustprinzips" (pp. 1–69; "11 May 1967") and "Das Ich und das Es" (p. 235–89; "7 April 1967 / C[linique du] P[rofesseur] D[elay]"). PC dated this book "1 April 1967 / [C]linique du] P[rofesseur] D[elay] (auf Grund einer Anweisung von Frau Fischer)" (because of Mrs. Fischer's instructions).

—A. Faller, *Der Körper des Menschen* (Stuttgart: Thieme, 1966). In this anatomy manual, in which numerous reading marks can be found in the chapters devoted to the heart and the lungs in particular, the first versions of the poems "Nah, im Aortenbogen" and "KOMM, wir löffeln / Nervenzellen" (10 May and 21 August 1967; *FS, NKGA*, p. 257 and 251), were written by PC on the flyleaf pages at the end of the volume.

—Thomas Mann, *Der Zauberberg* (Frankfurt am Main: S. Fischer, 1954). PC will reread two chapters from this novel on 10 April 1967; there are no reading marks.

—John Millington Synge, *Der Held der westlichen Welt und andere Stücke* (Frankfurt am Main: Suhrkamp, 1967). This volume shows numerous reading marks and is dated 26 April 1967 (p. 56).

2. Claude Lévi-Strauss, *La Pensée sauvage* (Paris: Plon, 1962). Among lines marked by PC, some can be read as elements of his own poetics, and one in particular clearly has an autobiographical significance for PC, recalling his situation regarding the Goll Affair: "L'homme qui fait une belle récolte est tenu pour un voleur chanceux" (The man who reaps a good harvest is taken for a lucky thief), p. 146.

3. PC will not write to his editor or send him the manuscript of *AW* until 23 March 1967.

329

[Paris,] Thursday, 10 February[1] 1967

My Darling,

Your letter just arrived: I learn that you are leaving Paris this evening, but you do not tell me where you are going. I am very distraught about that.

Give me your news regularly and tell me with whom Eric is staying.
Good Health! Good return!

> I hug you! Until soon!
> Paul

1. Actually Friday, 10 March.

330

> [Paris, 16 March 1967]

My dear Gisèle, it is Thursday, Sunday is your birthday,[1] I would like for these lines to be there, that day, beside you, to bring you my wishes: my fervent wishes.

> Paul

1. 19 March 1967, GCL's fortieth birthday.

331

> 78 rue de Langchamp
> Paris, 16th [arrondissement]
> Monday, 3 April 1967

Dear Paul,

I just returned to Paris, excuse me for not having been able to write. I find your letters, for which I thank you, also the note for my birthday, which touched me so much. When I left for Provence, I just couldn't take any more. Everything had become intolerable for me in Paris, the apartment, the phone calls, the people, I wasn't sleeping anymore, I couldn't hide from Eric the very heavy weight of suffering and worry. I couldn't take care of him as I needed to, calmly. I thought that I would find a place in La Messuguière, but a last-minute group having overrun everything, I ultimately turned up in a piteous state at Françoise's[1] house. Marie-Thérèse took care of Eric and he is staying with her, so he has been able to continue school until the Easter vacation. He accepted and understood my departure and was very pampered and spoiled by his aunt.

Going to see you in the hospital, feeling your hope being born again, not knowing how to respond, you know, troubled me very much. A true dialogue about the drama you had been through, that we had been through [sentence incomplete] Such a change in your attitude toward me, who couldn't forget the three so terribly painful days of incomprehension which made difficult, difficult for me any spontaneous gesture toward you.

I know what your love is, I hope that you don't doubt mine. Your drama, your fate, occupy all my thoughts, but in grave moments my inability to help you and the fact that my presence itself is so traumatizing for you,[2] the wall of incomprehension that rises between us, this total solitude, this failure I experience and that finally leads to such a dramatic situation, drive me to despair, are too much for me.

I would like in these moments at least not to plunge you deeper into your difficulties, into your suffering. It's hard, it's very hard.

Paul, dear Paul, do you understand how difficult, awful it is for me too?

I sent Eric, when you left, envelopes with your address so that he writes you, I hope he will have done so. Personally, I only received a few lines once. He does not like to write, but he seems very content to do a lot of skiing. I hope that he enjoys his vacation, which he needed so much, as much as possible.

I am thinking of you, I am thinking of you constantly, but the future, I don't know how to envision it for the moment. I know, believe me, how terrible everything you are going through is. It's hard for me, very hard. I will try to get back to work and, beginning Wednesday evening with Eric's return, to help him again with school, with what he needs help with.

The knowledge that I have from you, which you told me so often you had forgotten but recognized in my words as coming from you, is precious to me, and this loyalty to this knowledge of which as you told me you made me the guardian, will help me to help Eric.

As soon as he is back, I will tell you how he is doing.

Tell me how you are doing.

I am thinking of you, Paul.

Gisèle

1. Françoise Bonaldi, friend of GCL's, lived in Saint-Cézaire-sur-Siagne, not far from La Messu-guière.

2. The passages in Shakespeare's *Cymbeline* that PC had underlined three weeks earlier (reading dated 13 March 1967, see above, no. 328, n. 1), are extremely troubling in this context. For example: "CORNELIUS. First, she confess'd she never lov'd you, only / Affected greatness got by you, not you: / Married your royalty, was wife to your place, / Abhorr'd your person [...] / CYMBELINE. O most delicate fiend! / Who is't can read a woman? Is there more? / CORNELIUS. More, sir, and worse. She did confess she had / For you a mortal mineral which, being took, / Should by the minute feed on life, and ling'ring, / By inches waste you. In which time she purposed / By watching, weeping, tendance, kissing, to / O'ercome you with her show; and in time, / When she had fitted you with her craft, to work / Her son into th'adoption of the crown; / But failing of her end by his strange absence, / Grew shameless desperate, opened in despite / Of heaven and men her purposes, repented / The evils she hatched were not effected; so / Despairing died. / [...] CYMBELINE. Mine eyes / Were not in fault, for she was beautiful; / Mine ears that heard her flattery, nor my heart, / That thought her like her seeming. It had been vicious / To have mistrusted her. Yet, O my daughter, / That it was folly in me thou mayst say, / And prove it in thy feeling. Heaven mend all!" PC also marked with a line in the margin the beginning of Cymbeline's reply in the German translation of "Mine eyes [...] beautiful": "Meine Augen / Sind ohne Schuld, denn sie war schön." In this same mood, PC had marked and underlined almost all of Posthumus's monologue in Act 2, scene 5.

332

[Paris,] Tuesday, 4 April 1967

I thank you for your long letter, dear Gisèle. I was happy when, this morning, the nurse brought it to me; just as I was happy yesterday, when I received the letter from Eric with your handwriting on the envelope. Four weeks of waiting is, especially for someone so not used to that, a long wait. But here is a new thing in my life: I have learned to wait.

As for what you tell me in your letter, how can I respond? You tell me you don't know how to envision the future, I understand you, but understand well, Gisèle, that it is necessary to envision the future if there is to be a future. And I firmly believe that there needs to be one, for us three, one way or another. We will surely not be able to immediately find the solutions, but we have to see each other again, for an hour perhaps, from time to time. Then for longer: to find a solution.

You ask how I'm doing: I am sleeping well and during the day I manage to read.[1] (Thanks to the forwarded mail I have not been lacking in books at all—which now, here, encumber me.) And I think of us.

The doctor Si. who took care of me until today,* thought that I could and should resume my classes at the École toward mid-May (after the written exam of the agrégation) and continue them until the end of June, my recuperation residing in my work. I do not ask for anything better. But in order to prepare my classes I need to work at home, with my books—and you, are you prepared to meet me on this occasion? Make the effort, Gisèle: you will do it for us three.—I plan to speak to Doctor D. about the problem of the classes to be resumed and of the rest; he promised to receive me for an interview.

A little surprise for you: *La Gazette de Francfort* from 29 March published an etching by you, taken from *Atemkristall*, with a quite sensible note[2]—did you know about it? (Remember that we will be able to do more things like that.)[3]

This summer, I will have to occupy myself with the proofs for the new volume—which also marks a date in my life.[4] And I feel like translating poetry.[5] Perhaps, if you prefer, a friend will loan me, before and during the summer, his residence. Or I will rent a room.[6]

But there are also practical problems, in the immediate future: dirty laundry, *money* (André du Bouchet loaned me 10,000 fr[anc]s**) etc.—Try to come the day after tomorrow, Thursday, to the clinic for a little hour, from one thirty on; at three o'clock I go into town, to the dentist (who did a very good job. But there too, I need Insadol, etc.)

Hug Eric and thank him for his letter.

My wishes go toward you

Paul

1. PC is reading intensely. See no. 328, n. 1.
* she was just replaced by a new doctor

2. The fourth etching in *Atemkristall* was reproduced in the *Frankfurter Allgemeine Zeitung* of 29 March 1967.

3. PC and GCL will publish another collector's edition in 1969, entitled *Schwarzmaut* ("Black Toll").

4. On 23 March 1967, PC had sent his new publisher the manuscript of this "new volume," *Atemwende (Breathturn)*.

5. PC will translate, in this and the following year, Jules Supervielle, Giuseppe Ungaretti, and André du Bouchet.

6. PC will spend the entire summer of 1967 either in Sainte-Anne or in his office on rue d'Ulm. He will not rent a furnished studio until the end of November of this year.

** replies to letters

333

[To Eric Celan]

[Paris,] Tuesday, 4 April 1967

My dear Eric,

Tomorrow you get home, Mama will be there to receive you—welcome home.

Your letter reached me yesterday, with the card reproducing your nice hotel and this big dog whose master, I admit, I would gladly be. You are like me, I think: you like these big animals that are strong and loyal.[1]

Me, I am really doing better (and I am glad to let you know). I sleep well, sometimes I have extremely pleasant dreams—as I only rarely have—and during the day I read and I write. (Of course, I read more than I write;[2] the contrary would be desirable.) You know, I think that a new volume of poems should appear in September with Suhrkamp (my new publisher in Frankfurt), it's an important date in my life, for the book, in several respects, including, above all, that of its language, marks a turning point (which its readers will not be able not to realize).[3]

And you? How did this second trimester end? You remember, you promised me the details—I am waiting for them. And I am waiting for new fruitful efforts in school—there too I am counting on you.

Write to me often.

I hug you

Your papa

1. The postcard sent by EC, who is spending his vacation in the Alps, bears the image of a Saint Bernard.
2. PC had just written "Stille" (30 March 1967), "Die Eine" (1 April 1967) (*FS, NKGA*, p. 247) and, on this day, a poem that begins: "Bei Glüh- und Mühwein, nekronym / lang vor der Zeit" (*With Mulled- And Woe-, necronymously / long before the time*) (*NKGA*, p. 247; see also *BIT*, p. 172, *FB*, p. 143. The adverbial use of "nekronym" is tied to PC's reading of Lévi-Strauss (see above, no. 328, n. 2).
3. *AW* marks a rupture with the lyricism inherited from early-twentieth-century poets, such as Rilke or Mandelstam, which is still perceptible in *NR* (1963).

334

[Paris,] Friday, 7 April 1967

My dear Gisèle,

How, after all that we said to each other yesterday, should I speak to you today? I think of us three, of you, of Eric—numerous, numerous thoughts, around the heart, searching their places, their orbits.

Zwei Bitten: please send the telegram attached to this letter to the daughter of Ludwig von Ficker;[1] I cannot write her a letter; send it as a telegram-*letter*, it's a bit long, but less expensive.

Die zweite Bitte: two folders for the April and May mail. I am enclosing a few lines for our brave Eric.

Good work! Good health! Good calm!

Paul

[To Eric Celan]

[Paris,] Friday, 7 April 1967

My Dear Eric,

I was so glad yesterday when Mama showed me your grades: the progress is clear, it is there, it is well established. Now it is necessary to affirm it, maintain it, in some places—literature!—improve it. Which I do not doubt, you will do.

Apart from studies: I wish you good games! good books!

Your papa

1. "Zwei Bitten" means "two requests," "die zweite Bitte" means "the second request." Birgit von Schowingen had just sent PC a collected volume of the writings of her father, Ludwig von Ficker, the discoverer, publisher, and friend of Georg Trakl (whom PC had met in Innsbruck in July 1948): *Denkzettel und Danksagungen: Reden und Aufsätze aus den Jahren 1910 bis 1966 über Ferdinand Ebner, Theodor Haecker, Karl Kraus, Else Lasker-Schüler, Christine Lavant, Adolf Loos, Rainer Maria Rilke, Georg Trakl, Ludwig Wittgenstein u.a.*, ed. Franz Seyr (Munich: Kösel, 1967).

335

[Paris,] Friday, 7 [April 1967], twelve thirty

My dear Gisèle,

I am writing you a second letter because, upon reflection, an idea occurred to me, which might resolve the problem of the resumption of my work at rue d'Ulm between the end of May and the end of June.

I will not have any need to sleep twice a week at rue de Longchamp—as I envisioned yesterday—but it will suffice if we transport just once, preferably on a Sunday afternoon, books, dictionaries, texts, and typewriter into my office on rue d'Ulm, where, subsequently, I will go with the permission of Dr. D. to prepare my classes for the following day, while sleeping at the clinic.—

That seems to me to be a solution and I ask you to mention it during your meeting with D.

I would like to contribute, calmly, to your calm

Paul

336

[Paris,] Monday, 10 April 1967

Thanks my dear Gisèle, for the little planner that arrived this morning by mail, thanks for the big package that I just received.

How prompt You are! Thanks again.

I had a rather peaceful Sunday, the morning a bit lazy—the people on day release had not yet left—then, after lunch, various readings, including two chapters from *Zauberberg*—which I adored eighteen years ago: "Schnee" and "Walpurgisnacht" (the latter containing the mostly French dialogue between Hans Castorp and Clawdia Chauchat).[1] Well, I found that insipid, "old news," as Eric would say, not his, but, alas, already so little ours. Alas? No, there should be fewer regrets. But (self-made) harshnesses, but rocky protuberances emerging from depths, but rigorously anti-bourgeois spirit.

That led me to write two poems yesterday and one today—in all I have written fourteen since I have been here.[2]

The new doctor is very nice, I will probably see her next Saturday. You will probably already have seen Dr. D.

Tell me when the day of the exhibition of the portfolio[3] is: I would like to direct my thoughts there.

For Bochum,[4] I think that when it comes to "lady companions" Madame de la Motte remains the best choice:* she is from the area and knows the people, she likes what you do, she does not speak too much—a risk with Nadia, who is busy anyway with her work—she will really help you. As for Ruth, you can invite her, like Nadia, but no more than that.

Unless they let me accompany you and "frame you" with my poems[5] (which, for this occasion, I would choose from a new angle).

May you work and breathe in calm, with our son.

Paul

---

1. See above, no. 328, n. 1. Fernand Cambon, an *agrégation* student at the ENS in 1966–7, recalls a memory that echoes PC's words here: "To me personally—as far as I can recall—Celan only spoke once, during a chance encounter in the hallway. That was to ask me, and not only as a matter of form, what I was reading at the moment. It happened to be *The Magic Mountain*. Celan made a grimace of disapproval and gave rein, with a touch of sarcasm, to the words: 'Ach! Thomas Mann—der ist ein Pasticheur!' (Ah! Thomas Mann—he is a pasticheur!) He didn't say another word; but this quip sufficed to situate in a flash his radicality and his intransigence in matters of writing."
2. PC in fact likely means "the day before yesterday," namely: "Die herzschriftgekrümelte" (Crumbled by heart-writing) and "Unverwahrt" (Un-preserved); *FS, NKGA*, pp. 248, 249; and *FB*, pp. 146, 148). The fourteen poems mentioned here constitute the beginning of the third cycle of *FS*. The manuscripts of the poem PC says he wrote "today," entitled "Das unbedingte Geläut," are dated 8, 9, 10, and 11 April 1967.
3. See no. 305, n. 2, and Appendix, image no. 12.
4. From 9 May to 4 June 1967, GC will show nearly all of her prints made between 1954 and

*you have to invite her at your expense

1966 at the Städtische Kunstgalerie in Bochum. Twenty of these prints will be reproduced in the catalogue published on this occasion, which includes the bilingual titles provided by PC.
5. PC will not visit this exhibition and the envisioned reading will not take place.

337

78 rue de Longchamp
Tuesday [11 April 1967]

Dear Paul,

Thanks for your letters, I spoke with Dr. D., you will no doubt have spoken to him since. For Bochum, it seems that a leave of absence for several days, to go abroad, is still difficult. For the École, however, I think that he is thinking seriously about it. I will get in touch with Elmar[1] so you know where the students are and when the exams begin.

There is no exhibition planned in Paris for the Brunidor *Portfolio VI*, but in the coming days I expect to have a copy. It will be shown (in part?) in Bochum with *Atemkristall* and 70 etchings but...I have not received a reply to my last letters in which I asked for clarifications about the shipment. The print-shop must have finished everything. I already have a large part here, the rest I'll have tomorrow. The etchings that I was supposed to print myself are also ready. I am just waiting for the instructions from Bochum that do not arrive.

If I go to Bochum (will I be up to it? I'll see), yes I will send a message, as you tell me to, to invite Madame de la Motte (for what you have in mind: help), also Ruth and Nadia but I don't yet have an invitation or details.

In the meantime I had a few health worries which are gone now, I am waiting for the result of a test to be totally reassured. But I am doing well—very well. A job came along by chance, and I accepted it.[2] I thought in reality I would wait a while to go back to looking. But I have so few abilities that I could not let the opportunity go by of an offer for a small class that I had to take right away, with hours allowing me to work on etching too, if I manage to. Eric is delighted, finds it amusing, as for me I dive into a new job and that makes me panic as I don't know if I'll manage it. We'll see.

Today I responded, tomorrow I begin. It happened very quickly, in two days. A month ago I would have been too tired, I couldn't have done it, and the exhibition was not ready. Now is probably the right time. And in two and a half months I'll see if I can continue or not. It doesn't pay a fortune but there are four months of vacation when I can work for myself and I will only be occupied in the mornings from 9 to 12 and two afternoons from 2 to 5. Saturday free.

I think I had to accept. It's one of the rare things I can do and that leaves me time for myself.

I know your courage for continuing to read, to work, to write. I wish for you to be able to begin a real life again.

I wish you, Paul, all the best.

You are writing, you will write so much more!

Gisèle

Eric is doing very well, the work at school has begun very seriously again. The result of a German composition in my absence was not as brilliant as we could have hoped: only a 12. That compromises the end-of-year prize he hoped to have. He will write to you, he often plans to but he has a hard time making up his mind to do it.

Courage, Paul. Courage.

G.

1. Elmar Tophoven, who is replacing PC at ENS.
2. GCL will be a substitute teacher at a private school in le cours Victor Hugo, 16th arrondissement, until June 1968. She will also give private lessons to some of its students.

338

[Paris,] Saturday, 15 April 1967

My dear Gisèle,

Just a few words in response to your last letter and to the lines added to the letter from Unseld that arrived this morning.

I am a bit worried about the state of your health. You need to speak to me clearly about it, calling things by their name, as in the past. So tell me what it was and how you are doing.

On your pedagogical career all of my congratulations, all my best wishes! You have rare pedagogical gifts and you will succeed perfectly. Then, the four months of vacation are not far away. But what must take *priority* is your etching, in which I believe.

I saw André du Bouchet and I spoke to him of my situation, above all of my need to find myself a place to stay. He promised me that he would ask around, and I gave him a clipping of the *Figaro* regarding a studio that he plans to go see.—I allow myself to ask you the same thing with regard to the studio* near Trocadéro—I am enclosing the clipping. Go there, please, just for my orientation (generally, the prices vary between 50,000 and 70,000 francs).

The letter from Unseld is good—I plan on working a lot.

Good and calm days to you and to Eric

Paul

[In the margin:] D. has not yet called me. But I had the impression, following a remark by Mlle Arrieta, that they believed that I could *live* and *sleep* at rue d'Ulm—which is not feasible. Anyway, we will see.

How much does Marie-Thérèse rent out her studio for? (empty? furnished?)

* unfurnished rentals

339

[Paris,] Tuesday, 18 April 1967

My dear Gisèle,

Thanks for your so prompt letter. I am glad about the good news regarding your health, glad about your success at the school. But which school is it? And—I am indiscreet—what is your salary?

I almost saw Delay yesterday—but it was postponed to another day. A few words exchanged with D., whom I will see tomorrow, more extensively.

I am sending You in this envelope:

1. A letter from the ENS bursar. For the "account sheets," I don't really know what that is; here in any case are the statements from Crédit privé, plus a pay slip: it's all I have.

2. A letter to be sent to Unseld, which is stamped.

3. A letter to be sent *by airmail* to Moscow.[1]

4. Little advertisements / studio, including a "meridian of Paris[2]"...

Jean Bollack came—briefly—Sunday and is coming back next Sunday. André du Bouchet will come Thursday in eight days. Tomorrow I have, for the last time, the dentist.

All good lights for you and Eric

Paul

---

1. Letter not identified.

2. The name of this building does not fail to intrigue PC. PC's friend André du Bouchet will also write to PC about this possible lodging, emphasizing its name.

340

[Paris,] Wednesday, 19 April 1967

Dear Gisèle, can you, please, send these two letters[1] for me? You need to double-check the address for Insel Verlag (and, possibly, correct it) and put stamps on the letters (30 fr[anc]s each).

Can you find out some details about studios for rent etc.: lease agreements, charges etc., from your sister Marie-Thérèse, who is always in the know about these things?

Thanks for all that

Paul

---

1. The first letter, to Siegfried Unseld, specifies PC's requests regarding the creation of his book, in particular its binding, which should be in *"light gray linen"* like *SG* and *"not* the brownish yellow" of *NR*. The second letter has not been identified.

341

[Paris,] Wednesday, 19 [April 1967], afternoon

Dear Gisèle,

I was seen, this morning, by Professor Delay, for around fifteen minutes, in the presence of Dr. D. and of Madame Gu. (the new doctor). What can I say about it? I tried my best to respond. We discussed, also, the separation that you desire.

Professor Delay, very affable, at the moment of leaving, said he hoped I would "be doing better and better."

I attach to these lines a new advertisement (from the *Figaro* from today). This one seems to me to be much more advantageous than the rest. Perhaps you can make an appointment and go there to see what it is.

I thank you for that

Paul

342

[Paris,] 20 April 1967

My dear Gisèle,

I just got your—so little gladdening—letter from yesterday and I hurry to respond to you.

First of all regarding your work at the school: I suspected that these extra burdens would emerge. But try not to let yourself be submerged in that: You are not obligated to meet for too long with the students' parents.

For the statements and pay slips, I can only find, here, the statement from 31 March (Crédit Privé), which I am enclosing with these lines. Perhaps there is something in the correspondence folders for January and February at home. For the pay slips, look in my briefcase. If not, it was perhaps put in my mailbox at rue d'Ulm—Elmar[1] can take a look.

Otherwise there is the letter from the ENS, here is the copy: medical leave from 1 April to 29 June. I nonetheless count on resuming classes on 23 *May* (this date was indicated to me in the letter from Elmar that you forwarded to me the day before yesterday). D. agrees about this resumption, that is absolutely sure. But there is, among other things, also the problem of lodging. Before and after the end of the classes.

Professor Deniker wants to see me again as well: I recall having told you that he envisioned aftercare. As I see my state of being, I need books, a place of work, a bit of human contact, the deepening and enlarging of my work as a translator of poetry (Emily Dickinson, Supervielle, André du Bouchet), in agreement with Unseld.[2] The continuation of the new volume[3]—all that, to my mind, will not thrive at all in an aftercare program several months long...

Tell the young girl from Munich that there is a copy of *Der Sand aus den Urnen*** at the National Library of Vienna. Give her the address of Mlle Meinecke (Allemann's student, who is writing her dissertation about my poetry)[4] and tell her that I will send her, as soon as I can, photocopies of some poems published in Bucharest before my departure from there.[5]

Again about your school (what is its name?): you have only two more months. Then there will be vacation and time for *etching* and *reflection*.

I could help you still, Gisèle, I could. But I would not at all want to trouble you with anything in any way.

Hug Eric.

Calm, work, clarity, rest

Paul

---

1. Elmar Tophoven, PC's replacement at the ENS.
2. PC will publish the following year, with Insel and Suhrkamp, two volumes of translations: a selection of poems by Jules Supervielle and two cycles of poems by André du Bouchet. But he will not undertake new translations of Emily Dickinson (PC's reading marks in Dickinson's poetry and correspondence dating from the beginning of 1968, as well as his sparse notes, show that he never gave up on this project; see also *GN*, p. 512).
3. This "new volume," entitled *Fadensonnen*, will appear in 1968.
* [In the margin:] There are many uncorrected misprints in certain copies.
4. Dietlind Meinecke, *Wort und Name bei Paul Celan: Zur Widerruflichkeit des Gedichts* (Bad Homburg/Berlin/Zurich: Gehlen, 1970).
5. PC left Bucharest at the end of November 1947. He is referring to three poems that appeared in the review *Agora colecţie internaţională de artă şi literatură*, ed. Ion Caraion and Virgil Ierunca, Bucharest, [May] 1947: "Das Geheimnis der Farne" (*NKGA*, p. 37); "Ein wasserfarbenes

Wild" (with the title "Die letzte Fahne" in *NKGA*, p. 38); "Das Gastmahl" (*NKGA*, p. 39); the first publication of "Todesfuge" (*NKGA*, p. 46) in its Romanian translation by Petre Solomon, under the titled "Tangoul morții" (corresponding to its earlier title, "Todestango" [Death Tango] in the Bucharest journal *Contemporanul* of 2 May 1947.

343

[Paris, Friday, 21 April 1967]

Just a note, dear Gisèle, to accompany these very pretty stamps destined to enrich our son's collection. Contained in the envelope is a lovely poster for an evening of readings of my poems in Halle in East Germany. It's a gesture of courage and of solidarity to which I am very sensitive.

What preoccupies me a little is to know whether I will be able, despite the medical leave, to resume classes on 23 May. But I think that will be easy to solve.

I am thinking of your exhibition, which, you will see, will be another, more extensive, Hanover.[1]

All my wishes for serenity

Hug Eric

Paul

Friday, 21 April 1967

1. PC compares the Bochum exhibition (see no. 336, n. 2) with that of Hanover in May 1964 (no. 112, n. 2).

344

[Paris,] Monday, 24 April 1967

Dear Gisèle,

Thanks for the books sent by Jean,[1] thanks for your letter from Friday.

I saw Dr. D.: I will resume, this also with the agreement of Professor Deniker, my classes at rue d'Ulm, on *Tuesday, 23 May*. Here, furthermore, for *Moret*, the schedule (communicated by Elmar and which I am maintaining):

Tuesday:	9:30–10:30 beginners
	14:30–16:30 *agrégation* students
Friday:	14:30–16:30 *agrégation* students
	16:00–17:00 beginners
	17:00–18:00 advanced

In order to prepare my classes, I need to gather and organize my papers from the previous years (I will have around 12 French-German translation exercises,[2] which is a lot); to put into order my books from the ENS in the chambre de bonne and to choose which I have to bring; to add a certain number of other works and my typewriter.

To do that, I will need to go, and Dr. D. agrees, to rue de Longchamp twice: Sunday the 21st and Monday the 22nd. It is agreed, Professor Deniker having insisted on this, that I will not spend the night from Sunday to Monday at rue de Longchamp. So I will leave again Sunday evening and will return Monday morning. Would you have the time—and the desire—to convey me to rue d'Ulm on Monday afternoon?—tell me with simplicity.

Nothing precise has been arranged beyond that. Dr. D. asked me to wait with the search for lodgings. Nevertheless, and as Doctor D. understands very well, it is essential that I can, as soon as possible, resume all my activities as a writer and translator. Personally, I hope to find myself a lodging in early July, move in there—I will have a few purchases to make: table, chairs, bed, bookshelves—and work until September—when I will possibly go, on the invitation of friends of Franz Wurm's, to Ticino.[3] A prolongation of my stay in the clinic would likely be depressing.

May these good things be materialized.

Do not *send me any more books*: I already have a lot of clutter. Just forward me the mail and the journals.

Where do things stand for Bochum? Give me some details.

My wishes, all my wishes.

Hug Eric, my great historian (or composer of history). I hope to see him when I am there.

[Unsigned]

Please send me a money order of 30 Fr[anc]s by return mail.

P.S. Elmar asks me to meet him before the 23rd to give me the key—which is hardly possible. So I will ask him to drop it off.

1. Among the books sent by Jean Bollack, who had seen PC the previous day, 23 April 1967, were probably:
—Gershom Scholem, *Von der mystischen Gestalt der Gottheit. Studien zu Grundbegriffen der Kabbala* (Zurich: Rhein, 1962). PC had noted on the back of the flyleaf a draft of this letter: "Paris, 23 April 1967 / von Dr. Unseld." PC's volume presents numerous reading marks and the dates of reading: 1 May 1967 (p. 134 and 271) and 3 May 1967 (p. 191), as well as the date of 21 May 1968 (p. 249). Among the important passages underlined in this book is one devoted to the light of the Shekhinah ("Ziv"; see "Nah, im Aortenbogen" [Near, in the Aorta-Arch], *FS*, *NKGA*, p. 257; see also *BIT*, p. 200).
—Gerscholm Scholem, *Zur Kabbala und ihrer Symbolik* (Zurich: Rhein, 1960). The volume presents numerous reading marks, in particular in the chapter on the Golem and at the end of the last chapter (p. 259); the date of reading is 16 May 1967.
—Theodor W. Adorno, *Ohne Leitbild. Parva Aesthetica* (Frankfurt am Main: Suhrkamp, 1967). The volume presents some underlinings and the date of reading: 8 May 1967 (p. 181, at the end of the text).
2. PC was responsible for around twenty-five classes in oral French to German translation for the *agrégation* students at the ENS each academic year. The twelve themes evoked here correspond to the new texts he envisioned preparing for the academic year 1967–8, the other texts being reused. It is probable that PC includes among these twelve themes those that he will put in the program at the end of the academic year, that is to say, in May and June 1967. Most of the texts which PC selected for the translation exercises, but not all of the dates of the translation sessions, have been identified:
—Marguerite Duras, *Le Vice-consul* (1966), from "Elle marche" to "palmes bleues" (15 May 1967).
—Nathalie Sarraute, *Tropismes* (1957), Chapter 8 (27 November 1967); chapter 4 (4 December 1967); chapter 2, from "Ils s'arrachaient à leurs armoires" to "adressiez la parole à qui que ce fût."
—Jean Henri Fabre, *Souvenirs entomologiques* (1879–1907), "La Mante.—La chasse": from "Encore une bête du Midi" to "elle a presque une physiogomie" (December 1967); from "Le contraste est grand" to "en écrasant la bête" (8 December 1967 and 9 January 1968).
—Charles Baudelaire, *Fusées* (written in the 1860s), fifteenth part, from "Le monde va finir" to "même les erreurs des sens!—") (7 November 1967); fifteenth part (continuation), from "Alors, ce qui ressemblera à la vertu" to "parce que je veux dater ma colère/tristesse" (21 November 1967).
—Marcel Proust, *A la recherche du temps perdu. Du côté de chez Swann*, part 3 (1913), "Projet de voyage à Florence" from "Quand mon père eut décidé" to "les quarts d'heure qui s'écoulent" (21? August 1968).
Among the other texts reused this academic year, many have been identified with certainty

and include selections from Choderlos de Laclos, *Les Liasons dangereuses* (1782) (1963–4 and June 1967); Henri Michaux, *Un certain Plume, La Nuit des Bulgares* (1930) (1963–4 and 1967–8); Francis Ponge, *Le Parti pris des choses* (1942), *Le restaurant Lemeunier rue de la Chaussée-d'Antin* (dates not clear); Claude Lévi-Strauss, *Tristes Tropiques* (1955) (dates not clear); Paul Valéry, *Monsieur Teste* (1919), *Lettre d'un ami* (dates not clear); Albert Camus, *L'Exil et le Royaume* (1957), *La Pierre qui pousse* (June 1965 and 15 March 1968; on this book see above, no. 154, n. 2); Jean-Paul Sartre, *Les Mots* (1964).

The majority of texts given by PC to his students to translate echo PC's personal as well as pedagogical preoccupations. Texts such as those of Jean-Henri Fabre, which bear a close relation to three poems from *LZ*, "Herzschall-Fibeln," "Vervorfene," and "Die Mantis," written respectively on 23 September, 30 September, and 7 October 1967, are an eloquent example (see *LZ*, *NKGA*, p. 295 and 297). PC's choice of texts to be translated in his classes is often just as autobiographical in nature as when he reads texts "according to the angle of inclination of his existence" (to borrow a phrase from *Meridian*). One of the most emblematic texts in this respect is the excerpt from the beginning of *La Peau de chagrin*, where Balzac describes Raphaël de Valentin's suicidal thoughts (see above, no. 299, n. 5).

3. The photographers and filmmakers Miggel and Luzzi Wolgensinger. The Jewish poet Franz Wurm, originally from Prague, was a producer at Radio Zurich.

345

[To Eric Celan]

[Paris, 27 April 1967]

As a souvenir of a little flânerie in your springtime Paris, first with André du Bouchet, then alone like a grown-up, these three stamps—especially the one with Zola, just and courageous man[1]—picked up on rue Danton, at the post office, from where I sent Mama a little money earned with my pen.

Write to me!

Your papa

1. The author of "J'accuse" was dear to PC, who considered the Goll Affair to be a "true Dreyfus Affair—sui generis" (see no. 85, n. 2).

346

[Paris,] Friday, 28 April 1967

My dear Gisèle,

A few words to thank you for your letter, for the forwarded letter, for the money order that arrived this morning and that I will not touch, for administrative reasons, for three days—

André du Bouchet came to pick me up to go for a walk, to the Panthéon first in a taxi, then by rue de la Montaigne-S[ain]te-Geneviève toward the Russian library[1] where I bought for a lot of money—exchanging the big bill of my honorarium from *Ephémère*—volume two of the works of Mandelstamm.[2] A little coffee afterward, then a walk to rue Danton. André having a meeting, I left him there to send you a money order of 30,000 fr[anc]s. (I also settled my debt with André, so that I wound up no longer very rich, after two hot chocolates and buttered toasts.)—Then I saw the Michaux exhibition,[3] which disappointed me. So precise in his writing, Michaux espouses so many alterities in painting.

Walk from rue des S[ain]ts-Pères to the Raspail metro. I buy two kilos of oranges. Return, toward eight fifteen.

Regarding Dr. Leo: you well know that I still have to refuse the readings in Berlin and in Freiburg, then I have the École. But promise Dr. Leo that I will surely come in autumn.

Good spring, good seasons

Paul

[In the margin:] Jean, who is coming Sunday, declared himself ready to come with a suitcase to take away my dirty laundry and some books—remind him please.—Shirts will be an issue when I resume the École.

---

1. Les éditeurs réunis, 11 rue de la Montagne-Sainte-Geneviève (5th arrondissement).
2. *Sobranie socinenij v dvuch tomach. Tom vtoroj: Stichotvorenija, Proza* (Collected Works in Two Volumes. Second Volume: Poems, Prose), ed. G. P. Struve and B. A. Filippova (New York: Inter-Language Literacy Associates, 1966).
3. The exhibition of the album of etchings, *Parcours*, and recent prints, with a selection of Michaux's works from 1946–66.

347

[To Eric Celan]

[Paris,] Friday, 12 May 1967

My dear Eric,

I am so glad that I'll see you again next Thursday at André du Bouchet's house. We will have lunch there, then we will chat peacefully while we wait for Gilles[1] (who goes horseback-riding every Thursday afternoon).

We will also be able to run over to the post office on rue Danton, very close, to check which new stamps are missing in your collection.

I congratulate you on your accomplishments and your success in school. I am very pleased with it and a bit proud. Now, during Pentecost, you will enjoy a stay in Moisville with all your comrades. And in less than two months it will be the big vacation with its joys and pleasures.

I hug you

Your papa

1. The son of André du Bouchet and Tina Jolas.

348

[Paris,] 17 May 1967

Dear Gisèle,

Thanks for your letter: I find you to be more at ease with yourself and I am glad about that. And tomorrow I will have the joy of seeing Eric.

Your package just arrived: thanks again. You can be proud of the portfolio: your etchings, which came out and are presented very well, the typography and the binding—all that is perfect. I find the etchings completely worthy of their "sisters" outside the portfolio: you deprecated them in speaking of them. They are true successes.

But I am more than surprised that, on the title page, there is not the

least indication that, before the etchings, there is a poem by Paul Celan.*
I am frankly vexed by this and ask you for an explanation.

At the end of the week I hope to know a bit more about my fate.—You probably know that I will spend Saturday afternoon with Mlle Arrieta—I hope that you will be there, if only to help me a little to figure out my affairs. And this would also be simpler vis-à-vis Mlle Arrieta.

Have good days!

Paul

* [In the margin:] to my knowledge, this is not done.

349

[Paris,] Wednesday, 24 May 1967

Dear Gisèle,

It is a quarter to five. Monsieur Vial just brought up your package with the manuscript and what accompanied it. I thank you ardently for it.

I just finished a poem that I transcribe for you here.

DIE RAUCHSCHWALBE STAND IM ZENITH, DIE PFEIL-
SCHWESTER

DIE EINS DER UHR
FLOG DEM STUNDENZEIGER ENTGEGEN,
TIEF INS GELÄUT,

DER HAI
SPIE DEN LEBENDEN INKA AUS,

ES WAR LANDNAHME-ZEIT
IN MENSCHENLAND,

ALLES
GING UM,
ENTSIEGELT WIE WIR.

The chimney-swallow stood at the zenith, the arrow-
sister

The one of the clock
flew against the hour-hand,
deep into the ringing,

The shark
spat out the living Inca,

It was land-seizing time
in the land of humans,

Everything
circulated
unsealed like us.[1]

The times are hard. May Israel endure and live![2]

Hug Eric.
Good days

Paul[3]

---

1. See *NKGA*, p. 262; see also Joris and Fairley's translations, in *BIT*, p. 209 and *FB*, p. 225, respectively.
2. There had been a serious climate of tension in the Middle East for twelve days, between Israel and its neighbors, Syria and Egypt, at the moment when the Jewish State celebrated its nineteenth year of existence (14 May 1967). On 22 May 1967, President Nasser decided to close the Straits of Tiran, in the Gulf of Aqaba, to prevent access to the Red Sea from the Port of Eilat in southern Israel. On 24 May 1967, General de Gaulle received the Israeli minister of

foreign affairs, expressed to him his fear of a nuclear conflict and declared that France would not support Israel in the case of armed conflict with Egypt.

3. See no. 52, n. 2.

350

[To Eric Celan]

[Paris,] Friday, 25 May 1967

My dear Eric,

I just stopped at the post office at rue d'Ulm (to send the corrected proofs of my book[1] and a letter to Aunt Berta) and I discovered there the stamp of the Douanier Rousseau of which I am sending you two here.

Do you feel like having lunch with me next Thursday at Fontaine de Jade? (Afterward, we will go for a walk together.) If so, tell Mama so that she lets me know.

I hug you

Your papa

1. *AW.*

351

[Paris,] Wednesday morning, [31 May 1967]

Dear Gisèle, I got your letter yesterday evening, on my return from the École. So Thursday at twelve thirty I will be at the bus stop of the 63, at Alma. I think I will send you a pneumatic letter tomorrow in case these lines do not reach you.

My classes are going very decently, and I continue to write poems.[1]

There is a laundry problem. Could you come to pick up the dirty laundry here (or at rue d'Ulm) and drop off clean laundry for me, above all shirts? I worry that the laundry services damage the nylon shirts.

The package from Insel, but also the book by Marguerite Taussig[2] (which I received the other day) as well as the copy of *Liaisons Dangereuses*, which you will find in the "translation" shelf, in the room upstairs,[3] send these to me at rue d'Ulm (or leave them with the concierge of the École, at the entrance, under the flag). The letters too, address them and forward them to me at rue d'Ulm, they will reach me more quickly, since I am there 4 times a week.

Claude David spoke very nicely of me in an article in *Le Monde* from yesterday (in the context of a paper on Group 47 . . .).[4]

Give me your news.

Have good days!

Paul

I will see Dr. D. this morning.

---

1. PC has just written seven of the nine poems that comprise the fifth and last cycle of *FS:* "Die Rauchschwalbe" (4 May 1967; see no. 349), "Weiß" (25 May 1967), "Unbedeckte" (25 May– 2 June 1967), "Der Schweigestoß" (27 May 1967), "Haut Mal" (27 May 1967), "Das taubene- igroße Gewächs" (28 May 1967), and "Angewintertes" (30 May 1967); *NKGA*, pp. 262–4.
2. Book not identified.
3. Choderlos de Laclos, *Schlimme Liebeschaften,* trans. Heinrich Mann (Frankfurt am Main: Insel, 1967). The volume presents a few reading marks, including the date of 5 June 1967 in the introduction.
4. Claude David, "Le 'Groupe 47' vingt ans après" (*Le Monde des livres,* Wednesday, 31 May 1967). On PC's relationship with Group 47, see: no. 9, n. 3; no. 11, n. 2; no. 96, n. 4; no. 119, n. 5; and no. 122, n. 1.

352

[Paris,] Thursday evening [1 June 1967]

Just a note to accompany the letter from the "Groupe Chaillot"[1] (which was addressed to me) and to thank you.

The situation around Israel is very critical.[2]

I was touched by the stance taken by Eugène Ionesco in *Combat,* re- printed in *Le Monde* today.[3]

Say a word of thanks to Claude David—if you judge that you can do it.

I just found here an express letter from Unseld, submitting his prospectus to me: I am at the very top of the list, followed by the Polish poet Z. Herbert and by Max Frisch. Unseld is full of attentiveness.[4]

Have good days!

Paul

1. The group "Éclaireurs de France," a secular and coeducational scouting association from the Chaillot neighborhood (16th arrondissement).
2. Since May 27, 1967, Israeli troops have been stationed in the Negev desert. On the other side of the Epyptian-Israeli border, in the Sinai and in the Straits region, the Egyptian army is in a state of high alert. In Israel, the military pressure grows with plans for immediately entering into war. France, led by De Gaulle, refuses to take a side and thus says *no* to Israel. Three thousand people march on avenue de Wagram towards the Israeli Embassy.
3. Here are the excerpts from the article chosen by the editorial team of *Le Monde*, published under the title, "The moderation of reactions of the moral conscience makes me indignant": "Under the title 'The ignoble scoundrels,' M. Eugène Ionesco writes in *Combat:* / A people is threatened with being destroyed. A people that does not want the place of others and that has only asked for a little place to live in the world. A people that has the right to life just as must as others, and more than others. A people that does not want to have colonies or satellites. A people that has the right to live more than any other because it has been the most calumnied, persecuted, tortured. A people, the only one, which believes authentically in morality in politics, something spoken about so much at this moment because no one believes in it. [...] / Czechoslovakia, a quarter-century ago, was not aggressive either. The vile scoundrel, Hitler, Nasser's model, accused Czechoslovakia of being aggressive in order to seize it. [...] / The moderation of the reactions of the moral conscience of the world is an outrage for me. It has always been this way: who, in the West, protested against the persecutions, against the atrocities of the Nazis, before Germany threw itself against the West? It was only then, when the Westerners were attacked, that generous sentiments emerged."
4. On May 29, 1967, Siegfried Unseld writes in his letter accompanying the proofs of a text announcing the upcoming publication of *AW*: "You see that I put Your book at the top of the Suhrkamp program. That should be a demonstration."

353

[Paris,] Tuesday, 6 June 1967

Dear Gisèle,

Today is our son's birthday, and I am addressing these lines to you to congratulate you.

I am thinking of June sixth 1955, I see us again in the little notaries' car, then at the clinic on Boulevard Montmorency, at the arrival of the doctors, of the storm before Eric came into the world.[1]

I am thinking above all of your calm courage and of the simplicity with which you accepted very hard and difficult things.

May you accompany our Eric for long years still.

Paul

---

1. One of the two notaries associated with the Lestrange family, referred to by the family as "the little notaries," their neighbors in the countryside, had in great urgency driven the Celans to Clinique Villa Molière. EC was born prematurely under difficult conditions, after a Caesarian section. Christoph Schwerin, who accompanied them, relates these events in his memoir *Als sei nichts gewesen* (Berlin: Edition Ost, 1997), p. 204.

354

[Paris,] Tuesday, 6 June 1967

Dear Gisèle,

A note to ask you if Eric can have lunch with me Thursday. If yes, let me know through the Clinic. I need my address book—can you send it to me with Eric?

I will come down Thursday in the late morning—after the Big visit[1] and when I leave rue d'Ulm—the package of laundry to be washed, left in the Clinic office, I will mark it with your name.

Thanks for the book parcel. There was, sent by Unseld, a quite pretty edition of E.T.A. Hoffmann[2]—one day that I hope to see, Eric will take it and read it.

Have good days!

Paul

---

1. See no. 238, n. 2.
2. *Werke*, ed. Herbert Kraft and Manfred Weber (Frankfurt am Main: Insel, 1967). In the second volume, there are reading marks by PC in *Die Serapions-Brüder*.

355

[Paris, Tuesday, 6 June 1967]

It is five thirty, I am at the École—my two classes went well[1]—and here is your letter from the 5th waiting for me in the mailbox.

Thanks, Gisèle, for thinking, for feeling, for acting this way. Thanks, on this day, for including Eric in that.[2] Thanks for giving me an occasion to write to you a third time in a single day.

Toward noon, there was, in my mailbox, a roneoed paper saying:

So that
ISRAEL MAY LIVE
everyone at the
Concorde
Tuesday, 6 June at 19:00

I called Jean whom I'm meeting in a little while, at quarter to seven behind the Palais-Bourbon, to participate in the demonstration (which is, I think, organized by young people).[3]

Israel will vanquish and will live.

Hug Eric.

From the heart

Paul

---

1. On the content of these courses, see no. 344, n. 2.
2. PC responds to GCL's evocation of the events in Israel, the beginning of the Six-Day War on 5 June 1967, the bombing of Tel Aviv, the attitude of De Gaulle, and the stance of Eugène Ionesco, about which GCL notes that she speaks at length with EC.
3. In *Le Monde* from 8 June 1967, the demonstration was described in a section on "French Reactions to the War and the Debate in the Assemblée Nationale," in an article entitled "Nouvelles manifestations à Paris": "Three to four thousand people participated Tuesday evening in a demonstration in favor of Israel. / At 7 p.m. the demonstrators were gathered at place de la Concorde with the intention of filing towards the Palais-Bourbon. / But as a significant police presence, composed of the C.R.S. [Republican Security Services], mobile gendarmerie, and guardians of the peace prohibited access to the Concorde bridge and to the quai d'Orsay, the procession formed on rue Saint-Florentin. / At its head were several dozen cars on which young people, in groups, brandished Israeli and French flags. It was a deafening concert of horns and chants of 'Israel will vanquish!' Behind the cars marched several thousand people

[…]. The crowd chanted 'Nasser—assassin,' 'We are volunteers,' and 'Israel will live.' Other slogans were reprised: 'We want peace,' and 'Down with racism.' On the sidewalks, passersby applauded. […] Then the procession headed towards rue de la Victoire. / The horns stopped and the demonstrators no longer shouted. / In an impressive silence, they filed in front of the synagogue, stopped, and sang, the Israeli anthem in Hebrew, the Marseillaise in French. After a minute of silence, the organizers asked the demonstrators to disperse. It was 8:45 p.m."

356

[Paris,] Wednesday, [7 June 1967]
around three o'clock

I had to be seen by Doctor D. in the late morning, and hoped to have your response about the lunch tomorrow, with Eric.

Since I will not leave here probably until around noon tomorrow, you can still, tomorrow morning, let me know if Eric is free and if I can come pick him up, at *one o'clock*, at the 63 bus stop at place de l'Alma.

Have good days!

Paul

357

[Paris,] Friday, 10[1] June 1967

Dear Gisèle,

If you go to Moisville, try to find, in the big room upstairs, next to the bookshelf with my publications in reviews or almanacs, the offprints and bring them to Paris. But check first if, in the pile, there are the translations of Emily Dickinson and of Supervielle in the *Rundschau*.[2] If not, bring the respective issues of the *Rundschau*.

But I recall having published two poems by Emily D., one in a Fischer almanac, the other in an *Insel-Almanach*.[3] Both should be findable—try to find them for me.

You speak to me of your doctor—what does he say, how does he think you are doing? And who is it?

The cease-fire is here—thank God![4]

Have good days

Paul

1. Actually the 9th.

2. This year PC has published, in *Die neue Rundschau:*

   —*Acht Gedichte*, eight poems by Emily Dickinson (72nd year, volume 1, 1961, pp. 36–39; *GW* V, pp. 384–9); with the two poems mentioned below, this is the entirety of Dickinson translations published by PC).

   —*Gedichte*, eleven poems by Jules Supervielle (72nd year, volume 4, 1961, pp. 845–51); *GW* IV, pp. 357–67, 348–9, 368–9, 354–5, 352–3, 358–9, 366–7, 372–3, 374–5, 406–7, 410–1, respectively.

3. "Because I Could Not Stop for Death"—"Der Tod," in *Almanach* of S. Fischer, no. 73, 1959, p. 59; "At Half Past Three"—"Um halb vier," in *Insel-Almanach* 1963, p. 65 (*GW* V, pp. 383–4, 400–1).

4. On 9 June 1967, Syria and Egypt agree to a ceasefire. Israel, after this war that lasted six days, controls the Arab part of Jerusalem, the West Bank, Sinai, Gaza, and the Golan Heights.

358

[Paris,] Monday, 12 June 1967

Dear Gisèle,

I hope that you have had a good weekend with Eric in Moisville.—I am writing you from rue d'Ulm, where I found the Suhrkamp program with *Atemwende* at the top. It's a truly rich program and I am proud to be listed first.[1]

For my leaves of absence from Thursday the 15th to Friday the 16th I have the right to not go back to sleep at the clinic; I will take advantage of that to sleep at the Bollacks', and I ask you to add a pair of pyjamas to the washed shirts.

The arms have gone silent around Israel—may peace take hold, forever.

Good days

Paul

I am a bit surprised about the absence of any mail from the bank: perhaps you should add, after the name Antschel, a hyphen and the name Celan.

1. See no. 352, n. 4.

359

[Paris,] Tuesday, 13 June 1967

Dear Gisèle,

Thanks for your letter and the package.

To tell the truth, I find myself regarding whether Eric advances to the 7th grade or his repetition of 6th grade,[1] in the same dilemma as you.

I will think of about. And discuss it with the Bollacks and André.

Can Eric have lunch with me on Thursday? (I have a meeting at 4 thirty, with a friend of André's[2]). Let me know through the clinic by Thursday morning.

P.

The catalogue is quite good, the text by Leo not stupid at all (except for what it says about Friedlaender.[3]

Echoes will emerge, despite the sabotage.[4]

Thanks for the pretty address book.

---

1. Seventh grade in the US education system is the equivalent of the "5ème" in the French education system and US 6th grade is the equivalent of the French "6ème."
2. PC noted in his planner, for 15 June 1967: "6:30 Racine / Odéon [Café Le] Danton." Charles Racine, a poet of Swiss origin, was going to publish poems in issue no. 3 of *L'Éphémère*. André du Bouchet was a member of the journal's editorial board and one of its founders.
3. In his brief preface to the catalogue of the Bochum exhibition, the head of the Städtische Kunstgalerie sketches a definition of GCL's formal universe: "lyricism of lived experience, via rhythm and equilibrium in composition bound together into a rigorous syntax"; "hand-written spontaneity and approaches to sensuous luxuriance must pass through the filter of technical calculation and flawless manual mastery." Peter Leo also refers to GCL's "apprenticeship" with the "printmaker-poet Friedlaender."
4. Allusion to numerous hitches in the organization of the Bochum exhibition.

360

[Paris,] Wednesday, 14 June 1967

Dear Gisèle,

I had hoped to find my shirts yesterday evening—try to bring me them at the latest *tomorrow before noon*: I do not have any more clean ones.

This will be the last time I impose this work upon you.

Paul

I am waiting for an answer about the lunch with Eric.

361

[Paris,] Thursday, 15 June 1967

Just a note to tell you that your pneumatic letter reached me in time yesterday evening.

I will not sleep at the Bollacks'; this was not permitted. But I will dine with them and I will have the chance to discuss Eric's problems. Personally, and above all because Eric is leaning that way too, I am, all in all, for his repeating. But why not hope that he will succeed in his school exam?

My reading in Freiburg will take place between July 19th and 25th;[1] my stay in Ticino, in Tegna, from September 10th to 30th. But until then...I will see—I've been told—Doctor D. on Monday morning (he is in Guadeloupe), maybe I will see things more clearly. For the moment the clinic is very oppressive.

I'm not sure what to do about the clothes I need. It is starting to get hot, the two summer suits, the blue one and the gray one, would be useful to me. For Freiburg, I need the dark gray three-piece suit and long-sleeved shirts. Apart from that, the shirts. For Ticino, the Bavarian shoes, the long-sleeved English sweater, the (unlined) Windjacke.*[2] All that will probably have to be transported to Jean's, or to André's. I will see about the dates with Jean and I will speak to you again about it (personally in a letter and through his mediation by telephone).

For the meeting with Eric let us fix noon as the time (I cannot leave the clinic before the end of the Big visit[3]), I will stay an hour with him, you will have made him lunch beforehand.

Paul

The stamps for Eric come from Aunt Berta.

---

1. The reading in Freiburg will take place 24 July 1967: see no. 365, n. 2.
* The big brown suitcase and the leather suitcase
2. A windbreaker.
3. See no. 238, n. 2.

362

[Paris,] Friday, 16 June 1967

Dear Gisèle,

I am, after having spoken with Jean and Mayotte, but also, alas, after reading Eric's last letter, in favor of his repeating.

Thanks for your letter. This morning I received, at the same time, the attached letter. I think that you will be able to sell some etchings if you see M. Wille, the director of the Art Collections of the city of Göttingen. It would be worth the trouble, leaving Eric with the Bourgies, to come back to Paris for a day. Write immediately, set a date, explain that you are coming back from the country just for this and excuse me because of illness (or find something else to say).

The letters from the bank have reached me.

I think I finished my new volume yesterday. There is, also, a poem about Israel.[1]—But the clinic *weighs on* me.[2]

Good days

Paul

Will it be possible to see Eric Thursday between noon and one o'clock at Alma?

[In the margin:] Pierre Solomon, currently in Belgium, will come to Paris one of these days. I told him to write to me at rue d'Ulm.

[Added at the top of the letter:] Important: In one of the folders—*Insel*, I believe—in the drawer at the top of the filing cabinet, there is the paper that frees me from the payment of taxes in Germany. Try to find it and send it to me.

1. "Denk dir" (7 and 8 June 1967; *FS*, *NKGA*, p. 266). The last poem of *FS*, the second collection of poems PC published with Suhrkamp (Frankfurt am Main, 1968); see no. 366, n. 1.
2. PC has been hospitalized at Sainte-Anne for four months.

363

[Paris,] Friday, 16 June [1967]

Dear Gisèle,

Here is a new letter: a few lines accompanying the pay slip that I just found in my mailbox; it is from June. (The Clinic has still not delivered to me the certificate demanded by the École.[1])

Two more things I would like to ask you for: my translation files (in the wardrobe?), in the one with the translations of the Shakespeare sonnets, the offprint (*Rundschau*) of the Shakespeare sonnets.[2] I hope it is easy to find.

And also: the file with the English translations by Erna Baber.[3] Maybe the simplest thing would be for you to take it to the Bollacks. But it's not urgent-urgent.

Have a good weekend

Paul

1. The certificate for returning to work.
2. See no. 107, n. 3.
3. Erna Baber had published the translation of a selection of twenty poems from *MG*, *VS*, *SG*, and *NR*. PC writes to Felix Berner on 24 April 1968 regarding Baber and her translations:

"Three years ago, a young German woman from Siebengürgen who had grown up in the United States came to see me; she had translated a not inconsiderable number of my poems; I found these translations very successful; since then, English-speaking friends have confirmed me in this judgment; the whole thing is born of a true relation to the poems, of a real confrontation with them."

364

[To Eric Celan]

[Paris,] Monday, 19 June 1967

Thanks, my dear Eric, for your pretty gift. As you see, I am using it immediately, in writing you.

Tomorrow, the day of your exam, I will cross my fingers for you. Do not let yourself be intimidated by difficulties, you are perfectly capable, in French as in Latin, of resolving them. Keep calm and reflect on what you have in front of you.

I hope to be able to see you, for a little hour, Thursday at noon. Tell Mama to confirm this meeting with me as soon as she can.

So, for tomorrow: m...[13].[1]

See you Thursday, I hug you

Papa

---

1. "Merde à la treizième" or literally: "shit to the thirteenth power"—an expression that corresponds to the English expressions "break a leg" or "good luck."

365

[Paris,] Tuesday, 20 June 1967

Dear Gisèle,

Thanks for your letter from Sunday night.

I am very glad I will see Eric Thursday: I will take him out to lunch. But don't forget to give Doctor D. notice: it is important to him that all my movements be *coordinated*. He informed me that he planned to keep me at the Clinic for a few more weeks.

If you bring my two suits to the Bollacks, don't forget my passport and my four books.[1] (But the Bollacks are leaving too... I will perhaps have their key.)

The reading in Freiburg will take place the 21st or the 24th, this depends on Heidegger's presence.[2]

I ask you to send all my mail to the address of the *École*: I hope that even after the classes, I will have leaves of absence allowing me to work. I will occupy myself with Supervielle first of all.[3]

Good days

Paul

---

1. PC asks for the entirety of the books he has published to date—*MG* (1952), *VS* (1955), *SG* (1959), and *NR* (1963), with his reading in Freiburg in mind.
2. The reading will take place Monday, 24 July 1967, in Heidegger's presence (see no. 372, n. 3).
3. PC is bringing together his Supervielle translations, published in various journals and reviews, with a view to publishing them, with twenty-two new translations, as a book. See no. 415, n. 1.

366

[Paris,] 26 June 1967

Dear Gisèle,

I hope that You have had a good trip and that the house has received You well.

Werner Weber published my poem about Israel at the top of the literary page (clipping attached). Moreover, in the local edition of the *NZZ* he printed the poem, accompanied by an interpretation (which I ask you to send me when possible). What's more, a very warm letter from him.[1]

I am sending the same clippings to the aunt.[2]

This morning, I went to meet Petre Solomon at his hotel, he was going to see Ionesco, I will see him again tomorrow, the day of my last class at rue d'Ulm. (All the agrégation students are eligible for the oral exams.)

I translated a certain number of poems by Supervielle—that makes 29 in all[3]—and in a little while, at three o'clock, I will see Madame Supervielle, in the company, probably, of Denise and Pierre.[4]

Good days

Paul

[To Eric Celan]

[Paris, 26 June 1967]

My dear Eric,

I thank you for your nice card. I hope that the crawl will go well.

I bought you the latest stamps to appear, but I will keep them until your return.

Enjoy yourself!

Your papa

---

1. "Denk dir" (7 and 8 June 1967; *FS, NKGA*, p. 266) had appeared in the literary supplement of the *Neue Zürcher Zeitung* on Sunday, 25 June 1967. The poem had already been published the day before, on the front page of the local edition of the *Neue Zürcher Zeitung* (morning edition, 24 June 1967), accompanied by an article by the editor-in-chief of the literary pages of the *NZZ*, Werner Weber, entitled, "Zu einem Gedicht von Paul Celan." In his article, Weber recalls the political and military events that have inspired the poem, before commenting at length on the lines "Denk dir: / der Moorsoldat von Massada / bringt sich Heimat bei," in which Weber recognizes a bridge across time, connecting the resistance and collective suicide of the zealots in the fortress of Herod the Great, as recounted by the Jewish historian Flavius Josephus, with "the suffering of the prisoners" in the Börgermoor concentration camp, to which Wolfgang Langhoff bears witness in *Die Moorsoldaten* (1935). Neither the account by Josephus nor the work by Langhoff are in PC's library. See also "Just Think," *CSP*, p. 149.

2. Berta Antschel. See no. 21, n. 2.

3. PC has already published twelve translations of Supervielle and recently completed "Paris" (2 June 1967), "A un arbre"—"An einen Baum" (13 June 1967), "Pointe de flame"—"Flammenspitze" (16 June 1967), and "Montagnes et rochers, monuments du délire"—"Ihr Berge und ihr Felsen" (16 June 1967). See, respectively, *GW* IV, pp. 412–3, 416–7, 362–3, 370–1. The volume of Supervielle poems translated by PC contains thirty-five poems (see no. 415).

4. The daughter of Pilar and Jules Supervielle, Denise Supervielle, and her husband, the Germanist Pierre Bertaux.

367

[Paris,] 30 June 1967

Dear Gisèle,

Thanks for your letter, thanks for having recopied "Denk dir." It is, for me, an important poem.[1] I sent it to Duniu, to Alfi,[2] to the Aunt, I am getting ready to send it to Erich von Kahler.

You can bring me from the country all the Supervielles (including the little German edition—Fischer, Schulausgabe).[3] The meeting with Mme Supervielle went well.

I have *Mörike* for the 67/68 agrégation program, and I ask you to bring me the three or four volumes of the Tempel edition (orange, I believe).[4]

Another book that you will have a little trouble finding figures in my program: *Die Nachtwachen des Bonaventura*, a steel-blue book I believe, with a black insignia, quite skinny and svelte. It is on the side of the romantics.[5]

Yesterday, I put on my summer suit: it fits me perfectly. I will need, for the trip, my chestnut-colored cloth suitcase. Also my razor, my shaving brush etc.—I will have ten days of leave and I will go back—for how long?—to the Clinic upon my return.

I hope that you are enjoying the rural calm.

Good days

Paul

[In the margin:] I have bought, for Eric, a book by Israel Zangwill (tran[slated] from English): *Les enfants du ghetto*,[6] which I am sending to rue de Longchamp. It would be good for you to look at it a little: it is not the one I read in my childhood[7] and I am not sure how good it is; but it is a moment in Jewish life.

1. PC chooses to end *FS* with "Denk dir"(see no. 362, n. 1).
2. David Seidmann (nicknamed Duniu or Douniou) a friend and former classmate of PC's at the University of Czernowitz, originally from Bukovina, lived in Israel, like PC's maternal uncle, Ezriel Schrager (nicknamed Alfi).

3. Aside from the German edition, *Gedichte und Legenden* (various translators, S. Fischer, 1961), PC also possessed an English-language translation: *Supervielle*, trans. Teo Savory (Santa Barbara: Unicorn Press, 1967). The other six Supervielle volumes in the original French in PC's library are: *Gravitations* (Paris: Gallimard, 1925), which has a dedication "To M [name illegible], in homage, from Jules Supervielle"—PC also noted, in the table of contents of this volume, probably bought second-hand, the dates of his translations, all from 1960; *Les amis inconnus* (Paris: Gallimard, 1934); *1939–1945; Poèmes* (Paris: Gallimard, 1946); *Choix de poèmes* (Paris: Gallimard, 1947)—this volume presents sketches of translations and underlinings; *Naissances: Poèmes, suivis de "En songeant à un art poétique"* (Paris: Gallimard, 1951); *Le Corps tragique, Poèmes* (Paris: Gallimard, 1959)—this volume is dedicated "To Paul Celan / from poet to poet / and recalling our first encounter / Jules Supervielle."

4. *Gesammelte Werke* (Berlin: Tempel).

5. (Leipzig: Insel, 1919).

6. French translation by Pierre Mille (Paris: Éditions Georges Crès et Compagnie, 1918).

7. Edition not identified.

368

[Paris,] 7 July 1967

Dear Gisèle,

I see that you are back: I find your handwriting on the mail that you are forwarding me. Tell me how you are doing and how Eric is doing (and give me his address with the length of his stay there).[1]

I have bought my ticket for Freiburg; the departure is the 22nd and I will have around ten days; that way I will be able to see Allemann—who has just been appointed in Bonn*[2]—Unseld, and Klaus Reichert. Not to mention Elmar's friend,[3] Ludwig von Ficker's daughter[4] etc.

Give me the exact text of the imprint of *Atemkristall*—especially the number of copies (70 or 75?) and the publication date: I would like to put a note about that in *Atemwende*.[5]

The poem about Israel made, it is Weber who wrote me this, a big impact: "countless letters" + a reprint in Israel.[6]

For my trip, I ask you to transport to Jean:

1. suitcase in chestnut-colored cloth
2. my tour volumes + a Mandelstamm[7]
3. razor, shaving brush, soap
4. Swiss and German money (right-hand drawer of the desk).

I thank you for that.

Good days

Paul

[In the margin:] I send you Erich von Kahler's Grüße and Wünsche.[8]

1. GCL has just returned from Moisville; EC has left the night before for camp with the Eclaireurs.
2. That is to say, appointed professor at the University of Bonn.
 * but will come to Frankfurt
3. Gerhard Neumann.
4. Birgit von Schowingen-Ficker.
5. *Atemkristall* was printed in Paris on 23 September 1965, at Fequet et Baudier; the eight original copper prints by Gisèle Celan-Lestrange were printed on the handpress of Lacourière et Frélaut. According to Celan's note in *AW*, *Atemkristall* was printed in seventy-five numbered copies.
6. "Denk dir" and the interpretation by W. Weber (see above, no. 366, n. 1) were published in Tel Aviv under the title "Zu einem Gedicht von Paul Celan" in *MB. Wochenzeitung des Irgun Olej Merkas Europa* (Weekly Newspaper of the Organization of Jewish Immigrants from Central Europe), no. 26, 7 July 1967, and, with the title "Ein aktuelles Meisterwerk von Paul Celan," in *Die Stimme: Organ der Hitachduth Olej Bukowina* (The Voice: Organ of the Union of Jewish Immigrants from Bukovina), no. 211, August 1967.
7. In addition to his own poems (see no. 365, n. 1), PC asks for his translation of Mandelstam (*Gedichte*, 1959) in view of his public reading in Freiburg.
8. Literally: "greetings and wishes."

369

[Paris, 17 July 1967]

Dear Gisèle,

I thank you for having brought the two suitcase to Jean's[1]—I will take the bigger one, Saturday, when I go to Freiburg via Basel.

Franz Wurm charges me with the task of sending his "Grüße" to Heidegger, which hardly fills me with happiness. In truth, the real aim of this trip is Frankfurt, that's to say the meetings with Unseld, Reichert, Allemann.

This evening, I am dining with André, to whom I am bringing, as a surprise, the cycle "Le Moteur blanc" in my translation. Tomorrow, I will send the poems to Weber, for the *Zürcher Zeitung*.[2]

The time, sometimes, seems to me to be interminably long and empty, especially at the Clinic.—As soon as I have returned I will begin typing out *Fadensonnen*[3] and preparing my classes.

Tell me how you are doing and how Eric is doing.

I am thinking of you.

Paul

17.7.1967

[In the upper margin, to the right and upside down, crossed out:] Could you recopy for me, following the manuscripts at the house (*Atemwende*, 1st version), the poem: "Frankfurt, September"?

I just found it.

1. Jean Bollack.
2. A typed version of *Der weiße Motor*, by André du Bouchet (see *GW* IV, pp. 256–87). See no. 378, n. 1.
3. PC will send the final manuscript of *FS* to Suhrkamp on 6 December 1967.

370

[Paris,] 18 July 1967

Dear Paul,

Thanks for your little letter. Yes I understand that the reading in Freiburg in Heidegger's presence poses some difficulties for you. I hope nonetheless that it goes well. It's surely very useful that you can see Unseld. I see that you are continuing to work a lot. André du Bouchet must be happy about this new translation.

A little note from Eric, only the second, not very marvelous in form. But he seems very content. Speaks of numerous swims in the river, very successful cooking competitions, big games, and "relaxed" afternoons when he plans to "read, read." I think he is really content.

For me, nothing special. The etchings are back from Bochum without any note. Seven are missing. That's little! I suppose they've been sold. I wrote to demand receipts for unpaid photographs and wrapping and to ask for explanations about these etchings that are missing.

I try as best as I can to go back to work and spend my days at the very calm and cool printer's.

I wish you a good stay in Germany and fruitful contact with Unseld. I am delighted that you can work despite the very difficult current conditions and hope that you will be able to leave the hospital very soon.

All my wishes for you

Gisèle

Aunt Berta hopes that you will go to see her in London this summer.

371

[To Eric Celan]

[Basel, 22 July 1967]

From Basel, where I have stopped on my way to Freiburg, a souvenir of a very beautiful Klee exhibition[1]—in Moisville you must have had shown to you, by Mama, the big book we have on him.[2]

I hope that you're enjoying yourself.

I hug you

Papa

22 July 67

1. Postcard caption: "Paul Klee (1879–1940)—Kleines Tannenbild—Petit arbre au sapin—Little Painting with a Fir-Tree, 1922. (Kunstmuseum Basel, Vermächtnis Doetsch)."
2. Will Grohmann, *Paul Klee*, trans. Jean Descoullayes and Jean Philippson (Paris: Flinker, 1954).

[Paris,] Wednesday, 2 August 1967

Dear Gisèle,

I just got back, am at rue d'Ulm and hasten to send you a note.

I hope that you are all doing well in Moisville.

The reading in Freiburg was an exceptional success: 1,200 people who listened to me with bated breath for an hour, then, having applauded me for a long time, they listened to me again for another fifteen minutes.[1]

Heidegger had come up to me—The day after my reading I was, with M. Neumann, Elmar's friend,[2] in Heidegger's hut (Hütte) in the Black Forest. Then there was, in the car, a grave dialogue, with clear words from me. M. Neumann, who was the witness of it, told me afterward that, for him, this conversation had something epoch-making about it. I hope that Heidegger will take up his pen and that he will write a few pages echoing that, and warning too, in the face of mounting Nazism.[3]

Three days in Freiburg, then two at the Allemanns' in Würzburg, the rest, very crammed, in Frankfurt, where Unseld received me at the train station. Full of work plans. I hope that the clinic, where I am going in a little while, will let me go.

Write to me. I am glad that you were able to work.

Good days

Paul

---

1. The article published in the culture pages (*Feuilleton*) of the *Badische Zeitung*, "Der Dichter und sein Gedicht. Paul Celan las eigene Gedichte" (26 July 1967), evokes the reader and his audience in the following terms: "More than a thousand listeners had come to hear the poet Paul Celan read from his own poems, at the invitation of the German Department, in the University's main lecture hall on Monday evening. If curiosity indeed played a role in this, Celan is after all one of the most important German-language poets today; the number spoke for itself. After a short introduction by the Professor of Modern German Literature, Gerhart Baumann, in which Baumann saw in Celan's work a counterweight to our age's tendency to level out, Celan began, almost hesitatingly, softly and yet with precision, his style of speaking corresponding exactly to his writing style." The critic (the article is signed "v.") highlights PC's nuanced repetitions and the way he accentuated the moments of silence. The enthusiasm of the audience probably led PC to prolong his reading with "a number of recent poems" written between 1965 and 1967, taken from *FS*, the final text of which PC was about to establish.

2. Elmar Tophoven's friend, Gerhard Neumann, was then assistant to Prof. Gerhart Baumann at the University of Freiburg.

One can read this paragraph as a sort of commentary, paraphrasing and simplifying some of the lines of the poem "Todtnauberg" (*LZ, NKGA,* p. 286), written in Frankfurt the day before this letter was written, on 1 August 1967. In the first version of the poem, PC writes: "*Seit ein Gespräch wir sind, / an dem / wir würgen, / an dem ich würge/ , das mich / aus mir hinausstieß, / dreimal, viermal*" (*Since we are a conversation, / on which / we choke / on which I choke / that drove me / out of myself, / three times, four times*). This amplifies and glosses this famous line from Hölderlin's late hymn, "Versöhnender, der du nimmergeglaubt" (Reconciler, you who was never believed), which Heidegger comments on in his essay "Hölderlin und das Wesen der Dichtung" (Hölderlin and the Essence of Poetry) (in *Erläuterungen zu Hölderlins Dichtung,* 1951): "Seit ein Gespräch wir sind / Und hören können voneinander" (Since we are a conversation / And can hear from one another).

373

[Paris,] 4 August 1967

Dear Gisèle,

Our letters crossed.

I saw Dr. D. this morning, he told me that they won't give me a green light before September first.

But I will be able to leave, in around eight days, to see Aunt Berta, for eight to ten days.

My black suit is bothering me a bit—where does one buy a garment bag? (Then, unless I can reach Jean, who is back in Paris for a few days, I will hang it up on the coat rack in my room.)

The stay in London will surely be rather demanding—Régine and Léo, back from Vienna, will entertain me a bit...But in any case it will be better than the clinic where I have to make an effort that is starting to be beyond me.

A lot of people, the Allemanns first, the Neumanns, Unselds, the Höllerers, have asked me how you are doing.

I have a good deal of stamps for Eric. Hug him

Paul

374

[Paris,] 7 August 1967

Dear Gisèle,

Patricia's broken arm is really bad luck, and I hope that Madame Virou-leau took it well. How long do you plan to stay in Moisville? I'm leaving on Saturday for London, but don't know yet for how long, ten days perhaps, or twelve, I will find out Thursday at the big visit.

Did I tell you that Unseld accepts, in principle, a Supervielle with Insel and an André du Bouchet with Suhrkamp?[1] And also, but that depends above all on my faculties, a volume of Emily Dickinson.[2]—Will they let me leave September 1st? So I will be, to begin with, at Jean's…or at the École. On September 10th, I plan to go rest for three weeks in Ticino, I need it. And for you, it's the first day of school…All that means, *among other things*, that I will not see Eric again until my return from Switzerland…

I wrote, for a Romanian poet whose name you know, Ion Caraion, who is composing a volume about Brâncuşi, a little poem, a copy of which I am enclosing for you here.[3]

Hug Eric. Good days

Paul

"Bei Brâncuşi, zu zweit"

Wenn dieser Steine einer
verlauten ließe,
was ihn verschweigt:
hier, nahebei,
am Humpelstock dieses Alten,
tät es sich auf, als Wunde,
in die du zu tauchen hättst,
einsam,
fern meinem Schrei, dem schon mit-
behauenen, weißen.

4.8.67

"At Brâncuşi's, The Two of Us"

If of these stones one
let be divulged,
what silences it:
here, nearby,
on the hobbling stick of this old man,
it would open itself up, as a wound,
into which you would have to dive,
lonesome,
far from my scream, from what's already been
knocked together with it, white.[4]

1. PC will publish, the following year, a selection of poems by Jules Supervielle (*Gedichte*) and the translation of *Dans la chaleur vacante* (*Vakante Glut*) by André du Bouchet.
2. PC will not carry out this plan.
This poem will be published three years later, with a Romanian translation accompanying it, "La Brâncuşi, în doi," in *Masa tăcerii. Simposion de metafore la Brâncuşi* (The Table of Silence: Symposium of Metaphors for Brâncuşi), an anthology introduced and translated by Ion Caraion (Bucharest: Editura Univers, 1970), pp. 100–101. PC had met the Romanian poet Ion Caraion in 1946, in Bucharest's Surrealist circles. In this poem, PC recalls meeting Constantin Brâncuşi, together with GCL, on 24 February 1954. They met in the sculptor's studio when he was seventy-eight years old and no longer working (the studio was at 11 impasse Ronsin—once next to 152 rue de Vaugirard, this longer exists and the studio has been reconstructed outside the Centre Pompidou). PC's first encounter with Brâncuşi was on 15 July 1951, when PC visited him thanks to Jean-Dominique Rey, with a group of people including Nani Maier, Klaus Demus, the painter Traute Wolsegger, and the sculptor Josef Pillhofer. J. D. Rey recalls this visit to the Romanian sculptor in these terms: "Perhaps there were ten of us, one or two young women. Whether Ingeborg Bachmann, very close at the time to Paul Celan, was there that day, I wouldn't be able to say. In any case, Paul Celan accompanied us. All throughout our visit, the elderly sculptor with a Buddha's smile beneath the white scrub of his beard, did not speak a word other than to pay a few compliments to the young women. At one point, Celan mentioned Romania, but without awakening any apparent echo in Brâncuşi: ever silent, he turned *L'Oiseau dans l'espace* on its stand or caressed the skull of the *Princesse X*. Later, at the Luxembourg, Celan brought up Romania again and the famous *Colonne sans fins*" (*Supérieur Inconnu*, no. 15, p. 84); Ingeborg Bachmann was not among the visitors that day, as her letters to Paul Celan from summer 1951 show.
3. See "Two at Brâncuşi's," *BIT*, p. 253.

375

[To Eric Celan]

[Paris,] Tuesday, 91 August 1967

My dear Eric,

I was very delighted upon finding, this morning, your long and detailed epistle as well as the card with the pretty Norman cabin announcing to me your success in swimming. Congratulations!

I'm going to leave Saturday to pay a little visit to Aunt Berta and I bet that I will not return, as far as you're concerned, with empty hands. Indeed, if there are useful things to buy there for the house, talk to Mama about it so that she tells me in time.

I am enclosing with these lines a few picture postcards, brought back above all from Fribourg-en-Brisgau (in German: Freiburg im Breisgau) and from the Black Forest (Schwarzwald), including one with silver thistles (Silberdistel).[1] I hope that you will like them.

See you soon. I hug you

Papa

---

1. The postcard referred to by PC has the caption: "Schwarzwald—Silberdistel" (the species of thistle *Silybum Marianum*; see no. 87).

376

Moisville, via Nonancourt, Eure

Tuesday [8 August 1967]

Thanks, Paul, for the beautiful poem, for your letter. I wish you a good trip to England, a good stay there. I hope that Aunt Berta won't be too tiresome, too monopolizing. She is so full of good intentions! But so exasperating too. Well she is as we know her, and age doesn't help. But her heart is good, and she must be so happy about your arrival.

I am glad you can go to Ticino since you surely need good air, calm, and freedom.

Since your departure from the hospital finally seems close at hand, tell me what you need from the house to move in. Let's be simple, Paul, you know that everything we have is ours, and if it makes your move easier, don't hesitate to take it. Unless you prefer another kind of furniture. You'll see. You'll let me know.

Yes, of course, I understand that you want to see Eric before your departure to Switzerland, and the new term for me is the 15th, for Eric the 18th of September. But if you so desire, I can come back to Paris when you return from London for one day so that you can spend a few hours with him. You'll let me know.

I hope that the aunt won't harass you too much with presents for Eric, in any case, if you cannot do otherwise, winter pyjamas would perhaps be best, or a thin light-gray sweater for example.

Have a good stay. Take heart

Gisèle

377

[London,] Tuesday, 15 August 1967

Dear Gisèle, I am currently in Aunt Berta's house, she went shopping—it is just past eleven o'clock—and I am waiting to be treated to culinary delights, as always. But the extra-culinary treats have begun, and yesterday a new Burberry landed on my broad shoulders.

I am staying with Régine,[1] discreet as you know her to be, very agreeable. The mornings and afternoons I spend at the aunt's house, reading a work for the École.[2] Otherwise, there's the shopping (which will avoid you just as little as Eric). Today the son of my aunt from Chicago (Blanca)[3] is supposed to arrive in England, and we are—or rather Aunt Berta, very "concerned," is stuck to the telephone. The expected cousin is the brother of the one we met back then in Paris;[4] he is, I believe, an economist, and is arriving, provided with a scholarship, with his wife and two children, to live not in London but some remote place in England.

Last night, I dreamed—literally: dreamed—a little poem,[5] I woke up right away and was able to write it out: such things have happened to me only very rarely.

I left Paris under battering rain, but here the weather is rather mild and I hope that you all have good weather in Moisville. Has Patricia returned?

I am thinking of you both, I wonder how your new etchings are.

I hug Eric.

Good days

Paul

I thank you for coming back for one day so that I can see Eric. As soon as I am back and know what the doctors' intentions are, I will speak to you about it.—I return the 23rd.

1. Regine Schäfler, 37 Sandringham Court, Maida Vale, W9.
2. Book not identified.
3. Blanca Schrager, PC's maternal aunt.
4. Sidney Berman, the brother of David Berman.
5. "Wie du" (*LZ*, *NKGA*, p. 287): "WIE DU dich ausstirbst in mir: / noch im letzten / zerschlissenen / Knoten Atems / steckst du mit einem / Splitter / Leben." (AS YOU die out in me: / still in the last / worn away / knot of breath / you sit with a / sliver / of life); see also *BIT*, p. 260.

378

[Paris,] Wednesday evening [23 August 1967]

Dear Gisèle, I just got back and found your letter from yesterday—thanks. I had the pleasant surprise in London, of finding, in the *Gazette de Zurich*, in a very good spot, my translations of André.[1]

Tomorrow, at the Clinic, I will know which day next week I will be able to see Eric.

Give my regards to Erika, say hi to Jonas.[2]

Hug Eric.

Good days

Paul

1. The translation of the poem cycle *Le Moteur blanc* (*Der weiße Motor*) by André du Bouchet was published in its entirety on Saturday, 19 August 1967, on the front page of the literary pages of the *Neue Zürcher Zeitung*.

2. Erika Tophoven and her son Jonas.

379

[Paris,] Friday, 25 August 1967

Dear Gisèle,

I just found Eric's note, sent from the creperie in Dreux, and I am delighted. Tell him that—I will tell it to him again, in person, next Friday, that's to say September first, the day when I ask you to bring him to Paris.

I will wait for him at Alma (the 63 bus stop) at *twelve thirty*, I will go have lunch with him, take him to rue d'Ulm to get: a pullover (for him), chocolates + two sweaters for you,* and the stamps I bought him. Then I plan on walking with him along the Seine and bringing him to you around five o'clock.

I await your response.

Give my best to Erika and her son,

hug Eric.

I am thinking of you

Paul

It would be good if Eric brings his backpack!

* sweaters and chocolates are gifts from the Aunt!

380

[Paris,] Friday, 1 September 1967

Dear Gisèle,

I am at the École with Eric, after a meal at the Fontaine de Jade. I found Eric grown and very handsome.

Soon it's the first day of classes and I am sending you 30,000 francs for this. My book has been published: I received the first copy and I give it to you.[1] The note about *Atemkristall* is at the end of the table of contents.[2]

I am enclosing with these lines a prescription; it is what was given to me before Freiburg. For the trip to London, I was supplied with medications[3] by the clinic directly.

I am leaving Thursday for Switzerland for around three weeks. Beforehand, that's to say, Monday, I will see, regarding my discharge, Professor Deniker and Doctor D. (who is not very fond of the idea of my staying with Jean and Mayotte).[4]

I hope to be able to have a good school year and, to this end, I must leave the clinic as soon as possible.

My address in Switzerland: P.C., c/o M. Wolgensinger, CH-6652 *Tegna* (Ticino), Switzerland.

Good days

Paul

[Dedication in *Atemwende*]

To Gisèle,
on the Bridge of Years,[5]

Paul

1 September 1967

---

1. *AW* (Frankfurt am Main: Suhrkamp, 1967).
2. See no. 368.
3. Antidepressants and neuroleptics.
4. In the Bollacks' chambre de bonne, on the top floor at 54 rue de Bourgogne.
5. See no. 3, n. 2.

381

Dear Gisèle,

Just a note to ask you not to have my mail forwarded to Switzerland, but as up until now, to rue d'Ulm.

This poem by Supervielle[1] is really pretty and I think that it would be a good exercise for Eric to learn it by heart.

Good days

Paul

[To Eric Celan]

[Paris,] 2 September 1967

Dear Eric,

While reading, in view of their translation into German, poems by Supervielle, I came across a pretty short, very pretty poem—here it is, and, if you feel like it, learn it by heart.

I hug you

Papa

---

1. The (typed?) copy is no longer attached to the letter. It may be the poem entitled "L'Allée" for which PC noted the translation (Der Reitweg) in his copy of Supervielle's *Choix de poèmes*. See no. 367, n. 3; See *GW* IV, pp. 378–9: "Ne touchez pas l'épaule / Du cavalier qui passe, / Il se retournerait / Et ce serait la nuit" (Do not touch the passing cavalier's shoulder, / He would turn around / And it would be night).

382

[To Eric Celan]

[Locarno,] 8 September 1967

And here I am, already, wandering around, in Locarno, on Lake Maggiore, where I am offering myself a good Campari...maggiore

Your Papa

383

[To Eric Celan]

[Bellinzona,] 9 September 1967

My dear Eric, it is not very nice out, nonetheless I am wandering around or rather being taken around[1] in Ticino. Here I am in the main town of the canton: Bellinzona. On the card one of the three castles that dominate the town.[2]

Your Papa

1. By Franz Wurm and his photographer friends, Miggel and Luzzi Wolgensinger.
2. Postcard caption: "Bellinzona—Castello di Unterwalden."

384

[To Eric Celan]

[Bellinzona, 10? September 1967]

My dear Eric, here is the second of the three castles of Bellinzona.[1]

This morning, I was basking in the sun, now that it is raining, my friends offer me, in a café, a good "cappuccino."

I hug you

Your Papa

1. Postcard caption: "Bellinzona—Castello d'Uri o San Michele."

385

Tegna, 11 September 1967

Dear Gisèle,

A few lines to tell you that I am doing well here, in a pretty house, very spacious, very calm, surrounded by a garden, in the middle of a valley, at a low altitude, but a high dose of friendship.

Jean, who saw Doctor D., has perhaps told you that Deniker envisions my transfer to la Verrière (for an "aftercare program" probably),[1] but that D. and Mme Le Gu. are opposed to that.

So I will see upon my return. And I will probably ask the École to give me housing for a while.

Unseld insists that I come to his reception for the Book Fair, to read, in his house, before around fifty invited guests, the poems of *Atemwende*. (A reading of around thirty minutes.) I accepted in principle and hope that the doctors will agree too. It is planned for October 12th.

I wish you a good and "aquafortist" beginning of the school year.

Hug Eric.

Good days

Paul

I am staying here until the 20th, then it'll be Zurich.

This evening, we are invited at the Höllerers, who have a house in the neighborhood.[2]

---

1. PC will regularly go to La Verrière for psychotherapeutic sessions, but he will not be hospitalized there. See no. 208, n. 5.
2. The photographer Renate von Mangoldt, Walter Höllerer's wife, took a series of portraits of PC on the occasion of this encounter (see Appendix, image 9).

386

[To Eric Celan]

[Dedication in *Atemwende*][1]

For you, my dear Eric, who one
day will read and understand these poems

your father
Tegna, September 12th, 1967

1. See no. 380, n. 1.

387

[To Eric Celan]

[Zurich,] 20 September 1967

My dear Eric,

Here I am in Zurich, in the hotel[1] where we stayed seven years ago, when we came to receive Nelly Sachs. Very nearby, there was the Knie circus, your first big circus.[2]

I hope that the first day back at school went well and that you have good teachers.

I hug you and tell you

See you soon.

Your Papa

1. Hotel Zum Störchen (At the Stork) is on the banks of the Limmat river, on the site of the house where Paracelsus lived. See the poem by PC entitled "Zürich, zum Störchen," written after his first encounter with Nelly Sachs in May 1960 (*NR*, *NKGA*, p. 130).
2. EC had been to a "little circus" in August 1961 in Brest (see the poem written 15 August 1961, "Nachmittag mit Zirkus und Zitadelle," *NKGA*, p. 154; *SPP*, p. 182).

388

45 rue d'Ulm, [Paris,] 27 September 1967

My dear Gisèle,

Thanks for your two letters.

My stay in Tegna found itself shortened because of the fact that the Wolgensingers, my hosts, who are photographers and filmmakers, had to agree, overnight, to shoot another film for I don't know what big pharmaceutical company, about this company's multitude of branches—which, practically, means a voyage around the world. Before beginning it, Madame Wolgensinger went to take a little rest in a sanatorium.

Zurich was very friendly to me, I saw quite a few people,[1] spoke German, wrote poems.[2] And above all: Franz Wurm is a true friend. In his work room, where he meditates on the works of Kafka, Schönberg,[3] Wittgenstein, in a free, very visible corner: your *Kämpfender Atem*.

As luck would have it, I met, in a bookstore, Monsieur Larese[4]—very happy to see me again and buying, on the spot, several copies of *Atemwende*, which he had me sign for him and his friends. He told me he had called me one morning in the month of May. I told him to call in the evening, and it seems to me that he will do so after October 15th, during his next stay in Paris. Naturally, if there is an exhibition, he will want me to come give a reading. Perhaps you will find it possible to go there with me; otherwise, let's find a pretext, you will go to the exhibition opening, and later I will go to read poems in the context of your exhibition.

A similar project was proposed to me by Professor Baumann of *Freiburg*. Nothing specific yet, except that they intend to show your etchings there.

And for you, as with poetry for me, etching goes along with teaching.

I of course approve for you to show *Atemkristall*, in addition to your etchings, at the Salon de la Jeune Gravure.

Another thing: Altmann, in his last letter (from a few months ago), seemed to me to allude to a new book project.[5] I am ready to do it with you, the poems exist already, more than thirty aside from *Fadensonnen*,[6] so almost half of a third volume.[7] What's more, we need the money. Do you want me to write to Altmann?

I would very much like to see Eric as soon as possible: Thursday, October 5th, at one thirty at Alma; or, if that doesn't work, another day, in the evening, after he leaves school, around five thirty, for an hour and a half.

In a few hours I go back to the Clinic. I hope to obtain my discharge to be able to teach. I also hope to be able to go, on the 12th, to Frankfurt, and read my poems there. (The book, it seems, is selling quite well.)

I am thinking of you and wish you good, very good days,

Paul

1. Including Peter Schifferli, editor-in-chief of the literary pages of the *Neue Zürcher Zeitung*, Werner Weber, and the Germanist Bernhard Böschenstein. These conversations often took place in the Urban Hotel Garni, which was frequented by musical and literary circles.

2. "Das Wildherz," "Die Ewigkeiten," "Graumanns Weg" (*NKGA*, pp. 292, 293, 481). After this encounter with Franz Wurm, PC had bought Arnold Schönberg, *Texte. Die glückliche Hand. Totentanz der Prinzipien. Requiem. Die Jakobsleiter* (Vienna/New York: Universal Edition, 1926); PC's copy is dated "Zurich," 20 September 1967.

3. Franz Larese had a bookshop-gallery in Saint-Gallen.
4. PC and GCL had imagined a book composed of poems written in part in Moisville between summer 1966 and early winter 1967. This project will be abandoned and it will not be until 1969 that PC and GCL publish a new book together, entitled *Schwarzmaut*.
5. Eighty-one poems that will be collected later in strictly chronological order, under the title *Lichtzwang*.
6. LZ.

389

[Paris,] 29 September 1967

My dear Gisèle,

You know the author of the attached letter: he is a Yiddish poet, originally from Bukovina,[1] who, while in Paris two years ago, admired your etchings very much; we sent him the etching with the little poem.[2]

I suggest that you receive Madame Mark. The plan for showing your etchings in the American gallery is still quite vaguely formulated—it will become clearer. (*Resend* me the letter so that I can respond.)

The École demands 3 books from me:

Max Brod, *Heinrich Heine*

The review *Europe*, "Heine" issue

L. Marcuse, *Heine* (rororo).[3]

See if you can find them in Moisville or at home.

I also ask you to bring from Moisville *La Futaie* by Stifter[4]—you will find it near the German volumes of Stifter (green cloth), in the hallway.[5] I promised this book to Heidegger,[6] ordered it at Delatte, but without success. If you have the time, leave the book for me with the concierge at rue d'Ulm (immediately to the left, under the flag).

Doctor D. is leaving the clinic; his replacement is Doctor Co. I must obtain my certificate for the resumption of work, the École is demanding it from me very urgently.

Hug Eric.

Good days

Paul

1. In the letter, Freed Weininger, who had translated poems by PC into Yiddish, sends the contact details for Anna Mark, a painter originally from Hungary living in Paris. He hoped—in vain—that contact with this artist, whose work was then being shown at the Sisti Gallery in Buffalo, NY, could help GCL to have her work exhibited in the United States.
2. See no. 308.
3. Max Brod, *Heinrich Heine* (Amsterdam: Albert de Lange, 1934); "Henri Heine," *Europe*, no. 125–6, May–June 1956; Ludwig Marcuse, *Heinrich Heine in Selbstzeugnissen und Bilddokumenten (Rowohlts Monographien, 41)* (Reinbek near Hamburg: Rowohlt, 1963).
4. The French Stifter translation PC has in mind is in fact entitled *Les grands bois & autres récits*, trans. Henri Thomas (Paris: Gallimard, 1943). The volume contains three texts: *Der Hochwald* (referred to by PC as *La Futaie*), *Abdias*, and *Der Waldsteig* (*Le Chemin forestier*).
5. Adalbert Stifter, *Gesammelte Werke*, 6 vols. (Wiesbaden: Insel, 1959).
6. Martin Heidegger thanks PC for sending this book, on 30 January 1968, in the following terms: "I must still thank You for the copy of the French Stifter translation. It is a sign that a translation is impossible in this case and that the texts were chosen according to the prevailing conceptions." The letter is published in its entirety by Stephan Krass in the *Neue Zürcher Zeitung* of 3 and 4 January 1998. In fact, PC admired this translation and indeed all the translations by Henri Thomas (Bertrand Badiou conversation with GCL). It was no doubt not without ulterior motives, and with a certain mischievousness, that PC had given Heidegger a French translation of these three stories and thus proposed, to the Black Forest philosopher, rediscovering this German classic via a detour through the foreign.

389

[Paris,] Monday, 2 October 1967

My dear Gisèle,

Thanks for your two letters that arrived this morning.

You do not tell me if I can see Eric Thursday at one thirty or, if that is not possible, Friday around six in the evening. I am also free to leave Saturday and Sunday—if you are not going to Moisville, I could see him one of those days.

Regarding the book, you have time: the poems will not be published with Unseld until autumn *1969* at the earliest.[1]

The exhibition opening in Freiburg can take place in July, at a time when you will be free.

Send me *quickly* a note so that I can see Eric.

Good days

Paul

1. These poems will not be published until June 1970, under the title *Lichtzwang*. "Schwarzmaut" is the first cycle in *LZ*, and will be published separately in a collector's edition. It consists of fourteen poems by PC and fifteen etchings by GCL, and is published by Brunidor (Vaduz) on 19 March 1969, on GCL's forty-second birthday.

390

[Paris,] Tuesday, 4 October 1967

Thanks, dear Gisèle, for the good news. I will see D. and Co. tomorrow in the late morning and will probably find out something definitive.

Thursday, at 13:30, I will be at Alma to meet Eric.

Your "little series" of etchings: I know that it is important to you to publish it *alone*, without accompaniment. If however you decided to use it for the book,[1] I would be, know this, very glad.

Good days

Paul

1. See no. 388, n. 5.

391

78 rue de Longchamp, 4 October 1967

Dear Paul,

I would like you to know and to have no doubt about it. All that is in my power to do for you to have a free life again will be done. I have always been acting thus, for months. I think that you understand how essential it is for you to receive care when you are not well and how important, very important, it is for you to have medical attention even when you are doing well, like now.

If I decided to no longer live with you like before, it's because I think that not only have I not been able to help you, but even more that, so close to one another, we were hurting each other. If the doctors decide now that you can leave the hospital, I hope with all my heart that you will find a studio in which you can live, write, work, and feel well.

It's my greatest desire.

I think you can continue to trust Dr. D. I know that he wants to do everything to help you to live in freedom.

Don't lose your courage and send me a note, if you can, about all this

Gisèle

I did not find Max Brod on Heine.[1]

I don't think that we have *La Futaie* by Stifter.[2] I don't remember having seen it. I'm sending the only Stifter in French that I found. Is this it?

The paper from the École, about sick leave, a copy, and unsigned, was always sent in this way, I will put it in the file.

Have you replied to M. Graisowsky?[3] About the possible film or a meeting at least in Paris or Frankfurt? What should I tell him if he calls?

1. See no. 389.
2. See *ibid.*
3. Reference to a letter not published here. Horst Graisowsky, a young film director working for a German television channel, had written to PC to express his desire to make a film about PC's poetry.

392

[Paris,] 5 October 1967

Dear Gisèle,

Thanks for the letter you sent with Eric. I thank you for it. Believe me: I do not at all doubt your good intentions.

I saw Deniker, quite reticent, today during the visit; he told me, among other things, that he will see me again Monday. Then I leave to present my book in Frankfurt.[1]

Take care

Paul

[In the margin:] The Stifter is indeed the one I was thinking of. Don't look anymore for the Brod: I have returned it.

1. PC will present *AW* and read a selection of poems that have just been published with Suhrkamp at the Frankfurt Book Fair (see no. 394, n. 1).

393

[Paris,] 10 October 1967

My dear Gisèle,

Professor Deniker just told me that I will leave the clinic upon my return from Frankfurt—you can imagine how glad I am.

In the *F.A.Z.* Book Fair Supplement from today, first review of *Atemwende*, at the top.[1]

I telephoned Aunt Berta to tell her the good news of the discharge.

Hug Eric—

Good, very good days!

[Unsigned]

Tell me something regarding the Altmann project!

1. In his article entitled "'Atemwende.' Paul Celans neue Gedichte" (*Breath Turn*: Paul Celan's New Poems), which opens the literary supplement of the *Frankfurter Allgemeine Zeitung* from 10 October 1967, Peter Horst Neumann, after recalling the difficulties posed by this poetry, which places its reader in the position of interpreter, emphasizes how difficult it is to situate this book in PC's oeuvre, since it is the result, like the previous books, of an extreme experience: "This poetry continues to affirm itself in the no man's land between language and no-longer-language." In the middle of his article, Neumann focuses on an interpretation of the first stanza of "Weggebeizt" (*NKGA*, p. 185; see "Eroded," *BIT* p. 19) and in particular the line "Strahlenwind deiner Sprache" (the wind of rays of your language)) which evokes for Neumann "a sort of Pentecost miracle," whose light is however in contradiction with that of New Testament tradition: "It continues to 'bite' with the power of an acid, which, faced with this One Language, does not have any longevity or consistency. Such a language, which would be able to extinguish the colorfulness and beautiful appearance of every other, would be the language of God. A poetry that oriented itself according to this absolute language and the ban on images of the Torah, would have carried out a turning against art, against itself. But how could it then assert itself as poetry? / In fact, such a circle made of self-renunciation and self-affirmation has always been formed around Celan's poetry." Neumann, who will later publish an index of vocabulary in Celan's poetic works (*Wort-Konkordanz zur Lyrik Paul Celans* [Munich: Fink, 1969]), points out the importance of the word "Atem" (breath) in Celan's poems in *SG* and *NR*, as well as in *Meridian*.

394

[Paris,] Tuesday, 17 October 1967

My dear Gisèle,

Back since yesterday, I found your letter from the tenth and thank you for it. I received my discharge today, but am waiting still for Mlle Arrieta to send, with a view to my reintegration, my certificate for the resumption of work. This evening, I will make an appointment with Doctor D.

I understand your scruples about a new, joint book; also your "little series" deserves to be published individually; nonetheless I will bring up the subject with Altmann, who wrote me after having received *Atemwende* and who desires to see me.

Frankfurt went very well:[1] Unseld is a—my—true editor.

I would like to see Eric Thursday at one o'clock at Alma—tell me in a few lines if that's possible. If not, Friday, around six o'clock?

I telephoned Gerhard Neumann, Elmar's friend, regarding a possible exhibition of your etchings in Freiburg,[2] while informing him that we will not, probably, be able to go there at the same time; it would be July.

I think very much of you. Hug Eric.

Paul

1. PC's presentation of and reading from *AW* had taken place in the home of Siegfried Unseld, director of Suhrkamp, on 12 October 1967, during the Frankfurt Book Fair.
2. The exhibition of GCL's prints at the Kröner Galerie in Freiburg will take place in May 1968.

395

[Paris, 20? October 1967]

Dear Gisèle,

Would you have a pair of sheets that I could use? I bought myself one and could, if you don't have enough, buy myself a second one.

I will soon need a portion of my books in the chambre de bonne, some dictionaries and books from downstairs, my files of letters (including the translation by Erna Baber)[1] etc. Elmar wants to help me to transport them and I ask you to consider a day (before November 3rd, the date I resume my courses, if possible).

In ten days, I will see Altmann. I plan to ask him to print for me a single poem: the one I wrote after my encounter with Heidegger. It is a difficult thing to illustrate, nonetheless, if you think you can augment it with an engraved sign, I will gladly accept it.[2]

I understand that you want to go your own way with your etchings. The next volume will be published in autumn 1968, so there is no time practically speaking for a collector's edition before that.[3] There remains only the one I am working on currently and which will be published in 1969.[4] I could choose a certain number of pieces and decipher them for you in my way—orally if possible. Think about it.

Monday, I will see Doctor D. I will also see Henri Michaux. I am sending you 400 more francs with Eric.

I wish you good days

Paul

If you go to Moisville, bring me all the Supervielles. Thanks in advance.

1. See no. 363, n. 3.
2. The poem referred to, "Todtnauberg," was written in Frankfurt on 1 August 1967, one week after the encounter between PC and Heidegger in the "hut" (*LZ*, *NKGA*, p. 286). "Todtnauberg" will be published in a collector's edition without a print accompanying it on 12 January 1968 (Vaduz: Brunidor, 1968).
3. On this abandoned project, see no. 388, n. 5. *FS* will be published on 3 September 1968.
4. This book, *LZ*, will not be published until June 1970, after PC's death.

396

[Paris, 26 October 1967]

I saw, yesterday, on the table, a Klee—here is another, several others.[1]

Then I noticed your etchings, I picked them up a bit to look at them, as well as the one standing in front of the little table: they are very, very beautiful, I congratulate you on them.

Paul

Tell me if you can accept engraving a sign to accompany the poem on the encounter with Heidegger.[2]

26.10.67

1. Probably postcards but also perhaps the catalogue of the Paul Klee exhibition at the Basel *Kunsthalle* from June 1967. The Celans possessed Klee's writings and numerous works about this painter.
2. See above, no. 395, n. 2.

397

[Paris,] Sunday, 5 November 1967

Dear Gisèle,

Thanks for your letter and your invitation to the Exposition de la Jeune Gravure.

I would like to see Eric Wednesday evening, around six thirty, and take him out for dinner. If that is not possible, then Thursday toward one o'clock, or Friday around six thirty. Answer me by return mail please.

I am glad that you can show your work in Gothenburg.* One day, not too distant, you will show your work in Paris, I am sure of it.

Good days!

Paul

* You can, of course, show *Atemkristall* there.

398

[Paris,] Wednesday, 8 November 1967

Dear Gisèle,

Thanks for your letter—I will expect Eric Friday at Alma at 18:30.

(Excuse my untimeliness the other day—I had posted my letter Sunday, thinking that it would reach you Monday.)

If you go to Moisville, bring me, please, all the Supervielles (+ a German brochure with its translated poems, which should be with the other volumes)[1] and *Das grüne Heft* by Mörike (facsimile collector's edition, which, in a slightly larger format, must be lying among the German classics).[2]

I wish you good days

Paul

1. See no. 366, n. 3.
2. (Stuttgart: Württembergische Landesbibliothek, 1954).

399

[Paris,] Wednesday, 15 Nov[ember] 67

Dear Gisèle,

Thanks for your letter. I am happy about your success at the Salon de la Jeune Gravure.

I leave Saturday morning to go to Cologne for a Television recording.[1] Can you give to Eric, in your big handbag, my other gray pair of pants?* Thank you for that.

For the Supervielles—of which I am in great need—look, please, in the room upstairs, on the first bookshelves on the left (as you come in). There should be several volumes (three or four) including the first edition of *Gravitations* and a volume that Supervielle dedicated for me not long before his death.[2]—If not, they must be in the country. But if you do not find them, I will go recopy the parts I am missing in the French text—it is above all the first versions of a few poems from *Gravitations*—with Denise Bertaux.

I hope that you will soon have news from Freiburg.

Good days!

Paul

Another thing: Look please in my wardrobe, on the upper shelf, if there is an offprint of "Gespräch im Gebirg": Franz Wurm asks me for it and I would like to send it to him.

1. This is PC's reading of poems from *AW*, filmed 27 November 1967 at Westdeutscher Rundfunk.
* *and two pairs of pyjamas?*
2. *Le Corps tragique* (1959). Jules Supervielle had dedicated this volume for PC on 12 January 1960, around four months before his death on 17 May 1960.

400

[Paris, 18 November 1967]

Dear Gisèle,

Two blanks in our memories: the Supervielles, Eric must have told you yesterday, were left, by you, with the Bollacks. I found out on Thursday and I asked the Bollacks to tell you by telephone; they did not do it.

I am not leaving until next Saturday, after all (and return Monday evening).

Thanks for the pyjamas, the undershirt, the gloves, the pants.

Can you see if, among the files lined up in the wardrobe on the right of the desk, there isn't one containing a few translations of poems by *Jean Daive* (de Schrynmakers[1])? If you find them, give them to Eric, who will bring them to me Thursday, when we meet at Alma. It occurs to me to take him to the Russian Art Exhibition[2]—what do you think of that?

Bravo for the etchings at the Salon!

Good days!

Paul

I am glad that you can keep your job at the school.

1. Jean de Schrynmakers (who published under the name Jean Daive) had just published, in *L'Éphémère*, his translation of "Engführung," the poem comprising the last section of *SG* (no. 4, September 1967, pp. 74–89).
2. *L'Art russe des Scythes à nos jours. Trésors des musées soviétiques*, Grand Palais (October 1967–January 1968).

401

[Paris,] 21 November 1967

Dear Gisèle,

Tomorrow, could you give my (red) wool scarf to Eric—who will bring it to me at one o'clock? I thank you for that. After my return from Cologne, next week, I will probably come one day, maybe Thursday, to get my overcoat, since it is quite cold out. Eric can perhaps let me in.

Since yesterday, I have a little lodging—furnished room + bath-kitchen—at 24 rue Tournefort, five minutes from the École.[1] (But continue, please, to address my mail to me at rue d'Ulm, where I will be practically all the time, in my office, which is quite comfortable.[2])—I saw your etchings and I congratulate you on them.

Paul

---

1. PC writes to Petre Solomon two days later, "the 23rd, 9 in the evening," the day of his forty-seventh birthday: "Eric came to congratulate me, I took him to visit the small apartment that I just found a few minutes from here, on rue Tournefort. Twenty years of Parisian life, to end up in a 'studio'-kitchen, furnished, without any place for my books. But I have the office on rue d'Ulm" ("Corespondenta lui Paul Celan cu Petre Solomon," in: Petre Solomon, *Paul Celan: Dimensiunea românească* Bucharest: Editura Kriterion, 1987, p. 209–241; *Paul Celan: The Romanian Dimension*, trans. Emanuela Tegla). PC will live in this studio until the end of November 1969 and will write numerous poems there, which are mostly published in the posthumous *SP* (1971). See also the poem not chosen for publication, entitled "24 Rue Tournefort" (*NKGA*, p. 534).
2. From this point on, PC will spend more time in his office, on the ground floor of the south wing of the ENS, with a view of the Pasteur Courtyard. Numerous posthumously published poems, in particular from *SP*, are marked "rue d'Ulm." PC also regularly gave his class in this room, which was intended for this purpose as well.

402

[Paris,] 24 November 1967

Thanks for the two pretty etchings, dear Gisèle, thanks for your wishes.[1] (Are these etchings from October or from November? I would like to know. You dated them 23.10, but since your birthday wishes bear the same date, I ask you to clarify their date for me.)

Eric was, I think, very glad to see the *Grand Meaulnes*. Through him, I perceived the contours of a particular, very old emotion, from which you were not absent.[2]

I agreed with Eric to meet him on Thursday the 30th at one o'clock at Trocadéro, *in front of the tabac*, to take him to have lunch, then, perhaps, to the Russian Art Exhibition.[3] Then I would like to go up to the apartment to get the overcoat and a few files.

The Wolgensingers send him even more stamps.

I hope that the French translation of Nelly Sachs' poems will facilitate your reading of the original.[4] I think that you can put this book into Eric's hands too.

Good days!

Paul

1. For PC's forty-seventh birthday.
2. The film is Jean-Gabriel Albicocco's cinematic adaptation (1967) of the famous novel by Alain-Fournier (1913).
3. See no. 400, n. 2.
4. *Brasiers d'énigmes et autres poèmes*, trans. Lionel Richard (Paris: Denoël, 1967).

403

[Paris,] 3 December 1967

Dear Gisèle,

I went to Porte de Versailles to look for seats—in vain, there were no more for Sunday.[1] Since the following Sunday I will be in Berlin, Eric and I will have to wait for other choirs, other dances. So Eric will be able to participate in his scouts trip. But Thursday the 7th, I will be at Trocadéro at twelve thirty, to take him to have lunch with me.

I received a note from Neumann (Freiburg); his wife just brought a little boy into the world. In the coming days you will have details about your exhibition in Freiburg, directly.

I hope that Gothenburg is coming into focus. I will write tomorrow to Nelly Sachs, then will write her again about you.[2]

Good days!

Paul

1. PC hoped to take his son to a show performed by the choirs and the ballet of the Red Army.
2. PC will write to Nelly Sachs on 8 December 1967 without mentioning these plans for an exhibition, which he will do on 1 April 1968: "Gisèle has done a lot of work in recent years, there is much new work that is beautiful and—permit me to say it—unique in its way. Gisèle has exhibited at various places with success occasionally even with great success. [...] My dear Nelly, I am sure there are artists and critics among your friends whose attention you could draw to these exhibitions [in Skara, Hudiksvall, Kristianstad, and Gothenburg]. Do it, please!" See *Paul Celan / Nelly Sachs: Correspondence*, ed. Barbara Wiedemann (Riverdale -on-Hudson: The Sheep Meadow Press, 1998), pp. 63–64.

404

[Paris, early December 1967]

Dear Gisèle,

If I am not mistaken, we sent "Schlafbrocken" to Nelly Sachs last year.[1] Send her a little etching for her birthday, which is December 10th. I will write to her, then, when you know the exact date of your exhibition in Gothenburg, I will ask her to contemplate a second exhibition in Stockholm.—I did not put away the key for upstairs,[2] it must still be on the desk.

[Unsigned]

Nelly Sachs's address: Stockholm, Bergsunsstrand 23

[On the back of the envelope:] You must absolutely go see *the Russian exhibition*!

1. See *Paul Celan / Nelly Sachs*, p. 61. On "Schlafbrocken," see no. 308, n. 1.
2. The key to the chambre de bonne.

405

[Paris,] 14 December 1967

Dear Gisèle,

Here is *L'Éphémère* with the translation of "Engführung," here also the *Humboldt* review with, on page 86, two poems from *Die Niemandsrose* translated into Spanish.[1]

And here is my Berlin address: Akademie der Künste, *1 Berlin* (West), Hanseatenweg 10. I think that I will be there until after Christmas, then I will go for a few days to the Allemanns' (5 34 *Bad Honnef*, Böckingstr[aße] 2).

Please do not forward my mail, Eric will bring it to me when I return.

Have a good vacation, happy New Year!

Paul

1. "Habia tierra en ellos" (Es war Erde in Ihnen) and "Salmo" (Psalm), trans. Klaus Dieter Vervuert and Rodolfo Alonso, *Humboldt*, no. 32, 1967, p. 86. GCL had, thanks to a long stay in Spain in the early 1950s, become very proficient in the Spanish language. The issue also contains translations by PC of Yesenin and Mandelstam into German. On this journal, see no. 111, n. 3.

406

[To Eric Celan]

[Berlin, 22 December 1967]

My dear Eric,

Here I am in Berlin since Saturday after a very agreeable flight.

It is a beautiful city with very wide streets, with often very elegant houses set apart from one another, a lot of sky, clusters of pines and birch trees, many memories, many...[1]

Have a good vacation!

Papa

1. The birch trees evoke the landscapes of the East—Mandelstam's, Block's, Essenine's, and Tsvetaeva's Russia—but also Moisville. PC also refers to his stopover in Berlin, via the "Anhalter Bahnhof" (the station from which Kafka had earlier arrived from Prague; see no. 410, the Berlin poem "Lila Luft"). PC arrived in Berlin for the first time on 9 November 1938, the

day before Kristallnacht, on his journey from Czernowitz to Tours, France (via Paris), for his first year of medical studies. These events are referenced in the poem "La Contrescarpe": "Über Krakow / bist du gekommen, am Anhalter / Bahnhof / floß deinen Blicken ein Rauch zu, / der war schon von morgen. Unter / Paulownien / sahst du die Messer stehn, wieder, / scharf von der Entfernung" (Through Krakow / you came, at the Anhalter / Bahnhof / there flowed toward your gazes a smoke, it was already of tomorrow. Under / paulownias / you saw the knives standing, again, / sharp with the distance) (*NR, NKGA*, p. 164; see *CSP*, p. 83). See also Edith Silbermann, *Begegnung mit Paul Celan* (Aachen: Rimbaud, 1993), pp. 6of.

407

Berlin, Hanseatenweg 10, 23 December 1967

Dear Gisèle,

I heard just now from Beda Allemann, whom I just telephoned, that a letter from you is waiting for me at his house.—I will only have it in Paris, the 29th, the day I will return directly, without stopping in Bonn.

My reading went very well; in the press, the next day, there was an astonishing response which showed me that I was, still, present, at a level that, I admit, surprised me all the same.[1]

It was cold and I saw, for the first time, in twenty or twenty-two years, a winter made of snow and of snow.[2] And I caught laryngitis, which had to be treated intensively, which I had to have treated by the doctor. Inhalations, injections—successful, luckily. Postponement—to the 28th—of a TV recording, generously offered by Ernst Schnabel. But not possible anymore to go to Bonn to stay with the Allemanns. (I will go there 13 January, for a reading.)—

Two poems, including one about Karl Liebknecht and Rosa Luxemburg (murdered here 16 January 1919).[3]—

Péter Szondi,[4] courteous friend.

And another friend, whom you met in the past in Zurich, Walter Georgi (friend of Allemann's): he took us on a sailboat on Lake Zurich.[5] Remind Eric about it.

If you are there, I will telephone you upon my return to hear what is new with you as well as with Eric.

Happy New Year!

Paul

1. The reading organized and presented by Walter Höllerer took place 18 December 1967 at the Akademie der Künste. The *Tagesspiegel* reported on the event in a long article entitled "Der lesende Paul Celan. Begegnung mit dem König des Gedichts" (Paul Celan Reading: Encounter with King of the Poem), 20 December 1967. In the article, Joachim Günther evokes the presence of an audience as diverse as it was large ("from the Kreuzberg sweater literati to professors, publicists, and the spiritual aristocracy of ladies"), and this despite Celan's poetry's reputation for hermeticism. PC reads, for an hour and a half, poems taken from each of his published books (*MG, VS, SG, NR, AW*), but also other unpublished poems, from the future *FS* and *LZ*. He chooses to end his reading with a poem-dedication that he had just published in the journal *Akzente:* "Einem Bruder in Asien" (To a Brother in Asia), a poem related to the war in Vietnam written on 11 August 1967 (*LZ, NKGA*, p. 287). In his article, Günther paints the portrait of a Celan quite different from the one known from authorized portraits thus far: "Celan [...] is in his 48th year of life, when one almost necessarily, if one is no Steppenwolf, puts on weight, and the tensions between spirituality and physicality tend to come out in a stronger physiognomic dialectic of forehead and chin." Before this poet, of the family of Hölderlin rather than Goethe, of those who "settle at the abyss and at the edge of language," perceived at once as "shy" and "sure of himself," the audience stood up spontaneously, recalled Günther, as the students of Friedrich Gundolf did upon Stefan George's entrance into the classroom. To conclude, Günther analyses the way PC reads, emphasizing the lack of correspondence between his diction and the image of the lines, a form of semi-non-respect of versification, privileging the syntactical connections; he is surprised in particular by the absence of any oral manifestation of caesura in the words.

2. The poems from the end of 1967 and the beginning of 1968, including the two Berlin poems mentioned in note 3, will be published under the title *Schneepart* (*Snow Part*).

3. "Du liegst" and "Lila Luft" (see no. 410). On "Du liegst," see Péter Szondi's study, entitled "Eden," which contains recollections of PC's stay in Berlin, published in *Celan Studies*, trans. Susan Bernofsky (Stanford: Stanford University Press, 2003).

4. During this stay, PC will meet several times with Péter Szondi, who had organized a reading for 19 December 1967 in the context of his seminar at the Freie Universität Berlin.

5. PC will meet with the doctor and psychoanalyst Walter Georgi several times in Berlin. The boat trip on Lake Zurich with Georgi took place—in the company of Günter Grass—in June 1959. On this occasion, PC had given Georgi a dedicated copy of his translation of Rimbaud's *Le bateau ivre* (The Drunken Boat); see no. 61, n. 1.

408

Saint-Césaire-sur-Siagne, 28 December 1967

Dear Paul,

Your letter reached me this morning and I am delighted that the reading in Berlin went so well. You tell me: "There was an astonishing response that showed me that I was still present, and at a level that I admit surprised me all the same." How could you doubt that? I am delighted that you have such proof from time to time, but I beg you not to forget it, to know it. I understand so well that, in the solitude you live through and in the midst also of so much incomprehension, experiences of this kind are a great help. I would like for you to have them even more frequently. But that, in Berlin—that touches me particularly. I'm sorry that the Berlin cold was such that you did not hold up too well against it. I hope that now all is well but it's really too bad that you couldn't go to the Allemanns' and that the recording had to be postponed. You have, it seems, many trips coming up. I hope that each time will be, like in Berlin, an encouraging confirmation. It's all the same good that encounters with your poetry exist also for a more general public, through television. Among all those who will hear you, a few will know, will be touched. I think you are totally right to take on this possibility which, on the other hand, is not totally agreeable.

But you tell me nothing of Berlin. Was it livable?

Of course I remember Georgi, he had seemed very nice to me, I remember the walk at the lake when I was only half reassured and also a dinner afterward with him which I left early with Eric, who was sleepy. You must have continued walking with him.

I also caught a nasty flu the last day of school, and I was almost not able to leave. I'm still getting over that a little, and it really tired me out, which I didn't need. Here, I have seen my Corsican friends, with whom I spent a good afternoon. La Messuguière also, where I still have a few warm ties. Françoise is not doing too poorly right now and I am glad to be in the calm of her village, the mountaintops are snowy and the sky blue. I will return the 2nd in the morning. I still haven't heard from Eric, really, it's not nice of him to write so little. The mail must have been slowed down by the holidays, but still!

I am sending you another little etching.[1] All that is not really good. I hope I'll be able to work more and better when I return.

A very good year, I wish you again

Gisèle

---

1. An untitled etching.

409

[Paris, 1967 or 1968]

Thanks, dear Gisèle. I received only *one* letter from you, not telling me if I can take Eric to the cinema Thursday (and when). Send me a note about this.

Good days

Paul

410

[Paris, 8 January 1968]

Dear Gisèle,

I am sending you five poems[1]—excuse me for not translating them for you, I will do it another time.[2] I hope that they will speak to you, in themselves.

I will see Altmann after my return from Bonn.

Good work, good days!

Paul

8 January 1968

Treckschutenzeit,
die Halbverwandelten schleppen
an einer der Welten,

der Enthöhte, geinnigt,
spricht unter den Stirnen am Ufer:

Todes quitt, Gottes
quitt.

———

Paris, rue de Longchamp
3.12.1967[3]

432

Time of track-boats,
the half-metamorphosed tug
at one of the worlds,

the downlifted one, made contemplative,
speaks among the brows on the bank:

Quit of death, of God
quit.

Lila Luft mit gelben Fensterflecken,

der Jakobsstab überm
Anhalter[4] Trumm,

Kokelstunde, noch nichts
Interkurrierendes,

von der
Stehkneipe zur
Schneekneipe.
—
Berlin, 23.12.1967

kokeln (berlinois)—jouer avec le feu et la lumière / Trumm (singulier
de Trümmer)—moignon, ruine

Lilac air with yellow window stains,

Jacob's staff[5] over the
Anhalt ruin,

The hour of playing with fire, nothing yet
intercurrent,

from the
stand-up bar to the
snow bar.

Brunnengräber im Wind:

es wird einer die Bratsche spielen, tagabwärts, im Krug,
es wird einer kopfstehn im Wort Genug,
es wird einer kreuzbeinig hängen im Tor, bei der Winde.

Dies Jahr
rauscht nicht hinüber,
es stürzt den Dezember zurück, den November,
es gräbt seine Wunden um,
es öffnet sich dir, junger
Gräber-
brunnen,
Zwölfmund.
—

Berlin, 25.12. 1967

Well-diggers in the wind:

someone will play the viola, descending the day, in the tavern,
someone will stand on his head in the word Enough,
someone will hang with crossed legs in the gate, near the winch.

This year
does not rush past,
it reverses December, November,

it digs and turns over its wounds,
it opens itself to you, young
well of
diggers' graves,
twelve-mouth.

Das angebrochene Jahr
mit dem modernden Kanten
Wahnbrot.

Trink
aus meinem Mund.
—

Paris, 2.1.68
Rue d'Ulm,

Kanten—croûton[6]

The opened-up year
with the moldy crust
of madness-bread.

Drink
from my mouth.

Unlesbarkeit dieser
Welt. Alles doppelt.

Die starken Uhren
geben der Spaltstunde recht,
heiser.

Du, in dein Tiefstes geklemmt,
entsteigst dir
für immer.

—

Paris, rue d'Ulm, 5.1.1968

Illegibility of this
world. Everything double.

The powerful clocks
concede to the hour of division,
hoarsely.

You, wedged into your deepest,
climb out of yourself
forever.[7]

1. "Treckschutenzeit," *LZ, NKGA*, p. 308; for the other poems from *Schneepart*, see *SP, NKGA*, pp. 485–7.
2. PC did not leave behind translations of these poems.
3. This is most likely the only poem written in rue de Longchamp after PC and GCL's separation. PC wrote it hastily, as suggested by the envelope on which the first version was written, during a stop at their apartment.
4. Anhalter Bahnhof, the train station in Berlin (see no. 406, n. 1).
5. Literal translation of the name of the three stars at the center of the constellation Orion, known in English as Orion's Belt.
6. This seems to be an approximation or "French variant" for the word *Kanten*, rather than a translation; the English translation thus reflects only the German *Kanten*.
7. See Joris's translations in *BIT*, pp. 314, 323, 325, and 327; Fairley's in *Snow Part/Schneepart* (Riverdale-on-Hudson, NY: Sheep Meadow Press, 2007; hereafter *Snow Part*), pp. 9, 11, 13, and 15; and Gillespie's translation of "Illegibility," *CSP*, p. 195.

411

[Paris,] Tuesday [9? January 1968]

Dear Paul,

I very much liked the poem of the Encounter.[1] I am delighted that it is being published that way. It's very beautiful. The other poems reached me today. As soon as I can, I will devote myself to studying them better. I just spent two days with the remains of a cold that still gives me no respite and pull myself out of bed to give my class and go back to it right away afterward.

I was a little bit saddened by your reaction to Eric. I see only something very normal in Eric's passions, so short-lived![2] It's a sign of his trust in us that he shares them with us, and this openness that he has allows us to explain things to him and to give him our opinion. I always do so, even if, in many cases, I cannot agree with him. Believe me, what you tell him always makes him reflect, a conversation with him is never lost. What seems important to me is that he remains trusting and open, that he does not close himself off in a world where he would not feel our understanding.

I wish you a good reading. I thank you again for the poems. I decided to try to make etchings close to the poems that you will send me but can't promise I'll manage it.[3]

May all go well for you

Gisèle

---

1. GCL confirms receipt of the proofs of "Todtnauberg," the poem PC wrote on 1 August 1967 following his encounter with Heidegger on 25 July 1967 (*NKGA*, p. 286). PC will send the first collector's edition of this poem to Heidegger.
2. EC's enthusiasm for pop music and the hippie movement.
3. On the future *Schwarzmaut*, see no. 413, n. 3.

412

[Paris, 10 January 1968]

Dear Gisèle,

I just wrote a poem[1] made of simple words—I send it to you. I hope very much that it will please you.

I am thinking of you

Paul[2]

10 January 68, eight in the evening

Was näht
an dieser Stimme? Woran
näht diese
Stimme
diesseits, jenseits?

Die Abgründe sind
eingeschworen auf Weiß, ihnen
entstieg
die Schneenadel,

schluck sie,

du ordnest die Welt,
das zählt
soviel wie neun Namen,
auf Knien genannt,

Tumuli, Tumuli,
du
hügelst hinweg, lebendig,
komm
in den Kuß,
ein Flossenschlag,
stet,
lichtet die Buchten,
du gehst
vor Anker, dein Schatten
streift dich ab im Gebüsch,

Ankunft,
Abkunft,

ein Käfer erkennt dich,
ihr steht euch
bevor,
Raupen
spinnen euch ein,

die Große
Kugel
gewährt euch den Durchzug,

bald
knüpft das Blatt seine Ader an deine,
Funken
müssen hindurch,
eine Atemnot lang,

es steht dir ein Baum zu, ein Tag,
er entziffert die Zahl,

ein Wort, mit all seinem Grün,
geht in sich, verpflanzt sich,

folg ihm

———

Paris, 10.1.1968
Paul Celan

What sews
on this voice? On what
does this
voice sew,
on this side, on the other side?

The abysses are
sworn to white, from them
emerged
the snow needle,

swallow it,

you put the world in order,
that counts
as many as nine names,
named on bended knees,

tumuli, tumuli,
you
hillock away, living,
come
into the kiss,

A flipper blow,
constant,
lights up the bays,
you come
to anchor, your shadow
strips you down in the bushes,

arrival,
origin

a beetle recognizes you,
you loom
before one another,
silkworms
spin you both in,

the great
globe
grants you both passage,

soon
the leaf knots its veins to yours,
sparks
must pass through,
for as long as a spell of suffocation,

you have the right to a tree, a day,
it deciphers the number,

a word, with all its green,
goes into itself, transplants itself,

follow it[3]

1. "Was näht," *NKGA*, p. 487.
2. See no. 52, n. 2.
3. See *BIT*, pp. 326–8, and *Snow Part*, p. 19.

413

[Paris, March 1968?[1]]
Paul Celan[2]

"Schwarzmaut"[3]

→ Herbst 69[4]

Hörreste, Sehreste im
Schlafsaal eintausendundeins,

tagnächtlich
die Bären-Polka:
sie schulen dich um,

du wirst wieder
er.

[Paris, 9 June 1967]

[The word-for-word French translations in this letter are all by Paul Celan:]

Restes d'ouï, restes de vue dans
le dortoir mille et un,

nuit journellement
la polka des ours:

ils te rééduquent,

tu deviens à nouveau
lui/ il.

Residues of hearing, residues of sight[5] in
dormitory one thousand and one,

day nightly
the bear-polka:[6]
they reeducate you,

you become again
he.[7]

Ihn ritt die Nacht, er war zu sich gekommen,
der Waisenkittel war die Fahn,

kein Irrlauf mehr,
es ritt ihn grad—

Es ist, es ist,
         als stünden im Liguster die Orangen,
als hätt der so Gerittene nichts an
als seine
erste,
muttermalige, ge-
heimnisgesprenkelte
Haut.

[Paris, 9–10–11 June 1967; 10 September 1967]

La nuit le chevaucha, il était a venu à lui,
le sarrau des orphelins était le drapeau,

pas de course errante,
cela le rendait droit en le chevauchant—

C'est, c'est,
         comme si se tenaient dans le troène des oranges,
comme si celui chevauché de telle manière n'ait rien sur lui
que sa
première,
tachetée d'envies, grivelée de mystère / secret
peau.

The night rode him, he had come to himself,
the orphan smock was the flag,

no more running astray,
it rode him straight—

It is, it is,
        as though in the privet stood the oranges,
as though he who was so ridden had nothing on
but his
first,
mother's mark-sprinkled,
mystery-freckled
skin.

Muschelhaufen: mit
der Geröllkeule fuhr ich dazwischen,
den Flüssen folgend in die
abschmelzende Eis-
heimat,
zu ihm, dem—nach wessen
Zeichen zu ritzenden?—
Feuerstein im
Zwergbirkenhauch.

Lemminge wühlten.

Kein Später.

Keine
Schalenurne, keine
Durchbruchscheibe,
keine Sternfuß-
Fibel.

Ungestillt,
unverknüpft, kunstlos,
stieg das Allverwandelnde langsam
schabend
hinter mir her.

[Paris, 14 June 1967]

Tas de coquillages: avec
la massue faite de cailloux je fonçais dedans
suivant les fleuves dans
la patrie (de) -glace fondante
vers lui—qui doit être rayé / gravé d'après
le signe de qui?—
le silex (pierre à feu), dans
le souffle du bouleau-nain.

Des rats creusaient.

Pas de plus tard.

Aucune
urne-cupule, aucun
disque ouvragé
aucune fibule en forme de pied d'étoile.

Inapaisé,
sans liens, sans art,
ce-qui-métamorphose-tout
monta / marcha derrière moi,
en grattant / crissant (de son pas le sol).

Pile of shells: with
the pebble-mace I rushed in,
following the rivers into the
homeland of
melting ice,
toward it—which must be etched according to
whose sign?—
the flintstone in the
dwarf-birch breath.

Lemmings dug.

No later.

No
Bowl-urn, no
carved disk
no star-foot-
fibula.

Unappeased,
unattached, artless,
the all-metamorphosing climbed slowly
scraping along the ground
behind me.

Mit der Aschenkelle geschöpft
aus dem Seinstrog,
seifig, im
zweiten
Ansatz, auf-
einanderhin,

unbegreiflich geatzt jetzt,
weit
außerhalb unser und schon—weshalb?—
auseinandergehoben,

dann (im dritten
Ansatz?) hinters
Horn geblasen, vor den
stehenden
Tränentrumm,
einmal, zweimal, dreimal,

aus unpaariger
knospend-gespaltener
fahniger
Lunge.

[Paris, 15 June 1967]

Puisé avec / à la louche de cendres
dans l'auge de l'Etre,
savonneux, au
deuxième
abord coup, / l'un vers l'autre,

incompréhensiblement nourris à présent
loin
en dehors de nous et déjà—pourquoi?—
levés pour être séparés,

ensuite (au troisième
abord) soufflés
derrière la corne, devant
le tronçon des larmes, debout
une fois, deux fois, trois fois,

à partir d'un impair
germant-fendu
drapeleux [sic] / en bannière
poumon.

Scooped with the ash ladle
out of the trough of Being,
soapy, in the
second
attempt, toward
one another,

inconceivably fed now,
far
beyond us and already—why?—
lifted up to be separated,

then (in the third
attempt?) blown
behind the horn, in front of
the standing
truncheon of tears,
once, twice, thrice,

from unpaired
blooming-split
flaggy
lungs.

Mit Mikrolithen gespickte
schenkend-verschenkte
Hände.

Das Gespräch, das sich spinnt
von Spitze zu Spitze,
angesengt von
sprühender Brandluft.

Ein Zeichen
kämmt es zusammen   es: das Gespräch [PC's note in the margin]
zur Antwort auf eine
grübelnde Felskunst.

[Paris, 16 June 1967]

Lardées de microlithes / petites pierres
donnantes-données / offertes au don
mains.

Le dialogue qui se tisse
de pointe en pointe
roussi de
scintillant air d'incendie.

Un signe
le rassemble d'un coup de peigne
en faisant la réponse à
un art de roc qui rumine une pensée.

With microliths larded
giving-given
hands

The conversation that spins itself
from tip to tip,
singed by
scintillating fire air.

A sign
combs it together   it: the conversation [PC's note in the margin]
in answer to a
brooding rupestrian art.

In die Nacht gegangen, helferisch,
ein stern-
durchlässiges Blatt
statt des Mundes:

es bleibt
noch etwas wild zu vertun,
bäumlings.

[Paris, 20 June 1967]

Allé dans la nuit, aidant
avec une feuille perméable à l'étoile
en guise de bouche:

il reste
encore quelque chose à gaspiller sauvagement,
arbrement.

Gone into the night, helping,
a star-
permeable leaf
instead of a mouth:

there remains
something still to squander wildly,
treely.

Wir lagen schon tief in der Macchia, als du
endlich herankrochst.

Doch konnten wir nicht
hinüberdunkeln zu dir:
es herrschte
Lichtzwang.

[Paris, 24 June 1967]

Nous gésîmes [*sic*] déjà profondément dans le maquis, lorsque tu
t'approchas enfin en rampant.

Mais nous ne pûmes
ténébrer vers toi:
il régnait
contrainte de lumière.

We were lying deep in the maquis already, when you
finally came creeping this way.

But we could not
darken over to you:
there reigned
light duress.

Tretminen auf deinen linken
Monden, Saturn.

Scherbenversiegelt
die Umlaufbahnen dort draußen.

Es muß jetzt der Augenblick sein
für eine gerechte
Geburt.

[Paris, 27–28 June 1967]

Mines sur tes gauches
lunes, Saturne.

Scellées (de tesson) / d'éclats
les trajectoires de révolution / astron[omie] là dehors.

Cela doit être maintenant le moment
pour une juste
naissance.

Land mines on your left
moons, Saturn.

Sealed by shards
the orbits out there.

Now must be the moment
for a just
birth.

Wer schlug sich zu dir?
Der lerchengestaltige
Stein aus der Brache.
Kein Ton, nur das Sterbelicht
trägt
an ihm mit.

Die Höhe
wirbelt sich
aus, heftiger noch
als ihr.

[Paris, 1 July 1967]

Qui vint se joindre à toi?
La pierre en forme d'alouette
dans la jachère.

Aucun son, seule la lumière d'agonie
aide à la porter.

La hauteur
tourbillonne en se creusant,
plus violemment encore
que vous.

Who joined with you?
The lark-shaped
stone from the fallow.

No sound, only the light of agony
helps
to carry it.

The height
whirls itself
out, more violently still
than you both.

Abglanzbeladen, bei den
Himmelskäfern,
im Berg.

Den Tod,
den du mir schuldig bliebst, ich
trag ihn
aus.

[Paris, 5 July 1967]

Chargé de reflet, chez les
scarabées du ciel,
dans la montagne.

La mort,
dont tu m'es resté(e) redevable, je
la porte jusqu'à sa maturité.

Reflection-laden, with the
sky beetles,
in the mountain.

The death,
which you still owed me, I
bring it
forth.

Freigegeben auch dieser
Start.

Bugradgesang mit
Corona.

Das Dämmerruder spricht an,
deine wach-
gerissene Vene
knotet sich aus,

was du noch bist, legt sich schräg,
du gewinnst
Höhe.

[Paris, 8 July 1967]

Feu vert aussi pour ce
décollage.

Chant de roue de proue avec
Corona.

La rame crépusculaire répond,
ta veine
réveillée par son arrachement / ouverture
se dénoue,

ce que tu es encore, se couche obliquement,
tu gagnes
de la hauteur

Cleared also for this
take-off.

Nose wheel song with
Corona.

The twilight rudder responds,
your torn-
awake vein
unknots,

what you still are lies down aslant,
you gain
in height.

—

Baken-
sammler, nächtlings,
die Hucke voll,
am Fingerende den Leitstrahl,
für ihn, den einen an-
fliegenden
Wortstier.

[Paris, 8 July 1967]

Collecteur de balises, vers la nuit,
la hotte pleine,
à la pointe du doigt le rayon conducteur,
pour lui, l'unique
arrivant (au vol)
taureau-parole.

Beacon-
collector, towards night,
the load full,
on his fingertip the conducting ray,
for him, the only in-
coming
word-bull.

Aus Verlornem Gegossene[8] du,
maskengerecht,

die Lid-
falte entlang
mit der eignen
Lidfalte dir nah sein,
die Spur und die Spur
mit Grauem bestreun,
endlich, tödlich.

[Paris, 17 July 1967]

Toi, la coulée dans le perdu
ajustée au masque,

le long
du pli de paupière
avec le propre
pli de paupière être près de toi,

la trace et la trace
parsemer de gris,[9]
enfin, mortellement.

Cast in the lost, you,
fitted to the mask,

along
the lid-fold
with the own
lid-fold to be close to you,

the trace and the trace
strewn with gray,
finally, mortally.

Was uns zusammenwarf,
schrickt auseinander,

ein Weltstein, sonnenfern,
summt.

[Paris, 17 July 1967]

Ce qui nous jeta ensemble / réunit par un lancement
tressaillit et se défait,

une pierre du monde, loin du soleil,
bourdonne.

What threw us together,
shudders apart,

a world stone, far from the sun,
hums.

1. It is impossible to say when PC sent GCL the copy of this cycle of fourteen poems destined to be accompanied by prints. If one believes the date noted in pencil by PC on the title page, the word-for-word translation was added in fall 1969; it would not be until after the publication of *Schwarzmaut* (19 March 1969), then, that PC would have recorded in writing the oral translation referred to in his letter from 20? October 1967 (no. 395). See the manuscript of "Freigegeben" in the Appendix, image no. 16.

2. See no. 52, n. 2.

3. The cycle of poems entitled "Schwarzmaut" will be published in a collector's edition in March 1969. It will later constitute, with a few rare modifications, the first cycle (without a title) of *LZ* (June 1970).

4. "Autumn 1969." See above, n. 1.

5. On June 9, during the Six-Day War, Celan writes a draft of this poem on a torn-out page of *France-Soir*, although he has already noted its central formulation, "Hörreste / schulungsfähig," in his datebook for 1 April 1967. This draws on Freud's essay, "The Ego and the Id": "Die Wortreste stammen wesentlich von akustischen Wahrnehmungen ab, so daß hierdurch gleichsam ein besonderer Sinnesursprung für das System *vbw [Vor-bewusste]* gegeben ist" (in Joan Riviere's 1927 translation: "Verbal residues are derived primarily from auditory perceptions, so that the system Pcs [preconscious] has, as it were, a special sensory source."). PC's reading of this section is dated 7 April 1967; see Bertrand Badiou, *Paul Celan: Eine Bildbiographie* (Berlin: Suhrkamp, 2023), pp. 392–3; and *NKGA*, p. 980.

6. See Bertrand Badiou, *Paul Celan*, p. 393: "It is important to know that bear-trainers, to make the bears 'dance' rhythmically, would force them onto a glowing hot metal plate. Celan connects the dormitory, which in the clinic was under the roof, above the room that he would later occupy, with an unpleasant memory of a short stay there at the beginning of February 1966 (conversation with GCL, summer 1985)."

7. For this and all the following poems in this document, see the translations of the final versions by Joris, *BIT*, pp. 236–49; and Gillespie's translations of "We Already Lay" and "Released," *CSP*, pp. 177, 179. For the final versions of the poems, which comprise the first cycle of *LZ*, see *NKGA*, pp. 279–83.

8. The title recalls the technique in sculpture referred to in French as "la fonte de la cire perdue" (referred to as "lost wax casting" in English), in which bronze is cast by creating a model with a wax surface and enclosing it in a mold; the wax is then melted out and the metal poured in between the core and the mold.

9. This should read "parsemer de gris / la trace et la trace."

414

[London,] Wednesday, 10 [April 1968]

Dear Gisèle,

Thanks for your good letter, thanks for the forwarded letter.

This stay in London is doing me good. I have seen people, Fried—with whom I had a very frank and very fruitful (I think) debate about Israel,[1] Judaism, anti-Semitism (including that of the left)—Hamburger,[2] the Rabbi Friedlander[3] (friend of the very noble Martin Luther King),[4] others.

The aunt is spoiling me—which must not surprise you. But she is quite tired and I decided, also for this reason, to come home Tuesday the 16th. Before then, I will celebrate, this Friday, the "Seder" (the first night of Passover) with Léo and Régine, then I will see the Ehrenbergs.[5]

I am enclosing the response from Nelly Sachs.[6] It is, alas, disappointing. But the aunt and Régine, to whom I spoke of her, attribute it to her age, her illness as well. I learned, in effect, moreover, that she has been sick (she speaks of it herself). All the same have the boxes sent to the indicated galleries and send her (Nelly) a few (including one for Lenke Rothmann and one for Eva-Lisa Lennartsson).

Here, the magnolias[7] are in bloom—I would like to be able to feel it as I did long ago, in Czernowitz. The sky is without clouds, hair is generally cut short, the skirts considerably lengthened. The orange shirt is difficult to find.[8]

Hug Eric!

Good days!

Paul[9]

---

1. PC, who had been in contact with the poet and translator Erich Fried, who had emigrated to London in 1938, since the beginning of the 1950s, disagreed with Fried, who was very critical of the Six-Day War and its political consequences. On this topic, see Wolfgang Emmerich, *Paul Celan* (Reinbek near Hamburg: Rowohlt, 1999), p. 87.

2. Michael Hamburger, a poet of Jewish background born in Berlin, who emigrated to London in 1930, had translated poems by PC into English, including *Poems of Paul Celan* (2002).

3. Rabbi Albert H. Friedlander, of the Wembley & District Liberal Synagogue in London (326 Preston Road, Harrow) had written to PC, after their meeting, in April 1968 (the following translated from German): "We think often of Your wonderful visit. It must have been exhausting for You; but it was very important for us. Your message *must* be heard in our communities (it is of course a universal message—but You are also the greatest Jewish poet of our time). I use Your poems in my sermons, and also hope to write essays in order to guide the public to the profound meaning of Your words. The rabbis in particular should become aware of this. [...] I truly feel the duty to lead the Jewry of today to know Paul Celan."

4. Martin Luther King, Jr., had been assassinated six days earlier, on 4 April 1968.

5. Eva Ehrenberg and her husband, Victor Ehrenberg, professor of ancient history, University of London. Eva Ehrenberg is the author of a short autobiography, *Sehnsucht—mein geliebtes Kind. Bekenntnisse und Erinnerungen* (Ner-Tamdid, 1963). The last chapter cites PC's "Todesfuge" (p. 72).

6. See *Paul Celan / Nelly Sachs*, p. 64 (letter from Nelly Sachs 4 April 1968).

7. See lines 1–9 of the poem written during this stay in London, on 14 and 15 April 1968, "Mapesbury Road" (*SP, NKGA*, p. 495; *BIT*, p. 348, *Snow Part*, p. 60).

8. Even though orange was in fashion this year, PC would have trouble finding the shirt that his son wanted, before finally finding one in a store frequented by hippies. PC had a preference for the color orange, especially that of the Capuchin monks: see the first line of the poem "Hendaye": "Die orangene Kresse" (*FS, NKGA*, p. 230). This is the reason for the choice of this color for the cover of the anthology of his poems published that year (*Ausgewählte Gedichte. Zwei Reden* [Frankfurt am Main: Suhrkamp, 1968]).

9. See no. 52, n. 2.

415

[Dedications in Jules Supervielle, *Gedichte*, selection of poems translated by Paul Celan[1]]

For you, Gisèle,

> Paul
> [Paris, end of April? 1968]

For you, Eric,

> Your father
> [Paris, end of April? 1968]

1. (*Poems*), trans. Paul Celan (Frankfurt am Main: Insel, 1968). This volume brings together translations of thirty-five poems by Jules Supervielle.

416

[Paris,] 2 May [1968]

My dear Gisèle,

Here is Nelly Sachs's address—write to her, she will be delighted.

I am very glad that the book is being made[1]—it is almost there, your etchings are truly very beautiful; with the acid, the poems have bitten (into) your copperplates, following the trace of your hands, preceded by them, accompanied by them

Paul

They have just confirmed to me the Ungaretti.[2]

---

1. On *Schwarzmaut*, see no. 413, n. 3.
2. Insel has confirmed the arrival of PC's manuscript. The volume will be published as Giuseppe Ungaretti, *Das verheißende Land, Das Merkbuch des Alten*, trans. Paul Celan (Frankfurt am Main: Insel, 1968).

417

Hanover, 2 July 1968

Dear Gisèle.

First of all, here is the text from Monsieur Baumann: it is, as I told you, a very beautiful text[1] and I think that if you sent an etching to Monsieur Baumann, that would make him very happy. Here is his address: Professor Dr. Gerhart Baumann, Freiburg im Breisgau, Andlawstraße 7.

Very good reading in Freiburg, in front of an audience that was almost as large as last year;[2] kindness. Monsieur Kröner was there, he came to congratulate me, then he offered me an advance of a thousand marks for your etchings which I did not accept, first because it was only an advance—indeed he hopes to continue to sell your etchings—and then because I did not want to take too much money with me; I had also imagined going back through Freiburg. In Frankfurt, work made quite a few demands on me, I was not able to see Vonderbank, but I will return the day after tomorrow, after the reading here. In Kiel, yesterday, the audience, large, was attentive also. I will stay in Frankfurt until the morning of the tenth. I still have to correct the proofs of *Fadensonnen*, of the André du Bouchet volume,[3] the Ungaretti.[4] Two readings, one at the university, the other in front of young booksellers. Unseld insisted that I accept a reading in Tübingen and that is where I will read on the tenth. Then I think I will allow myself some vacation.

If you write to me after your return from Paris—you will be there the sixth, right?—send the letter express (as well as the mail) so that it reaches me in time. I will then let you know where you will be able to reach me.

I am writing a letter at the same time to Eric and hope that he will respond to me soon.

Good days

Paul

1. Gerhart Baumann's article, "'Atemkristall': Graphik und Gedicht," written for GCL's exhibition at the Kröner gallery, 25 May 1968, was published later, dedicated to GCL, in Baumann's *Entwürfe: zu Poetik und Poesie* (Munich: Wilhelm Fink, 1976), pp. 144–6. The following are two translated excerpts: "One may not seek complaisance, but rather that magic of melancholy, which is unassailable precisely because all heaviness is suspended in it. The restrained gray tones and a luminous darkness, grill-work, net, and mesh—they favor metaphors which possess an exciting thickness and at the same time an ungraspable ghostliness: petrified branches, rocks rendered skeletons, plantlike air bubbles, frozen bird-flights, algae with animal-like faces and shark teeth, flying flippers, bird-souls, solidified 'currents of melancholy' [see *AW*, *NKGA*, p. 180; *BIT*, p. 7], 'Chunks of sleep' [see no. 308], 'Unconsoled,' along a void [allusion to two titles of prints by GCL: 'L'Inconsolé' and 'Einer Leere entlang—Le Long d'un vide']; uncanny tensions are condensed; the undetermined is grasped with precision, sensibility and sobriety meet" (p. 145); "A microcosm of cell nuclei spreads itself out, molecules search for the lost link, splinters of a hidden mythology. Poems corroded by acid, fables of drypoint needle, capriccios in aquatint" (p. 146).

2. See no. 372, n. 1.

3. André du Bouchet, *Vakante Glut—Dans la chaleur vacante*, trans. Paul Celan (Frankfurt am Main: Suhrkamp, 1968).

4. See no. 416, n. 2.

418

45 rue d'Ulm, Paris, 23 July 1968

Dear Gisèle,

I wrote to Eric, but I still do not have any response from him. I think you must have heard from him, and I ask you to please tell me how he is by return post.

I would also like to know the exact date of his return to Paris, maybe I will be able to see him before leaving for Vaduz.

Good days

Paul

419

45 rue d'Ulm, Paris, 6 August 1968

Dear Gisèle,

I came back to Paris, not having found in Vaduz the chance to take a true vacation.

The exhibition was rather composite, a bit "pop" I would say, different from what I do. But these things are being done, and I will have to take them into account in my poems, like every current event.

Your etchings, around a dozen, were well presented, in a kind of little "salon" that contained, like the others, a plaster sculpture; the book was on a lectern and people leafed through it.[1]

There were a lot of people at my reading, it was a world quite different from the previous readings, but attentive.[2]

I plan to read and write now, then see my students. Then go on vacation.

Tell me what Eric's plans are, tell me how he is doing, how you are doing.

Good days

Paul

---

1. The exhibition organized by Robert Altmann in Vaduz took place from 3 to 15 August 1968 and was entitled *Das Buch als Kunst. Ausstellung bibliophiler Ausgaben: Editions Brunidor und Collection de l'avante garde* [*sic*]. See also, on this subject, Robert Altmann, *Memoiren* (Geneva/Milan: Skira, 2000), pp. 65–8.
2. The reading took place on Sunday, 4 August 1968. The critic of the *Liechtensteiner Volksblatt* paints a portrait of both the poet and his audience in the article published 8 August 1968, "Wer ist unsichtbar genug, euch zu sehen. Alois Büchel besuchte die Dichterlesung mit Paul Celan (im Rahmen der Ausstellung 'Das Buch als Kunst')": "Somewhat sunken into himself, his head bent forward, sits the poet. The infinite discretion of his movements is perhaps the most striking thing, then a—for the observer—somewhat gauche timidity (as long as he remains silent), which would like to conceal itself from this reality, in order to be strong in another one. His concentration is complete, it leaps across to the spectator; no background noise can be heard in the well-attended auditorium, other than the monotone, penetrating, and incantatory voice of Paul Celan, which comes from the night. His voice, a cello, binding one tone to another with slowly drawn bows, after having been savored. Seldom staccato, sometimes—and intentionally—somewhat unctuous in intonation. Compound words are recited in the fugue of his diction—the word 'fugue' should be understood in the musical sense. Paul Celan is at once the resonance and the cello bow: with his bow he tears away reality and reconstitutes it in new worlds, new harmonies. Literally: Paul Celan is a magician of the word, but also a

magician of the public reading: he gathers from time to time the concentration of his listeners, which threatens to fade away before these difficult figures of language." Büchel recalls Goethe's visit to Vaduz and claims that one day PC will have the same importance in the awareness of German speakers; before situating PC's poetry, he evokes the poet's trajectory, his origins, and his poetic origins: Georg Trakl, Else Lasker-Schüler, but also, shockingly, Yvan Goll.

420

[To Eric Celan]

45 rue d'Ulm, Paris, 6 August 1968

My dear Eric,

Thanks for your good letter. It reached me the day of my departure from Vaduz, where the hotel conditions were not such that I would have been able to take a real vacation.

The exhibition was rather peculiar, the things quite different from one another. That poses problems, in its way, and because it is there, I will take it into account, also, in my poems, which seek to be current.

I am happy with your progress and am sure that in English too you will make progress. I will help you to do so.

I am thinking very much of you and give you a big hug. Write to me often. See you soon!

Your papa

421

45 rue d'Ulm, Paris, 23 August 1968

Dear Gisèle,

Thanks for your letters and the forwarded mail. These summer days are not easy to fill, my readings should be more numerous, I hope to be able to deepen them, converse with my books, with numerous recent, current books. The problems of poetry pose themselves to me with a great acuity, the events—you imagine how much I am affected by those in Czechoslovakia—occupy me in the middle of what I write, of what I am trying to write.[1]

I reread, quite often, the poems written after *Fadensonnen*,[2] sometimes

with the temptation, with the longing, to give some of them a better con-
tour. A few days ago, I found again, for new poems, the compact diction
that I wished to find. It will be a new book.[3]

I saw my students again,[4] the work with them gladdens me, it is going
very well, we will continue still for a while, then my vacation plans will
become clearer, I hope.

Good days

Paul

1. On 21 August 1968, Russian tanks entered Czechoslovakia; on 22 August 1968, the Commu-
nist Party of Czechoslovakia organized the resistance against the occupier. The same day, PC
had just finished writing a poem that does not seem to be explicitly tied to the events in
Czechoslovakia ("Zerr Dir," *SP*, *NKGA*, p. 509). On the other hand, the poem written the
evening before, on 21 August 1968, shows how PC is occupied with these current events in
his writing: "Leuchtstäbe, / deren / Gespräch, / auf Verkehrsinseln, / mit endlich beurlaubten
/ Wappen-Genüssen, / Bedeutungen / grätschen im aufgerissenen Pflaster, / das Küken / Zeit,
putt, putt, putt, / schlüpft in den Kraken-Nerv, / zur Behandlung, / ein Saugarm holt sich /
den Jutesack voller / Beschlußmurmeln aus / dem Klöten-ZK, / die Düngerrinne herauf und
herunter / kommt Evidenz." (Luminous staffs, / whose / conversation, / on transport islands,
/ with heraldic pleasures, / finally on leave, / meanings / straddle ripped-up cobblestones, /
the chick / time, peep, peep, peep, / slides into the octopus-nerve, / for treatment, / a tentacle
extracts / the jute-bag full / of murmurs of decisions out of / the balls-C. C. / up and down
the dung furrow / comes evidence); *SP*, *NKGA*, p. 508; see also *BIT*, p. 384. ZK is short for
"Zentralkomitee" (the Communist Party's Central Committee); reversed, it reads "KZ,"
short for "Konzentrationslager" (concentration camp). A poem written the day after this
letter also seems to echo these events ("Kalk-Krokus," *SP*, *NKGA*, p. 509; *BIT*, p. 388).
2. The poems that will make up *LZ*. PC will still send the manuscript for this book to his pub-
lisher, but he will not correct the proofs.
3. These "new poems" are "Ich schreite" (early August 1968), "Leuchtstäbe" (21 August 1968),
"Ein Leseast" (20–22 August 1968), and "Zerr Dir" (23 August 1968), SP, *NKGA*, pp. 507–9.
They will be part of the fifth and last cycle of *SP* (*NKGA*, pp. 506–13), which will not be
published until 1971, one year after PC's death.
4. During this summer, following the events of May, which led to changes in the academic
calendar, PC is preparing students for the oral French to German translation exam of the
agrégation in German. He gave classes on 20 and 21 August, and has given one on this very
day, 23 August 1968 (on the content of these classes, see no. 344, n. 2).

422

[To Eric Celan]

45 rue d'Ulm, Paris, 23 August 1968

My dear Eric,

Thanks for your letters. To tell the truth, even if the days have been long, I had not entirely noticed that so many had passed since your first letter from Moisville.

These days, for me, are very much like one another: I read, I write, I go for a few walks or go grocery shopping, I offer myself a film from time to time. Not many people in my neighborhood; only recently has it begun to be repopulated.

This past week, I saw my students again, I am working with them and that is a pleasure for me.

I am happy with your progress, happy as well at the thought that you are not at all bored. I am sure you will pass your exam. Take good walks, have a good stay with your friend—

My thoughts do not leave you. Work well, amuse yourself well, write to me.

I hug you

Your papa

423

45 rue d'Ulm, Paris, 15 September 1968

Dear Gisèle,

Thanks for your note received yesterday. I am glad to learn that Eric is in good form.

Have you received my letter, which I sent you as soon as I received your letter from 20 August? I asked you in it what Eric's plans were and I expected you to tell me how long he was going to stay with his friends, what his address was, when he was going to take his exam, etc. I would have wanted, of course, to see him upon his return to Paris.

I am telling myself that, Eric probably having to take his exam one of these days, you did not go to Moisville for the weekend and I am addressing this letter to you at rue de Longchamp.

I would be glad to see Eric Wednesday or Thursday for lunch (or dinner), or Friday for lunch—let me know in response if it is possible.

Good days

Paul

424

[Paris,] Monday [7 October 1968]

Dear Gisèle,

Thanks for your letter and, especially, for Eric's good news. I noticed, while reading his last letter, that his handwriting has firmed up and his spelling improved, and you can well imagine that I am happy about that.

I will come to Trocadéro at noon on Thursday, to have lunch with Eric.

Thanks for your encouragement. I am thinking of you.

Paul

425

[To Eric Celan]

[Paris,] Monday, 7 October 1968

My dear Eric,

I am very happy with your progress as you describe it and as your writing shows.

I hear you are free next Thursday and I will come to Trocadéro at noon to have lunch with you.

You can well imagine that I am delighted.

I hug you

Your papa

Maison Roux,[1]
Chemin de la Rive Bergère, La Colle-sur-Loup
28 October 1968

Dear Gisèle,

Here I am in a region you no doubt know, comfortably settled in, beneath an often-blue sky. Cagnes, Nice, Vence, Grasse, Les Gorges du Loup, the Maeght Foundation: all that within easy reach, seen, seen again, meditated on.

Nothing pretentious, the "picturesque" quickly faded, the trees, the stones, the bushes in good company,[2] perceivable this side of metaphor. But which you have to go find in the bus or in the car. But also the Coast, quite "materialized," the agglomerations and agglutinations. The gaze that slides, that recoils, that passes beyond the immediate.

No doubt you are enjoying, with Eric, the short vacation at the beginning of the month. Can you, by return of post, send me, in a single envelope, the letters that have arrived so far? (With the exception of those from the bank.) And, if there are any, the books? Thank you.

I am thinking of you

Paul

[To Eric Celan]

Maison Roux,
Chemin de la Rive-Bergère, La Colle-sur-Loup
28 October 1968

My dear Eric,

Here I am in the Midi, for a week already, not all the way on the Coast, but above it, between Cagnes and Vence—or more or less—comfortably settled in the sky is there with its "bluenesses," the village does not have a false charm, it is without pretention, one main, commercial street, then a few alleys, rising and falling, nothing excessive, pines, of course, but no parasols, the backcountry very beautiful, very naked, nature, still, as one rarely sees it.

Tell me how you are doing, how your work is going. You are already on vacation, I wish for you to enjoy it fully. Write to me.

I hug you

Your papa

---

1. PC is the guest of the Maeght Foundation. He will stay here from 21 October to 11 November 1968.
2. PC echoes GCL's description of the Provence landscape; see no. 317.

427

Hôpital Vaucluse
1st Pavilion Sect. C, Épinay-sur-Orge
Monday, 25 November 1968

Dear Gisèle,

I find myself for around twelve days now in the hospital[1] whose address precedes these lines.

My thoughts, you can well imagine, go ceaselessly toward you and toward Eric. Can you, by return of post, tell me how you are doing? I would be particularly glad if Eric added a few lines in his hand for me.

Visiting hours here are Thursday and Sunday, from 14:00 to 16:30. The closest train station is Sainte-Geneviève-des-Bois.

I hug Eric. An intense thought, with so many others.

Paul

---

1. Following a crisis of delusion on rue Tournefort on 14 November 1968—during which PC attacks a neighbor on his floor whom he imagines is hurting his son—PC is taken, in the presence of Dr. D. and the social worker of the Clinique de la Faculté, Reine Arrieta, to the psychiatric infirmary near the Préfecture de Police, on rue Cabanis, next to Sainte-Anne hospital. There, PC remains in complete silence, which he interrupts only to murmur "Je suis français," "J'ai été opéré d'un poumon" ("I am French," "My lung was operated on"—PC had an operation on his left lung after his suicide attempt at the end of January 1967; see no. 323, n. 1). The doctors decide to intern him in the psychiatric hospital of Vaucluse. PC is hospitalized once again under the formal condition known as "placement d'office," compul-

sory internment, which is applied "in the case of imminent danger attested by the certificate of a doctor or by public notoriety." The patient cannot leave the hospital without a "medical certificate from the doctor of the establishment indicating that the sick person has been healed or has improved" (see *Manuel de psychiatrie*, ed. Henri Ey, P. Bernard, Ch. Brisset (Paris: Brosse Masson et Compagnie, 1963). See above, nos 208 and 220. PC's state is referred to by the doctors as "delirious melancholy" (Bertrand Badiou conversation with GCL).

428

[Paris,] 26 November 1968

My dear Paul,

I have not heard from you for a long time. I hope your stay in Provence will have been good, that you will have been able to work, write, and also enjoy being in nature and rest. I thought you would return to Paris around the 15th, so we, Eric and me, sent a sign for the 23rd[1] to rue d'Ulm. Not knowing if you are back, I am sending this letter to La Colle-sur-Loup, just in case, to ask you also if I should forward your mail, and where? Among others there are two letters from Madame Sperber[2] and I imagine that they are perhaps urgent.

I believe I have finished the etchings for the book and I would like for you to see them. Altmann calls me regularly to know how far along I am, I told him last time, that's to say fifteen days ago, that I am now waiting for your feedback and your feelings to know if I should continue to rework some of them or if on the contrary you approve of them. I worked a lot and I sincerely believe that something is now there that is close to the poems.[3]

Eric continues to receive many good grades a school. A 15 today in composition: the best grade, his assignment was read in class. Yet I find that he doesn't make much of an effort. But it's fine. He is eagerly awaiting his skiing vacation.

I hope to hear from you soon.

See you soon

Gisèle

---

1. For his forty-eighth birthday, GCL had just sent PC a copy of the series of ten etchings (augmented by one etching that had earlier been part of the series) made in 1966. In October 1979, GCL will give it the title *Suite Moisville*.

2. In her letters, Jetty Sperber asks for PC's support to have Insel publish a selection of poems by her late husband, Alfred Margul-Sperber. In the first letter, Sperber reminds PC that Margul-Sperber had helped him to "take his first steps in the literary world" and that his "so harmonious pseudonym" was invented in their house in Bucharest (in fact, Sperber herself had suggested that PC create his pseudonym by reversing the syllables of the Romanian spelling of his family name: Ancel—Celan). She is also very sick, and asks for medicine.

3. The fifteen etchings of *Schwarzmaut* (see nos 413 and 441).

429

[Paris,] 28 November 1968

My dear Paul,

I just received your letter. I am sorry, Paul, that you are in the hospital again. I was, lately, very worried not to have heard from you. I thought you would let me know when you were back, that you would call. I received no response to my last letters, or to what I sent you for the 23rd at the address of the École. Eric, too, had written, had remembered your birthday. I didn't know you were back. I had called André around ten days ago, since I was worried, he had received a note from you from Provence, he told me that you were working, that you were traveling around a lot. I hoped that all was well.

So nobody, it seems, had heard from you, and you have been hospitalized for ten days. But what happened, Paul? And above all, how are you doing now? Are you well cared for? When do you think you can leave?

I have been thinking of you very much lately. I am thinking of you. I am thinking of you. Tell me how you are doing.

Tell me if I should send you the mail? Do you need anything that I can do?

I am thinking of you

Gisèle

430

[Épinay-sur-Orge,] 29 November 1968

My dear Gisèle,

Thanks for responding by return post. Your letter and Eric's are a great comfort to me. I have never ceased thinking of you both, and to read your letter is to know you are close, to know you are well.

I am well taken care of, but the days are long and I do not know, for the moment, when I will leave hospital.* That's why I told you the visiting days, hoping that you will stop by with Eric, next Thursday perhaps (or the day after tomorrow, Sunday). If you do, please bring me some fruit and writing paper.

It is nice of you to offer me your help; I think that for starters you could give the secretariat of the École a call (and the concierge so that he holds onto my mail).

I was going to respond to your letter, the only one I received at La Colle [-sur-Loup], anticipating my thoughts, with its calm, its details—then I decided to go home.

Dear Gisèle, once again: it is a great comfort for me to have Your letters. Respond to me soon. My thoughts seek you, you know it well

Paul

* which is a psychiatric hospital

[To Eric Celan]

[Épinay-sur-Orge,] 29 November 1968

My dear Eric,

Thanks for your letter: I am infinitely glad to have it, to read your letter. Glad also, of course, about your good results at school. But you will, I am sure of it, be able to do better yet. (Speaking of which, what is your grade in English?)

Soon you'll have vacation—where do you plan to spend it? I would be happy to see you beforehand. Thanks for your birthday present; I will find it when I leave and we will see each other for a little party.

Work well, amuse yourself well, think of me.

I hug you

Your papa

431

[Épinay-sur-Orge,] 29 November 1968

Dear Gisèle,

This post-script to my letter from before:

Upon reflection, I think it is preferable that Eric does not come to visit me for the moment,* and I think also that you yourself are hesitating to come, which I also understand well.

But please send me a little money, by postal money order, thirty francs for example. Also, if it is not too inconvenient, *Le Monde* (or any other newspaper you find interesting). And a little pad of stationery with envelopes. No mail for the moment, aside from your letters and Eric's.

Before my departure, I had paid the taxes (which arrived addressed to both our names in the same envelope) by check. I was surprised that you had to pay them separately.

I am thinking of you.

Paul

* but if he *desires* to come, bring him please.

432

[Paris,] 2 December 1968

My dear Paul,

You know well how hard it was for me to see you again where you were. But I am glad, I tell you again, to have found you better than I had feared. I hope with all my heart that you will recover again quickly and that you will be able to resume a normal life, in which you can work and write. I know very well how hard life is for you, I know the weight of suffering that is your lot and I revolt often, believe me, against this injustice. It is so difficult to help someone. That's hard to live through, too, you know. And to know you are so wounded, in so much pain, is hard for me to live through too.

I got in touch with Roland, with André,[1] and I did what you asked me to do. André will speak to you about it, that poses no problem. None. We must, I think, be happy about that.

I told Lortholary the news,[2] who was sorry to hear that you were in the hospital and who wishes you a quick recovery. The resumption of classes hasn't really taken place yet in any case, so it's not much of a bother if you can't give the classes. As soon as I can, I will go to pick up the mail. I have sent a note to Beda Allemann, as you asked me.

André will come to see you next Thursday.

I am thinking very much of you, Paul, of your hardship, of your suffering. I would like so much for you to be doing well and for life not to be so harsh with you.

Courage. See you Sunday

Gisèle

---

1. The psychiatrist Roland Beauroy, Mayotte Bollack's brother, and André du Bouchet.
2. Bernard Lortholary, PC's former student, head of modern language teaching at the ENS in Paris.

433

[Épinay-sur-Orge,] 5 December 1968

My dear Gisèle,

Thanks for your letter, thanks for everything you do for me.

Here, nothing has changed. The days are still long, and my back still hurts. Right now, it is just before three in the afternoon, I am here waiting for André's visit, but I am not sure that he will come; it seems to me rather, according to his letter, that he will try to come eight days from today. Give him a call, please, to tell him not to come Sunday, at the same time as you. And tell him that for the administration I am Paul *Antschel**

What else to tell you? I have confided so many thoughts to you. And my thoughts, now, go toward you and toward Eric. Until Sunday

Paul

Bring me a cup made of plastic.

* The letters must be addressed to this name.

434

[To Eric Celan]

[Épinay-sur-Orge,]
Sunday, 15 December 1968

My dear Eric,

It is a great joy for me to see you succeed so well in your studies—and congratulations on making the honor roll. (Indeed, I expected that, you see.)

I find your handwriting has very much improved, it is beginning to really be yours, and in these times when so many things, including, and this is not at all surprising, handwriting, are becoming depersonalized, it is particularly heartening to see your handwriting firm up and take shape.

I am also glad about your reading. Gorki and Turgenev[1] are naturally human, Gorki especially, the *tone* in which he tells stories is richly authentic, the problems he takes on, he lives them truly, everything begins with what is lived through, that's very important. Turgenev is more intellectual, more considered, more abstract perhaps, but always close to humans and to their preoccupations. Of course, the world has evolved since Gorki and Turgenev; but to know them, to go deeper into them, is to be able to measure and to assess what changes, what evolves, what remains in a new form, often different and identical at the same time.—I will continue to suggest books to you, but soon you will choose them yourself, and, I am sure, you will know how to orient yourself. Think also of poetry, of that which is always in search of truth and which I will help you to discover.

I wish you a very good vacation in Austria, I hug you very tight

Your papa

1. PC is responding to a letter in which EC writes: "Mama, following your advice, has bought me Russian books, by Gorki and also Turgenev, whose *Sketches from a Hunter's Album* I am reading now." Regarding Gorki, the book in question is *My Childhood* (1913), and a selection of stories, novellas, and poems (1892–4).

435

[Épinay-sur-Orge,]

Friday, 20 January[1] 1968

My dear Gisèle,

Thanks for your letters and the books, which I have started to read.[2]

You told me that you might come for the visit of Thursday, 26 December—I would be particularly grateful to you if you came. Of course, your vacation takes precedence, you should only come if you are in Paris.

I am so glad about Eric's success! He will surely have a good vacation.

I am thinking of all that we said to each other, I am thinking of you, Gisèle, very much.

Paul

1. Actually December.

2. Probably: *Marina Tsétaeva*, trans. Elsa Triolet (Paris: Gallimard, 1968); Isaac Asimov, *Geschichte der Biologie* (Frankfurt am Main: S. Fischer, 1968). The latter volume is underlined in relation to a poem written in January 1969, "Kralliger Licht-Mulm" (*NKGA*, p. 554).

436

[Paris,] 23 December 1968

My dear Paul,

I send you all my best wishes for 1969, may this little etching[1] convey them to you better than I know how.

Sixteen years ago, it was also a December 23rd: ours.[2] What haven't we been through since! Let this new year be less hard.

I know the words that you hope for and that I cannot say. I know where your gaze is turned without being able to respond to it: it is very cruel, life.

In my sorrow and grief, I don't have the words, knowing that you are where you are, I cannot tell you what it is for me; your courage and your patience despite all that!

I am thinking of you.

Gisèle

Thanks for your letter from Friday the 20th, which arrived this morning.

437

[Épinay-sur-Orge,]
Thursday, 26 December 1968

My dear Gisèle,

Thanks and thanks! For your letter, your etching, for everything you tell me by sending them. Thanks to Eric for his present, for his wishes.

The December 23rd that you evoke is still ours and will always be ours, it accompanies us in order to offer itself to us, it inscribes itself in our words, in our gestures, in all our life does.

Your etching is very beautiful, I look at it and I read in it, I recognize you in it. My dear Gisèle, I wish you a good new year. Hug Eric.

Paul

438

[Cap d'Antibes,]
Sunday,[29 December 1968]

My dear Paul,

Here I am again with the pines and the red earth, sun too, but it's cold out. Decidedly, I do not like this place, where rich property owners jealously guard their pieces of beach. You can't reach the sea, you run into fences, and you have to walk on the road, with the cars, to go along it. But the house is calm, I am resting, and they are welcoming. The television is on too much for my taste, but it is also possible to listen to music. I came with *Fadensonnen*, with the few handwritten poems you had copied out again for me, I am also reading a book by Kundera.[1]

A note from Eric dating from the day of his arrival, still tired from the train ride, but in the meantime, many slopes will have surely filled him with enthusiasm.

And you, Paul, I hoped to hear from you, maybe I will tomorrow. I hope you have received my little etching, which I am not sure is good. You'll tell me.

I am thinking of the long hours, one after another, which must follow one another, each equally boring. I am thinking of you. When I return I will again try everything so that you don't remain eternally where it is so hard for me to know you are.

Let's hope for better days. See you Sunday

Gisèle

---

1. *La Plaisanterie*, trans. Marcel Aymonin (Paris: Gallimard, 1968), published as *The Joke* in English. The French translation had been published only a few weeks earlier.

439

[Épinay-sur-Orge,]
Wednesday evening [8 January 1969]

My dear Gisèle,

You have a flu, you have trouble with your teeth: why am I not there to take them away, the flus and troubles, to comfort you! I hope that, already, you are doing better and, egotistically, I hope that you will come on Sunday.

With me, my eye trouble has proved to be a common conjunctivitis, which silver nitrate drops (silver sulfate?) will make disappear. My reading: Marie Luise Kaschnitz's diary, nice and superfluous.[1] To tell the truth, it is also a certain idea of the essential that has often dictated my returns to Paris to me—of the essential and of its *stature*.

I've reread, after so many years, Klaus's volume of poetry:[2] there are, alas, few pages that hold up. At the time I saw in it aspects of a forerunner, and when I asked you for the book, I expected to find it again. What, then, does poetry have to be nourished with, in order for it to keep what is indomitable about it?

I am enclosing with the letter the lists[3] of books and of manuscripts that you have been so kind as to send me: I have marked what I would like to look at and keep on Sunday.

You help me very much, my dear Gisèle.

Hug Eric.

Paul

I am taking advantage of Jean Daive's visit to send you these lines.

Post-script, Thursday noon: I just came from the mentioned doctor—result: I will soon recommence my work. It's incredible, but I am not dreaming. Until soon!

1. *Tage, Tage, Jahre, Aufzeichnungen* (Frankfurt am Main: Insel, 1968).
2. Klaus Demus, *Das schwere Land* (Frankfurt am Main: S. Fischer, 1958).
3. Lists not preserved or identified.

440

[Épinay-sur-Orge,]Monday, [20 January 1969]

My dear Gisèle,

Jean[1] having cancelled, I am writing to Jean Daive to ask him to come Thursday. Perhaps you can call him to remind him.

Hug Eric, my thoughts seek him, seek you

Paul

1. Jean Bollack.

441

[Paris,] Friday evening, [7? February 1969]

My dear Paul,

Here's the mock-up of the book.[1] I find it very beautiful. I think the order of the poems shouldn't be changed, there is only the etching at the top after the poem "Mit Mikrolithen gespickte" (p. 7) which doesn't seem to totally go with the poem. But the others, I cannot bring myself to change them, I truly believe that each one has at least something that truly goes with the poem preceding it. So I think that it's preferable not to change anything. But you'll see.

When you have decided, send the mock-up to Fequet, and give Altmann a call to let him know.

It seems to me it's missing a text at the end, with the number of poems and Fequet and Baudier, typographers, the number of etchings and Frélaut and Lacourière, printers. Can you point that out to them?

I am sending your social security card, the pay slip from October 1968. I don't have the one from August—you must have not sent it to me, we didn't see each other either during that time. I'm sure you have it, but you can always ask the École for a duplicate.

The URSSAF number is: 951-75-105-E-029–CK.

I wish you all the courage you need for your classes, for your work, for everything. Excuse this poorly written letter, I am really tired.

Gisèle

---

1. A collector's edition of *Schwarzmaut*, bringing together fourteen poems by PC and fifteen etchings by GCL, was to be published by Brunidor in Vaduz on 19 March 1969, GCL's forty-second birthday.

442

Paris, 25 February 1969

Wanderstaude, du fängst dir
eine der Reden,

die abgeschworene Aster
stößt hier hinzu,

wenn einer, der
die Leier zerschlug,
jetzt spräche zum Stab,
seine und aller
Blendung
bliebe aus.

[Word-for-word French translation by Paul Celan:]

Arbuste itinérant, tu t'attrapes
l'un des discours,

l'aster abjuré
s'y joint,

quand[1] un qui
brisa la lyre
se mettait maintenant à parler à la canne,
son aveuglement et celui de tous
n'auraient pas lieu.

Wandering shrub, you catch yourself
one of the speeches,

the forsworn aster
joins up here,

if one who
smashed the lyre
were now to speak to the staff,
his and everyone's
blinding
would not take place.[2]

1. This should read "si."
2. See also *BIT*, p. 403.

443

[Paris, 7 March 1969]

My dear Gisèle,

I am sending you your reviews.[1] I think you can send Erlangen the one that appeared in the *F.A.Z.*: "Flügelflächen und Stege."[2] And, of course, Monsieur Baumann's text.[3]

All my wishes

Paul

7 March 1969

1. In view of a possible exhibition in Erlangen, GCL had been requested to send clippings of reviews of her work, and she had asked PC (letter from 3 March 1969) whether he "would you be so kind as to read them and return them to me Thursday and indicate which seem good to you."
2. The article entitled "Flügelflächen und Stege. Radierungen von Gisèle Celan Lestrange" had appeared in *Frankfurter Allgemeine Zeitung* on 20 April 1968, on the occasion of the exhibition of around fifty of GCL's etchings at the Karl Vonderbank gallery in Frankfurt. Its author (C.L.), having emphasized GCL's technical mastery, identifies the presence of two basic forms in her artistic imaginary: winged surfaces (Flügelflächen) and footbridges (Stege). The connection between GCL's work and PC's poetry is evoked mainly through interpretations of *Atemkristall* (see no. 107, n. 6 and Appendix, image 11) and *Schlafbrocken* (see no. 308, n. 3).
3. See no. 417, n. 1.

444

Paris, 21 March 1969

Gehässige Monde
räkeln sich geifernd
hinter dem Nichts,

die sach-
kundige Hoffnung, die halbe,
knipst sich aus,

Blaulicht jetzt, Blaulicht,
in Tüten,

Elend, in Kopfstein-
Trögen flambiert,

ein Wurfsteinspiel
rettet die Stirnen,

du rollst die Altäre
zeiteinwärts.
/ Paris, 21.3.69 /

[Word-for-word French translation by Paul Celan:][1]

Des lunes haineuses
s'étirent en bavant
derrière le néant,

l'espoir expert,
le demi-espoir
s'éteint,

lumière bleue, maintenant, lumière bleue,
[dans des sachets]

misère, flambée
dans des bacs faits de pavés,
un jeu de pierres à lancer
sauve les fronts,

tu roules les autels
vers l'intérieur du temps.

Hateful moons
stretch themselves out slobbering
behind nothingness,

the expert
hope, the half-hope,
goes out,

Blue light now, blue light,
in bags,

misery, singed
in cobblestone-troughs,

a game of throwing stones
saves the foreheads,

you roll the altars
inward in time.[2]

---

1. The manuscript of "Gehässige Monde" accompanied by its word-for-word translation in the margin, was doubtless transmitted to GCL by EC. Cf. the final version of this poem, published posthumously, *ZG, NKGA*, p. 557.
2. See also Joris's translation of the final version in *BIT*, p. 403.

445

Dover—London, 29 March 1969

Im Zeithub,[1]
beim Weltentziffern,

die Möwe hängt sich herein,
die Kreide formiert sich,

vom Eis gegenüber
nickt der selbst-
und gemeingefährlichste aller
Namen.

Dover—London 29.3.69

[Word-for-word French translation by Paul Celan:]

Dans la montée du temps,
en déchiffrant le monde,

la mouette s'y suspend,
la craie se constitue,

de sur la glace en face
fait signe le plus dangereux
pour lui-même et autrui de tous les
noms.

In the upthrust of time,
while deciphering the world,

the seagull hangs itself in,
the chalk forms itself,

from the ice opposite
nods the most self-
and other-dangerous of all
names.

1. See *NKGA*, p. 579.

446

[London,] 2 April 1968[1]

My dear Gisèle,

I just received Eric's letter, which I am sending you in this envelope. He seems to be very content and I am delighted about that. I hope that he wrote to you at the same time.

The air, in London, is lively, invigorating, the aunt[2]—she "grousses" you—auntissime, Léo and Régine very nice, I am dining with them this evening, for Passover, and will tomorrow too.

I saw the Rembrandts again, at the National Gallery.[3]

I hope you are really enjoying your vacation.

I am thinking of you

Paul

[London,] 3 April 1969

My dear Eric,

Thanks for your letter. I am very happy to know you are content, well settled in, at ease and skiing.

As for me, it's a very calm life that I am leading here, while walking around a bit, but above all while being pampered by the aunt.

Give my best to Jean-Pierre and to his father.

I hug you

Your papa

---

1. Actually 1969.
2. See no. 21, no. 2.
3. PC had already gone back to the National Gallery the previous spring to see the Rembrandts. On 5 May 1968, PC inserted, under this date in his office datebook, a postcard acquired at the National Gallery, captioned "Rembrandt, *Self-Portrait*, 1669." A year earlier, in May 1968, PC wrote this short text in French, perhaps intended for Gisèle, evoking one of Rembrandt's self-portraits, which he had contemplated many times with her:

45 rue d'Ulm, Paris, 10 May 1968

Je regarde l'autoportrait
de Rembrandt (celui de Cologne),

son regard et sa bouche
distendus par les contingences,
sa tête et un peu de son
manteau dorés par les
contingences, rongés par elles, songés
par elles, son bâton éclaboussé de deux
gouttes, trois gouttes de cette
même substance.

(I am looking at the self-portrait / by Rembrandt (that of Cologne), / his gaze and his mouth / distended by the contingencies, / his head and a bit of his / coat gilded by the / contingencies, eaten away / by them, dreamed by them, his stick splattered with two / drops, three drops of this / very substance.)

Among the Rembrandt paintings shown in 1969 are *Anna and the Blind Tobit* (1629–30; NG4189), *Belshazzar's Feast* (1636; NG6350); *Self-Portrait at the Age of 34* (1669; NG672); and *A Man Seated Reading at a Table in a Lofty Room* (c. 1628; NG3214), now no longer attributed to Rembrandt, which had inspired a poem the previous year ("Einkanter," 20 July 1968; *SP*, *NKGA*, p. 505; *BIT*, p. 376).

447

[London,] 6 April 1969

My dear Gisèle,

I am sorry to learn this news about Marianne—I address, through you, my thoughts to her.

Three more London days. Tuesday I will see Madame Ehrenberg, who broke a hip in December. Sadnesses. The aunt quite demanding, valiantly.

Your gouache is very beautiful, I am delighted that you can discover yourself in this other way.

Until soon

Paul

448

London, 6 April 1969

"Kew Gardens"

Jetzt, wo
du dich häufst, wieder,
in meinen Händen,
abwärts im Jahr,

löst die angestammelte Meise
sich auf in lauter
Blau.

London, 6.4.69

[Word-for-word French translation by Paul Celan:][1]

Maintenant que
tu t'amoncèles, de nouveau,
dans mes mains,
vers le bas, dans l'année,

la mésange à laquelle s'adressent les balbutiements
se dissout en du seul
bleu.

Now that
you are accumulating, again,
in my hands,
downwards in the year,

the stammered-at titmouse
dissolves itself into mere
blue.[2]

1. See *NKGA*, p. 580; PC wrote the translation in the margin of the page.
2. See also Fairley's translation in *Snow Part*, p. 193.

449

Paris—Dampierre-en-Burly[1]—Paris, 12 April 1969

Gold, das den nubischen
Handrücken fortsetzt—den Weg,
dann den Fußpfad zu dir, hinweg
über den Stein, den zugeschrägten,
aus Traumentzug-Zeiten,

zwei Sandschollen, umgeweht,
stehen dir bei,

sternverseucht legt sich ein Luch
um eine der Kiefern,

der Chor
der Platanenstrünke
buckelt sich ein zum Gebet
gegens Gebet,

aus gesiegeltem
Floßholz
bau ich dir Namen, die pflockst du
fest, bei den Regenfeimen,

es werden die Kampfgrillen kommen,
aus meinem Bart,

vor den Denkkiemen steht
die eine

Träne.
Paris—Dampierre-en-Burly—Paris
12.4.1969

[Word-for-word French translation by Paul Celan:]

Or qui continue
le dos de la main nubienne—le chemin,
puis le sentier vers toi, par-dessus
la pierre chanfreinée,
datant des temps du rêve retiré,

deux mottes de sable, renversées par un souffle,
t'aident,

infesté d'étoiles, un marais
se dispose autour de l'un des pins,

le chœur
des moignons de platane
fait le gros dos en vue de la prière
contre la prière,

de bois à radeaux
scellé
je te bâtis des noms, tu les attaches,
des piquets, près des meules de pluie,

les grillons à combat viendront,
quittant ta barbe,

devant les ouïes à penser se tient
la seule
larme.

Gold, that continues
the back of the Nubian hand—the way,
then the footpath to you, away
over the stone, the beveled one,
from times of dream privation,

two clods of sand, blown down,
stand by you,

star-infested, a swamp lays itself
around one of the pines,

the choir
of plane tree stumps
buckles over to pray
against the prayer,

from sealed
raft-wood
I build you names, you stake them
down, near the rain-stacks,

there will come the crickets of struggle,
out of my beard,

in front of the thought-gills stands
the only
tear.[2]

During this time, PC is regularly invited by his friend Edmond Lutrand and his wife Rita to
their country house in the Loiret commune. The independence and the calm he found in this
house built on the edge of a pond, near the Loire river, allowed him to write several poems,
published after his death in *Zeitgehöft: Späte Gedichte aus dem Nachlaß* (Frankfurt am Main:
Suhrkamp, 1976; hereafter *ZG*) and *GN*; see the most recent edition in *NKGA*, pp. 557–67;
for "Gold," see *NKGA*, pp. 558–77).
3. See also Joris's translation of the final version in *BIT*, p. 404.

450

[Paris,] 16 April 1969

Dear Paul,

I just saw Claude David, who tells me that he is about to decide on an apartment, so to sell his on avenue Émile Zola,[1] he also has in mind an upcoming devaluation and thus the need to act as soon as possible. So he wanted let you know about it. He needs to decide on Monday, and, as soon as he has a buyer, he will sell the other one. That could take a few days, but several clients are interested. He is selling it for 23 million.[2] The service charges are, I think, rather high, and there is the heater that was changed and remains to be paid for in ten years (500 000 F). It would be good if you could see others first, I think you can really find something just as good and maybe a little smaller and a little less expensive, but I still wanted to tell you in case you don't want to consider anything else.

I will call Altmann this evening.

If you would like to see the apartment on rue [sic] Émile Zola again, call Huguette[3] or Claude, you aren't committing yourself to anything if you see it again.

See you soon

Gisèle

---

1. A few weeks later, GCL will buy this three-room apartment, on the third floor of a building at 6 avenue Émile Zola (15th arrondissement), near Pont Mirabeau. PC will not move in until 6 November 1969, with much difficulty. GCL was at the time secretary to David, head of the Institut d'etudes germaniques, who was behind PC's recruitment as lecturer in German at the ENS.
2. Twenty-three million francs in 1969 is roughly equivalent to three hundred thousand dollars today.
3. Huguette Ochs, David's wife.

451

rue d'Ulm, 21 April 1969

Welt
fingert an dir: befrag

ihre Härten,
die umnagelte Mandel: bei ihr
vergewissere dich,
daß du zu dir kommst, an deinen
lichtfühligen Rändern.

21. April 1969
Rue d'Ulm

[Word-for-word French translation by Paul Celan:][1]

De l'univers (Du monde)
te tâte de ses doigts: questionne
ses duretés,

l'amande "circoncloutée": auprès d'elle
assure-toi
que tu viens à toi, par tes
bords sensibles à la lumière.

World
feels you with its fingers: question
its durities,

the almond encircled by nails: with it,
assure yourself
that you come to yourself, at your
photosensitive edges.

---

1. The manuscript of "Welt," accompanied by a word-for-word translation, was given to GCL by EC. See *NKGA*, pp. 558–9.

[Paris,] 1 May 1969

My dear Paul,

You just said to me: Don't you also have difficult hours? Oh, Paul, if you only knew! I cannot speak much about it and, to hold up, I also choose to seem fine, to pretend...I don't fool myself, even if I fool others, and often it's harder afterwards. But the walls of my room alone witness the hours of my greatest distress.

Work is a refuge, the one as well as the other,[1] with the illusions that it represents, but all the same, I don't deny it, it helps. But etching is becoming distant, distant, the gouaches too, after that surge of activity, have become impossible for me. You know how badly one puts up with oneself when one isn't working, and how dearly one has to pay for this chance (what would be the right word?) to work. I put up so badly with these silences of the copper plate, as though contact can no longer be established, I miss that too right now. What's more, once again I am not reading anymore, once again I don't manage to listen to music. The two cantatas you gave me,[2] hardly a month ago, I loved them so. Can I admit that today they simply bored me? But why am I telling you all that? I know well what you are experiencing and how much more unjust and cruel your fate is than mine.

Your phone call...

I just put the Beethoven concerto back on again,[3] which moves me very much after all. Bach with his immense knowledge also has this acceptance, this resignation, which is sometimes difficult for me to put up with. Beethoven is wilder, more human; in pain and in revolt I feel closer to his music than to Bach's. To listen to Bach you have to be doing well. For me in any case. What I'm saying must be very false. But I have felt it this way often for several months.

I ask you truly to take this step toward the new apartment with simplicity. Don't introduce any moral considerations and notions of merit, I beg you. Why couldn't you work there too? And why would it be worse not to be able to work there? Accept that in the midst of all these difficulties there is all the same a place for little miracles, try to be able to recognize them. I assure you that they exist despite everything. I know that this apartment won't resolve all your difficulties. I have no illusions about that and I consider this possibility of living in a less unpleasant place to be a very little thing, but the very little things also have their modicum of importance. This apartment is a crumb, Paul, yes, a crumb, nothing more, but a crumb all the same.

Tomorrow I will be at the Grand Palais. I will finish six hundred forms for the students' grades. At noon I will probably take myself in hand to return to Bauhaus. The Klees are very beautiful, and to see them again brings a few true moments to life. With Kandinsky, there is the true respect that renders you very little, but also the difficulty in approaching his work, which still remains a gap for me. I don't enter entirely into it.

I didn't ask you if you were going to the Lutrands' next weekend, I would be delighted if you could enjoy being in nature a little. I was very sensitive to it this year in the springtime, what with the differences in climate there were contrasts that did not leave me indifferent.

I leave you now. I wish you all the best. Try, as I do, to also see the things that are not bad, they exist. I don't expect miracles all the time: I haven't changed, I don't count on them and I don't live in hope of them, but there are little miracles that come along and I recognize them. There are, Paul, especially when one isn't expecting them. I wish you many of them, they bring a few moments to life, even a few hours, that's already something. Life probably cannot give much more, this so cruel, detestable life.

Gisèle

1. GCL's work as a printmaker, and her job as secretary at the Institut d'etudes germaniques at the Grand Palais, which she started in October 1968.
2. GCL could be referring to two records of J. S. Bach cantatas, interpreted by the Leipzig Saint Thomas choir and the Gewandhaus Orchestra conducted by Kurt Thomas (1964): *Was mein Gott will, das g'scheh allzeit* (BWV 111) and *Jauchzet Gott, in allen Landen* (BWV 51), as well as *Gott ist mein König* (BWV 71) and *Also hat Gott die Welt geliebt* (BWV 68).
3. Beethoven's *Violin Concerto in D Major*, interpreted by David Oistrakh and the Orchestre national de la Raddiodiffusion française, under the direction of André Cluytens.

453

4 May 1969

-i-[1]
ein Trosthappen balzendes
Nichts

Von der sinkenden Walstirn
les ich dich ab—
du erkennst mich,

der Himmel
stürzt sich
in die Harpune

sechsbeinig hockt
unser Stern im Schaum,

langsam hißt einer, der's sieht,
den Trosthappen balzendes
Nichts

——

4.5.69

Von der sinkenden Walstirn
les ich dich ab—
du erkennst mich,

der Himmel
stürzt sich
in die Harpune,

sechsbeinig
hockt unser Stern im Schaum,

langsam
hißt einer, der's sieht,
den Trosthappen balzendes Nichts.

——

Paris, 5.5. 1969

[Word-for-word French translation by Paul Celan:]

Sur le front de la baleine allant au fond,
je te lis—
tu me reconnais,

le ciel
se précipite / se perce
dans le harpon / du harpon,

avec ses six pieds
notre étoile s'accroupit dans l'écume,

lentement
hisse quelqu'un qui voit cela,
la bouchée de néant qui s'accouple / en rut.

On the sinking whale-forehead
I read you—
you recognize me,

the sky
hurls itself
into the harpoon,

six-legged
our star crouches in the foam,

slowly
someone who sees it hoists
the consoling mouthful of nothingness in rut.[2]

1. On the significance of "i" see no. 34, n. 3. See the final version of this poem in *NKGA*, p. 559.
2. See also the final version as translated by Joris in *BIT*, p. 407, and by Gillespie in *CSP*, p. 207.

454

rue d'Ulm, 9 May 1969

Über dich hinaus
liegt dein Schicksal,

weißäugig, einem Gesang
entronnen, tritt etwas zu ihm,
das hilft
beim Zungenentwurzeln,
auch mittags, draußen.

———

9. Mai 1969
Rue d'Ulm

[Word-for-word French translation by Paul Celan:][1]

Par-delà de toi
gît (s'étend) ton destin,

aux yeux blancs, échappé à un chant
quelque chose se joint à lui
et aide
au déracinement des langues,
même à midi, dehors.

Out beyond you
extends your fate,

white-eyed, escaped from a song,
something steps over to it,
which helps
with the uprooting of tongues,
even at noon, outside.[2]

---

1. The manuscript of "Über dich hinaus" accompanied by its word-for-word translation was probably given to GCL by EC. See "Du liegst hinaus," the final version of this posthumous poem, *NKGA*, p. 559.
2. See also the translation of "Du liegst hinaus" in *BIT*, p. 407).

455

[To Eric Celan]

45 rue d'Ulm, Paris, 20 July 1969

My dear Eric,

It is Sunday, the day is long, I am in my office, at my work table, I just translated two Russian poems[1]—their author, a very great poet—is named Velimir Khlebnikov, and my thoughts go toward you.

I was glad to know, after your first letter, that you are feeling well, that you are enjoying yourself with the Bartsches.[2] Surely you have since gotten used to having your bed made the German way, surely you have accomplished, aside from ping-pong so to speak, other feats—above all regarding the German language. I often think that one day this language will become very close to you, that you will evolve in it with beautiful ease.

(I forgot to tell you, before your departure, that you will probably be addressed with the informal "you"—you should likewise use the informal "you" with the Bartsch children, but say "vous" to their parents.)

Perhaps you are watching, on TV, the feats of Armstrong[3] and his companions...

Give my best—meine herzlichen Grüße—to your hosts. Write to me. I hug you

Your papa

1. "Кузнечик"—"Das Heupferdchen" ("Grasshopper") and "Кому сказатеньки"—"Wem bloß erzählchen." ("Who Wants to Hear a Story"). The same day, PC will send the translation of these two poems to Peter Urban, editor of an edition of Khlebnikov that will not be published until 1972 (Reinbek: Rowohlt; see *GW*, pp. 296–7 and 298–9, and *FREN* pp. 329–36).
2. In order to improve his German, EC is staying with Erika and Jürgen Bartsch, friends of Elmar and Erika Tophoven's.
3. On Wednesday, 16 July 1969, at 1:32 p.m. (Paris time), *Apollo 11* took off for the Moon. On Monday, 21 July 1969, at 3:50 a.m. (Paris time), Neil Armstrong set foot on its surface.

456

[To Eric Celan]

45 rue d'Ulm, [Paris,] 25 July 1969

My dear Eric,

Where are we? There was your second letter, so "French," and there was the news, very "American," about the feat of Armstrong and his companions.—I will concentrate on your letter.

I think that you will end up taking this German food for what it is: food. And I congratulate you on being wary, on this and every other topic, of what you call, while smiling, your "chauvinism." You are not a chauvinist[1] and you never will be.

Did you follow the flight to the Moon and the Moon landing on television? I did, for the Moon landing it was my little transistor radio that informed me, for the return, friends, the Lutrands, had invited me over.

I am very satisfied that you are learning German, including "Paraplü."[2]

I hug you,

see you soon

[Unsigned]

All my best to the Bartsches

1. On 18 July 1969, EC wrote to his father: "I am doing well. Nonetheless, slightly chauvinistic instincts are awakening in me! Actually, I have not been able to avoid thinking of the good French food after having gobbled down a revolting thing that you must be familiar with in the guise of a dessert […] particularly disgusting."

2. In the letter to which PC refers, EC wrote: "I am doing well and manage to understand vaguely *der deutsche Jargon* […] the Bartsches told me that in Cologne-German, you can say *ein Paraplü* and I plan to pose the question of the *Paraplü* to my German teacher, who will no doubt be a bit stupefied."

457

[To Eric Celan]

[Paris,] 29 July 1969

My dear Eric,

Thanks for your two notes, the second reached me this afternoon. I won't tell you anything new when I tell you that I don't find you to be particularly talkative, in either language. But, who knows, perhaps your rich talents as a narrator will flourish one day, under the influence perhaps of Isaac Babel, who tells things well, doesn't he.[1]

Have you been to Cologne—I mean: in the city, have you seen the Cathedral and the other beautiful churches?[2] Probably, but you keep your impressions to yourself.

The clip from the *Canard* that you send me is not very "great."[3] Of course, there are so many things to resolve on this earth; but of course, this first Moon landing is not nothing either. But you will see things yourself.

I have come back from a long walk in Paris: wind, not too much, a light, fine rain—we could have walked together, I thought about that.

I will come to the train station when you return.

Give my best to all the Bartsches.

I hug you

Your papa

1. PC is doubtless thinking of EC's reading of the following books by Isaac Babel: *Cavalerie rouge* (*Red Cavalry*), trans. Maurice Parijanine (Paris: Gallimard, 1959) and *Contes d'Odessa suivi de Nouvelles* (*Odessa Stories*), trans. A. Bloch and M. Minoustischine (Paris: Gallimard, 1967).

2. PC likely means the Roman churches of Cologne, including the Sankt Maria im Kapitol. See no. 119, n. 3.

3. EC attached to his letter Moisan's 23 July 1969 cartoon in *Le Canard enchaîné*. The astronaut, having descended to the lunar surface from the Concorde, is trying to contact Earth by telephone: "—NASA? It's for an important message." EC accompanies this drawing with the following commentary: "I followed the moon landing [l'alunissage], which was indeed quite blurry. But I think that before landing on the moon, it would be better to moon [lunir, 'furnish'] the Earth's inhabitants with quite a few things they don't have. Indeed, as the *Canard enchaîné* says (of which I send you a copy), 'Proletariats of all countries, moonite [alunissez-vous]!'."

458

[To Eric Celan]

[Interlaken, 20 August 1969]

Facing the snow,
a thought for
you,

Your father

459

[Bern,] 25 August 1969

Dear Gisèle, thanks for your letter. Neither aunt nor barometer indicates sunny weather, but there are collective excursions that will take us to Zurich tomorrow, where I will spend two days at the end of the month too,[1] before returning on the first.

All my best to Marianne

Paul

1. In his datebook, PC mentions a stay in Zurich on 29–30 August 1969, as well as a meeting with Gershom Scholem on 30 August 1969.

460

[To Eric Celan]

Tel Aviv, 1 October 1969

My dear Eric, here I am, after an extremely agreeable flight, in Tel Aviv.[1]
Here, much kindness, many good faces. Greetings—

Your papa

1. PC has traveled to Israel on the invitation of the Israeli Writers' Association, 30 September–17
   October 1969. He will give a reading in Jerusalem on 9 October 1969, and in Haifa on 13
   October 1969; in Tel Aviv, he will give a short speech to the Hebrew Writers' Association (see
   SPP, p. 441) on 14 October, and a reading on 15 October. This stay inspires a group of poems
   published after his death in *ZG* (see for example *NKGA*, pp. 567–8, 569, and 571).

461

[To Eric Celan]

Jerusalem, 6 October 1969[1]

My very dear Eric,

Jerusalem is an admirable city—you too, you will come one day to see it.
I hope you are doing well.
I hug you

your papa

1. This postcard, with the caption: "הקיתעה ריעה ,םילשורי—Jerusalem—View of the Old City—
   Jérusalem—Vue sur la vieille ville," is the last known document addressed by PC to his son.

462

[Paris,] Sunday [7 December 1969]

My dear Paul, I am sending you with Eric a copy of *Atemkristall* (Altmann
has number 1)—a copy of *Schlafbrocken*, and also of *Schwarzmaut* (when
you have a chance, when you go to pick yours up at Fequet's—and you
should do that—you can give one back to me).

I find it very sad that you don't have these publications with you.[1] I hope you don't mind that I send you them.

Good luck with Eric. I spent more than two hours yesterday with his English, and we worked this morning too.

Take heart, Paul.

Gisèle

[In Paul Celan's writing:] 7.12.69

---

1. That is to say, in his new apartment at 6 avenue Émile Zola, where PC has been living since 6 November 1969.

463

[Paris,] Wednesday, 14 January 1970

My very dear Gisèle,

This moment which I can, perhaps, situate. You know my purpose, that of my existence; you know my raison d'être.

The "kilodrama" has happened. Faced with the choice between my poems and our son, I have chosen: our son.[1] He is entrusted to you, help him.

Do not leave our (solitary) level: it will nourish you.

I have loved no woman as I have loved you, as I love you.

It is love—an over-contested thing—that dictates these lines to me.

Paul[2]

---

1. According to GCL's oral testimony to André Bouchet, PC had expressed this choice in these terms during moments of delusion, saying that poetry required that he make "Abraham's sacrifice" again (EC conversation with André du Bouchet). See no. 208, n. 3. See the manuscript of this letter in the Appendix, document 17.
2. See no. 52, n. 2.

464

What can I offer you, my dear Gisèle?

Here is a poem written while thinking of you—here it is as I noted it down, right away, in its first version,[1] unaltered, unchanged.

Happy Birthday![2]

Paul

> Es wird etwas sein, später,
> das füllt sich mit dir
> und hebt sich
> an einen Mund
>
> Aus dem zerscherbten
> Wahn
> steh ich auf
> und seh meiner Hand zu,
> wie sie den einen
> einzigen
> Kreis zieht
>
> 13.XII.69
> avenue Émile Zola

[Word-for-word French translation by Paul Celan:]

> Il y aura quelque chose, plus tard,
> qui se remplit (se remplira) de toi
> et se hisse(ra)
> à (la hauteur d') une bouche

De mon (Du milieu de) délire (ma folie)
volé(e) en éclats
je me dresse (m'érige)
et contemple ma main
qui trace
l'un, l'unique
cercle

There will be something, later,
which fills itself with you
and hoists itself
up to a mouth

Out of shattered
madness
I stand up
and contemplate my hand,
how it traces the one,
single
circle[3]

---

1. See the manuscript of the poem, "Es wird etwas sein, später" in the Appendix, image 18. PC attached three documents to this letter: the manuscript of this poem, his word-for-word translation, and a typed copy of the original text. Cf. the last version of this poem, published posthumously, entitled "Es wird" in *NKGA*, p. 574. These are the last known documents sent by PC to GCL.
2. 19 March 1970 is GCL's forty-third birthday.
3. See also *BIT*, p. 443.

465

[Paris,] 20 March 1970

My dear Paul,

the tulips, their red, their life, this morning, beginning at six, after the hours of so little sleep, they were with me.

The poem accompanies me too.

. . . .

Thanks, thanks again.

Have a good stay in Germany

Gisèle[1]

---

1. On the night of April 19–20, 1970, Paul Celan took his life by throwing himself into the Seine, probably from the Pont Mirabeau.

ADDITIONAL CORRESPONDENCE (DATE UNCERTAIN)

466

I love You with all my heart, my darling. See You very soon.[1]

[Unsigned]

---

1. GCL believed that this note, not delivered by the postal service, may be from 1961. The particular short trip to which it makes reference could not be identified, and it is therefore published among these additional notes.

467

Happy New Year![1]

---

1. GCL believed that this note, not delivered by the postal service, is from 1 January 1967, but it has not been possible to establish this with certainty.

468

[To Eric Celan]

Good life, Eric[1]

[Unsigned]

Happy New Year papa

                    Eric

1. GCL believed that this note, not delivered by the postal service, may be from 1967.

469

Thanks for all the things prepared
    Paul
    Good days![1]

1. GCL believed that this note, not delivered by the postal service, may be from 1967.

470

Leave *the key to the chambre de bonne on the desk*!
Prepare the large Scottish suitcase and the large brown suitcase
Prepare coffee in the kitchen and little petits fours for Mademoiselle Arrieta
cigarettes
a bottle of grape juice
Check the typewriter!
Prepare 100 sheets of paper +
1 Angoulême notebook
1 pack of carbon paper
1 regular notebook

My Basque beret

My summer gloves
t[urn over] *p*[please]

the list of persons
having telephoned me

prepare:
my leather briefcase
my summer scarf[1]

If you go to Moisville, bring me, please, all the Emily Dickinson volumes (especially the French translations)[2] and the large selected poems by Supervielle.[3]

Thank you for that

P.

---

1. GCL believed that the list may be from 1967.
2. None of the "French translations" of Emily Dickinson were kept in the Celans' library; it is possible that PC is thinking of translations published in journals, or that it is actually a question of German translations. PC had four different editions of Dickinson in English and two in German translation:
   —*The Complete Poems*, with an introduction by her niece Martha Dickinson Bianchi (Boston: Little, Brown, and Company, 1927);
   —*Selected Poems* with an introduction by Conrad Aiken (New York: The Modern Library, Random House);
   —*Selected Poems and Numbers*, ed. Robert N. Linscott (New York: Doubleday, 1959);
   —*The Complete Poems of Emily Dickinson*, ed. Thomas H. Johnson (Boston/Toronto: Little, Brown and Company, 1960);
   —*Gedichte*, ed. and trans. Lola Gruenthal (Berlin: Henssel, 1955);
   —*Briefe und Gedichte. Der Engel in Grau. Aus dem Leben und Werk der amerikanischen Dichterin Emily Dickinson*, ed. and trans. Maria Mathi (Mannheim: Kessler, 1956).
3. See no. 367, n. 3.

471

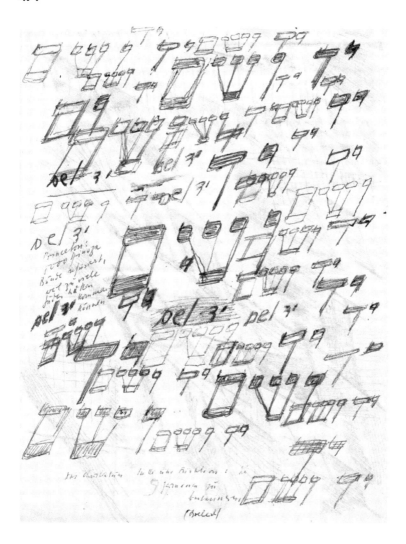

This page and next: Drawing by PC on the theme of Yad Vashem ("memorial and name" or "hand and name"), accompanied by various notes (21 x 27 cm, double-sided; pen with blue ink). Date uncertain (1968–1970).

Bibliography

WORKS BY PAUL CELAN IN GERMAN

AW

Atemwende (Frankfurt am Main: Suhrkamp, 1967); in *NKGA*, pp. 177–218.

ED

Eingedunkelt, in *Aus aufgegebenen Werken*, ed. Siegfried Unseld (Frankfurt am Main: Suhrkamp, 1968), pp. 149–61; in *NKGA*, pp. 267–72.

FS

Fadensonnen (Frankfurt am Main: Suhrkamp, 1968); in *NKGA*, pp. 223–66.

GW

Paul Celan, *Gesammelte Werke*, ed. Beda Allemann and Stefan Reichert, with Rolf Bücher, 5 volumes (the last two bilingual volumes are devoted to PC's translations from French, Russian, English, Italian, Romanian, Portuguese, and Hebrew; Frankfurt am Main: Suhrkamp, 1983).

LZ

Lichtzwang (Frankfurt am Main: Suhrkamp, 1970); in *NKGA*, pp. 277–309.

M

Der Meridian. Rede anläßlich der Verheißung des Georg-Büchner-Preises 1960 (Frankfurt am Main, S. Fischer, 1961); in *GW* III, pp. 187–202.

MG

Mohn und Gedächtnis (Stuttgart: DVA, 1952); in *NKGA*, pp. 31–59.

NKGA

Paul Celan, *Die Gedichte: Neue kommentierte Gesamtausgabe in einem Band*, ed. Barbara Wiedemann (Berlin: Suhrkamp, 2018).

NR

Die Niemandsrose (Frankfurt am Main: S. Fischer, 1963); in *NKGA*, pp. 127–71.

SG

Sprachgitter (Frankfurt am Main: S. Fischer, 1959); in *NKGA*, pp. 93–122.

SU

Der Sand aus den Urnen. Gedichte (Vienna: A. Sexl, 1948), in *NKGA*, pp. 11–23.

VS

Von Schwelle zu Schwelle (Stuttgart: DVA, 1955); in *NKGA*, pp. 65–92.

Published Posthumously

FREN

"Fremde Nähe." Celan als Übersetzer. Eine Ausstellung des Deutschen Literatur-archivs in Verbindung mit dem Präsidialdepartement der Stadt Zürich im Schiller-Nationalmuseum Marbach am Neckar und im Stadthaus Zürich, ed. Axel Gellhaus et al. (Marbach am Neckar, 1997).

FW

Das Frühwerk, ed. Barbara Wiedemann (Frankfurt am Main: Suhrkamp, 1989).

GA

Paul Celan—Die Goll Affäre. Dokumente zu einer "Infamie," collected, edited, and with a commentary by Barbara Wiedemann (Frankfurt am Main: Suhrkamp, 2000).

GN

Die Gedichte aus dem Nachlaß, ed. Bertrand Badiou, Jean-Claude Rambach, and Barbara Wiedemann, notes by Barbara Wiedemann and Bertrand Badiou (Frankfurt am Main: Suhrkamp, 1997).

SP

Schneepart (Frankfurt am Main: Suhrkamp, 1971); in *NKGA*, pp. 485–513.

ZG

Zeitgehöft (Frankfurt am Main: Suhrkamp, 1976); in *NKGA*, pp. 557–77.

WORKS BY PAUL CELAN IN ENGLISH

BIT
Breathturn into Timestead: The Collected Later Poetry, intr. and trans. Pierre Joris (New York: Farrar, Strauss and Giroux, 2014).

CSP
Corona: Selected Poems of Paul Celan, trans. Susan H. Gillespie (Barrytown, NY: Station Hill Press, 2013).

FB
Fathomsuns and Benighted, trans. Ian Fairley (Manchester: Carcanet Press, 2001).

MERIDIAN
The Meridian: Final Version—Drafts—Materials, ed. Bernard Böschenstein and Heino Schmull, trans. Pierre Joris (Stanford: Stanford University Press, 2011).

POEMS
Poems of Paul Celan, trans. Michael Hamburger (New York: Persea Books, 2002).

SELECTIONS
Paul Celan: Selections, edited and with an introduction by Pierre Joris (Berkeley/ Los Angeles: University of California Press, 2005).

SNOW PART
Snow Part/Schneepart, trans. Ian Fairley (Riverdale-on-Hudson, NY: Sheep Meadow Press, 2007).

SPP
Selected Poems and Prose of Paul Celan, trans. John Felstiner (New York: W.W. Norton, 2001).

CORRESPONDENCE

Paul Celan / Franz Wurm, Briefwechsel, ed. Barbara Wiedemann with Franz Wurm (Frankfurt am Main: Suhrkamp, 1995).

Paul Celan / Ingeborg Bachmann: Correspondence, trans. Wieland Hoban (Kolkata, India: Seagull Books, 2019).

Paul Celan/Nelly Sachs: Correspondence, intr. John Felstiner, trans. Christopher Clark, ed. Barbara Wiedemann (Riverdale-on-Hudson, NY: The Sheep Meadow Press, 1998).

Photographs

1. Photograph of Friederike Schrager, Paul Celan's mother, before her marriage to Leo Antschel. On the back of the photograph, Celan noted: "Mama, während des ersten Weltkriegs, in Böhmen" (Mama in Bohemia during World War I); private collection of Eric Celan; see no. 114.

2. Friederike and Leo Antschel, Celan's parents, Czernowitz (first half of the 1920s?); Eric Celan and Hubermann collection.

3. Paul Antschel, fifteen years old, Czernowitz, dated "Oktober 1935" on the back.

4. Paul Celan in Vienna, 1947–8.

5. Paul and Gisèle at their apartment on rue de Lota, 1954.

6. Paul, Gisèle, and their son Eric in rue de Montevideo, December 1955.

7. Celan at home, rue de Longchamp, 1958. Photo by Gisèle Celan-Lestrange.

8. Gisèle and Paul Celan at the exhibition organized by the Hanover Kestner-Gesellschaft in May 1964. (See no. 112.)

9. Celan in Tegna (Ticino), September 1967. Photo by Renate von Mangoldt, Zurich. (See no. 385.)

Works by Gisèle Celan-Lestrange

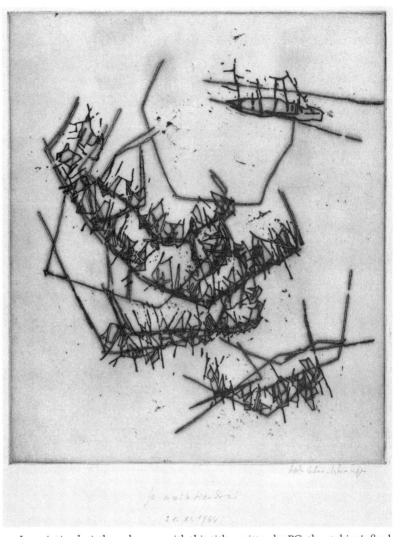

10. *Je maintiendrai*, the only copy with this title, written by PC; the etching's final title is *Souvenir de Hollande—Erinnerung an Holland*, 1964 (30 x 26 cm).

11. *Atemkristall*, September 1965 (27 x 34 cm), series of eight etchings (26 x 18.5 cm) accompanying the cycle of twenty-one poems by PC. Etching 1/8.

VI /xv   VI   *Gisèle Celan-Lestrange*

12. *Portfolio VI*, 1967 (43 x 34.5 cm): six etchings accompanying the poem by PC: "Diese / freie, / grambeschleunigte / Faust." Etching 6/6 (30.5 x 24 cm).

13. *Schwarzmaut*, March 1969 (24 x 34 cm), series of fifteen etchings accompanying the cycle of fourteen poems by PC. Etching 11/15 (26.5 x 18.5 cm).

Letters and Postcards from Paul Celan
to Gisèle Celan-Lestrange and Eric Celan

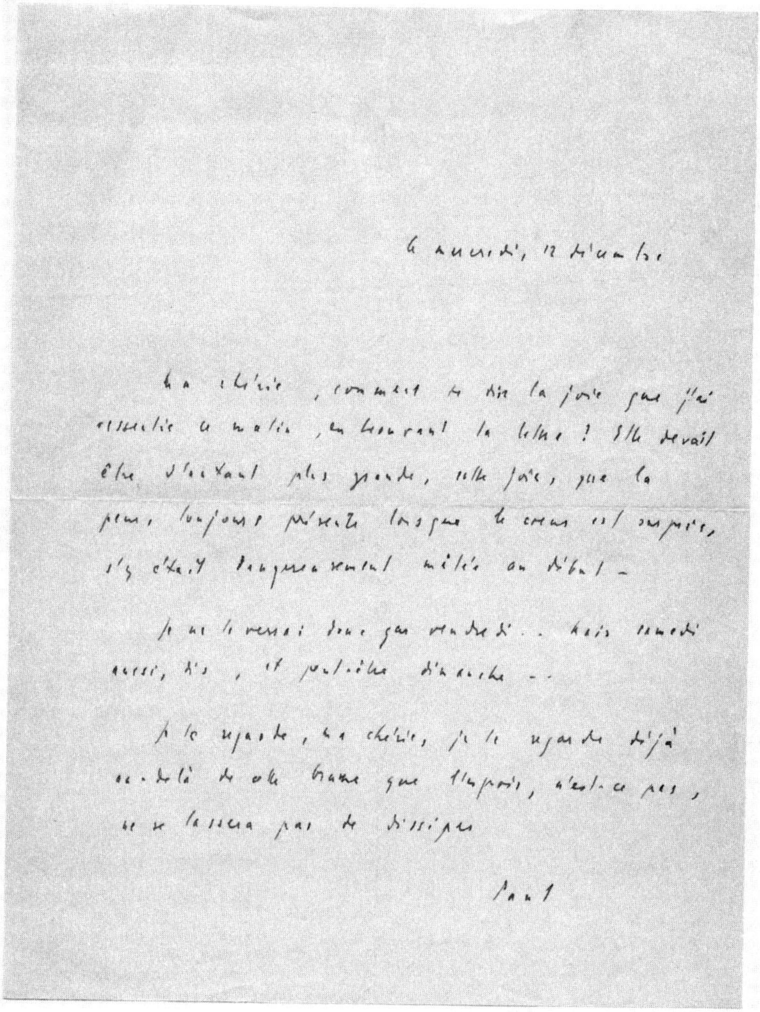
le mercredi, 12 décembre

Ma chérie, comment te dire la joie que j'ai ressentie ce matin, en trouvant ta lettre ! Elle devait être d'autant plus grande, cette joie, que la peine, toujours présente lorsque le cœur est surpris, s'y était longuement mêlée au début –

Je ne te verrai donc pas vendredi.. Mais samedi aussi, dis, et peut-être dimanche..

Je te regarde, ma chérie, je te regarde déjà au-delà de cette brume que tu perçois, n'est-ce pas, ne se lassera pas de dissiper

Paul

14. Letter to Gisèle from 12 December 1951. (See no. 2.)

15. Postcard to Eric, 22 October 1965. (See no. 189.)

FREIGEGEBEN auch dieser
Start.

Bugradgesang mit
Corona.

Das Dämmerruder spricht an,
deine wach-
gerissene Vene
knotet sich aus,

was du noch bist, legt sich schräg,
du gewinnst
Höhe.

– 11 –

16. "Freigegeben"—the eleventh poem in the *Schwarzmaut* cycle. (See no. 413.)

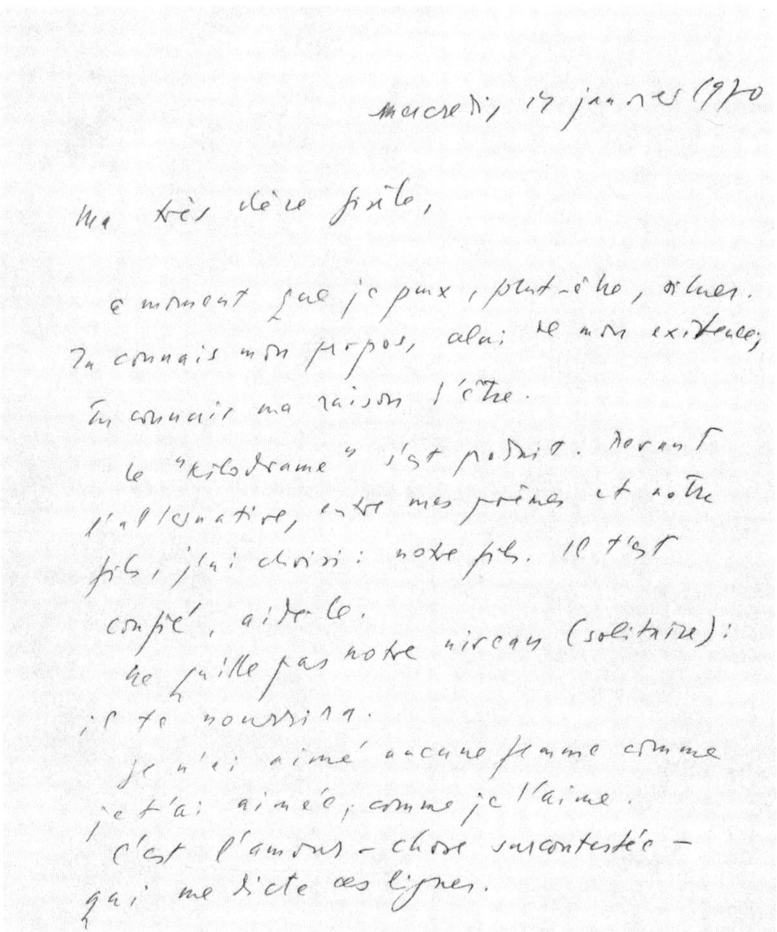

mercredi, 14 janvier 1970

Ma très chère Gisèle,

e moment que je peux, peut-être, oublier.
Tu connais mon propos, celui de mon existence;
tu connais ma raison d'être.
Le "mélodrame" s'est produit. Devant
l'alternative, entre mes poèmes et notre
fils, j'ai choisi: notre fils. Il t'est
confié, aide-le.
Ne quitte pas notre niveau (solitaire):
il te nourrira.
Je n'ai aimé aucune femme comme
je t'ai aimée, comme je t'aime.
C'est l'amour – chose incontestée –
qui me dicte ces lignes.

Paul

17. Letter from 14 January 1970. (See no. 463.)

18. "Es wird etwas sein, später," poem from 13 December 1969. (See no. 464).

OTHER NEW YORK REVIEW BOOKS / POETS TITLES